The Day Is Ours!

The Day Is Ours!

An Inside View of the Battles of Trenton and
Princeton, November 1776–January 1777

◆◆◆

WILLIAM M. DWYER

Rutgers University Press   New Brunswick, New Jersey, and London

First published in paperback in 1998
by Rutgers University Press, New Brunswick, New Jersey

First published in hardcover in 1983
by The Viking Press, New York, New York

Library of Congress Cataloging-in-Publication Data
Dwyer, William M.
    The day is ours! : an inside view of the battles of Trenton and Princeton,
  November 1776–January 1777 / William M. Dwyer.
       p.   cm.
    Originally published: New York : Viking Press, 1983.
    Includes bibliographical references and index.
    ISBN 0-8135-2608-6 (pbk. : alk. paper)
    1. Trenton, Battle of, 1776.   2. Princeton, Battle of, 1777.
I. Title.
E241.T7D88   1999   98-24044
973.3′32—dc21   CIP

British Library Cataloguing in Publication Data is available

Grateful acknowledgment is made to the following for permission to reprint copyrighted material:
Princeton University Press: Excerpts from *This Glorious Cause: The Adventures of Two Company Officers in Washington's Army,* by Herbert T. Wade and Robert A. Lively. Copyright © 1958 by Princeton University Press.
Samuel Stelle Smith: Selections from *The Battle of Trenton, The Battle of Princeton, The Hessian View of America,* and *At General Howe's Side 1776–1778,* by Samuel Stelle Smith.
Yale University Press: A selection from *Diary of the American War: A Hessian Journal,* by Capt. Johann Ewald, translated and edited by Joseph P. Tustin.

Manufactured in the United States of America

For Marjorie Wright Dwyer
and Suzanna Duncan Dwyer
and in memory of
First Lieutenant Edward Thomas Dwyer, Jr.,
U.S. Army Air Corps (5 August 1918–1 October 1944)

Foreword

In the course of researching this book I took a sunny afternoon off to play tennis with a friend who is a writer and educator. He knew I was at work on a book and, in the locker room before our match, he asked what it was about, if indeed that was any of his business.

Anticipating his reaction, I was reluctant to answer but after some hesitation decided to say that it was about the battles of Trenton and Princeton.

He was incredulous. Surely, he said, I couldn't be serious. Why, every schoolchild knew all about that business. What more could be said about Washington crossing the Delaware and so forth?

A fair question, and this book is my answer.

It is not the book that I set out to write. Originally, I intended to write a book about the early years of Mercer County, a subdivision of New Jersey created in 1839. In my visits to various libraries, however, I found myself reading less about the mid-nineteenth century and more about the autumn of 1776. As I extended my research I was struck by the extent of disaffection with the common cause that existed in 1776, a year whose "spirit" is still widely hailed. The more I researched the more I found myself agreeing with such perceptive and informed observers as Congressman Robert Morris and Alexander Graydon, who served as a Continental captain in 1776. "The year 1776 is over," Morris wrote General Washington on January 1, 1777. "I am heartily glad of it, and hope you nor America will ever be plagued with such another." Looking back in 1815, Graydon observed: "The times were not all fire and fury, as certain modern pretenders to the spirit of Seventy-six have almost persuaded us they were."

To his dismay, General Washington learned in the autumn of 1776 that, with the unstoppable British army coming on, he could count on little more than a handful of men. Thousands of able-bodied men of military age were buying their way out—legally, by paying a nominal fee. Thousands were simply refusing to serve or sending along a slave, a servant, an apprentice boy, or a poor relative as a substitute. Thousands more were serving with the British or preparing to. After a few fevered months, the American Revolution was not a popular war; there are indeed many indications that it was no more fervently supported by the general populace than a war that would be fought two centuries later halfway around the globe.

In the autumn of 1776, however, there did exist (as, it appears, in every major crisis) a few good men who could be counted on—in James Wilkinson's phrase, "the little band that faced the storm." By way of diaries, journals, letters, and memoirs, I was privileged to meet some members of this little band. Fortunately for oncoming generations, some of these men and boys, most of them projected from routine, even humdrum, lives into the big doings of a war, recorded some of their experiences in one form or another and thereby provided fresh and valuable insights into "the times that tried men's souls"; their observations add a dimension to the story of those times, giving the reader a sense of involvement and immediacy not to be derived from the formal accounts. So, I found, do some of the accounts written by Hessian and British soldiers, and so do those written by civilians, young as well as old, female as well as male.

Ultimately, having accumulated such a store of insightful and enlightening material, I felt compelled to bring together these accounts, many of them widely scattered, and to share with my contemporaries the genuine, unadorned stuff of history they contain. In doing so, I have attempted to let the participants tell their own stories, with as little intrusion on my part as possible.

One of the first and most interesting of the American soldiers I came to know was a fifteen-year-old boy who set off to fight for his country and, along the way, found himself being "greatly caressed" by townspeople who were "astonished such a little boy, and alone, should have such courage." His ingenuous account of the jaunt that took him from Boston, Massachusetts, to Trenton, New Jersey, is both illuminating and deeply affecting.

Farther on, I met an eighteen-year-old sergeant who knew how to deal not only with Hessian cannoneers but also with "crabbed old" officers and tavernkeepers unwilling to sell ham, cheese, or anything else to soldiers offering the only money they had, Continental paper. Anyone who has ever been in military service will empathize with this sergeant. Among the others I encountered were: a young private who would never forget brushing against General Washington's horse at the beginning of the often ignored *second* battle at Trenton; a young lieutenant marching farther each day from his home and then into battle after receiving word from his wife that their infant son had died; and a Presbyterian minister in his sixties who wrote his will and bade farewell to his young wife and five children before leading some men of his congregation off to reinforce Washington's dwindling army. I met many other Americans of more than passing interest, such as painter Charles Willson Peale in the role of lieutenant and mother hen for a company of young Philadelphians; politico Joseph Galloway, who went over to the British and told them how to end the war; and Colonel Nicholas Haussegger, who tried to surrender an entire battalion to the enemy (and, in part, succeeded).

In addition, I came to know some British fighting men and such Hessians as Private Johannes Reuber, Captain Johann Ewald, and Captain Friedrich von Muenchhausen. Reuber tells what it was like to have to surrender to rebels and to be marched off as a prisoner. Ewald provides a great deal of new light on the New Jersey campaign. Aristocrat Muenchhausen tells, among other interesting bits, of having "the honor to receive a small contusion" on his knee when a cannon ball "took away the hind leg" of his horse at Trenton.

I encountered some remarkable females as well: ten-year-old Martha Reed, whose home in Trenton was suddenly invaded one December night by a pack of Hessian "giants and giantesses"; Mary Peale Field, an opportunistic widow who knew how to cope with intrusive British officers and who befriended a Hessian captain she described as "the sweetest little Dutchman you ever see"; and widow Margaret Morris, a devout Quaker who helped an Anglican minister who was being hounded by a band of Tory-hunters. And then there is the beautiful young widow whose charms dazzled a Hessian colonel and indirectly contributed to General Washington's victory at Trenton.

I hope the reader will enjoy meeting these people as much as I did.

I hope, too, that the reader will heed the following lines, which express my own sentiments better than I ever could and which were written by William Camden in the foreword to his *Britannia*, published in 1637: "To accomplish this worke the whole maine of my Industrie hath been implied . . . with a firme setled study of the truth. . . . I right willingly acknowledge that I may erre much. Who shooting all day long doth alwaies hit the mark? . . . Others may be more skilfull and more exactly observe the particularities of the places where they are conversant; if they, or any other, whosoever, will advertise mee wherein I am mistaken, I will amend it with manifold thankes . . . if it proceed from good meaning, and not from a spirit of contradiction and quarrelling, which doe not befit such as are well bred, and affect the truth."

So be it.

W. M. D.

Lawrenceville, N.J.
May 1983

Contents

PART FOUR:
SOME LUCKY CHANCE MAY TURN UP

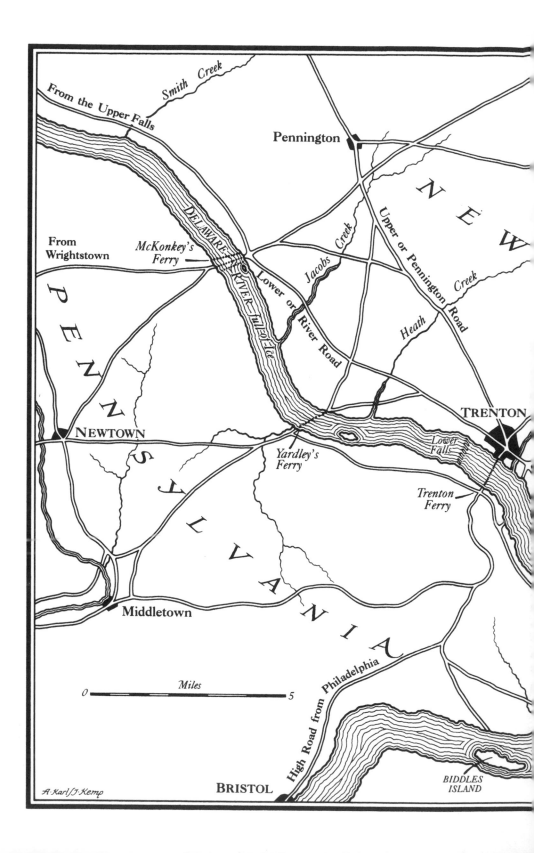

Smith Creek

From the Upper Falls

Pennington

DELAWARE

N E W

Upper or Pennington Road

Jacobs Creek

Creek

From
Wrightstown

McKonkey's
Ferry

Lower or River Road

Heath

P E N N S Y L V A N I A

NEWTOWN

Yardley's
Ferry

Lower
Falls

TRENTON

Trenton
Ferry

Middletown

Miles

0   5

High Road from Philadelphia

A·Karl/J·Kemp

BRISTOL

BIDDLES
ISLAND

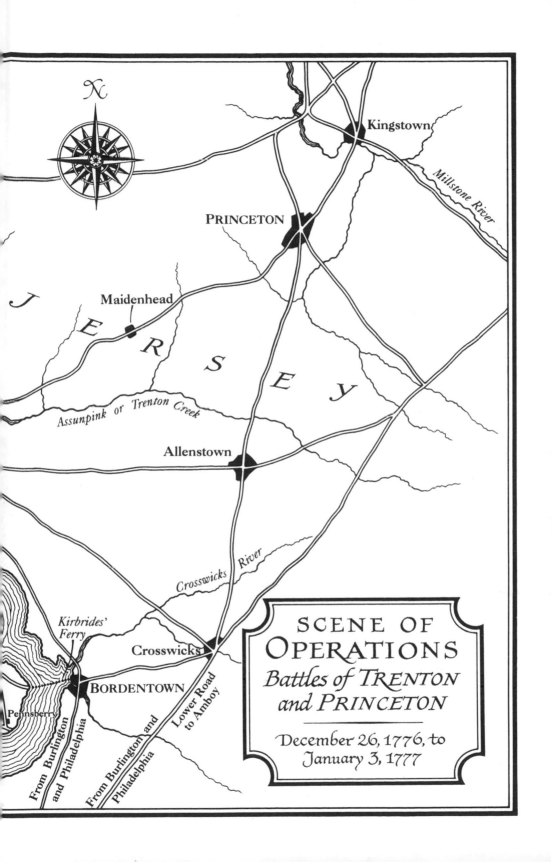

N

Kingstown

Millstone River

PRINCETON

Maidenhead

J E R S E Y

Assunpink or Trenton Creek

Allenstown

Crosswicks River

Kirbrides' Ferry

Crosswicks

Pennsberry

BORDENTOWN

From Burlington and Philadelphia

From Burlington and Philadelphia

Lower Road to Amboy

SCENE OF OPERATIONS
Battles of TRENTON and PRINCETON

December 26, 1776, to January 3, 1777

PART ONE

——◆◆◆——

A Game
Pretty Near Up

CHAPTER 1

Ye Should Never Fight Against Your King

Joseph White, an ordinary young man destined to take part in some extraordinary military action, was one of many New Englanders who volunteered for army duty around the first of May, 1775. It was a time of rising war fever and virulent anti-British sentiment; about a fortnight earlier, on April 19, the long-smoldering differences between the American colonies and the mother country had erupted into bloody skirmishes at Lexington and Concord. The revolution, finally, was on; public indignation about British "atrocities" was aflame; the spirit of '75 was spreading through the colonies.

White was eighteen years old and living at home in Charlestown, Massachusetts, when he enlisted for eight months of duty as a bombardier in a regiment of artillery. As things were to turn out, however, he did little bombarding. Early on, the adjutant of the regiment came by one day and said he had heard that White was a good speller. White (who was fond of taking "knaps") said he could spell "most any word." Fine, said the adjutant, then why not come and be his assistant? He would pay White five shillings a week, plus rations—officers' rations. How could a raw private resist such an offer?

White accepted it and quickly adjusted to a new life-style. With the help of the extra shillings he was presently able to buy a handsome uniform coat—an officer's coat it was, though White was still very much an enlisted man. It wasn't the uniform of his regiment either, and it didn't match the rest of his getup. But that didn't matter to White, or to anyone else. In this man's army a coat was a coat, and this one had buttonholes trimmed with gold lace, and the purchase price included a tricorne hat trimmed in gold.

With the new uniform and a title he adopted, "assistant adjutant," Private White proceeded to lead what he called the life of a "featherbed soldier." He slept in the cozy quarters of the commissary-general of military stores and he feasted on officers' rations. One of his new duties was to pick up the general orders of the day at the quarters of the regiment's deputy adjutant general—"a sour, crabbed old fellow." One morning White encountered the old crab himself and the following dialogue ensued:

"What do you want?"

"The general orders."

"What are you?"

"I am an assistant adjutant of the regiment of artillery."

"An assistant adjutant? I never heard of such an officer."

On another morning during the featherbed period, opportunity knocked again and White promptly answered. Colonel Richard Gridley, commanding officer of the regiment, sent for either the adjutant or an assistant. The adjutant being absent, White donned his coat and tricorne and hurried off to the colonel's quarters. There Colonel Gridley explained that he had a message, an oral one, that was to be given directly to His Excellency General Washington himself, not to one of his aides. "Tell him what I want," the colonel instructed White. "You must see him yourself."

After receiving the message, White hurried off to the house where both General and Mrs. Washington were quartered. He was admitted, but only after "a great deal of ceremony." At the foot of the stairway leading to the second floor, White encountered one of the general's aides. The general was upstairs, the aide said, and offered to deliver the message: "Tell me and I will go up and tell him." But this wasn't good enough for White: orders were orders; he had to see the general himself.

As the discussion continued, General Washington, apparently having overheard some of it, came to the head of the stairs. "Tell the young man to walk up," he called out.

White ascended the stairs and found himself face to face with the commander in chief—six feet two inches, about two hundred pounds, and, at age forty-four, still bearing himself like an athlete. As White "told my business," Washington apparently took note of the messenger's callow features and the gold-trimmed officer's getup. The general was puzzled.

"Pray, sir," he finally said, "what officer *are* you?"

"Assistant adjutant of the regiment of artillery," White replied.

"Indeed," Washington said, "you are very young to do that duty."

Yes, White agreed, he was young but "growing older every day." As he awaited the reply to his message, White noticed that the general "turned his face to his wife, and both smiled. He gave me my orders, and I retired."

About a year later, in the autumn of 1776, White would again find himself on the scene briefly with the commander in chief, but this time under tragically altered circumstances. White was among those standing nearby on November 16, 1776, as Washington and his aides witnessed the latest in a series of discouraging losses: the fall of Fort Washington. Between the autumn of 1775 and the autumn of 1776, the American rebellion had all but collapsed. The invasion of Canada, viewed by some as a campaign to add a "fourteenth colony," proved by the early summer of 1776 to be a disaster. Early in July 1776, William Howe, the British commander in chief, landed unopposed on Staten Island with some 9,000 troops. These were followed by thousands more—Hessian auxiliaries as well as British—and by the middle of August Howe was in command of more than 30,000 well-trained professionals. On August 27 the British and Hessian troops soundly defeated the Americans in the Battle of Long Island. In subsequent weeks, as thousands of American soldiers left for home, with or without permission, and as American morale foundered, General Washington was forced to evacuate Manhattan. On October 28 at White Plains the Americans were again defeated. Now, on November 16, they suffered the worst defeat of the revolution so far, the loss of Fort Washington, on the Hudson River about ten miles above what was then the city of New York (near today's 164th Street). With Hessian troops doing most of the fighting, the British army overwhelmed the Americans within a few hours. It was a debacle and one that could have been avoided if an indecisive Washington had followed his own judgment instead of bowing to that of Brigadier General Nathanael Greene. Greene, twenty-eight, an anchorsmith and former Quaker from Rhode Island, had insisted that the fort's garrison could withstand a British attack and persuaded Washington, who had his doubts, not to evacuate it. In Washington's words: "I had given it as my opinion to General Greene, under whose care it was, that it would be best to evacuate the place; but, as the order was discretionary, and his opinion differed from mine, it unhappily was delayed too long, to my great grief."

A few days before Fort Washington was attacked, Washington and a corps of troops had crossed the Hudson River to New Jersey and marched about five miles inland to encamp in and around Hackensack. On November 16, the day the fort was attacked, Washington was at Fort Lee, on the New Jersey Palisades, almost directly across the Hudson from the fort under attack.*

Among those standing near the commander in chief as he watched the fall of Fort Washington were General Greene, General Israel Putnam, General Hugh Mercer, and their aides—and Joseph White, now nineteen and a sergeant. White had completed his eight-month enlistment in December 1775 but, instead of going home, had "engaged to do the duty of an orderly sergeant for the year 1776." After experiencing the usual vicissitudes of army life and suffering "a dangerous sickness," he had recently made his way to Fort Lee for a period of recuperation. And now, here he was, once more in close proximity to General Washington. "The general," White observed, "seemed in agony when he saw the fort surrendered."

It was late in the afternoon when the white flag was raised over Fort Washington, signaling the surrender of more than 2,800 troops. One of those captured, young Oliver Woodruff of Livingston County, New York, would years later recall the sad day's doings: "We received a supply of cartridges and were ordered to eat our breakfast before daylight. As soon as daylight appeared, we were on our alarm posts. We had lines to defend a good distance from the fort. The British before sunrise appeared in three different places. The battle began with cannon shot, after some time with small arms, and continued until four o'clock in the afternoon, when the British sent in a flag and the firing ceased, and the fort was given up."

Another of the captured Americans, sixteen-year-old John Adlum, of York, Pennsylvania, observed that some American officers were so upset that they had "tears trickling down . . . their cheeks" and he "saw a Hessian officer with one of ours taking an inventory of our artillery, etc. And, very soon after, General Knyphausen himself

---

*The forts had been built in the hope of preventing British ships from sailing up the river and cutting American communications. The plan had fizzled; the British had sailed past the forts unimpeded.

with several of his officers came into the fort.* When Colonel
Swoops stepped up to him and offered his hand to General Knyphausen . . . he replied by saying, 'Naw, naw, naw, I no shake
hands mit a rebel.' "

Some of his fellow soldiers, Adlum noted, were drunk, "but I
believe they were all foreigners as I do not recollect of seeing one of
the Americans intoxicated." While waiting to be marched off to a
prison, Adlum "saw a number of barrels of biscuit and now knowing
that we were prisoners I cut open the lining of my coat and filled the
skirts of it with from a peck [to] a half bushel of biscuit and I
advised my companions to do the same. . . .

"After a little while we were called out of the fort. We were
drawn up in different lines, each regiment or detachment by itself
though contiguous to each other. . . . A guard of Hessian grenadiers
with brass caps were placed in our front and over our troops, who
were ordered to follow. . . .

"I stood looking on as our troops moved forward. When there was
a considerable number of private [British] soldiers and women . . .
drawn up, whom we had to pass, some of the women observed that
it was a shame to let our troops carry off their packs. Some of the
Hessian soldiers began to cut the knapsacks off the backs of our
men with their swords . . . and I was afterwards informed that some
of our soldiers was severely cut with the swords of the Hessians."

Presently, along the route of march, Adlum and the rest of the
captured soldiers were verbally abused by curious crowds, including
people they had presumably been fighting for: "There was great
numbers of people collected on various parts of the road, very few of
whom seemed to sympathize with us, but numbers were disposed to
say ill-natured things to us by saying that we ought to be or would
be hanged and called us by opprobrious names of rebel,† with a
damn added to it by some." The mob included some camp follow-

---

*Baron Wilhelm von Knyphausen, sixty, second in command of the German
troops in America, led the attack on Fort Washington. He had been soldiering ever
since joining the Prussian army in 1734. In America he would become best known
as a result of a widespread report that he spread butter on bread with his thumb.

†Although *rebel* was a likely term for one taking part in a rebellion, the appellation
was resented by many Americans. "Britain has most unjustly pronounced us rebels,
and treated us as such," the Reverend Jacob Green, minister of the Presbyterian
Church in Hanover, N.J., complained in 1776. In the same year, Captain Alexander Graydon found *rebel* "extremely offensive to my ear . . . however appropriate it
might be."

ers: "The Hessian women were particularly abusive. When we got to the environs of the city we were assailed by a number of soldiers' trulls and others who the soldiers called Holy Ground Ladies.* Numbers were calling out, 'Which is Washington? Where is he?' . . . and treated us with volleys of indecent language."

An American officer in the line of march, Captain Alexander Graydon, would never forget some of the women: "It was obvious that in the calculation of this assemblage of female loyalty, the war was at an end, and that the whole of the rebel army, Washington and all, were safe in durance. Which is Washington? Which is Washington? proceeded from half a dozen mouths at once, and the guard was obliged to exert itself to keep them off. Some of them assailed us with vollies of Billingsgate." At one point a British colonel riding horseback alongside the line of prisoners lost his patience with one of the tormentors. He "had enough to do to silence one of them, calling out repeatedly: 'Away with that woman! Take her away! Knock her down, the bitch! Knock her down!' "

A Scottish sergeant offered Captain Graydon some advice along the route of march: "Young man, ye should never fight against your king!" A British officer "rode up at full gallop, exclaiming, 'What? Taking prisoners? Kill them! Kill every man of them!' "

Turning toward him, Graydon took off his hat and said: "Sir, I put myself under your protection." It worked: "No man was ever more effectually rebuked. His manner was instantly softened. . . . After a civil question or two, as if to make amends for his sanguinary mandate, he rode off."

Within a few weeks hundreds of the Americans trudging in that line toward New York would die of cold, disease, and starvation in prison ships and improvised prisons.

---

*New York's brothel district (in today's terms the area surrounding the Woolworth Building) was a slum, most of which was owned by the Trinity parish.

◆◆

CHAPTER 2

All Who Are My Grenadiers, Forward!

An "almost inaccessible rock . . . surrounded by swamps and three earthworks, one above the other"—that is how Fort Washington looked to Lieutenant Andreas Wiederholdt on the morning of November 16, 1776, as he led an advance guard of thirty Hessians toward the place. "In spite of this," he later wrote in his journal, "every obstacle was swept aside, the earthworks broken through, the precipitous rocks scaled, and the [American] riflemen were driven out of their breastworks, from where they had been supported by their artillery, and we gained this terrible height."

Wiederholdt made it to the top uninjured "except for a little scratch on my face caused by a broken twig." A captain and a lieutenant following close behind him were among those fatally wounded in the ascent.

The attack had begun with heavy artillery fire, according to Private (later Corporal) Johannes Reuber, one of the Hessian soldiers who had followed Wiederholdt's party up the steep slopes. Two warships had suddenly begun to cannonade the fort, Reuber noted in his diary, "and at the same time matters broke loose on land with cannon firing and ships firing while all the force advanced up the mountain as stones and rocks tumbled down." Not to mention enemy fire: "One man fell down mortally wounded and another was shot dead instantly. We had to drag ourselves up by grasping the wild boxwood bushes because it was so steep that we could not keep our balance. Trees and rocks kept tumbling down and it was hard to make any progress. At last, however, we proceeded to mount the height. Then Colonel Rall gave the command: 'All who are my grenadiers, forward!' Thereupon the drummers struck up 'March,' the horn-players blew 'March,' and all of us who were still alive shouted 'Hurrah!' "

Now the rout was on as Reuber and the rest charged forward with their bayonets ready for action. The Americans, except those who fell wounded in the charge, raced to the temporary sanctuary of the fort. Although the Americans were advantageously positioned inside the fort, they were outnumbered by about 8,000 to 3,000; fighting for the day would soon be over.

Reuber was a member of Colonel Johann Gottlieb Rall's grenadier regiment, a well-trained unit that would be cited for exceptional bravery in that action.* The grenadiers had been drilled to form in close ranks and advance en masse in battle. When the enemy was within range, they fired their muskets in unison and then charged forward as a body, screaming and holding their bayonets forward and parallel to the ground. The awesomeness of such charges was enhanced by the grenadiers' getup. Their coats of blue wool were almost covered with broad belts. They wore towering brass-fronted headgear that made even short men appear tall. They dyed their mustaches with the same concoction used for blackening their shoes.† Their long hair, according to a contemporary description, was "plastered with tallow and flour and tightly drawn into a long appendage reaching from the back of the head to [the] waist."

In the final charge of the rebels at Fort Washington, Reuber noted, "not a shot was fired." He and the rest of the grenadiers relied as usual on the bayonet in chasing the Americans into the fort. Then: "We took positions in a ditch that the Americans had dug around the fort, and here we were ordered to stop our advance. The Americans had outrun us but now they were commanded to consider themselves prisoners of war. General Knyphausen ordered that the fort had to capitulate within two hours."

Knyphausen demonstrated his accustomed bravery throughout the action, according to Lieutenant Wiederholdt: "At all times he was to be found in the thickest of the fight, the place where resistance and action were the hottest." At the approaches to the fort the rebels had made defensive barriers of felled trees and other

---

*A century or more earlier grenadiers had been selected for their size and strength, particularly for their ability to hurl "hand bombs" a great distance. Though such grenades were no longer in use, the term "grenadiers" still usually indicated elite troops, but not necessarily tall ones. Grenadier Reuber, for example, was five feet one, and most of the rest of the Rall Regiment were only a few inches taller.

†One recipe for shoe blackening, recorded in the diary of Captaine d'Armes Jeremias Kappes of the Knyphausen Regiment, called for: "1 oz black ash, 2 oz brown sugar, 1 oz gum arabic, ½ pt beer."

objects. Urging his troops onward, Knyphausen "tore down the barriers with his own hands. . . . He was also exposed like a common soldier to the frightful cannon and shrapnel fire as well as the rifle fire, and it is a wonder that he came off without being killed or wounded."

Wiederholdt himself had survived fire just as deadly. After leading the vanguard to "this terrible height," he noted, "we . . . pursued the enemy who were retreating behind the lines and batteries, we routed them from there also, and took the batteries . . . and we followed the fleeing enemy to the fort proper. There we seated ourselves at the side of the precipitous mountain to protect ourselves from the cannonade from the fort. . . . The fort was summoned to surrender and, half an hour later, 2,600 men came marching out of it, laid their rifles down at our feet and surrendered as prisoners of war to His Excellency Lieutenant General von Knyphausen, who was present and signed the capitulation.* The entire fort with all stores of ammunition and provisions, which were considerable, was handed over to us."

A career soldier like most of his fellow Hessian officers, Wiederholdt was forty-four and a veteran of about twenty-five years of service. Although he had achieved a distinguished record he had not been promoted since 1760. Like many another Hessian officer, he found service in America attractive because, with Europe temporarily at peace, America was where the action was—promotions were far more easily gained there than at home. But what a paradox America was. Why were these people, so well treated, enjoying so much freedom, ungrateful enough to rebel against their king? Why, while they ranted about freedom and liberty, did they treat their black slaves worse than animals were treated in Germany?

Although the attacking force was made up of about 5,000 British troops and 3,000 Hessians and other German auxiliaries, the British suffered far fewer casualties than the Germans. In their accustomed manner they succeeded in prodding the Germans into a state of ferocity.† As a result the Germans suffered an inordinately high rate of casualties: of the 78 members of the British force reported killed,

---

*Actually, as noted, some 2,800 men surrendered.

†"The British Light Infantry formed in the rear of the Hessians and drove them on to our troops with their bayonets," according to the aforementioned American captive John Adlum.

58 were Germans; of the 374 reported wounded, 272 were Germans. Most of the other casualties were Scottish. The English troops, apparently having done more prodding than fighting, suffered relatively light casualties. (Of the Americans, about 50 were killed and an unknown number wounded.)

In the Battle of Long Island, about ten weeks earlier, Hessian troops had seen their first action in America and had faithfully followed British instructions to show no mercy to the damned rebels. "The Hessians and our brave Highlanders gave no quarter," an officer of Major Simon Fraser's (Seventy-first) Scotch Battalion reported following that battle. "It was a fine sight to see with what alacrity they dispatched the rebels with bayonets, after we had surrounded them so that they could not resist. We took care to tell the Hessians that the rebels had resolved to give no quarter to them in particular; which made them fight desperately, and put all to death who fell into their hands."

Colonel Henrich Anton von Heringen, who led one of the Hessian regiments in the Long Island action, also made note of the prodding: "The English soldiers did not give much quarter and constantly urged our men to follow their example."*

Even before the Hessians arrived in America, reports of their savagery had been circulated. According to a typical report, their "native ferocity, when heightened and whetted by the influence and malice of the sceptered savage of Great Britain, thirsting for the blood of his faithful American subjects, will exhibit such a scene of cruelty, death and devastation as will fill those of us who survive the carnage with indignation and horror, attended with poverty and wretchedness." The Hessians, in a typical report,† indulged in "rapine and bloodshed" and delighted in torture.

Following the Battle of Long Island, American newspapers charged the Hessians with unspeakable crimes. According to a

---

*Germans captured about two months after the Battle of Long Island said the British were still at it. James Thacher, a physician serving with the Americans, reported that the captured German "officers and soldiers, by a finesse of the British to increase their ferocity, had been led to believe that Americans are savages and barbarians, and, if taken, their men would have their bodies stuck full of pieces of dry wood and in that manner burned to death."

†Published in the *Norwich Packet* of July 8, 1776, a few weeks before the first Germans arrived in America.

typical piece of propaganda, the Hessians not only stabbed Americans begging for mercy but actually pinned their victims to tree trunks.*

Inside Fort Washington, after the rebels surrendered, a British officer surveyed the carnage and observed of the Americans that "many were without shoes or stockings, and several were observed to have only linen drawers on, with a rifle or hunting shirt, without any proper shirt or waistcoat." Frederick Mackenzie, a British captain, looked on as the captured rebels were prodded into formations for the march to New York City, where they would be imprisoned. "Few of them . . . appear to have washed themselves during the campaign," Mackenzie noted. "A great many of them were lads under fifteen, and old men. . . . Their odd figures frequently excited the laughter of our soldiers."

Outside the fort, Johannes Reuber and the rest of the Rall Grenadier Regiment stood in formation near the main entrance. Facing them from the other side of the entrance was another formation of Hessians, the troops of the Lossberg Fusilier Regiment. The Hessians' blue uniforms contrasted sharply with the varicolored garb of the rebels passing through. "The Americans," Reuber would note in his diary, "came out of the fort and had to march between the two regiments and as they passed through they had to take their rifles and belts and put all their armature down on the ground. As this was being done, the English troops came from the left flank and took the Americans away. . . . Then another regiment came out of the fort and had to do the same thing, and this continued until the fort was empty."

Some of the Hessians victimized the helpless rebels, according to Major (later Lieutenant Colonel) Stephen Kemble, an American serving as General Howe's deputy adjutant general. "To our shame," he reported, though the Americans "capitulated for the safety of their baggage, they were stripped of their wearing apparel as they marched out by Hessians, till a stop was put to it by making them take a different route."

After the last of the prisoners were marched off, Johannes Reuber and the other grenadiers of Colonel Rall's regiment entered the fort

---

*"The [American] riflemen were mostly spitted to the trees with bayonets," Colonel von Heringen reported after the Battle of Long Island. Such exaggerated reports contributed to a proliferation of tree-trunk stories.

and made preparations for a well-earned night of rest. The fort would be their home for about three weeks.

Rall's troops had by this time been in America for about three months, having arrived in New York harbor as part of a force of some 8,600 German auxiliaries in mid-August. These were the first German troops to reach America and this was the sixth time within a century that Hessian troops had been hired out to England to fight on foreign soil. Eventually England would hire about 30,000 Germans to serve during the revolution, some 19,000 of them being Hessians.*

Grenadier Johannes Reuber was one of thirty soldiers who had left their homes in Niedervellmar, a village outside the town of Cassel, to serve in America. In Niedervellmar, as in the other communities of Hesse-Cassel, males between the ages of sixteen and thirty were liable for military service. Most of the enlisted men who actually served were from poor families—families owning property worth less than a specified amount of money. Students, widows' sons, miners, and foresters were usually exempt from service. So were men owning farmland, and servants in the employ of aristocrats. Twelve heads of families were among the thirty soldiers who left Niedervellmar with Grenadier Reuber: they didn't own enough property to be exempted.

Reuber was one of the youngest of the grenadiers, having gone into service in the autumn of 1775 when he was sixteen. Most of those who joined at an early age were farm boys who, like Reuber, saw the respected profession of soldiering as a likely way of getting ahead. In the diary he was to keep throughout his years of service Reuber comes across as an earnest, no-nonsense, loyal soldier who never questioned orders and who idolized such a commanding officer as Colonel Rall. He was probably typical of the young Hessians in this regard and in his inability to understand why Americans, living in what seemed to be a land of plenty, would rebel against their sovereign.

---

*Although the mercenaries came from several areas of Germany, the term Hessians was often applied to all of them. According to the German historian Friedrich Kapp, Hesse-Cassel sent 16,992 troops, Hesse-Hanau 2,422, Brunswick 5,723, Anspach-Bayreuth 2,353, Waldeck 1,225, and Anhalt-Zerbst 1,160. Some 5,000 eventually deserted and more than 7,500 died in America. For the services of the mercenaries the princes who hired them out were enriched by a total of more than £4,584,400.

According to Reuber's diary, his training company had become part of Colonel Rall's grenadier regiment on January 2, 1776. These were dedicated young soldiers: "Every day . . . we trained in bitter cold and deep snow until we were as good as the other field regiments." February 29: "We heard a rumor that we were to be shipped to America." "All of us," he wrote on March 3, "were bewildered, realizing that 'this was it.' We were serious and depressed but there was nothing else to do but remain patient. That evening an order was received that we were to leave for Cassel the next morning to be inspected by Landgrave Frederick."

After parading past the Landgrave the next day, Reuber and the rest "left town through the Leipzig Gate" and set off on a march that would bring them to Bremerlehe (Bremerhaven) more than a month later, on April 9. Some of the soldiers on the march from Cassel and other garrison towns—about twelve in each battalion—were accompanied by their wives, a few by their children as well. A number had married shortly before leaving home in order to bring their women along. (A few of the women would give birth en route to America.) Some of the officers brought along their dogs as well as their wives. Twenty-four enlisted men deserted along the way.

In many towns there were tearful departure scenes, such as the one described by Lieutenant Heinrich von Bardeleben: "Disconsolate mothers, lamenting wives and weeping children followed the regiment in crowds, and impressed on us most sensibly the whole of this sad scene."

Reuber either did not observe such scenes or, in his diary at least, chose to ignore them. On arriving at Bremerlehe on April 9, he and the rest of his unit "were inspected by English officials and then had to pledge allegiance to the King of England." Three days later they "boarded the large ships," seventeen in all. They arrived eleven days later at the harbor of Portsmouth, England. Here they waited and waited—"just marking time and trying to be in good spirits," as good soldier Reuber put it—as a large convoy was assembled to transport British as well as German troops to America. It was not until May 11, according to Reuber, that the convoy, made up of some 150 transports and escorted by relatively fast-moving warships, finally set off on what was at times to be a horrendous voyage. Throughout, Reuber put his trust in God and, at least in his diary notes, never complained or bemoaned his fate, even when the ship encountered heavy storms. "The Lord," he noted, had "everything arranged." On the first night at sea, the moon "illuminated our way and our hearts were full of thanks to God who helped to start us on our voyage under the best of circumstances." Seasickness became a widespread problem early on, and during the worst of the storms many men were injured and a few died.

In his diary Reuber never complained about the food either, although, as others reported, the water became undrinkable and the biscuits maggoty. "At 8 in the morning," he noted one day, "the steward issues bread, meat, butter and cheese . . . and a little can of rum and vinegar for each man." On Sundays, he wrote, the menu included not only a good portion of meat but also pudding "mixed by the old soldiers themselves." Even when the seas were at their roughest he knew he could count on the Almighty: "The Lord . . . stopped the wind and we relaxed."

Finally, four months after departing from Germany, the ships carrying the German troops reached New York harbor with the rest of the convoy. "Now," Reuber wrote on August 15, "we saw a great number of ships . . . in the harbor. . . . Our command ship fired thirty-two shots in celebration and all the others joined in by firing. . . . With the help of the Almighty we had come to a happy end of our voyage. The name of the Lord was praised. God has helped us thus far and will protect us from bad luck in this land where we will fight the enemy."

Within a fortnight grenadier Reuber and many other German troops took part in the Battle of Long Island. A few weeks later they saw further action, including the battle at White Plains, and on November 16 Reuber and the rest of Colonel Rall's regiment enhanced their growing reputation as ferocious fighting men during the attack on Fort Washington. That day, Ambrose Serle, secretary to General Howe, declared, "the Hessians behaved with incomparable steadiness and spirit." To honor the Hessian officer in command of the attack, Fort Washington was renamed Fort Knyphausen. Not many weeks later, however, the vaunted Rall and Knyphausen regiments would be held in such disgrace that the man who hired them out, Frederick II, the Landgrave of Hesse-Cassel, would demand a searching investigation of their performance in battle.

CHAPTER 3

A Set of Rascals Skulked
Out of the Way

The British army was coming! Sergeant Joseph White, still recuperating from a "dangerous sickness" at Fort Lee, New Jersey, received the alarm from an express rider who galloped into sight, crying out: "Turn out! Turn out! We are all surrounded. Leave everything but your blankets. You must fight your way through or be prisoners."

Early in the morning of November 20, four days after taking Fort Washington, the British army, about 5,000 strong, had crossed the Hudson River from New York to New Jersey undetected. In a fairly dense fog the troops came ashore at a crude dock area known as Lower Closter Landing, about six miles above Fort Lee (but via the roads of the time a march of about ten miles). A short time after the invaders scaled the steep, 300-foot slopes of the cliffs along the riverbank—the Palisades—their leading troops were observed and word of the invasion began to spread through Bergen County.

Upon receiving the alarm, Sergeant White and some 2,000 others garrisoned at Fort Lee (except the soldiers who were too drunk on the sutlers' liquor to know or care what was going on) made hasty preparations to flee. "We were on the march in about ten minutes," White would recall. The order to abandon the fort came from General Washington, who was back in Hackensack when he received word that the enemy had landed. "I immediately went over," Washington would report the next day, "and as the fort was not tenable on this side and we were in a narrow neck of land, the passes from which the enemy were attempting to seize, I directed the troops . . . to move over to the west side of the Hackensack River."

The retreating soldiers, commanded by General Greene, fled down the western slope of the Palisades and on through the English Neighborhood (a sparsely settled area, now encompassing Englewood, Leonia, and Ridgefield). Their destination was the New Bridge span over the Hackensack River, situated about four miles north of the village of Hackensack and a march of about seven miles from the fort. At one point during the retreat, according to Sergeant White's recollection, a British force allowed the Americans to flee unmolested: "They let us march by them, leaving all the camp equipage." The abandoned equipage included eighteen sorely needed artillery pieces, a thousand or more barrels of flour, hundreds of tents and entrenching tools, tons of baggage, and large iron kettles bubbling with victuals.

Andrew Hunter, Jr., a twenty-four-year-old Presbyterian chaplain serving with a New Jersey unit, and two associates came close to walking into the enemy's hands. "In the morning," he noted in his diary, "we had an account of the enemy's landing . . . and about 10 o'clock we had orders to retreat, taking what baggage we could with us which was very little compared to what we left behind. . . .

"Colonel Brearly, Mr. Hollingshead and myself, having missed the route of the troops, had nearly gone into the enemy's camp, had we not been prevented by some women whom we met running crying in the road." Thanks to the women's warning, they changed direction and set off to rejoin Washington's retreating troops.

One of the versions of the abandonment of the fort was written by an anonymous soldier from Pennsylvania who, like many of his contemporaries, had his own way with words. In a notebook that he titled "Gornall of They campagn" he described the scene thus: "They Generalls orders was make they best way the cud and severalls left their goods in they camp and made of and there was a great many was taken that got drunk with they sutlers liquir and nocked they heads ought of the hogsheads."

The Americans were not to be trapped in the fort, but would they be able to get safely across the river at New Bridge before the British came on in force? A defeat here, following the debacle at Fort Washington and the other demoralizing losses, might be disastrous to the cause. The main body of the British army, however, was slow in coming. This enabled General Greene to make a return trip to Fort Lee: "I returned to the camp two hours after the troops marched off. Colonel Cornwell and myself got off several hundred; yet, notwithstanding all our endeavors, still near a hundred remained hid about the woods." Greene described these men as "a set of rascals that skulked out of the way for fear of fighting."

If the fort had been manned by Continental soldiers—full-time regulars—defense of the position would have been possible, according to Greene. But, Greene complained, the garrison had been made up "mostly of the Flying Camp, irregular and undisciplined; had they obeyed orders, not a man would have been taken."*

Except for a few units on patrol or reconnaissance missions, the British appeared to be intent upon reaching Fort Lee rather than seeking out and skirmishing with the Americans. The main body of the British moved southward toward Fort Lee while most of the fleeing Americans moved northward toward New Bridge by way of another route. Among those retreating with the troops was Thomas Paine, a newspaper correspondent from Philadelphia. He had enlisted in August 1776 and about a month later had become an aide to General Greene. Earlier in the year he had written "Common Sense," a fifty-page pamphlet that became a battle cry of the movement for independence. Now, serving both as a correspondent for the *Pennsylvania Journal* and as Greene's aide, he was keeping notes on the retreat and, by campfire at night, writing a pamphlet that would begin, "These are the times that try men's souls . . ."

Like Sergeant White, who said the British "let us march by them," correspondent Paine noted the enemy's reluctance to bring on a confrontation. On arriving at the New Bridge crossing he was relieved as well as perplexed to find that British troops "quietly suffered our troops to take possession" of the bridge. He had "expected we should have a brush" here. "However, they did not choose to dispute it with us,† and the greatest part of our troops went over the bridge, the rest over the ferry, except some who passed at a mill on a small creek, between the bridge and the ferry, and made their way through some marshy grounds up to the town of Hackensack, and there passed the river."

---

*The Flying Camp was established by Congress early in the summer of 1776 as a mobile reserve force to provide reinforcements in the New York area as needed and to oppose any effort by the British to enter New Jersey. It was made up of militiamen (weekend soldiers rather than "regular" Continentals) who signed up for a few months of duty. The original plan called for 10,000 troops to be recruited from New Jersey, Pennsylvania, Maryland, and Delaware and to be commanded by Brigadier General Hugh Mercer of Virginia. Its members, rarely numbering more than 3,000, were by and large better known for fleeing than fighting.

†In his memoirs James Wilkinson also made note of this: "The Americans . . . were suffered to escape across the Hackensack River without being brought to action." Later: "That we were surprised is admitted on all hands, and that the enemy had us in a *cul de sac*, from which he permitted us to escape is equally true." Wilkinson was not at the scene but apparently received this information from some who were.

When the crossings were completed, delaying actions were ordered. The boats used by the troops crossing to Hackensack village, about four miles downstream from New Bridge, were withdrawn from the enemy's reach. So was the ferryboat, a horse-drawn contrivance. Upstream, a detachment was left to defend the span at New Bridge, which the Americans had failed to demolish.

The fleeing troops, except for the intoxicated and the skulkers, had escaped entrapment; for the time being they were safe, and, as Tom Paine saw things, the situation was in hand: "The simple object was to bring off the garrison and march them on till they could be strengthened by the Jersey and Pennsylvania militia, so as to be enabled to make a stand."

Perhaps with the Hackensack River as a barrier, the Americans would be able to make a stand against what appeared to be a reluctant enemy force. Perhaps the militiamen of Bergen County would turn out to help in the defense of their home territory.

———— ♦♦♦ ————

CHAPTER 4

Spare the King's Subjects

Did the British really want to crush the rebel army and thereby end the rebellion, or didn't they? That question occurred to an extraordinarily able and perceptive Hessian captain, Johann Ewald, before the end of the first day of the incursion into New Jersey, November 20. On two occasions that day Ewald was ordered not to molest fleeing rebel parties. What kind of warfare was this? Ewald was the commanding officer of an elite company of Hessians eager to demonstrate their superiority over the Americans. He had come to America to assist in putting down a rebellion, not to coddle a passel of wretches who were fighting against their own king.

Ewald had been soldiering ever since the age of sixteen—half of his life—but he had never encountered such nonsense as this. While still in his teens he had fought for the Prussians against the French in the Seven Years War and had been wounded in action, cited for bravery, and promoted to the rank of ensign. Later, he studied engineering and wrote a book on military tactics. One dark night in 1770 he perpetuated a military tradition by engaging in a semidrunken duel with a friend outside an inn, and now his left eye was made of glass.

Slender, erect, serious on duty, strict with his troops, courageous, straightforward, intelligent, and a man of the finest manners—thus he would be described in a biography written by his son. Ewald was a fearless and aggressive leader in battle—at times, in the opinion of superior officers, too aggressive. Always ready for action, he carried two pistols and a big broadsword. One day, as von Ewald, he would be a celebrated general.

The jagers (from the German *Jäger*, hunter) such as those Ewald commanded were also known as *chasseurs* (French *chasseur*, huntsman), and because of the forest green of their uniforms they were nicknamed "Greencoats." They wore black tricorne headgear and green coats with carmine collars, cuffs, and lapels over green vests trimmed with gold. They carried rifled guns that had hexagonal bores and more accurate sights than those of the smoothbore muskets. In hand-to-hand combat they wielded hunting swords instead of bayonets. They were called to action not by the usual bugler or trumpeter but by a horn-blower using a crescent-shaped instrument made of brass.

At this time the jagers were foot soldiers; Captain Ewald was the only member of the Second Jager Company who was mounted. (Later in the war, Ewald commanded detachments that included mounted jagers.) They were expert marksmen; many had been game wardens, hunters, or foresters. They were trained to reconnoiter enemy outposts, to act as advance, flank, or rear guards during troop movements, to protect foraging parties, and to carry out other hazardous duties.

The First Jager Company, commanded by Captain Carl August von Wreden, had arrived at New York harbor in mid-August 1776 with the first corps of troops from Germany. In the Battle of Long Island, which took place only a few days later, Wreden's jagers fought with such daring and skill that the British high command immediately dispatched word to London requesting the hiring of a thousand additional jagers. From the Long Island action onward, Wreden's jagers were among the most respected of the British troops. (And by the enemy perhaps the most detested. Jonathan Gillett, a young soldier from Connecticut, was captured on Long

Island, as he reported, "by a party called jagers, the most inhuman of all mortals. . . . They first disarmed me, then plundered me of all I had: watch, buckles, money and some clothing, after which they abused me by bruising my flesh with the butts of their guns. They knocked me down. I got up and they kept on beating me almost all the way to their camp.")

Captain Ewald and his Second Jager Company—125 young men bearing such names as Bauer, Buchwald, Doerinckel, Gurckel, Haschell, Meister, Mergel, Reichmeyer, Ruppel, and Trautvetter—had reached New York harbor late in October 1776 as part of the second corps of German auxiliaries. Within a few days, Ewald's elite Greencoats, like Wreden's, proceeded to distinguish themselves as fearless, dedicated warriors, fiercely proud of their special status and of their Hessian heritage. In New Jersey both companies would gain further laurels.

Ewald and his company had left Hesse-Cassel on May 9, 1776. They were on the move for three weeks, marching through Götting-en, Hanover, and on to Cuxhaven on the estuary of the Elbe River. About a week later, after passing inspection, Ewald and his men boarded *Two Brothers*, a rickety three-masted schooner, one of several that the English had hired from the Dutch. In convoy with seventeen other vessels, the *Two Brothers* arrived at Portsmouth, England, after a voyage of thirteen days. After being expanded to sixty-four vessels, the convoy set sail for New York on June 28. Because of calms, "constant adverse winds," and other complications, the fleet was unable to head out into the Atlantic until July 28, a month after leaving Portsmouth. The rest of the voyage required almost three months, and during this time the fresh provisions and wine ran out. So did the patience of the jagers; as the days dragged on with no land in sight, they protested that the fleet had already passed America, and nothing the sailors said could convince them otherwise. Many of the men became violently ill; some of them died. "Scurvy was raging among our men so violently," Ewald observed at one point, "that in the past eight days ten men had died and almost twenty more looked forward to death, which in their misery they regarded as fortunate."

Along with the rest of the German troops commanded by Lieutenant General Wilhelm von Knyphausen, Ewald's jagers disembarked near New York early in the morning of October 22. By nightfall, after traveling part of the way by boat, they went into bivouac near New Rochelle, New York. There, to the dismay of neighboring farmers, they made their first night raid. While some of the jagers gathered wood and got huge fires crackling, others, as Captain Ewald noted, went on the prowl: "No sooner had several fires blazed than we heard the cries of chickens, geese and pigs which our resourceful soldiers had discovered. Within that hour, several roasts hung from long sticks before each fire. The whole camp was as busy as an anthill." Ewald could not help but admire such enterprise: "From this one can see how easily a good soldier knows his way about."

Early the next day, October 23, their second on American soil, Ewald's jagers set off to take part in a reconnaissance mission near Mile Square (later part of Yonkers). It was a march of a little more than two hours and it led to a heated and bloody skirmish with the rebels. This was the first day of what was to be a long and close relationship between Ewald and his commanding officer, Colonel Carl Emil Ulrich von Donop, and, because of Ewald's overaggressiveness, it got off to a squally start. In the skirmish Ewald found himself and some of his jagers hemmed in by heavy fire. "Suddenly Colonel Donop appeared with a few dragoons and shouted at me to retreat." Ewald replied that he could not, except at a great loss. Exasperated, Donop shouted, "You want to conquer America in one day! You write rules and then violate them," and rode off.

By the time the firefight ended, six of Ewald's men were dead, eleven wounded, and two captured—a costly encounter, and Ewald was reprimanded as well as praised for bringing it on. For his jagers Ewald had high praise: "The morale of the men was extraordinary, for during the twenty-one weeks they spent on the ship they had become languid and weak. Yet, on this day, they had to stay on their feet from morning until night. They kept complaining that they were so tired they would drop. I had only to remind them that they were Hessians, whereupon their strength always revived. None of us had eaten a bite of bread since morning. . . .

"Meanwhile, no matter is so serious that it does not have a pleasant side. Through it I gained such great respect with the enemy that they held me in all honor there; and each jager, who had fought with five to six men during the skirmish, regarded himself as invincible from this time on."

The jagers went on to enhance their reputation in the battle at White Plains on October 28 and in the taking of Fort Washington on

November 16. Now, four days later, they were in the vanguard of the British force that crossed the Hudson River to New Jersey for the attack on Fort Lee. Colonel Donop, second in command to Cornwallis on this mission, had by this time come to view Ewald as a daring and dedicated leader, but he continued to watch for signs of Ewald's overaggressiveness. An aristocrat and a thirty-seven-year-old career officer, Donop had served as adjutant to Frederick II, the Landgrave of Hesse-Cassel, before departing for America with the first contingent of Germans. Like many others, he thought it would be a short war and a great opportunity for advancement. He looked forward to promotion and to returning to court life in Germany with high honors.

Cornwallis's force, some 5,000 troops, was made up of English and Hessian grenadiers and five English brigades, according to Ewald, in addition to the jagers. "At daybreak," he noted, "this army crossed the river in flatboats, the crossing being covered by several frigates on the left. We climbed ashore along a steep bluff and scaled the rocky and bushy height as quickly as possible."

"We landed in the Jerseys," Lieutenant Henry Stirke of the British Tenth Regiment of Foot observed, "after passing a very disagreeable night in the flat boats under a thick heavy rain." Stirke and his fellow light infantrymen had been serving with distinction ever since landing in New York from Halifax during the summer. Only two days before the taking of Fort Lee, Stirke had been promoted from ensign to lieutenant. This is how he described the scaling of the Palisades: "The guards, with the British and Hessian grenadiers and the cannon succeeded us; which were obliged to be drawn up almost a precipice, above a half mile in length, by men as it was impassable for horses. (The 10th and 17th companys were to make the first landing with orders to push up the hill with as much expedition as possible to take post and maintain it 'till sustained.) Our landing was not opposed (though under so many disadvantages) certainly owing to their not expecting us in that quarter."

John Aldington, a Tory from Bergen County serving with the British, knew the area well and, along with a few other local British sympathizers, was on the scene to assist in leading the troops up the long, narrow, twisting path. (Years later, in England, when Aldington claimed remuneration for services rendered during the war, he received this endorsement from Cornwallis: "I hereby certify that Major John Aldington was a zealous Loyalist and that he guided the troops under my command when I landed in the province of New Jersey in the year 1776.")*

Of the successful scaling of the New Jersey Palisades, Commander in Chief Howe would report the following to Lord George Germain in London: "The seamen distinguished themselves remarkably upon this occasion by their readiness to drag the cannon up a rocky narrow road for near half a mile, to the top of the precipice which bounds the shore for some miles on the west side."

Colonel Donop was less than elated about Cornwallis's choice of landing area in New Jersey, describing it as an "extraordinarily high and scarped, rocky coast" and as a "dreadful and impracticable place." The troops, he would presently note in a letter, "had to pass one at a time up a steep path that was hardly four feet wide. The rebels must have considered this an impossible landing place because they had no guard here. Fifty men would have been enough to stop our entire corps. In spite of this, however, two light six-pounders in addition to two howitzers and four English three-pounders were dragged up by sailors and soldiers. This lasted until about 1 o'clock in the afternoon. In the meantime the jagers and light infantry were advancing through the woods to the right to the nearest houses where they made a few prisoners after firing a few shots."

Captain Ewald and his jagers were indeed advancing to the right and, as usual, seeking contact with the enemy. After having scaled "the rocky and bushy height," Ewald noted, "we found at the top several plantations in a district called Dunne fledt [Tenafly] where the jagers and light infantry deployed in a semicircle behind the stone walls and posted sentries by platoon at distances of three hundred paces. Fort Lee lay two hours away from us on the left.

"As soon as the grenadiers joined us, the corps advanced a half hour farther into the country, and both jager companies were posted on the highway somewhat forward. . . . I saw a plantation . . . whither I proceeded with several jagers to learn from the inhabitants just where I was. The owner of the house approached and informed me that this highway ran to New Bridge, a small place where there

*Aldington's involvement would not be made known until 1963, when Dr. Richard P. McCormick, a Rutgers University historian, discovered his claim, bearing Cornwallis's endorsement, in the British Public Office in London.

was a bridge over the [Hackensack] river, which joined another road
. . . that one must take to get to Fort Lee.

"During this conversation I discovered a great glitter of bayonets
and a cloud of dust in the distance.—Who is that?—That must be
the garrison of Fort Lee!—Can't we cut them off from the bridge?—
Yes, you have only two English miles from here to there!*—I ran
back to Captain Wreden and told him of my discovery. He believed
that these people were the second column of our army. I wanted to
know the truth and I took several jagers with me to draw near this
column in the flank, crawling from stone wall to stone wall, and
discovered that it was American.† I began to skirmish with them and
sent back a jager to fetch more men, but instead of the jagers, I
received an order from Lord Cornwallis to return at once. I had to
obey, and informed him what I had discovered.—'Let them go, my
dear Ewald, and stay here. We do not want to lose any men. One
jager is worth more than ten rebels.' " Lieutenant Johann Heinrichs, on the march with Wreden's jagers, had an explanation:
"Cornwallis had orders to follow the enemy until they should make
a stand, whereupon he was to retire and not molest them."

Ewald, it appears, had discovered the party of retreating Americans near a place known as Liberty Pole, where the route followed
by the British crossed the one along which the Americans were
fleeing toward New Bridge. Instead of pursuing the retreating
rebels, however, the British decided to continue toward Fort Lee. It
was around 2:00 p.m., according to Colonel Donop, when the main
body of troops got into formation in two columns and set off for the
final lap of the march to the fort. Captain Wreden's jagers formed
the advance party and Captain Ewald's covered the right flank.
Along the way, Ewald caught sight of a "column of the enemy army
[and] moved further to the right in hopes of catching some baggage.
A coach and four with several men actually fell into my hands, but I
hardly wanted to pursue my game further, and I received new
orders to keep closer to the column."

At this point Ewald realized he had the answer to the question
that had been troubling him: the British had no intention whatever

---

*Ewald had a working knowledge of English at this time; by the war's end he
was fluent in the language.

†Possibly the "several hundred" stragglers collected by General Nathanael
Greene when he returned to Fort Lee several hours after it was evacuated.

of stamping out the feeble rebel army and with it perhaps the whole revolution. "Now I perceived what was afoot," he confided to his journal. "We wanted to spare the King's subjects and hoped to terminate the war amicably, in which assumption I was strengthened the next day by several English officers."

Except for such thwarted forays as those attempted by Ewald's jagers, there was little contact with any rebels. Very few were captured, according to the journal of the Minningerode Grenadier Battalion, "because a very extensive forest favored their retreat."

"At first," Colonel Donop would report, "several troops of the rebels could be seen here and there but they never stood fast long. At 4 o'clock in the afternoon our advanced guards, without losing a man, reached the summits of . . . Fort Lee. . . . At the foot of the mountain an important storehouse for corn was found, and in almost all the houses large quantities of provisions were stored. At the summit . . . there were huts and tents for more than 6,000 men and quantities of all sorts of provisions and a large amount of ammunition."

Inside the abandoned fort a British officer came upon "some poor pork, a few greasy proclamations, and some of that scoundrel Common Sense Man's letters, which we can read at our leisure, now that we have got one of the 'impregnable redoubts' of Mr. Washington's to quarter in." Another British observer found the fort "evacuated by the rebels so precipitately that the pots were left absolutely boiling on the fire and the tables spread for dinner of some of their officers. In the fort they found but twelve men, who were all dead drunk.* There were forty or fifty pieces of cannon found loaded, with two large iron sea mortars and one brass one, with a vast quantity of ammunition, provisions and stores, with all their tents standing."

In one of the houses near the fort that night there occurred the beginning of what Colonel Donop called "a small curious story"— one that involved a bit of treachery on the part of the woman of the house: "During the first night the Block [grenadier] battalion was

---

*In all, according to another British officer on the scene, two hundred inebriated Americans were captured in and near the fort. According to him they said, "Brother soldier, we'll have a dram," upon being captured. A Hessian grenadier made no mention of drunkenness but reported: "We . . . made prisoners of more than two hundred men."

posted at some houses. The colonel [Lieutenant Colonel Justus Henrich Block], who was excessively exhausted by the very fatiguing march, took his night's lodging in one of these houses. The next morning about 9 o'clock the hostess informed him that a Rebel was in the room. The colonel looked around in all directions and could hardly conceive where the rebel could be until finally the woman opened a corner cabinet in which a young man with a rifle gun stood. Half fainting, he crawled out and begged that his life would be spared. He was an ensign of the Marylanders. The colonel could hardly convince him that he did not have to fear for his life. He then had him sent to Lieutenant General Cornwallis."

The plunderers were on the prowl that first night in New Jersey, according to Captain Ewald: "All the plantations in the vicinity were plundered, and whatever the soldiers found in the houses was declared booty."

The orders for the next day, November 21, included an appeal for control of the looters: "As the inhabitants in general are well affected to government, Earl Cornwallis expects that the commanders of brigades and corps will exert themselves to prevent their being plundered."

Colonel Donop blamed the British for the plundering: "The local area seems to be very fertile and is well cultivated and I hope that this expedition will contribute greatly to our better subsistence in the upcoming winter quarters so that the infamous plundering, which the English are again uncommonly engaged in in spite of all orders to the contrary, will be entirely eliminated. Up to this time the Hessian grenadiers cannot be charged with anything on this account and it actually gives me much satisfaction that . . . Lieutenant General Cornwallis personally declared to me . . . that he had had a number of marauders arrested but there were no Hessians among them."

There was more than a bit of irony in the fact that the man in command of the incursion into New Jersey was Lord Cornwallis, a thirty-eight-year-old member of a distinguished English family. A contemporary described him as "short and thick set, his hair somewhat gray, his face . . . well formed and agreeable, his manners remarkably easy and affable—much beloved by his men." As a member of Parliament he had for a decade or more opposed harsh measures imposed on the colonists in America. In a typical instance he denounced such acts as "reprehensible," and praised the protesting colonists as "free Englishmen, such as we, who are simply standing up for their rights." In 1766 he had voted with a minority of five against an act giving Parliament the right to tax the Americans. His feelings were obvious, but when duty called, good soldier Cornwallis responded, and now he was commanding a force capable not only of imposing harsh measures but also of crushing the rebel army and ending the rebellion. But, as Captain Ewald wondered, did the British high command want to end it that way?

———— ♦♦♦ ————

CHAPTER 5

Whether They Will Obey Orders, God Only Knows

"It was about dusk when the head of the troops entered Hackensack," a townsman would recall of the arrival of the American force on November 20. "The night was dark, cold and rainy, but I had a fair view of them from the light of the windows as they passed on our side of the street. They marched two abreast, looked ragged, some without a shoe to their feet, and most of them wrapped in their blankets." They had crossed the Hackensack River at New Bridge and marched four miles southwest to Hackensack village with "Washington at the head of his army, consisting only of 3,000 men."*

General Washington spent the night of November 20–21 at the home of Peter Zabriskie, situated on the village green. This had been his headquarters since November 14, the day he crossed the Hudson River from New York to New Jersey with a corps of troops. His table at the Zabriskie home was being supplied by Archibald

---

*Around this time about 4,500 troops were with General Washington. A thousand or more, under the command of Lord Stirling, were in and near Brunswick and Rahway and on guard against possible enemy amphibious operations. Most of the rest of the army was still in New York: about 7,000 troops with Major General Charles Lee in the White Plains area and some 4,000 with Brigadier General William Heath in the Peekskill area.

Campbell, the keeper of a tavern nearby. "Washington . . . had with him his suite, life-guard, a company of foot, a regiment of cavalry and some soldiers from the rear of the army," the townsman observed. That night, he continued, "the British encamped on the opposite side of the river. We could see their fires about one hundred yards apart, gleaming brilliantly in the gloom of the night, extending some distance below the town and more than a mile toward the New Bridge."

For a time General Washington was hopeful of making a stand at the Hackensack River. However, it was not much of a barrier, its width in this area varying from a mere 100 to 200 feet. The river, in Washington's words, was "fordable in a variety of places, being knee-deep only." Because of the easy fording, he continued, a great number of men would be required "to defend the passes and these we had not." One reason for the shortage of defenders was that, so far, the New Jersey militia had not "stepped forth in season (and timely notice they had)." Another was that many troops had been dispatched elsewhere in New Jersey: "Our force was insufficient because a part was at Elizabethtown, Amboy and Brunswick, guarding a coast which I thought most exposed to danger." There had been reports that another British force might strike at one of those places.

There would be no stand at Hackensack. Washington ordered further retreat and on the morning of November 21 he joined the exodus toward the next river, the Passaic (then also known as the Acquackanonck River or Second River)—a march of about twelve miles along crude roadways cut through the flat and forested countryside.

"In the morning before the General left," the townsman noted, "he rode down to the dock, . . . viewed the enemy's encampment about ten or fifteen minutes and then returned to Mr. Campbell's door and called for some wine and water. After he had drank and Mr. Campbell had taken the glass from him, the latter, with tears streaming down his face, said, 'General, what shall I do? I have a family of small children and a little property here. Shall I leave them?' Washington kindly took his hand and replied, 'Mr. Campbell, stay by your family and keep neutral.' Then, bidding him goodbye, rode off."

In falling back, the Americans were again in danger of being caught by the British between the Hackensack and Acquackanonck rivers. For some reason, however, the British paused in their advance and the Americans were able to retreat unmolested.

Newark, on the King's Highway about fifteen miles southwest of Hackensack, was to be the next stop in the Americans' retreat. They crossed the Acquackanonck bridge, a frail wooden structure about twelve feet wide, and hastened on. A detachment at the rear remained long enough to set fire to the bridge. The leading elements reached Newark late on November 22, the main body on the following day.

Perhaps at Newark New Jersey's militiamen would turn out in force and enable the Americans to make a stand. But how effective would these part-time soldiers be against the enemy's well-trained professionals? Through bitter experience General Washington had learned that such soldiers, subject only to state or local authority (and often not even that), were not generally to be relied upon. He had found them to be "timid and ready to fly from their own shadows" in battle. Moreover, "the sudden change from their manner of living . . . brings on . . . such an unconquerable desire of returning to their respective homes that it not only produces shameful and scandalous desertions among themselves, but infuses a like spirit in others."

Even so, Washington would welcome a turnout of militiamen at this stage of the retreat because the states were failing to produce men for service as Continentals or "regulars." "It is a matter of great grief and surprise to me," he had written his brother from Hackensack on November 19, "to find the different states so slow and inattentive to that essential business of levying their quotas of men." Throughout the states the levy quotas were being by and large ignored; many able-bodied men were dodging service by paying a nominal fee or by sending along a substitute.

As for the reliability of militia companies in New Jersey, Washington had been given fair warning by no less an authority on the subject than William Livingston, a brigadier general of militia who had been elected governor on August 27. In an express dispatch written on November 7 at White Plains, New York, Washington had assured Livingston that he would send troops to New Jersey if an incursion there by the British appeared likely. In replying two days later, Livingston wrote: "At any time of an apprehended invasion, I shall be ready to call out what numbers of the militia you think proper to repel it . . . but whether they will obey the orders, God only knows, and that they will be worth but little if they do, I experimentally know." Livingston noted that a bill for better regulating of the militia had failed to pass the House of Assembly. As for the officers being elected under the present law, they were described by Livingston in a letter to a friend as "scurvy subalterns" who were being appointed by the rabble, or in Livingston's term, "the mobility."*

Such feelings to the contrary, Livingston had made an urgent appeal to New Jersey's militia colonels on November 16, the day Fort Washington fell. He predicted that the enemy would soon "endeavor to make an incursion into this state. . . . To check their progress, General Washington . . . has transported a considerable body of Continental troops to the eastern parts of this state, who, with the assistance of our militia, will doubtless be able to give them such a reception as their rashness deserves."

Livingston went on to remind the militia officers that the world was watching: "As the eyes of all Europe are fixed on the brave Americans as a people resolved, at all hazards, to maintain that Independence which British injustice and British cruelty compelled them to adopt, as we ought not to be unwilling to do for our descendants what our ancestors have done for us . . . it is expected that the militia of New Jersey will not forfeit, by any unworthy conduct, the favorable sentiments entertained of their prowess, but . . . will shew, on this important occasion, a spirit becoming a people disdaining slavery, and ready to risk their lives in the cause of freedom, of virtue and posterity. In full confidence of not being disappointed in those expectations, you are hereby directed to have the battalion under your command ready to march on the shortest notice."

But in New Jersey, as elsewhere, were not the men who were willing to fight (or who had been coerced into enlisting) already in the army? How many would in this season leave their families and risk their lives against a vaunted enemy force? Livingston and Washington would know within a few days. They would also know

---

*About the Philadelphia militiamen lately on temporary duty in New Jersey, Livingston had complained: "The worst men . . . would still be pejorated by having been fellow soldiers with that discipline-hating, good-living-loving, to eternal-famed damned coxcomatical crew we lately had here from Philadelphia."

how many of the amateur soldiers of the Flying Camp would be willing to remain on duty after November 30, the final day of their enlistment period. Many were already openly anticipating a return to family and fireside.

How, with a dwindling army, could Washington hope to stop an enemy reported to be adding reinforcements almost daily?

——— ◆◆◆ ———

CHAPTER 6

Their Army Is Broken All to Pieces

The leading elements of the British army, mostly Hessians, began to take possession of Hackensack around noon of November 21. So reported the same townsman who had earlier witnessed the arrival of Washington's troops in the town. "In the afternoon," according to the eyewitness, "the [village] green was covered with Hessians, a horrible sight to the inhabitants. There were between 3,000 and 4,000, with their whiskers, brass caps and kettle or bass drums."

To some inhabitants it apparently was not a horrible sight. Captain Ewald found Hackensack to be "full of Loyalists" who confirmed the report that Washington's force was weak and that "large numbers deserted his colors daily." Lieutenant Wiederholdt found the town to be "a place of about 160 houses and many well affected people, mostly Dutch." Many of the townsmen "came in to take the Oaths of Allegiance," according to British Lieutenant Henry Stirke.*

The British advance toward Hackensack had started around nine o'clock that morning, the morning after their capture of Fort Lee. A formidable force was dispatched to take possession of New Bridge on the Hackensack River: "two light infantry battalions, together with the two English grenadier battalions and the 1st Jager Compa-

---

*William Howe, the British commander in chief, was preparing a proclamation that would offer amnesty to those willing to swear allegiance to George III. Some Americans were already doing so.

ny," according to Colonel Donop. Their immediate mission was to take New Bridge before the rebels could demolish the bridge there.

The opposition was feeble, according to Lieutenant Stirke: "the rebels, on our appearance, began to set fire to their stores and some houses; but on our advancing to the bridge they fled without effecting as much mischief as intended, as a good part of the stores fell into our hands. On the march one of our flanking parties fell in with a rebel advanced guard and killed two or three of them." Reinforcements, he noted, were already arriving: "This day a body of Light Dragoons joined us."

Cornet Banastre Tarleton also noted the arrival of reinforcements: "More troops are coming in from General Howe and we expect a stroke of some consequence every hour. General Washington trembles for Philadelphia. It is now late in the year but no talk of winter quarters. Great courage animates all the British troops."

On November 22, Tarleton and other members of the Sixteenth Light Dragoons, commanded by Lieutenant Colonel William Harcourt, led a reconnoitering party deep into rebel territory: "We penetrated 12 miles into the country to Acquackanonck [Passaic], where we found rebels posted. We alarmed them, cut a few sentries down and saw their position. . . . We then retreated without any loss or wound except one horse's ear."

Captain Ewald and his jagers were meanwhile stationed in an isolated position about five miles north of New Bridge, protecting the army's right flank. At a farmhouse where he was quartered Ewald went out of his way to show how well-behaved some Hessians could be: "the area was heavily wooded and hilly, and the owner of the plantation where I stayed was a captain of the enemy. Consequently, I had nothing to hope for from these people but that they would get the enemy on my neck. To be sure, I could plunder these prosperous inhabitants according to our rules, but to convince these people that there were human persons in our army, and to invite their good will and gratitude, I gave them every protection, and they forfeited nothing by my visit but several dozen chickens and one young ox."

Leading elements of the British army, including Captain Ewald and his jager company, advanced around two o'clock in the afternoon of November 23 "past New Bridge and Hackensack and camped on the hills around the village." Two afternoons later, the main body followed. "My brigade," Colonel Donop reported, "left the [English Neighborhood] camp and, together with the English brigade of guards, marched over New Bridge to Hackensack. General Leslie occupied my former camp at Neighborhood and General Grant advanced at the same time with his brigade to New Bridge." Cornwallis's force had meanwhile been strengthened by the arrival of even more reinforcements from New York: the British Second and Fourth brigades and a battalion of the Seventy-first Regiment. Orders of the day for November 25 specified that the sick were to be put on wagons and taken to "ye hospital as soon as possible," and that "no women will be allowed with ye Regt." Hessian as well as British women were among the camp followers.

On November 26 the British main body left the Hackensack area and set off toward the Acquackanonck River, a march of about five hours through mostly flat country. The advance began early, as noted by Captain Thomas Glyn of the British First Regiment of Foot: "The right column consisting of the Light Infantry and British Reserve under Lord Cornwallis marched at 4 this morning. . . . The left column consisting of the Chasseurs, Brigade of Guards and Hessian Grenadiers . . . marched at 5 along the high road."

In the Hackensack area, a British officer reported, the troops came upon a great amount of equipment that had been abandoned by the fleeing rebels. The roads, he said, were "thick strewed with muskets, knapsacks, etc. But the number of cattle taken in the Hackensack meadows, which had been driven from Pennsylvania and some part of the Jerseys for the use of the grand rebel army, is truly astonishing and amount to many thousands."

At New Bridge the rebels had been routed before they were able to demolish the bridge. This, the British learned, was not to be the case at the only available bridge over the Passaic. The river at this point was wider than the Hackensack—about 400 feet—but it was shallow enough to be fordable at many places, though not easily fordable in the chill of late November. "The rebels breaking down the bridge," Lieutenant Stirke noted, "obliged us to ford the river about a mile above the village [of Passaic]. Our field pieces played into the woods above the ford to prevent the lurking *Scoundrels* from annoying us in crossing the river."

Captain Glyn was among those lucky enough to find another way across the river: "The enemy appeared on the heights above the town but retired upon the approach of the right column who fortunately seized upon a sloop which enabled us to pass the river. We encamped on the heights of Acquackanonck.''

Colonel Donop's hardy Hessian troops and the rest of his force "had to wade through the river," he reported. "This was something quite rare for us and even though the water was fairly deep, everything turned out well enough. When all had rallied on the opposite bank, General Lord Cornwallis continued his march un-hampered until he reached the village of Acquackanonck (Passaic).'' Carl von Heister, a Hessian lieutenant, observed that the troops "had to walk through the frigid water up to their hips. It certainly speaks well for the quality and fitness of this army that the troops accomplished this without the least discontent.''

Obviously, such well-trained troops as these were going to be too much for the fleeing rebels. Reports of Cornwallis's triumphant advance indicated that the damned rebellion would soon be ended. Robert Auchmuty, a Loyalist living in Boston, received a typical report of progress written by a British officer on November 25: "His Lordship's face seems to be set towards Philadelphia, where he will meet with no kind of opposition. . . .

"You see, my dear sir, that I have not been mistaken in my judgment of this people. The southern people [those living below New England] will no more fight than the Yankees. The fact is that their army is broken all to pieces, and the spirits of their leaders and their abettors is also broken. . . . I think one may venture to pronounce that it is well nigh over with them. All their strongholds are in the hands of his Majesty's troops. All their cannon and mortars, and the greatest part of their stores, ammunition, etc. are gone. The people in the country almost universally sick of it, in a starving condition, and cannot help themselves. And what is to become of them during the approaching inclement season God only knows.''

CHAPTER 7

No Lads Show Greater Activity in Retreating

A tall, raw-boned, eighteen-year-old lieutenant named James Monroe had seen action at such places as Harlem Heights and White Plains.* Before the end of 1776 he would play a major role in an extraordinary turn of events. He was in Newark as a member of the crack Third Virginia Regiment and there, late one afternoon, he had a close-up view of General Washington: "I saw him . . . at the head of a small band, or rather, in its rear, for he was always near the enemy, and his countenance and manner made an impression on me which time can never efface. . . . I happened to be on the rear guard at Newark and I counted the force under his immediate command by platoons as it passed me, which amounted to less than 3,000 men. A deportment so firm, so dignified, so exalted, but yet so modest and composed, I have never seen in any other person."

Composed as he appeared to be, General Washington was by this time deeply troubled by the bad news arriving, it seemed, from every direction. As he retreated each day deeper into New Jersey discouraging reports abounded. The men of Bergen County were flocking to the British "almost in captain's companies," Colonel Ebenezer Huntington reported. He added that "by the best information the greatest part of the people are friendly to the British and will do them all the service in their power." Bergen County "is to raise a regiment to join the British army. . . . One Buscart or some such hard name is appointed a colonel and . . . they have given a specimen of their valor by shooting a Whig."†

Similar disaffection with the cause was reported from Monmouth County, to the south, where Tory bands were openly supporting the British. Colonel Isaac Smith of Trenton, commanding officer of a Hunterdon County militia battalion, had just been ordered by

---

*The future president had left his studies at William and Mary College in September 1775 to enlist.

†Andrew Van Buskirk was helping the British arrest Whigs in Bergen County and was recruiting a Loyalist regiment that would serve ably as part of the British army.

Governor Livingston "to detach one company of 50 men . . . to be stationed at or near Shrewsbury to intercept and put a stop to intelligence said to be carrying on between the Tories and Lord Howe's fleet."

From Perth Amboy, Brigadier General Adam Stephen reported that his troops were in a mood to execute "a parcel of Tories" from the shore area of Monmouth County—thirteen men who would be charged with such offenses as "forming a secret encampment in the woods for the purpose of aiding and assisting the British Army." They had been apprehended along with nine British sailors.

Stephen ordered a detachment of his troops to escort the thirteen alleged Tories across the state to Burlington. The detachment carried this message from Stephen to Governor Livingston: "I send you a parcel of Tories with depositions relative to their behaviour taken in their presence. . . . I hope your government will fall on some method of punishment that will make them useful to the state; perhaps send them aboard the Navy. At any rate prevent their return. Insignificant as they are, should they be permitted to return, the soldiery will put them to death.

"The men are greatly irritated at finding a number of disaffected and mischievous persons daily supplying the enemy and cannot with cheerfulness submit to rough the rigours of war and forgo domestic felicity to fight the battles of a people who are not willing to distinguish their friends from their foes."

A militia captain in Monmouth County reported that the inhabitants of the Deal area informed him that they "did by no means thank him for guarding them and that they would much rather have the [British] Regulars than the Yankees there." In Shrewsbury, a short distance from Deal, a militia colonel became so discouraged that he gave up his commission, it was reported, "making great complaints, 'to say no worse,' as he expresses himself, of his people, so few of whom, he tells us, are ready to turn out (hiding themselves and deserting their houses) whenever he marches to defend the shores." From the Monmouth County Courthouse (Freehold) area it was reported that Charles Read, a militia colonel, had "submitted to the enemy," and that his second in command had refused "taking the oath to the state."

Closer at hand, the news was no better: New Jersey militiamen were simply not turning out, and there was little or nothing General Washington could do about it. During the stay at Newark there

were the usual desertions, but one day a large contingent of reinforcements arrived. These were some of the troops commanded by
Lord Stirling.* They had marched in from Brunswick (as New
Brunswick was then usually called), about twenty miles southwest
of Newark. Even with them, Washington had a force of only about
5,000, not nearly enough to face the oncoming enemy, and within a
few days some 2,000 members of the Flying Camp would be free to
go home.

Shortly after reaching Newark, Washington sent off two of his
ablest officers in search of sorely needed reinforcements. He dispatched Brigadier General Thomas Mifflin with an urgent message
for help from Congress, then meeting in Philadelphia. He sent
Colonel Joseph Reed off to see Governor Livingston and to urge
him and the legislature, meeting in Burlington, to rouse the state's
militiamen to action. "The critical situation of our affairs and the
movements of the enemy make some farther and immediate exertions necessary," an exasperated Washington wrote Livingston.

Despite the worsening state of affairs, there were those who
agreed with the Continental officer who on November 23 wrote: "I
believe the generals intend to make a stand at this place. . . . I hope
these losses will rouse the virtue of America. If she does not exert
herself now, she deserves not the independence she has declared. I
have still hopes of success."†

Lieutenant Colonel Samuel Blachley Webb, a twenty-three-year-
old aide-de-camp to General Washington, also was hopeful that a
stand could be made at Newark. "You ask me a true account of our
situation," he wrote on November 24 to Governor Joseph Trumbull
of Connecticut. " 'Tis next to impossible to give it to you; I can
only say that no lads ever shew greater activity in retreating than we
have. . . . Our soldiers are the best fellows in the world at this
business. . . . Our whole body did not amount to 2000 at the time
the enemy landed in the Jerseys, of consequence we had it not in
our power to make a stand till we arrived at this place where we

---

*Brigadier General William Alexander, fifty, a prominent Whig from New
Jersey, had claimed a British earldom in the 1750s and, despite the fact that he
never received the title, he was known as Lord Stirling. He had been captured
during the Battle of Long Island and released a month later.

†This letter would later be used for its propaganda value in the *Pennsylvania
Journal.*

have collected our force and are not only ready, but willing to meet the lads in blue and red as soon as they think proper. . . . If they come on soon we shall, I trust, give a good account to our country."

As things were to turn out, however, Washington would not choose to make a stand at Newark against a British force now reported to number more than 10,000 and growing daily. To some it appeared that the enemy's intended destination was Philadelphia. "There is very good intelligence that the enemy intend to make a push for Philadelphia," another Continental officer wrote.* "We have not force enough to oppose their march by land. We look to New Jersey and Pennsylvania for their militia, and on their spirit depends the preservation of America. If in this hour of adversity they shrink from danger, they deserve to be slaves indeed! If the freedom that success will ensure us, if the misery that awaits our subjection will not rouse them, why, let them sleep on till they awake in bondage."

For some reason the British appeared to be reluctant to come on. Was it the weather, the almost daily rains? Were they following orders not to overrun the Americans? "Three days after our troops left Hackensack," Thomas Paine observed, "a body of the enemy . . . made their approaches slowly towards Newark and seemed extremely desirous that we should leave the town without their being put to the trouble of fighting for it."

Before ordering his main body of troops to abandon Newark on November 28, General Washington received more bad news: an armed uprising by Tories in and around Monmouth County Court-house. For the job of putting it down he called on Colonel David Forman, a Monmouth County resident serving in General Nathaniel Heard's militia brigade (which had reinforced Washington's army in New York). With his detachment, Colonel Forman marched off and methodically carried out orders to "apprehend all persons who appear to be concerned in any plot or design against the liberty or safety of the United States," and in mercilessly doing so he gave his victims further reason for calling him "Black David."

There was meanwhile little encouragement from the officers Washington had sent off in search of reinforcements. In Philadelphia General Mifflin was dismayed to find "the divided and lethargic state of my countrymen, who appear to be slumbering under the

---

*This letter, too, would later appear in the *Pennsylvania Journal*.

shade of peace, and in the full enjoyment of the sweets of commerce." In Burlington, Colonel Reed found no reason to hope for
"the farther and immediate exertions" that Washington had called
for.

This is how the anonymous soldier from Pennsylvania described
the beginning of the retreat from Newark to Brunswick in his
"Gornall": "Just in the evening when we were all drawn up in one
line then there was orders for the two bregads to stand guard all
night and entriys through the town and we wass to lye on our arms
and to bee reddy in one minute warning. Then in the morning
before day we ware all under arms and our orders was to march to
Brunswig."

The retreat was by this time coming to be known to many of
Washington's troops as the Mud Rounds. Frequent rainstorms had
made the crude and rutted roads—bad enough even in the best
of conditions—all but impassable in many places. It was tough
going; as Sergeant Joseph White would recall, "The sufferings
we endured is beyond description—no tent to cover us at night—
exposed to cold and rains day and night—no food of any kind but a
little raw flour."

Even under the harsh circumstances, Thomas Paine continued to
hope for the best: "From Newark our retreat was to Brunswick and
it was hoped the assistance of the Jersey militia would enable
General Washington to make the banks of the Raritan the bounds of
the enemy's progress."

———— ◆◆◆ ————

CHAPTER 8

The Rebels Fly Before Us

"At 9, all the army marched in two columns towards Newark where
it was said the Rebels would stand." So Lieutenant Archibald
Robertson, the British army's chief engineer, noted in his journal on
November 28. Having, for some reason, allowed the rebels to
remain in Newark undisturbed for almost a week, Lord Cornwallis
finally gave his reinforced army the order to advance. "The right

column," Robertson continued, "commanded by Count Donop,* consisting of Hessian grenadiers, one battalion, light infantry 17th Regiment, and some dismounted dragoons, and one company of jagers, marched by the back neighborhood. The left with Lord Cornwallis marched within a mile of the Passaic, keeping the heights."

The rebels, it soon became clear, were not going to defend Newark. "The enemy corps withdrew at our approach," Captain Johann Ewald noted. Colonel Donop elaborated: "We progressed through woods and bypaths to Newark Mountains. The rebels did not interfere with us except for a few stragglers whom we made prisoners. My brigade encamped for the night at Newark Mountains. . . .

"We marched at daybreak of the 29th and took the route through Newark to Elizabethtown. . . . Most of the inhabitants in this area had fled with bag and baggage, partly because they were rebel sympathizers and partly because of fear of the Hessians who had been described to them as real monsters."

Along the route of march, Captain Ewald was pained to observe the kind of destruction that contributed to the monster image: "On this march we looked upon a deplorable sight. The region is well cultivated, with very attractive plantations, but all their occupants had fled and all the houses had been or were being destroyed."

Ewald's next stop was the country manor of William Livingston, the rebel governor, outside Elizabethtown—a likely target for plunderers, but not for Ewald: "Someone gave me a hint that this man was one of the first and most fiery rebels. But I was not inclined to turn robber, and everything was left undisturbed except a few provisions.

"Early on the morning of the 30th the army marched in one column to the vicinity of Rahway and Woodbridge, where it went into cantonment."

By this time, in addition to the regular troops, there were Loyalists marching with Cornwallis—Americans who had gone over to the British. One of the most prominent was Cortlandt Skinner, a forty-nine-year-old member of one of New Jersey's wealthiest families. Before the outbreak of war, Skinner had served as New Jersey's

---

*Colonel Donop was an aristocrat but not a count. He was, however, often identified as one.

attorney general and, for a time, as Speaker of the House of Assembly. Early in 1776, at the request of the British commander in chief, William Howe, he had begun to form what was to become the largest Loyalist unit raised during the war. In September 1776 he had been given the rank of brigadier general. Lord Cornwallis, in making his way across the unfamiliar New Jersey terrain, was greatly aided by what he would describe as Skinner's "perfect knowledge of the country."

Numerous residents of New Jersey, though civilians, were also assisting in the advance of Cornwallis's army. Some of them—Cavalier Jouet, for one—were enjoying a taste of revenge. Jouet, a member of a wealthy family in Elizabeth, had been taken up late in July 1776 "as being," in the words of Brigadier General William Livingston, "by general reputation a malignant Tory, and having taken great pains to prejudice people under his influence against the American cause. In my opinion it is very improper for him to continue in this town in the present situation of affairs." Jouet was banished from Elizabeth and made to put up a thousand dollars to guarantee his good behavior.

Now, however, with the British army coming through town, he returned to Elizabeth and volunteered his services. He collected intelligence for the British, he guided detachments on missions into the country, and he pointed out the homes of particularly obnoxious rebel families for the special attention of plundering soldiers. As a colonist loyal to his king, he was helping to put a quick end to the troubles. Like many another American, Jouet felt the rebellion had gone on far too long. It was time for reconciliation.

In the opinion of many British officers, such as Frederick Mackenzie, it was time to crush the rebellion. "This," he said, "is now the time to push these rascals, and if we do, and not give them time to recover themselves, we may depend upon it they will never make head again."

Meanwhile, as the British advance continued without opposition, reports of the rebels' skittishness were proliferating. Captain William Bamford, on duty as town major of British-occupied New York, expressed the view of many in a letter written on November 23: "As we go forward into the country the Rebels fly before us and when we come back, they always follow us; 'tis almost impossible to catch them. They will neither fight nor totally run away, but they keep at such a distance that we are always above a day's march from them. We seem to be playing at Bo Peep."

Judge Thomas Jones, a New York Loyalist, recorded a tale typical of those making the rounds: "So great was the panic among the rebels that a captain of theirs, with about fifty men, near Hackensack, took to their heels upon the approach of six wagoneers dressed in red coats."

Another such tale was recorded by one of the Hessians taking part in the advance across New Jersey, Lieutenant Andreas Wiederholdt: "Some Light Dragoons of the enemy were sent on patrol to reconnoiter our encamped army, or rather, our advanced posts. . . . It happened that the silly Americans had an odd impression and fear of us Hessians. They did not believe that we looked like other human beings, but thought that we had a strange language and that we were a raw, wild, and barbaric nation.

"This patrol had to pass a forest at night, and they followed their route quietly and full of fear. They believed that they soon would approach our Hessian advance posts. Suddenly a bull frog croaked loudly. In dismay, they answered, 'Friend.' At this answer, the frog croaked a second time. They now believed that it was a Hessian picket, whereupon they stopped and cried out, 'Yes, yes, gentlemen, we are your prisoners.'. . . They got off their horses and waited for somebody to advance and take them prisoners. . . . Finally they realized their mistake and were ashamed and said: 'God damn, it is only a bullfrog.' "

Oh, those rebels!

———◆◆◆———

CHAPTER 9

They Perpetrate the Grossest Robberies

While Lord Cornwallis continued his impressive advance in New Jersey, His Excellency, the Honourable William Howe, General and Commander in Chief of His Majesty's forces in North America, from Nova Scotia to the Floridas, was busily engaged at his headquarters in New York: preparing to send off 6,000 troops to Rhode Island for occupation duty; maintaining correspondence with London and, among others, with Washington, the rebel general; and preparing the proclamation that would offer amnesty to those in New Jersey who would lay down their arms and swear allegiance to their king. In addition to being commander in chief, Howe had been designated a peace commissioner.* His superiors in London had conferred the title, a nebulous one that carried no real authority to negotiate effectively. Nevertheless, Howe, still harboring hopes of a peaceful settlement of differences, took it seriously. New Jersey, where Cornwallis was reportedly being well received by many "friends of government," appeared to be a likely setting for a peace offensive.

Among the letters that Howe wrote on November 11 was one addressed to General Washington. It concerned plans for an exchange of captured officers. On that day Howe also sent off to Washington a letter that the rebel general had written to Mrs. Washington. Howe returned it unopened.

That letter was part of a packet that had been given to an express rider early in November, when Washington was still in the New York area. Most of the messages in the packet were to be delivered in Philadelphia. En route, the express rider stopped at a tavern in Bristol, Pennsylvania, about eighteen miles northeast of Philadelphia. He left the packet in the bar room momentarily and, carrying one of the letters, went off to arrange for its delivery via the ferry to Burlington, directly across the Delaware River from Bristol. While he was out, someone made off with the packet and a few days later it was received at General Howe's headquarters.

Busy as he was with military affairs, Howe was continuing to find time for an affair of another kind. A ladies' man and a vigorous forty-seven, he was described by a contemporary as "a fine figure, full six feet high, and well proportioned. . . . His manners were graceful and dignified." According to the talk of the bustling town, he was spending an inordinate amount of time at the gaming table and abed with an accommodating and generously endowed woman named Elizabeth Lloyd Loring. Known as a "flashing blonde," a "brilliant and unprincipled woman," and, to staff officers, as "The Sultana," Mrs. Loring had been at Howe's side since the previous winter in Boston. It was common knowledge that her husband, Joshua Loring, in a trade-off for her charms, had been given a lucrative position as commissary of New York prisons and other favors. As Judge Thomas Jones put it, Joshua Loring "fingered the cash, the general

---

*So had his brother, Admiral Richard Howe, on duty at this time in New York.

enjoyed madam." Howe's longtime dalliance would inspire such quatrains as the following:

> *Sir William, he, as snug as a flea,*
> *Lay all this time a-snoring*
> *Nor dreamed of harm, as he lay warm*
> *In bed with Mrs. Loring.*

Before being ordered to America, Howe had represented Nottingham in Parliament. Like Cornwallis, he had, as a Whig, openly sympathized with the plight of the Americans; on several occasions he had condemned what he considered to be harsh measures taken against the colonists. He had been quoted as asserting that he would never take sides against the Americans. How then could he have accepted the assignment to command His Majesty's army in America? "My going thither," he would later explain, "was not of my seeking. I was ordered and could not refuse without incurring the odious name of backwardness to serve my country in distress."

Howe's decision to send 6,000 troops to Rhode Island was vigorously opposed by the man he ordered to lead the troops there, General Henry Clinton. Clinton proposed that, instead, Howe have him land with his force at Perth Amboy, New Jersey, "and endeavor to intercept Washington in his retreat to the Delaware." A logical move, but Howe vetoed it and ordered Clinton to prepare to set off for Rhode Island on December 1.*

Before leaving on this mission, Clinton would report, "I had little doubt . . . of his Lordship's overtaking them before they could reach the Delaware, or of his at least crossing the river with them and laying hold of Philadelphia. . . . And I own these favorable appearances flattered me with expectations that the rebellion was on the brink of being wholly crushed by the annihilation of that corps."

General Howe, however, was, as usual, more concerned with reconciliation than annihilation. An earlier attempt at peacemaking had resulted in an aborted conference held on Staten Island on September 11, 1776. Howe and his brother had offered to talk reconciliation with representatives of the Continental Congress.

---

*The Rhode Island expedition would accomplish little more than to tie up the services of the 6,000 troops in needless occupation duty. Clinton would be proved right.

John Adams, Benjamin Franklin, and Edward Rutledge met on the appointed day with Admiral Howe, General Howe being unable to attend. For some reason, at this late date, the admiral learned for the first time that the Declaration of Independence had been adopted. The "inadmissable ground of independency," as he called it in reporting to London, left no room for discussion. Moreover, as Admiral Howe forthrightly admitted, he and his brother had no real power to negotiate on their own. The conference got nowhere. A short time later a British handbill appeared in New York bearing the charge that "they, the Congress, disavowed every purpose for reconciliation not consequent with their extravagant and inadmissable claim of independence."

Undeterred, General Howe had ordered the drafting of the amnesty proclamation, which would go into effect in New Jersey on November 30. The colonists would be given sixty days in which to swear allegiance to George III, and for this they would be given Protection papers guaranteeing the safety of their lives and property. In New Jersey, a colony that, left on its own, might never have joined the rebellion, General Howe would "afford protection to the inhabitants that they might experience the difference between his Majesty's government and that to which they were subject from the rebel leaders."

One of Howe's main concerns at this time was the possibility of plundering and worse by his troops in friendly New Jersey. There had been far too much of it—around New York, especially, according to such British partisans as Ambrose Serle—on the part of the Hessians. Serle, secretary to Admiral Howe, found it "impossible to express the devastations which the Hessians have made upon the houses and country seats of some of the Rebels. All their furniture, glasses, windows, and the very hangings of the rooms are demolished and defaced. This, with the filth deposited in them, makes the houses so offensive that it is a penance to go into them." In another journal entry Serle added: "Sad complaints are made about the Hessians who plunder all men, friends of government as well as foes, indiscriminately."

In an effort to discourage plundering, General Howe issued another in a long-standing series of strongly worded orders: "The frequent depredations committed by the soldiers in pulling down fences and houses in defiance of repeated orders has induced the Commander-in-Chief to direct the provost to go his rounds attended by an executioner, with orders to hang up, upon the spot, the first man he shall detect in the fact, without waiting for further proof by trial. The commanding officers are to take particular care that the soldiers are acquainted with this order."

Such a threat had been carried out during the previous summer, according to British General James Robertson: "When I landed first, I found in all the farms, the poultry, cows, and farm stocked. When I passed sometime afterwards, I found nothing alive. . . . I saw some men hanged by Sir William Howe's orders for plundering." Sir William, according to Robertson, "wished to prevent [plundering] and . . . he took the means that occurred to him to do it."

Some British officers, however, such as Francis Rawdon-Hastings, better known as Lord Rawdon, actually encouraged plundering: "We should whenever we get further into the country give free liberty to the soldiers to ravage it at will, that these infatuated wretches may feel what a calamity war is," he wrote. Johann von Kraft, a Hessian lieutenant on duty in the New York area, recorded some of the calamitous results: "The English soldiers, especially those of Lord Rawdon's Corps (Volunteers of Ireland) perpetrate the grossest robberies and even kill."

A great deal—perhaps the outcome of the whole revolution—depended upon what was happening and about to happen in New Jersey. Would the people, friends of government as well as Whigs, be abused and thus alienated from the cause of government? Would Howe's proclamation offering amnesty be effective? Would Howe persist in ordering Cornwallis to advance no farther into New Jersey than Brunswick?

——— ◆◆◆ ———

CHAPTER 10

A Push for Philadelphia?

"The enemy are advancing and have got as far as Woodbridge and Amboy and, from information not to be doubted, they mean to push for Philadelphia." So General Washington reported from New Brunswick early on Sunday, December 1, a day that was to be perhaps the most discouraging of the fifty-mile retreat from Fort Lee. The Americans had made a timely exit from Newark on November 28. On that day, the enemy's "advanced guard were entering the town by the time our rear guard got out," Washington reported. Once more, however, the British tarried and the Americans were permitted to retreat unmolested, arriving in Brunswick on November 29. In coming to New Jersey, General Washington had anticipated that as many as 5,000 local troops would turn out. As he was now learning, that had been an unrealistic expectation for, with few exceptions, the Jerseymen willing and able to fight were already serving. In a letter written on November 30 Washington expressed his disappointment: "I had hoped we should meet with large and early succours by this time; but as yet no great number of the militia of this State has come in. . . . Added to this, I have no assurances that more than a very few of the troops composing the Flying Camp will remain after the time of their engagement is out. . . . If those go whose service expires this day, our force will be reduced to a mere handful."

Still other troops were meanwhile succumbing to the "devil of desertion," as some called it. "I am told," Washington reported, "that some of General Ewing's brigade, who stand engaged to the 1st of January, are now going away." Of the continuing desertions, soldier John Chilton wrote to a friend: "You will wonder what has become of the good army of Americans you were told we had. I really can't tell; they were in some imaginary."

By December 1, almost all of the Flying Camp soldiers—2,026 of them—had gone or were about to go home. The exodus occurred, General Greene complained, "notwithstanding the enemy were within two hours' march and coming on." Washington was thus left with about 3,000 men, and not all of them fit for duty—in Greene's phrase, "a very pitiful army to trust the liberties of America on."

Cowards and sunshine soldiers, Greene and some other officers called the departing members of the Flying Camp. But their time was up. What else was expected of them—of a boy named Michael Graham of Lancaster County, Pennsylvania, for example? "About the last of May or first of June, 1776," he would recall, "being then a little turned of eighteen years of age, I turned out a volunteer in a company commanded by Captain Collier (pronounced Colyer). We composed a part of the corps denominated the Flying Camp. We marched by Lancaster, Philadelphia, Trenton, Princeton, Brunswick, Amboy, Elizabethtown, and Newark to New York where we joined the main army."

In the disastrous Battle of Long Island, young Graham was among those who barely escaped capture by the vastly superior British force. After further action—occasional skirmishes with Hessian units and the battle at White Plains—Graham found himself part of the force retreating across New Jersey: "Soon after we crossed the Raritan, the British came in sight. Here some maneuvering and cannonading took place. . . . This was the last sight I saw of the British that campaign. From Brunswick we marched through Princeton to Trenton. This as well as I recollect was about the first of December. Our time had now expired. We were discharged, and I returned home." Graham had served the time he had volunteered for. It was time for others to take their turn. (Later in the war he would serve a second tour of duty.)

A seventeen-year-old ensign from Maryland named William Beatty was also among those who left for home after serving their time. He had enlisted early in 1776 and had been appointed an ensign in the Maryland Flying Camp. "The third of July I received my warrant," he reported. "In seven days recruited my quota of men, marched for Philadelphia the 13th August, where the company joined the regiment to which it belonged." Beatty saw his share of action. After a period of "being very unwell" and "lying two weeks at a Dutchman's" near Hackensack, he rejoined his regiment: "We now began our retreat through the Jersey . . . intolerable bad road. . . . From Newark our army retreated in two columns. . . . While our army lay in the neighbourhood of Newark, the sick were sent to Morristown. Two or three days after our arrival at Brunswick being the first of December and the expiration of the Flying Camp troop's time, our brigade marched to Philadelphia leaving our brave general with a very weak army. . . . After the Flying Camp's arrival to Philadelphia, I was employed in assisting to pay and discharge the company until the 10th of December when I set out for home where I arrived the 14th following."

(Like Graham and many others who went home when their time was up, Beatty would be back. In the spring of 1777 he would recruit a whole company and go off to battle again. He would endure many engagements and serve with distinction until he was killed in action one day in April 1781.)

The departure of some of the units on December 1 was no great

loss. There was, for example, a battalion from Delaware commanded by Colonel Samuel Patterson. Looking back on the battalion's
performance, Patterson concluded: "Had I known the men in general, I would not have went with them."

Patterson, the owner of a grist mill on the Christiana River, had
led his battalion, about 500 strong, from Delaware to Philadelphia
early in the summer of 1776. During a brief stay in Philadelphia
more than 200 of his men threatened mutiny. They laid down their
arms and said damned if they would go any farther unless they were
paid the same bounty being given Pennsylvania militiamen, a matter of a few extra dollars. Patterson had to use threats and even
bayonets to get the men into the boats waiting to carry them up the
Delaware River. Unless they got moving, he fumed, he would send
for regular troops and have the mutiny-prone disarmed and arrested.
"I at last got them down to the wharf," Patterson reported, "fixed
bayonets at the head of it and sent them off." This, however, was
not the end of his troubles in Philadelphia: "Captain Woodgate's
arms not being done, I kept his company to go with me, but this
morning I learned, to my astonishment, that his whole company,
save eleven men, had deserted during the night."

The battalion's performance apparently did not improve with
several months of field duty. Colonel Patterson was especially
critical of the young farmers "from below"—that is, from Delaware's Kent and Sussex counties. "If ever I come campaigning
again," he observed, "I should never be for bringing up the men
from below. They are not fit for fatigue, have no constitutions, and
are always dissatisfied. Almost fifty or sixty of them every day sick
and unfit for duty, and fond of desertion." There were a few, he
admitted, who were "excessive good, others perhaps another day
may be brave, not at present. In my opinion they had better have
stayed at home."

With the enemy coming on, Washington again sent an appeal to
New Jersey Governor Livingston: "I cannot help calling on you in
the most urgent manner, and begging you to fall upon proper means
to draw forth the strength of your province to my support. . . . The
militia from the Counties of Morris and Sussex turn out slowly and
reluctantly, whether from the want of officers of spirit to encourage
them or your summons not being regularly sent to them, I cannot
say. But I have reason to believe there has been a deficiency in both
cases."

Then there was the problem that centered on Charles Lee, forty-five, a brilliant but cantankerous officer who in 1772 had retired on half pay from the British army. Now a major general in command of some 7,000 seasoned American troops, he had served with distinction in the south and at White Plains, New York. He and his Continentals were encamped in and around White Plains, some twenty miles north of New York City. Washington needed these reinforcements badly and as early as November 10, before the loss of Fort Washington and Fort Lee, he had urged Lee to come to New Jersey "with all possible dispatch." For reasons of his own, Lee had chosen to ignore this summons, as well as increasingly importunate messages that followed. In Brunswick on December 1, with the British moving steadily closer, Washington tried once more: "I must entreat you to hasten your march as much as possible, or your arrival may be too late to answer any valuable purpose."

On the same day Captain Israel Carver, a Tory residing in Brunswick, summed up the situation in a letter to a friend: "Since the rebels abandoned Fort Lee, they have been hurrying through the Jerseys, closely followed by Cornwallis and his *magic lights*. The arch-rebel Washington is now at Brunswick but how long he will remain the devil only knows (for the Lord won't have anything to do with him). Yesterday we heard that our friends were coming on, and in that event we shall soon lose the company of the Congress *tatter de mallions*, which certainly most of the people here do not feel sorry for . . .

"Ned has just come in from Bonum [East Brunswick] by the back road and says that the British troops are now passed through that town and will soon be here."

Ned was right. Around noon green-coated Hessians in the British vanguard were reported to be only three miles off. About an hour later enemy soldiers were observed as they approached the east bank of the Raritan River, opposite Brunswick. "The enemy are fast advancing," Washington began a hurried dispatch to Congress, "some of 'em are now in sight."

"In the afternoon . . . the British appeared on the bank of the Raritan River," Lieutenant Enoch Anderson of the dwindling Delaware Regiment would recall. ". . . a severe cannonading took place on both sides, and several were killed and wounded on our side. Orders were now given for a retreat. It was near sundown. Our regiment was in the rear. Colonel Haslet came to me and told me to take as many men as I thought proper, and go back and burn all the tents. 'We have no wagons,' said he, 'to carry them off, and it is better to burn them than they should fall into the hands of the enemy.' Then I went and burned them—about one hundred tents.

"When we saw them reduced to ashes, it was night and the army far ahead. We made a double quick-step and came up with the army about eight o'clock. We encamped in the woods, with no victuals, no tents, no blankets. The night was cold and we all suffered much, especially those who had no shoes.

"The next day we got to Princetown, and here we had comfortable lodgings in the College. . . . The British were now in chase of us. . . . We continued on our retreat—our Regiment in the rear, and I, with thirty men, in rear of the Regiment, and General Washington in my rear with pioneers, tearing up bridges and cutting down trees, to impede the march of the enemy. I was to go no faster than General Washington and his pioneers."

Within a few days the commander in chief would admit, but only privately, that the game was "pretty near up."

PART TWO

Not All
Fire and Fury

CHAPTER 11

As the Fire Came Closer, Many Drew Away

There had been, an abundance of contemporary evidence makes clear, far more "spirit"—more enthusiasm for standing up to Great Britain—in 1774 and 1775 than in the latter months of 1776. This, in part at least, is explained by the fact that the shooting war was not begun in earnest until the latter half of 1776. As many a member of the "mobocracy"* came to know, it required somewhat more fortitude to face the bayonets of a vaunted and oncoming enemy than to prance about a Liberty Pole† or tar and feather a suspected Tory.

In 1774 there had been a groundswell throughout the American colonies in favor of opposing the harsh measures imposed by the English. In December 1773 the Boston Tea Party had brought the long-troubled relations between the colonies and the mother country to the breaking point: it was no joke, three hundred and forty-two chests of British tea worth some 9,000 pounds sterling thrown into Boston Harbor. This act of defiance set the stage for an eventful 1774, the year when a Maryland legislator, undoubtedly speaking for many, declared: "All America is in a flame. . . . the colonies are ripe for any measures that will tend to the preservation of what they call their natural liberty."

In retaliation for the tea incident, Britain imposed a series of acts, which came to be known as the "intolerable" and "coercive" acts. First they closed Boston harbor until the colonists agreed to pay for the dumped tea. Next they limited town meetings in Massachu-

---

*A term used by Whigs as well as by Tories.

†Liberty Poles had been erected since 1766 as symbols of protest against what Americans believed to be acts of British tyranny.

setts. Then came other onerous measures, including the Quartering Act, which provided that British soldiers could take quarters not only in public buildings and inns but also in private homes without even asking the consent of the owners. This one, moreover, applied not just to Massachusetts but to all of the colonies.

Instead of bringing the colonists into line, these strictures, as soon became obvious, brought them together as never before in their determination to resist "the tyrannous acts of the British Parliament." Throughout the colonies, legislators adopted resolutions to come to the assistance of the beleaguered Bostonians, to defy intolerable acts, to form a union. Before the end of 1774 the Continental Congress met in Philadelphia and adopted the Declaration of Rights and Grievances. At a meeting of the Virginia Convention in 1775, Patrick Henry gave the colonists a slogan: "Give me liberty or give me death."

James Moody, a wealthy New Jersey farmer, was among those who thought the anti-British activists were going too far. "Pretended patriots and forward demagogues," he would later claim, were "able to throw the whole continent into a ferment in the year 1774, and maddened almost every part of the country with associations, committees, and liberty-poles, and all the preliminary apparatus necessary to revolt. The general cry was, *'Join or die!'* "

An infuriated George III also thought the separatists had gone too far. He vowed "to put an end to present disturbances in America." In a message to Lord North, his prime minister, he declared: "The die is now cast. The Colonies must now either submit or triumph."

Samuel Adams and the rest of the agitators for independence—a minuscule minority of the colonists at the time—suddenly gained extensive support on April 19, 1775, the day of the bloody and widely publicized skirmishes between American militiamen and British regulars at Lexington and Concord. The reaction was immediate and widespread. Dr. Benjamin Rush's comment was typical of many who had previously been neutral: "I continued a spectator of the events which passed in our country in the winter of 1775. The battle of Lexington gave a new tone to my feelings, and I now resolved to bear my share of the duties and burdens of the approaching Revolution. I considered the separation of the colonies from Great Britain as inevitable. The first gun that was fired at an American cut the cord that had tied the two countries together."

"This tragical event," Dr. James Thacher, a physician serving

with American troops, declared, "seems to have electrified all classes of people. . . . Expresses are hastening from town to town, in all
directions through the country, spreading the melancholy tidings
and inspiriting and rousing the people To Arms! To Arms!" Judge
Thomas Jones, an outspoken opponent of the movement for independence, reported the reaction in New York: "They received the
news with avidity . . . paraded the town with drums beating and
colours flying. . . . The whole city became one continued scene of
riot, tumult, and confusion. Troops were enlisted for the service of
the rebellion, the Loyalists threatened with the gallows, and the
property of the Crown plundered and seized upon wherever it could
be found."

The second Continental Congress met on May 10, 1775, three
weeks after Lexington, promptly authorized establishment of the
Continental Army, and appointed Virginia squire George Washington as commander in chief. On the same day, far to the north,
Americans led by Brigadier General Benedict Arnold and Ethan
Allen, a colonel of militia, made a spectacularly successful raid on
the British garrison in Fort Ticonderoga.

As Washington made his way northward from Mount Vernon to
take command, American troops were holding their own in the
Battle of Bunker Hill (fought on Breed's Hill, overlooking Boston).
The battle proved to be inconclusive but it provided the Americans
with something to boast about. The British suffered more than
1,000 casualties, more than twice the American losses. "Upon the
whole," said General Nathanael Greene, "I think we have little
reason to complain. . . . I wish we could sell them another hill at
the same price."

Independence-minded colonists took heart. The American forces
around Boston grew to 17,000. Within a short time General Charles
Lee was crowing: "Not less than a hundred and fifty thousand
gentlemen, yeomen and farmers are now in arms, determined to
preserve their liberties or perish."

On March 17, 1776, after a stay of eight months, the British
evacuated Boston, a move that further encouraged rebellious Americans. On Dorchester Heights above the city two weeks earlier the
Americans had emplaced some fifty cannon that Colonel Henry
Knox and his men had lugged from Fort Ticonderoga. Rather than
face those guns and risk a defeat, General William Howe decided to
set sail with his army for Nova Scotia.

New life was injected into the common cause when Congress adopted the Declaration of Independence on July 4. "The declaration . . . has produced a new era in this part of America," Dr. Rush wrote. "The militia of Pennsylvania seem to be actuated with a spirit more than Roman. Near 2,000 citizens of Philadelphia have lately marched towards New York in order to prevent an incursion being made by our enemies upon the state of New Jersey. The cry of them all is for BATTLE."

Those soldiers, however, were crying for anything but battle a short time thereafter when Howe returned with a reinforced army of more than 31,000 and proceeded to inflict one defeat after another on the Americans. The boasts of '75 about a quick end to the war, about patriot sharpshooters easily disposing of the king's men, now had a hollow sound. There were growing numbers of neutralists, whose feelings were approximated in a statement attributed to a Philadelphia attorney named John Ross, a man who, it was said, "loved ease and Madeira much better than liberty and strife." Ross (an uncle-in-law of seamstress Betsy Ross) was being widely quoted as observing: "Let who will be king: I well know that I shall be the subject." Around the same time, journalist Thomas Paine, to his dismay, encountered a tavernkeeper who undoubtedly spoke for many when he dismissed the revolutionary effort with these words: "Well, give me peace in my day."

Colonel Joseph Reed raised a question that was on many minds in the final months of 1776: Where were all the chauvinistic loud-mouths of '75? "When I look round," he wrote from camp, "and see how few of the numbers who talked so largely of death and honour are around me, I am lost in wonder. . . . Your noisy Sons of Liberty are, I find, the quietest in the field."

A Whig lawyer-statesman named Elias Boudinot noted a similar change since the war-fever days of 1775: "A few weak violent men . . . were not only for raising a regiment of soldiers but expressly moved for an order to burn every man's house who should refuse to join in the opposition. It required prudence and patience to get rid of the effects of these hotheaded measures. But I could not help remarking that these very men were the first to join the enemy as soon as they appeared in force."

Captain Alexander Graydon would never forget an acquaintance "who was ever among the foremost in patriotism. . . . Yet this gentleman, so full of zeal in seventy-five, was so thoroughly emptied of it in seventy-six as to translate himself to the royal standard in New York."

Even in the fervid days following adoption of the Declaration of Independence John Adams had complained that he observed little of the "pure flame of patriotism" but "much of the ostentation and affectation of it."

Recollecting the good old days of 1775, Dr. Rush declared: "Our country was then untainted by speculation. A selfish spirit was scarcely seen. . . . Every man who acted for the public was then honest and earnest. Benevolence was actuated by new objects." In the final month of 1776, however, Rush excoriated "furious Whigs who considered the tarring and feathering of a Tory as a greater duty and exploit than the extermination of a British army. . . . These men were generally cowards, and shrunk from danger when called into the field by pretending sickness or some family disaster."

The Reverend Nicholas Collin, pastor of Swedes Church in Swedesboro, a village in southern New Jersey, observed in his journal: "When war began many theretofore advocates of fighting took to the woods. After the English army had defeated the American, captured New York and spread itself over Jersey, there was constant alarm. Formerly nearly all had been eager but now, as the fire came closer, many drew away, and there was much dissention among the people. Many concealed themselves in the woods, or within their houses, other people were forced to carry arms, others offered opposition and refused to go."

This is how the well-informed Congressman Robert Morris explained the collapse: "Our people knew not the hardships and calamities of war when they so boldly dared Britain to arms. Every man was then a bold patriot, felt himself equal to the contest, and seemed to wish for an opportunity of evincing his prowess. But now, when we are fairly engaged—when death and ruin stare us in the face, and when nothing but the most intrepid courage can rescue us from contempt and disgrace, sorry am I to say it, many of those who were foremost in noise, shrink, coward-like, from the danger, and are begging pardon without striking a blow."

◆◆◆

CHAPTER 12

The Devil of Desertion

One day in the spring of 1776 Lieutenant Colonel Philip Johnson issued a call to muster for the members of his militia unit in Lebanon Township, an area of well-kept farmland in the rolling countryside of Hunterdon County, about twenty miles north of Trenton. The colonel wanted to make an appeal to his part-time soldiers—farmers or farmhands, almost all of them—to volunteer for a short period of active duty with General Washington's army. Reinforcements were, as Johnson knew, sorely needed, and he hoped to enlist at least a few of the men. On the appointed day some of the militiamen turned out but, to a man, they refused to sign up and they were emphatic about it. "One half of two companies came with clubs. Colonel Johnson was knocked down by them and was afterwards obliged to retreat. The same day one of the captains was much beat by them."

That is how Colonel Edward Thomas described the doings in a letter to his friend William Livingston, then a brigadier general of militia (he would become governor of New Jersey about two months later). Colonel Thomas, like Livingston a prominent resident of Elizabethtown, was commanding officer of Essex County's First Regiment of Foot Militia. He had come to Lebanon Township on private business and had learned of the mutinous clubbing while staying as a guest in the home of the main victim, Colonel Johnson.

"There are numbers," Colonel Thomas declared in his letter, "that say if they are taken away at this season of the year they may as well knock their families in the head, for that they will be ruined."

In the same letter, written on June 30 (four days before Congress adopted the Declaration of Independence), he informed Livingston that an officer from Lebanon had gone to New Jersey's Provincial Congress (meeting in Burlington) and obtained an order to arrest the offending farmers. "Five was taken yesterday and sent with a guard of twenty men to Burlington. There are a party of one hundred and fifty militia out after more." Two of the five marched off to Burlington were members of the prominent Woof family—men of property.

Those refusing to serve claimed "that they was eight hundred strong, had plenty of ammunition, etc. But when the militia collected, they dispersed, and several that was called Tories have since appeared to be staunch Whigs and as long as they are kept in fear I suppose will continue such."

Colonel Thomas added that militia companies throughout Hunterdon County (which then encompassed a large area to the south, including Trenton) were "not above half full although some of the companies hath augmented the bounty to eight pounds prock [proclamation money]. In Somerset [County] I believe 'tis not much better."

Nor was it much better in, among other places, Delaware. In April 1776 a recruiting officer made this report to the Committee of Secrecy, War and Intelligence in Wilmington: "I am sorry to inform you that the militia are not so ready to turn out on this important occasion as I could wish, owing, I am certain, to their being at this season engaged in the farming business."

Through the summer and into the autumn of 1776, farming continued to have priority over army service in many areas. Even soldiers on active duty were slinking off to help with the family crops. Far too many militiamen serving with the Flying Camp, General Hugh Mercer complained, were "perpetually fluctuating between the camp and their farms."

Early in October in Haverstraw, New York, Colonel Ann Hawkes Hay, in command of the local militia regiment, was dealing with farm-related problems in addition to those related to his first name.* Even though Haverstraw, on the west bank of the Hudson River, had been fired upon by British vessels and was a possible landing place for the enemy, Hay's men were woefully unprepared, almost half of them not even having weapons. Moreover, after he repeatedly summoned the regiment to muster, only thirty-eight bothered to turn out. As for active service, it was out of the question and for a familiar reason: if they left their farms, the men said, their families would starve. All they wanted, according to Hay, was the "peace, liberty and safety" offered by the British. Some declared that Congress had been wrong in rejecting British offers of reconciliation.

There was more than a bit of truth in the claim of many farmers

---

*He had been named for a wealthy friend of the family.

that their families would suffer severely if they went off to war. The amount of work then required to keep a farm in operation and a family fed, sheltered, and clothed was staggering and exhausting. Many a farmer worked from sunrise to sunset: in addition to the back-breaking chores of the soil, there were such tasks as making dippers and bowls from gourds and tool handles from hard wood. Some had to weave their own cloth. Leaving farm and family to enlist, in the eyes of many, was an act of desertion rather than patriotism.

Hard-pressed farmers, however, were not alone in refusing to turn out; officers like Captain Alexander Graydon were becoming well aware of that. One morning in the spring of 1776, Graydon set out from Philadelphia with a lieutenant, a corporal, and a drummer boy, in the hope of enlisting some men in his company. His destination was Frankford, a village about six miles to the northeast. They were wearing the brown-trimmed-with-white uniform of the Pennsylvania Third Regiment, and Graydon and the lieutenant even had their dress swords, or hangers as they were usually called. Arriving in Frankford, they stopped at a likely place; a tavern with, as it turned out, a full complement of eligible, able-bodied young men. In his accustomed manner Captain Graydon ordered drinks for his prospective recruits and, after the usual interval, began his appeal. "A number of fellows," he would later recall, "indicated a desire to enlist, but although they drank freely of our liquor, they still held off. I soon perceived that the object was to amuse themselves at our expense, and that if there might be one or two among them really disposed to engage, the others would prevent them. One fellow in particular, who had made the greatest show of taking the bounty, presuming the weakness of our party . . . began to grow insolent, and manifested an intention to begin a quarrel, in the issue of which he no doubt calculated on giving us a drubbing."

Graydon resolved at this point that "if a scuffle should be unavoidable," he and the lieutenant would use not only their fists but also their hangers. "At length the arrogance of the principal ruffian rose to such a height that he squared himself for battle and advanced towards me in an attitude of defiance. I put him by, with an admonition to be quiet, though with a secret determination that, if he repeated the insult, to begin the war, whatever the consequence. The occasion was soon presented; when taking excellent aim, I struck him with my utmost force between the eyes and sent him staggering to the other end of the room. Then, instantly drawing our hangers and receiving the manful cooperation of the corporal and drummer, we were fortunate enough to put a stop to any farther hostilities. . . .'' Presently they were on their way back to Philadelphia empty-handed—another fruitless day.

"This incident," Captain Graydon later recalled, "would be little worthy of relating, did it not serve in some degree to correct the error of those who seem to conceive the year 1776 to have been a season of almost universal patriotism and enthusiasm. It was far from prevalent in my opinion among the lower ranks of the people, at least in Pennsylvania. . . . The true merits of the contest were little understood or regarded."

In the ensuing weeks Graydon persisted, but the results of his efforts were negligible. In a typical venture he and another captain spent several days down on the eastern shore of Maryland, scouring communities in search of recruits—"beating up," as Graydon called it. For all of their efforts, however, they succeeded in enlisting just one man—a questionable choice, as things were to turn out. A Maryland townsman, Graydon would recall, "helped us to recruit a fellow, he said, who would do to stop a bullet as well as a better man, and as he was a truly worthless dog . . . the neighborhood would be much indebted to us for taking him away." Graydon and the other captain took along "our solitary recruit, for whom we tossed up." In winning the toss, Graydon asserted, "I was, in fact, but a very small gainer": the townsman's judgment would prove to be right; the recruit "was never fit for anything better than the inglorious post of camp colour man."

Looking back years later on such experiences, Graydon would declare: "The times . . . were not all fire and fury, as certain modern pretenders to the spirit of Seventy-six have almost persuaded us they were."

By the final month of 1776 a revolution so vociferously hailed in the spring of 1775 was collapsing; resistance to British power was dissolving, and the end was in sight. Most Americans, even General Washington for a time, had expected a short war. Now they were sick of it; it had gone on far too long; public indignation, as usual, had not lasted long. It was time, many felt, to make peace, for how could a band of ragged nonprofessionals ever hope to stand up against the greatest expeditionary force ever sent out of Great Britain?

It was a time—the final months of 1776—not only of mass

desertions but also of widespread evasion of army service. Out of a white population of more than 2,000,000, no more than a handful of dedicated fighting men could be counted on.* Moreover, thousands of Americans were joining the British; in some states more Americans were enlisting with the British than in American units.† John Adams would later estimate that one third of Americans supported the revolution, one third remained loyal to the crown, and the rest were neutral. Indeed, late in 1776, far fewer than a third—perhaps fewer than a tenth—of the eligible and able-bodied men were willing to turn out.

Throughout the states, particularly the middle states, open defiance of local-committee orders was a commonplace occurrence. There were some men who declined to join the local militia and emulated a Philadelphian who "refused to deliver his gun and uttered expressions discovering a violent enmity to the Libertys of America." He escaped punishment by "declaring himself sorry for his indiscreet conduct." A Philadelphian named Samuel Delap was less fortunate, finding himself behind jailhouse bars "for drinking the king's health and damnation to the rebels at the sign of the Harp and Crown in Third Street." Some men not only refused to serve but also declined to give a blanket for use by a man who would. In Delaware Tory mobs were tearing down Liberty Poles and taking over courthouses. One group was reported to be molding bullets, flocking to "a headquarters of insurrection," and vowing: "By God, there never will be any peace till the Whigs and Presbyterians are all cut off."

Dr. Benjamin Rush observed in the autumn of '76 that "Maryland had yielded a little to the gloomy complexion of public affairs. She had instructed her delegates in Congress to vote for an accommodation with Great Britain . . . and one of those delegates said to me . . . that General Howe's proclamation contained everything we could wish, and that we ought now to submit to Great Britain."

---

*From the black population of about 500,000 only a few were accepted for enlistment in American units. Uncounted hundreds joined the British or were coerced into doing so. They were usually put to more menial jobs than soldiering.

†Before the revolution's end New York alone would furnish an estimated 15,000 to the British army and some 8,000 Loyalist militiamen. In all, about 50,000 Americans would join the British.

Resistance to orders took some bizarre forms in Maryland. On a mid-November day Captain James Bosley, "appointed by the Committee of Baltimore County to collect fines from non-enrollers," called on one, farmer Vincent Trapnell. According to an eyewitness, Trapnell not only refused to pay the fine but said "that he would be damn'd if he did not blow Bosley's brains out. However, his wife met him at the door crying out to him for God sake not to get the gun." Trapnell thereupon "snatched up a large stick, . . . run up to Bosley and laid on with both of his hands . . . which cut him very bad upon his head. I suppose he lost half a pint of blood from the wound." Bosley said he would report the attack to "the Gentlemen of the Committee." Trapnell "damned all the Committee for a pack of damn'd rogues, and they might kiss his asse," meanwhile "pulling his coat apart behind." Threatening to kill the captain, Trapnell then chased him from the farm, "throwing at Bosley stones and every thing that came in his way."

Around the same time in Baltimore County another truculent farmer, Henry Guyton, dramatized his displeasure when a courier arrived with notice that the patriot committee was going to bring legal action against him. Guyton's reply, according to the courier, was that "he would wipe his ass" with the law. As for the patriot committee, Guyton "turned up his ass and said a fart for them that I will give it to you."

Even in New England, often described as a hotbed of rebellion, there was considerably less than universal support of the common cause in 1776. Early in the year, General John Sullivan complained that "not near half the Massachusetts militia could be prevailed upon to tarry and many of them went off one day before their time was out." As for his own New Hampshire troops: "I . . . had them drawn up and endeavoured every way to induce them to tarry and finally prevailed on all but about 350 who were determined to quit us at all events. These worthless scoundrels though willing to sacrifice their liberties could not suffer the least delay of payment for their service."

Following the Battle of Long Island on August 27, Connecticut troops went home en masse. "As for the militia of Connecticut," Major Lewis Morris, Jr., reported, "Brigadier Wolcott and his whole brigade have got the cannon fever and very prudently skulked home."

Late in 1776 Dr. Rush reported learning "from two New England officers that the four Eastern States [of New England] will find great difficulty in raising their quota of men, owing to that excessive rage for privateering, which now prevails among them. Many of the Continental troops now in our service pant for the expiration of their enlistments in order that they may partake of the spoils of the West Indies. At a moderate computation, there are now not less than ten thousand men belonging to New England on board privateers. New England and the Continent cannot spare them. They have a right at this juncture to their services and to their blood."

In Virginia, another "hotbed," recruiting officers were bemoaning the fact that, late in 1776, no one would enlist. The "supineness" of the people was evident throughout America. "The only source of uneasiness amongst us arises from the number of Tories we find in every state; they are more numerous than formerly and speak more openly." So Benjamin Franklin and Robert Morris reported in September 1776 to Silas Deane, America's man in France.* "If America falls," they added, "it will be owing to such division more than the force of our enemies."

The paucity of reliable officers was one of the army's greatest problems. Writing to his brother and not for publication, General Washington complained that "the different states nominate (as officers) such as are not fit to be shoeblacks." Colonel Joseph Reed berated officers who "failed in their duty by absence from camp on pretence of sickness." As for those in camp: "I am sorry to say too many officers from all parts leave the army when danger approaches." Throughout the army, according to Reed, "a spirit of desertion, cowardice, plunder, and shrinking from duty when attended by fatigue or danger prevailed but too generally."

Before leaving New York for New Jersey, Reed himself had almost been done in by a would-be deserter. Having confronted the man skulking toward the rear, Reed ordered him to return to his unit. Instead, as Mrs. Reed reported in passing along the story, "the fellow presented his musket within half a yard of his [Reed's] head, but it happily missed fire."

A captain named Farmer made this report from camp near New York around the same time: "A party attempted to desert, about thirty, but were prevented by force. A corporal at their head thrust

*Franklin himself would leave for France with two other diplomats on October 26.

his bayonet at Lieutenant Lang, which he parried. The corporal is in custody. The same corporal cocked his piece at Ensign Davis and attempted to fire."

Throughout the states, other officers put bits of the bad news on paper: "Enclosed is a list of officers who will not serve." "What must be done with deserters from the militia?" "I proposed marching . . . but the men and officers utterly refused going." "The captains complain of great backwardness of the people." "The three battalions mutinied, and appeared on the parade under arms. After this, they deserted in parties, with their arms." "I am convinced that the militia will go home bodily before three days." "My battalion of the Flying Camp . . . has received the bounty and the greatest part thereof deserted."

General Washington found himself, late in the autumn of 1776, not only contending with "the devil of desertion" but also competing with states that were paying militiamen, for home duty, higher bounties than he could offer for hazardous duty. Moreover, as he toiled to hold together what Colonel Reed described as "the wretched remains of a broken army," he was receiving little help from Congress. With inflation rising and Continental money falling in value, Congress was not able to provide the promised train of artillery or even uniforms or blankets. Members were still debating whether to give the commander in chief the authority he needed for securing troops and appointing officers. Some congressmen were calling for his dismissal. Others were simply staying home: there were days, at this critical time, when there was barely a quorum in Philadelphia. Charles Thomson, the secretary of Congress, was referring to times such as this when, some years later, he responded to a suggestion that he write a history of the revolution. "No," he replied, according to Dr. Benjamin Rush, "I ought not, for I should contradict all the histories of the great events of the revolution, and show by my account of men, motives and measures, that we are wholly indebted to the agency of Providence for its successful issue. Let the world admire the supposed wisdom and valor of our great men. Perhaps they may adopt the qualities that have been ascribed to them, and thus good may be done. I shall not undeceive future generations."

The congressmen on duty sympathized with the plight of the underequipped army, and in one of their resolutions they denounced profiteers, who, "with views of avarice and extortion, have monopolized and engrossed shoes, stockings and other necessaries for the army, whilst the soldiers . . . fighting for the liberties of their country are exposed to the injuries of weather at this inclement season." Congressman Matthew Thornton observed that "an inexcusable neglect in the officers, want of fidelity, honor and humanity in the Doctors and avarice in the Suttlers has slain ten soldiers to the enemy's one." A distraught officer reported: "We have neither beds or bedding for our sick to lay on or under . . . the dead and dying laying mingled together." Another sought relief for "ye 200 sick men . . . now lying in a barn . . . without even straw—many on the bare earth without boards."

This was a time when, even in Boston, "gentlemen" were buying their way out of military duty and when some affluent families were finding it convenient to send their sons off to Europe for a better education. For these and other reasons it was also a time when an inordinately high number of men and boys from poor families were serving in the army. Some had been more or less dragooned into service. Many volunteered; the army looked good to immigrants and others who were unemployed or plodding away at dull, poorly paid jobs. Some found in military service an opportunity to combine patriotism with enlightened self-interest. A recruiting pamphlet told of two young "friends of the country" who met one day in 1776. One of them, unable to find a job, said he had decided on soldiering as an ideal way "to get my living by." Enlisting, he observed, would allow him to leave the ranks of the unemployed and demonstrate his support of the cause of "Independency."

For many the army offered not only a better life—money plus free food and clothing—but also an opportunity to escape from unpleasant social situations or lives of drudgery. Joseph Plumb Martin happily left the sweat and strain of labor on his grandfather's farm in Milford, Connecticut, to enlist in the army, serving—for a fee—as another man's substitute. As long as he was going to sign up anyway, he figured, why not get as much as he could for it? A young man named John Burrows (who would grow up to become a general) and his brothers escaped an unpleasant situation at their home in Colvin's Ferry, Pennsylvania (Morrisville), opposite Trenton, by enlisting in the summer of 1776. "My kind stepmother having deceased," Burrows would recall, "my father married a third wife, very unlike his last. She had six children and he had six. Upon which occasion, his children, not feeling comfortable at home, and the news of the British landing on Long Island, we all . . . marched in the militia; and when our term expired we joined the Flying Camp." Two of the Burrows brothers had been captured by the British at Fort Washington. John and two other brothers were retreating with Washington's army across New Jersey.

One can only guess at the number who, like Joseph Garison, preferred to serve as soldiers rather than as apprentices or servants. Garison, "an apprentice lad . . . aged near 20 years but small of his age," had run away in March 1776 from the farm of his master, Cornelius Austin of Salem County, New Jersey. In a newspaper notice written in October 1776, Austin made this comment: "It is supposed he is enlisted in the provincial service, where he will do some good if he cannot help it. Whoever will bring home the said lad to his master shall have two pence reward, and one penny for his trouble."

Some men sent along black slaves to serve in their place—a slave named Samuel, for example. Samuel, twenty-nine, was working on his master's farm in Somerset County, New Jersey, when, one day in the spring of 1776, a man named Casper Berger came along and offered to buy him. Berger said he would pay a substantial sum— ninety-two pounds, ten shillings—on one condition: that the slave would serve as a substitute in the militia for the duration of the war. This was acceptable to Samuel's owner, so the deal was made. Samuel served during the Battle of Long Island, came home to do some farming, then went off on another tour of duty, a routine he would continue for several years.

"Men of fortune," according to Captain Alexander Graydon, ". . . though evidently most interested in a contest whose object was to rescue American property from the grasp of British avidity, were willing to devolve the fighting business on the poorer and humbler classes." Perhaps, he felt, this was related to the fact that in the Continental Army of 1776 "the eye looked round in vain for the leading gentry of the country." Although it was then "little known or suspected," the army was deficient in "young men of figure." And this, he said, was true not only of the middle states: "New England was far behind the other provinces . . . in the quality of her officers. . . . Neither did the fighting department appear to be fashionable among the gentry of Virginia. . . . She furnished some gentleman aides-de-camp and volunteers . . . but [in] the serious, drudging business of war . . . she evinced but little brilliancy." Washington, too, lamented the dearth of gentry on duty, observing that it was imperative to get "gentlemen and men of character to accept commissions." Colonel John Cadwalader, himself a member of Philadelphia's gentry, castigated patricians who had "procured appointments of little consequence, which they plead in excuse for serving in the field."

Aware of some of the inequities, some enlisted men on active duty made organized protests. Perhaps the most vocal group was the Committee of Privates from Philadelphia, who described themselves as "tradesmen and others who earn their living by their industry," and who had left behind families "destitute of every means of acquiring an honest living." The committee included "a great many apprentices."

In the summer of 1776 the privates called for universal military service. Why shouldn't everyone serve? The legal fine for refusing to serve was far too low, they said, and it offered "the lazy, the timid, and disaffected" an easy way to avoid service and an opportunity to "ridicule those whose patriotism" led them to enlist. The privates charged that "some of the most considerable estates in the Province" were represented among the Non-Associators. These affluent stay-at-homes ought to be made to pay fines "proportioned to each man's property," and these funds ought to be used to support the families of men on duty, "as no man who is able, by his industry, to support his wife and children could ever consent to have them treated by the Overseers of the Poor, as the law directs."

The privates petitioned the Pennsylvania Assembly for the right to vote, declaring "that it has been the practice of all countries, and is highly reasonable, that all persons . . . who expose their lives in defense of a country, should be admitted to the enjoyment of all the rights and privileges of that country. . . . All Associators should be given the right to vote."

Fair enough, but this request, like others made by the privates, was ignored. If you did not meet the property ownership requirements, you did not vote. Members of the gentry of Philadelphia, some of them influential Whigs, dismissed the Committee of Privates as "in general damned riff-raff—dirty, mutinous, and disaffected."

PART THREE

A Handful Daily Decreasing

CHAPTER 13

They Don't Want to Finish the War!

Cornwallis's army reached Brunswick on Sunday, December 1, one day after the issuance of the proclamation offering a pardon and protection papers to anyone willing to swear allegiance to the king. In the ensuing days hundreds of rebels would take advantage of the offer.

"The light infantry had moved towards Brunswick," Lieutenant Robertson noted in his journal on December 1, "and on information that it was evacuated, Lord Cornwallis turned off at Woodbridge with the Hessian Grenadiers and pushed on to Brunswick, but found the rear guard of the rebels still there and five pieces of cannon with which they gave us a cannonade. The jagers prevented their destroying the bridge over the Raritan."

Near the bridge there were about twenty houses on each side of the river. "The houses on the opposite side," Captain Ewald observed, "had been occupied by enemy riflemen and those on this side by jagers under Captain Wreden, whom I joined just as soon as I had rendered my report to Colonel Donop. The firing continued on both sides until late in the night."

Of the cannonading exchange, Lieutenant Henry Stirke of the British Tenth Regiment noted: "We fired on them across the river from our field pieces; which was returned for some time. As the Rebels took care to demolish part of the bridge, we could not prevent their carrying off some of their stores, etc. The Hessians lost a captain, killed by a rifle, and a Grenadier by a cannon ball."

The fatally wounded Hessian captain was Friedrich Karl von Weitershausen, commanding officer of a company of grenadiers. "When he . . . handed over his instructions and turned his horse to ride away, he received such an unfortunate shot through the chest and spine from a rifleman that he died from it." So it was reported in the battalion journal. Weitershausen "wanted to watch the action and lost his life by a rifle shot that shattered his spine," according to Captain Ewald. The rebel marksman who shot the captain, another Hessian officer reported, "had concealed himself under the bridge." He added that Weitershausen "had written to his wife by the last packet, asking her to follow him to America." (It is not known how she responded to this request.)

Ewald's and Wreden's jagers, on the prowl as usual, "captured two sloops below the bridge, loaded with stocks of clothing and wine. There was a large quantity of shoes and long trousers on board, which came at just the right time because our men could no longer proceed in their own boots.

"During the dark night the Americans left the right bank of the Raritan River. Captain Wreden immediately crossed the damaged bridge with his jagers and took post on the height . . . and the bridge was quickly repaired." So Ewald noted in his diary.

With the rebels well on their way toward the Delaware River, the main body of Cornwallis's army crossed the Raritan bridge on December 2 and took up quarters in Brunswick. "The bridge being repaired," Captain Hall (first name unknown) would report, "this division of the army passed over the river and entered the town, which the rebels had quitted, leaving their hospital full of sick and wounded. . . . As Lord Cornwallis had orders to proceed no further than Brunswick, here the pursuit ended for the present."

Meanwhile, the Howe brothers' proclamation was offering the king's subjects an opportunity, in General Howe's words, to "reap the benefit of his Majesty's paternal goodness, in the preservation of their property, the restoration of their commerce, and the security of their most valuable rights, under the just and moderate authority of the crown and parliament of Great Britain." The Howes offered forgiveness and protection to anyone willing to "testify his obedience to the laws by subscribing a declaration in the following words: 'I, _____, do promise and declare that I will remain in a peaceable obedience to his Majesty, and will not take up arms, nor encourage others to take up arms in opposition to His Authority. . . .' " It was simple: all a rebel had to do was to promise to remain in peaceable obedience and he would be guaranteed protection of life and property. The offer—more generous than the damned rebels deserved, some thought—was an immediate success. The war, many rebels apparently felt, was almost over anyway, so why not join the winning side and get protection papers, too?

Among those assisting the British in processing the protection papers was a well-to-do Loyalist named Bernardus LaGrange. In 1775 he had been carted about the streets, jeered by a mob as a damned Tory, and forced to leave town. Now he was back in Brunswick and, as he noted, "honoured . . . in being appointed to administer the oaths of allegiance, and to deliver protections to such persons as came in." He happily noted that he was carrying out his new duties with "unwearied assiduity." All was not exactly bliss, however. Although he was back in his commodious home and reunited with his wife and children, his family was being confined to one room. The rest of the house was aswarm with no fewer than "seventeen Hessian officers and some twenty of their servants and carters."

One of those who eagerly accepted the Howes' offer was a farmer named John Bray. From his home at Raritan Landing, near Brunswick, he passed on the word to his uncle, Andrew Bray, of Lebanon Township, New Jersey: "You are acquainted that the British troops have possession of this place and you may depend that they will go through the country wherever they attempt it and [such] great destruction follows wherever they go that I would recommend it to all my relations and friends to come in and receive Protection. The Proclamation which no doubt you have heard of is free to all during its limitation. Great numbers flock in dayly to headquarters which is at this place. You can come down and receive Protection and return home without molestation on the part of the King's troops and you best know the situation of the Provincial Army. Do advise Couzin Johnny and Thomas and Couzin Thomas Jones for if they do stay out to the last they will undoubtedly fair the worst. 40,000 Hessians have offered their service to the King of England of which 24,000 are to embark in the spring but I hope the matter will be settled before that time."

Each day rebels lined up in Brunswick, and other towns occupied by the British as well, to pledge allegiance and receive in return the sheet of paper that would protect their families and their property. In all, some three thousand would sign up in towns on or near the route of the British advance. Others were going to British headquarters in New York to sign up. Since most of the men who took advantage of the Howes' offer represented not just themselves but entire families, a high percentage of the population of the occupied areas—more by far than the three thousand signers—took advantage of the proclamation.

Captain William Bamford, of the British Fortieth Regiment of Foot, was "sure such terms offered when we are in the height of success must induce these deluded rabble to seize so fair and easy an opportunity of reinstating themselves in the happiness they once enjoyed. . . . Those who remain in arms . . . deserve no mercy." A few days after the proclamation was issued Bamford would note its wide acceptance: "Great numbers of people in the Jerseys have come on . . . and taken quit passes of their habitations. Too great an indulgence for their past behavior."

Ambrose Serle, on duty in New York as civilian secretary to Admiral Richard Howe, thought the proclamation to be impracticable, and, like Captain Bamford, considered it too great an indulgence: "Some of the old friends to government are much displeased at its publication." The proclamation, he declared, "violently offends all those who have suffered for their attachment to government. They say that *they* are now the only sufferers while the rebels, being rebels, have secured on both sides all their property."

As the British marked time in Brunswick, there arrived at Lord Cornwallis's headquarters a party of prominent Philadelphians, including a remarkable lawyer named Joseph Galloway. Said to be second only to Benjamin Franklin in political importance in Philadelphia, Galloway had been a member of the Pennsylvania Assembly from 1757 to 1774 and served as Speaker of the House from 1766 to 1774. Like many another wealthy conservative, he had opposed the move for independence, sincerely believing that more could be gained for the good of America through negotiation than through revolution. In the First Continental Congress (1774) he had called for dominion status for the colonies in his much discussed "Plan of Union with Britain." It was defeated, but by only one vote.

Even when the war fever was spreading in 1775, Galloway continued to proclaim his support of the mother country, and he was frequently subjected to jeers and insults. One morning as he was about to leave his house he found a surprise at his front door. "Late in the evening," he informed a friend, "a box was left at my lodgings nailed and directed to me. Upon opening it next morning I found in it a halter, with a threatening letter." Inside the box with the halter and letter there was a mock insurance policy. Galloway, it declared, would not be alive in six days. The letter advised: "Hang yourself or we shall do it for you." The threat, Galloway said, "had no other effect on me than to fix me in my former resolutions to oppose those lawless measures at all events."

Eventually, however, Galloway decided he had had enough; it was time to escape "the distressing and ungrateful drudgery of public life," as well as the threats and insults. He decided not to run again for the Assembly and he turned down a seat in the Second Continental Congress. He got away from it all by spending most of his time at his 444-acre estate in Trevose, a village in lower Bucks County, about midway between Philadelphia and Trenton.

Galloway had for many years been a protégé, close friend, and staunch political ally of Benjamin Franklin, who was twenty-four years his senior. As fellow members of Pennsylvania's General Assembly, they had often led the good fight to repeal the tax exemptions and other special privileges accorded Governor John Penn and his family and other wealthy proprietors. In May 1775, after returning from a decade of service in London, Franklin rode out of Philadelphia one day to visit Galloway at his home in Trevose. In accepting Galloway's invitation for the visit, Franklin had written, "I am concerned at your resolution of quitting public life at a time when your abilities are so much wanted." In unavailing attempts to revive the old partnership, Franklin made two more trips to Trevose early in the summer of 1775. Franklin's son William, the royal governor of New Jersey, by now an ally as well as a friend of Galloway's, was present at the second meeting. The wine was flowing and the conversation was amiable but Franklin *père* eventually brought up the subject that was to divide them. "The glass having gone about freely, he, at a late hour, opened himself and declared in favour of measures for attaining to Independence." He "exclaimed against the corruption and dissipation of the Kingdom, and signified his opinion that . . . the Colonies . . . would finally prevail. He urged Galloway to come into Congress again." His arguments failing to persuade his friend, Franklin "broke off with Galloway."*

As Galloway would later recall the scene, the former political allies "parted as they met, unconverted to the principles of each other." Franklin was no more successful in attempting to convert

---

*So Massachusetts Governor Thomas Hutchinson, exiled in London, would note in his diary on January 6, 1779, after conversing that day with Galloway.

his son, who returned to New Jersey and the perilous job of maintaining royal rule there.*

Despite their differences, Franklin and Galloway remained friends, even after the Declaration of Independence was adopted about a year later. In October 1776, a short time before departing for a special mission in France, Franklin rode out to Trevose again. This time he brought along a trunk containing almost twenty years of his correspondence and the only manuscript copy of his autobiography. These papers, Franklin felt, would be safer in Galloway's "house (which was out of the way of any probable march of the enemies' troops) than in my own."†

Despite his ongoing friendship with Franklin and other supporters of the revolution, Galloway became a target for abuse from some of his neighbors; his Tory reputation had followed him into the country. Mobs gathered in front of his home and shouted threats. There were attempts to set fire to his property. One evening late in the autumn of 1776 a group of patriots imbibing at a nearby inn, described as "drunken Dutchmen," decided to get the damned Tory Galloway and hang him from the nearest tree. Only a swift and surreptitious message from the innkeeper saved him.

Shortly thereafter, on November 28, about a month after Franklin's final visit, Galloway made the move he had been contemplating for some time: he set off to join the British as they came across New Jersey. His wife, Grace, remained at the Trevose estate despite fears of being assaulted by "radical thugs," but Elizabeth, their only child, accompanied her father, along with the Allen brothers, Andrew, William, and John, members of a leading Philadelphia family, and a boy from another prominent family, Edward (Neddy) Shippen. They crossed the Delaware River from Pennsylvania to New Jersey and made their way almost thirty miles to Cornwallis's headquarters, moving in the direction opposite to that being taken by the retreating rebel army.

---

*Governor Franklin, an able administrator (and, according to his father, at this time "a thorough government man"), maintained his office longer than most royal governors, but in June 1776 the Provincial Congress of New Jersey declared him an enemy and ordered his arrest. He eventually sailed to England and remained there until his death in 1813.

†As things were to turn out, the papers might have been safer in Philadelphia. They were scattered and many of them lost when Galloway's house was later ransacked.

They joined the British a short time after Cornwallis and his army reached Brunswick. To his dismay, Galloway learned that the British were merely marking time here, awaiting word from Commander in Chief Howe. Why, Galloway wanted to know, did they not pursue the fleeing rebels and deliver "a fatal blow to the rebellion"? Howe, Galloway would later charge, "suffered his enemy to escape without pursuit. In the midst of victory the ardour of his troops was suppressed, and the chase forbid. . . . The rebel army was merely a new raised undisciplined corps, which a victory and vigorous pursuit never failed to destroy, or finally disperse.

"At Brunswick . . . Lord Cornwallis was upon the heels of the enemy. The destruction of a bridge over the Raritan saved them only for a few hours; their further security was owing to the orders received from that Nobleman [General Howe] to halt at Brunswick. The Raritan is fordable at that place in every recess of the tide; and had the noble General [Cornwallis] been left to act at his own discretion, he might, and no doubt would, have pursued his enfeebled and panic-struck enemy to the Delaware, over which they never could have passed without falling into his hands.

"At Brunswick the British army halted near a week. Washington's, consisting of 3,000 men, lay at Prince Town, seventeen miles, and at Trentown on the Delaware, twenty-nine miles distant, with all his heavy cannon and baggage. Many persons were astonished at his temerity in remaining a week so near the superior force of the British army, with a large river in his rear to cross. . . . But he, on this as on every other occasion, relied on the indolent progress of the British army."

An official British report a few years later would support Galloway's charge: "As the orders of his Lordship [Cornwallis] were positive not to advance beyond Brunswick, he here sent dispatches to the Commander in Chief [Howe], expressing sanguine hopes, that by a continued pursuit he could entirely disperse the army under General Washington, and seize his heavy baggage and artillery before he could pass the Delawar. But General Howe would not revoke his order, saying only that he would join his Lordship immediately: but this junction did not take place till after an important interval of several days, and the Americans were once more saved by the cold and dilatory policy of the English General."

Noting the arrival of Galloway and the Allens, Captain Ewald reported in his diary that they implored Cornwallis "to press General Washington as closely as possible so that we might overtake him in the vicinity of the Delaware River, by which his retreat would be cut off. There we could surely destroy or capture his disheartened army." Cornwallis was unmoved; the army would remain in Brunswick; the commander in chief's orders.

"Mr. Galloway," according to Ewald, "was so enraged over the delay of the English that he said out loud, 'I see, they don't want to finish the war!', which every honest man must think.

"For, seriously, why did we let the corps of five to six thousand men withdraw so quietly from Fort Lee?

"Secondly, why did we tarry so many days until the enemy had peacefully crossed the Second River?

"Thirdly, why did we march so slowly that the enemy could cross the Raritan safely?

"And fourthly, why did we not pursue the enemy at once, instead of lingering here for five days?

"One had to conclude, therefore, that we had hopes of ending the war amicably, without shedding the blood of the King's subjects in a needless way."

———— ◆◆◆ ————

CHAPTER 14

The Enemy's Approach Alarmed Our Fears

The college in Princeton had routinely reopened early in November 1776, a time when the war seemed a distant thing. "The students of the College of New Jersey," read the usual announcement in the *Pennsylvania Journal*, "and all who intend to enter there this fall are desired to take notice that the vacation will be up and college orders begin to take place on Monday the 14th of November. They are also desired to remember that on Wednesday the 6th the chambers will be fixed and assigned, so that those who do not appear that day will lose all claim from their former possession unless they have leave of absence previously asked and obtained. The Grammar School will begin at the same time, where boys are taught the Languages, Writing and Arithmetic with the utmost care."

Classes were resumed on November 14 with some 140 young men in attendance. They ate, slept, studied, and attended classes as well as religious services in Nassau Hall, an elongated, four-story stone edifice said to be the largest building in America. About half of the young men had come from Virginia and other places in the south that were many wearying days of travel away. By the end of November most of them would be on the road again.

A Princeton scholar who was keeping a journal during the increasingly critical days made this note on November 29: "New Jersey College, long the peaceful seat of science and haunt of the Muses, was visited with the melancholy tidings of the approach of the enemy. This alarmed our fears and gave us reason to believe we must soon bid adieu to our peaceful departments and break off in the midst of our delightful studies. Nor were we long held in suspense."*

The Reverend John Witherspoon, president of the College of New Jersey, called the students together on the twenty-ninth to give them the bad news. "Our worthy president, deeply affected at this solemn scene, entered the hall where the students were collected and in a very affecting manner informed us of the improbability of continuing there longer in peace; and after giving us several suitable instructions and much good advice very affectionately bade us farewell. Solemnity and distress appeared almost in every countenance. Several students that had come five and six hundred miles and just got settled in college were now obliged under every disadvantage to return with their effects or leave them behind, which several, through the impossibility of getting a carriage at so confused a time, were obliged to do, and lost their all."

In the succeeding days most of Princeton's two hundred or so families fled from the town. Several Quaker families remained; as neutrals, sworn not to take part in the rebellion, they would take their chances with the oncoming troops. A few other families—among them Loyalists still hopeful that there could be a reconciliation with the mother country—also decided to remain. Surely, the Loyalists felt, the king's men would treat them well.

At the age of fifty-four, John Witherspoon had been president of

*The author of the journal is generally thought to be William Churchill Houston, a thirty-year-old instructor who had been graduated from the college in 1768 and who was a captain in the Second Regiment, Somerset County Militia.

the College of New Jersey for ten years. He was one of the two members of Congress who would presently flee from Princeton with their families. The other was Richard Stockton, forty-six, a wealthy and distinguished attorney who a dozen years earlier had helped to persuade Witherspoon to leave his native Scotland and assume the presidency of the college in Princeton. Both men had signed the Declaration of Independence.

Stockton was a fourth-generation American, a wealthy aristocrat and master of an imposing estate known as Morven near the western edge of Princeton.* On August 27, 1776, he had come within one vote of being elected New Jersey's first nonroyal governor. In an election held by members of the legislature, Stockton and William Livingston each received the same number of votes in the first round of the balloting. The following day the election went to Livingston. Stockton was offered the prestigious position of chief justice of New Jersey but turned it down. He remained a member of the Continental Congress, serving with distinction on several committees. Late in September he and Congressman George Clymer traveled north with orders to investigate the condition of the troops on duty near the Canadian border. They found the soldiers to be in great want, especially of winter clothing, and on their return they urged Congress to make better provisions for the army.

Near the end of November, back home in Princeton, Stockton decided it was time to flee; the British would be here any day now. His wife, Annis Boudinot Stockton, supervised the packing of the many family treasures and saw that others were buried in Morven's spacious garden. And then the Stocktons were off—not, for some reason, across the Delaware and into Pennsylvania, where almost everybody else was going; instead, they headed southeast, and rode some thirty miles into Monmouth County, a section of New Jersey known for its high concentration of Tories. Perhaps the reason was that Richard Stockton knew that he and his family would receive a warm reception there from old friend John Cowenhoven, whose mansion, Federal Hall, could easily accommodate them all. In any case, on November 29, Richard and Annis Stockton, with four of their children (who ranged in age from three to fifteen), drove off, after saying goodbye to their twelve-year-old son Richard. For some

---

*From 1958 to 1981 it served as the home of New Jersey's governor. It is now a museum maintained by the New Jersey Historical Society.

reason the boy was left at Morven, in the company of one of the family's slaves.

During the second night the Stocktons spent in the Cowenhoven home, around two o'clock, a small band of armed Tories invaded the place. They dragged both Richard Stockton and John Cowenhoven from their beds and rode off with them. The raiders had been led to the scene by a Monmouth County Tory named Cyrenus Van Mater.*

The raiding party took Stockton and Cowenhoven to Perth Amboy, some forty miles to the northeast, and turned them over to the British authorities there. This was to be the beginning of a journey that would end with Stockton, ill and infirm, a prisoner of the British in New York. Apparently breaking under the strain, Stockton would be released about a month later. But at a price. To gain his freedom, he would sign a Proclamation paper ("I, Richard Stockton, do promise and declare, that I will remain in a peaceable obedience to his Majesty . . ."), thus becoming the only signer of the Declaration to recant, to swear allegiance to Great Britain. Soon thereafter he would be back in Princeton reunited with his family, but, in the view of some, living under a cloud of suspicion. He would never again serve in Congress.

American troops—some of them wounded, some ill, some deserting, some looting—had begun to pass through Princeton several days before the Stocktons left the village on November 29. The main body of the dwindling American army followed two days later, looking like anything but a match for the oncoming enemy, some of them wearing little more than blankets. Newspaper notices describing some of the deserters illustrated the variety of American "uniforms." One man "had on when he deserted an old wool hat bound with yellow binding, a coarse blue coat . . . no under jacket, old

---

*About eighteen months later, in June 1778, a grand jury indicted Van Mater for "giving information to the enemy and therefore being the cause of their taking" Stockton and Cowenhoven. Found guilty, Van Mater was sentenced to six months in jail and fined 300 pounds. But he was apparently in jail only a short time. "We hear," the *New Jersey State Gazette* reported on July 8, 1778, "that the enemy, in their late passage through [Monmouth] county, released Van Mater; who having piloted them through his neighborhood, went off with them to New York, leaving a large real and personal estate behind him, which we presume will be forfeited for his crimes."

leather breeches, his shirt very dirty . . . coarse light blue stockings, pretty good shoes, and old brass buckles." Another wore "a brown hunting shirt and trouser, without fringe, an old felt hat, old shoes, and had a black eye." Another "had on a light coloured frock, yellow breeches, old hat," another, "a purple frock and trowsers, old hat, good shoes."

"Indeed," Major James Wilkinson would recall of this time, "the splendid appearance and triumphant march of the British battalions in pursuit of our half-naked, sickly, shattered force, overspread the country with terror."

The plunderers among Washington's troops, and there were many, added to the terror. Though on the run and falling back from Brunswick, they found time to plunder many a house and barn, victimizing Whig as well as Tory. In addition to wagons, horses, saddles, harnesses, hay and oats, they carried off beds, tables, desks, chairs, looking glasses, griddles, pots, pans, storage chests, stockings, coats, cloaks, sides of leather, tanned calfskins, and panes of glass. Some of them knocked chimneys to the ground and carried off the bricks.

Numerous farmers in the Princeton area had already lost out in encounters with American troops—Jacob Van Dike, of Ten Mile Run, for one. He would testify that he had "most chearfully and willingly afforded all the comfort in his power" to American soldiers passing through. But, early one evening in September 1776, a battalion of Virginia regulars had, without his permission, stomped into his pasture field with about a hundred horses. They tore down his fences and burned them for firewood through the night "without his consent or knowledge" and he "was denied the least satisfaction by the commanding officer."

A few weeks later a company of Americans came along looking for pasture for their ninety-nine oxen. Van Dike offered them "a twenty shilling bill if the oxen should be drove to some other place where pasture might be hired." The soldiers turned down the offer, treated Van Dike "with bad language," and drove the oxen onto his property "in a most arbitrary manner."

During the retreat from Brunswick, farmers in the Princeton area suffered further losses. The "press men" of Washington's army seemed to be everywhere—collecting horses, wagons, fodder, provisions, sometimes issuing payment slips, sometimes not. At the farm of John Striker, a short distance from Princeton, they seized, among other items, an eleven-year-old horse and "1 negro man, 23 years old." Shortly thereafter, one of Striker's neighbors would report seeing the dragooned black man "with the Continental army driving waggin."*

In the Princeton area as elsewhere, horses and wagons were at a premium. Their owners were trying desperately to get their property away from the reach of the American collecting parties. Some owners deliberately disabled their wagons and carriages. According to a contemporary report, General Washington "got few carriages but what he took by force. The people hid their wagon wheels. He compelled them to produce them. They then broke their wheels and disabled their wagons, which rendered it very difficult for him to be supplied with wagons."†

The Princeton scholar who was keeping a journal described an instance of successful resistance. With the war coming closer, he had decided it was time to get out of its path: "As all hopes of continuing longer in peace at Nassau were now taken away, I began to look out for some place where I might pursue my studies, and as Mr. J. Johnson had spoken to me to teach his son, I accordingly went there and agreed to stay with him til spring. Next day I sent my trunk and desk to his house and settled all my business at the college.

"On Sunday evening [December 1] General Washington retreated from Brunswick. I then went to Johnson's and, having now no hopes of remaining there, was preparing to send my things farther out of the way, but we had not been long talking before the press men came for Mr. Johnson's wagon and horses, and with much difficulty we put them off for this time. Soon after, they came again, when we had but little hopes of keeping the wagons and horses. But knowing unless we got off our things while we had our wagons, they must necessarily fall into the enemy's hands, I took the opportunity while the press men were debating with Mr. Johnson, and took the

---

*Blacks were considered fair game by both armies. Around the same time Joseph Holmes, Jr., of Upper Freehold, about sixteen miles to the southeast of Princeton, found himself at the mercy of a band of Tories who, he reported, "seized on my Negro man, two horses and waggon, and sent them into the service of the British army." As they advanced across the state, the British were reported to be routinely pressing black men into service.

†Joseph Galloway would so testify before a committee of Parliament in 1779.

wagons out of the stable and went off with them into the woods, and though they ran after me, they neither found me nor the horses.

"After they were gone we packed up our things. I carried them by hand to the woods where we had concealed the wagons. Near daybreak we got all the things ready to move and drove to Amwell, where we arrived a little before sundown."

The College of New Jersey's Nassau Hall served as a temporary barracks for the retreating Americans and suffered considerably at their hands. Ebenezer Howard, a graduate of the college and a supporter of the American cause, would be appalled by the devastation during a visit a few months later: "The College is in a very ruinous situation, but this suffered more from the licentiousness of our own troops than from the ravages of the enemy." At Princeton, as one American observed, despite what seemed to be impending disaster, there was time for a bit of horseplay: "We are in a terrible situation, with the enemy close upon us and whole regiments . . . leaving us. Tomorrow we go to Trenton." But: "A Tory . . . was brought in here today by a party of the Pennsylvania boys. . . . This afternoon, after taking off his breeches and giving him an absolution by setting him on the ice (to cool his loyalty) they set him to work bringing in fagots. He seems pleased with his new office, knowing that he got off easy."

"Three villains" among the American troops were reported to have invaded the home of Nowel Furman, near Princeton, on December 3. "After abusing the family in a barbarous manner," according to a reward notice in the *Pennsylvania Evening Post,* "they took with them goods to the amount of between one and two hundred pounds, consisting chiefly of large pocket handkerchiefs of several kinds of red and blue stripes, . . . four dozen razors, one pair of four thread fine black worsted hose, black leather pocket books, pocket almanacks, a few pieces of children's garters . . ."

John Denton, a Princeton bookseller who offered a reward for their capture, went on to describe the thieves in the newspaper notice: "One of the above rogues is an Irishman, a middle sized man, well set, has bushy sandy hair, and supposed to be marked with the small pox; had on a blue coat. His name is said to be Watson and I have been informed he belongs to Capt. Brown's company of Pennsylvania riflemen, under Col. Broadhead. The second person I cannot describe. The third is a tall slim man, with light coloured clothes. They have with them two rifles and three longs swords, without scabbards. They put the goods in bags or knapsacks.

"They were seen near the Baptist meeting-house at Hopewell on Wednesday evening [December 4], but could not be taken for want of men of resolution."

Late in the afternoon of Friday, December 6, with the enemy reported to be coming on, John Witherspoon and his wife made hasty preparations to leave Princeton. Witherspoon was a likely enemy target; a few weeks earlier he had been burned in effigy (along with Generals Washington, Lee, and Putnam) by enemy troops. The college president was, as John Adams observed, "as high a son of liberty as any man in America." With the help of two students, Benjamin Hawkins and John Graham, the Witherspoons loaded household goods into a large wagon. They had to abandon sheep, cows, chickens, and the rest but they took along four colts. Young Hawkins drove Mrs. Witherspoon off in a two-wheeled, one-horse "chair," Graham, the other student, rode the wagon, drawn by a team of horses, and Witherspoon was astride a sorrel mare. Night had fallen by the time they rode off.

On the road from Princeton west to the Delaware River, the Witherspoon party encountered another Presbyterian minister, the Reverend Elihu Spencer, pastor of the church in Trenton. Dr. Spencer was on his way toward Princeton, to see his two daughters and grandchild, who lived there, safely out of the path of the enemy. One of the daughters, Margaret, was the wife of Jonathan Dickinson Sergeant, an attorney serving in the Continental Congress in Philadelphia.

The trip would not be necessary, Spencer learned from Witherspoon; his daughters had already left Princeton. A friend of the family, Dr. Absalom Bainbridge, had roused Mrs. Sergeant in the middle of the night and arranged for her, as well as her infant child and her sister, to flee in a carriage. They were right now heading for the Delaware River and Pennsylvania, Witherspoon told Spencer. He advised Spencer to hurry back home, get his family, and do the same.

Like Witherspoon, Spencer had good reason to flee the British advance. There was, according to a family record, a reward of a hundred guineas offered by the British government for his capture. Like many other Presbyterian clergymen, Spencer had been an early advocate of separation from the mother country. In 1775 he and another outspoken Presbyterian, the Reverend Alexander McWhorter of Newark, New Jersey, had been given a propaganda mission by the Congress. They were, as Spencer's daughter would recall, "appointed by Congress to visit the more remote parts of Virginia, Georgia, North and South Carolina for the purpose of informing the settlers there who were at the time exceedingly ignorant of the cause of the Revolution and of the necessity of standing forth in defense of their right and country."

Ever since making that trip, according to the family record, Spencer had been a marked man. McWhorter, too: he had left Newark and was accompanying Washington's retreating troops.

Back in Trenton, Spencer and his family packed up and hurried off from the parsonage. There was no choice but to leave home, church, livestock, everything, at the mercy of the invading troops. The Spencers rode off toward the river in a carriage. A few hours later, in a crowded and chaotic scene at a ferry above Trenton, they found their daughters and grandchild. "So many frightened people assembled," one of the daughters would recall, "with sick and wounded soldiers, all flying for their lives, and with hardly any means of crossing the river. We were unspeakably delighted when we got over safely and into a little hut, where we spent the night with a company of American soldiers."

Eventually the Spencers would find temporary haven in a village in Delaware called St. George's. Dr. Spencer had been the pastor there before being transferred to the church in Trenton.

The Witherspoons found their haven in Pequea, a village in Lancaster County, Pennsylvania. Here they were warmly welcomed by the Smith family. Back in July 1775 the Witherspoons' daughter Ann had married the Reverend Samuel Stanhope Smith and moved to Pequea.*

Mrs. Witherspoon remained at Pequea until the following summer, when she returned to her plundered home and farm in a desolated Princeton. Her husband, the only member of Congress in clerical garb, served in that body until 1782, meanwhile attempting in vain to reopen Nassau Hall, which had suffered at the hands of the enemy and even more when occupied by American troops. Between congressional sessions and assignments he found time to

---

*Years later, in 1792, Smith succeeded Witherspoon as president of the College of New Jersey.

correspond with his two daughters and three sons, the eldest of whom, James, was killed in action in October 1777. In a letter written on March 17, 1777, to his son David he referred to the fate of Richard Stockton, with whom he had signed the Declaration of Independence: "Judge Stockton is not very well in health and much spoken against for his conduct. He signed Howe's declaration and also gave his word of honor that he would not meddle in the least in American affairs during the war."

---◆◆◆---

CHAPTER 15

The Rebels Were Always Barely Ahead of Us

At General Howe's headquarters in New York, a twenty-three-year-old Hessian aristocrat, Captain Levin Friedrich Ernst von Muench-hausen—"Fritz" to his friends—was keeping a record of the British army's progress. "Lord Cornwallis," he noted on December 1, "advances still farther . . . has arrived at Brunswick, after having covered the areas of Hackensack, Bootbridge, Bergen, Elizabeth Point, Elizabethtown, and Amboy. There have been no important engagements up to this time, only small skirmishes."

December 3 and 4: "Lord Cornwallis is standing quietly at Brunswick; he has orders not to advance, but to rebuild the disman-tled bridge over the Raritan River, near Brunswick."

A serious type, Muenchhausen was becoming bored with the routine of his headquarters job and with the "frivolous" life of New York—nothing but "balls, concerts and meetings." In addition to the usual tiresome staff duties, there was the bother of censoring the letters written by rebels imprisoned in New York, a task "which keeps us busy many an annoying night." And then there was that damned Ludwig, Muenchhausen's shiftless and ungrateful servant. Ludwig had "good food and drinks in the kitchen of the general and furthermore I give him one guinea a month. . . . For this I ask him to take care of my belongings, washing, etc. . . . But he is indolent and spends too much time with the girls."

Captain Muenchhausen had arrived from Germany about four months earlier, in August 1776, as a company commander in the Hessian Leib Regiment. In the middle of November General Howe selected him, because of his linguistic abilities, as an aide-de-camp. His main job was to translate Howe's messages and orders into German and those of Lieutenant General Leopold Philipp, Freiherr von Heister, commanding general of the German forces in America, into English.

Muenchhausen kept a daily account of headquarters life in a diary that he sent from time to time to his brother Wilhelm, an official in the royal court at Hannover. On Thursday, December 5, there was some welcome news to report: Muenchhausen and several other aides were to go into the field with the commander in chief himself: "In the morning, unexpectedly, General Howe went to Jersey in a sloop, taking us with him. We landed at Elizabethtown Point and . . . went to Amboy, where General Howe and his suite lodged with General Grant, who with his 4th brigade of English, had been left behind at Amboy by Lord Cornwallis, with instructions to cover the rear. This was most necessary since all the information we received regarding the corps of General Lee indicated that he intended to cross the Hudson River to get into the rear and on the right flank of our corps."*

With Captain Muenchhausen and other aides and a unit of fresh troops, General Howe left Amboy in the morning of Friday, December 6. "At nine o'clock," Muenchhausen noted, "we were off to Brunswick. General Grant was ordered to advance with us, leaving behind the 46th Regiment. . . .

"At four o'clock in the afternoon we arrived at Brunswick where we met Lord Cornwallis with his corps. Immediately upon our arrival the Hessian grenadiers received orders from General Howe to move out to the right one hour's march." General Howe and the main body of troops proceeded to cross the repaired bridge over the Raritan River. After a brief march they bivouacked for the night on the heights beyond Brunswick. Howe's column—all English troops—would set off the next morning along the main stagecoach route toward Princeton. Howe put Cornwallis in command of the column he had ordered to march off to the right. In addition to

---

*Almost a month after first being summoned by General Washington, Lee and his corps finally had crossed the Hudson to New Jersey on December 2 and 3.

Hessian grenadiers this column included the Forty-second Regiment of Scottish Highlanders, two troops of the Sixteenth Regiment of Dragoons—and Captain Johann Ewald's company of jagers. The Cornwallis column, with Ewald and his men in the van, marched up the Raritan River for an hour, then bivouacked on the road for the night. From there they would advance along a route more or less paralleling the road to the south to be taken by Howe and his column.

The next morning, Saturday, December 7, Cornwallis, Ewald, and the rest of the right-wing column set off toward Princeton. Around the same time Howe's main column left Brunswick for the same destination. Along the way, there was, as usual, a special mission for Captain Ewald: to take twenty of his jagers and twenty dragoons, infiltrate rebel territory off to the right, and seize a rebel described as "a very disaffected man." Ewald and his party rode off and, with the help of a guide picked up along the way, reached the disaffected man's house without incident. There they came upon the man's wife and children and servants about to depart. Their extensive belongings had been loaded on seven wagons.

The man Ewald was seeking had fled. So he was told. But he decided to make sure: "I rummaged through the entire house while the mistress of the house followed at my heels with three children, and with tears in her eyes continually begged me not to take away everything from her. I assured her that I wanted nothing but her husband, which, however, she did not seem to believe. She gazed in astonishment when I marched off again, leaving her wagons and coach standing, and contenting myself with forty-five bottles of Madeira wine which I divided among my men, and for once drank myself."

Captain Muenchhausen was at Howe's side in the lower column of troops marching toward Princeton. "The Hessian grenadiers and jagers," he noted, "who had advanced yesterday, made up the second column, marching one hour's distance to the right. Our column, of Englishmen only, accompanied General Howe. We marched in trains except for two battalions of light infantry, two battalions of grenadiers, 150 mounted light dragoons with eight 3-pounders, all of whom marched in battle order, ahead of us.

"The rebels were always barely ahead of us. Since General Howe was with the vanguard, we advanced very slowly, and the rebels had time to withdraw step by step without being engaged. Jersey is a beautiful though mostly flat country, but there are numerous small woods and dense thickets. In one of these woods several of our scouts were killed. They were supposed to have scouted to the front and sides, but they had not done so efficiently enough. They were suddenly surrounded, and so were lost. Following this incident, the troop of 150 rebels hastily retired without our being able to chastise them."

Farther on, along the main road to Princeton, there was no resistance at all. The rebels were on the run. Nor was there any resistance along the route to the north being followed by Captain Ewald's jagers and the other units in the Cornwallis column. The British army, at long last, was on the move again. The word spread fast: The British were coming, and the Hessians, too! Soon they would be in Princeton.

----◆◆◆----

Chapter 16

They Pillaged Friend and Foe

It happened early in December at a farmhouse near Princeton according to a report that would appear in the *Pennsylvania Journal* of February 5, 1777: "One afternoon a large number of British light horse came to a farmer's house (whose mother, an aged widow woman, lay very sick with a fever) and put up for the night.

"A Colonel and about a dozen other officers took possession of their parlour and bedrooms, except the one where the sick woman lay. After their horses were fed with the hay and grain of the farmer's . . . they plundered the cellar of about 50 pounds of sugar, 60 pounds of butter, a quantity of cheese, hog's fat, candles and meat, not leaving the family an ounce of either. . . . In a few hours there was not a mouthful of victuals left in the house for the family to eat, and although the daughter of the sick woman applyed to the Colonel several times with tears in her eyes . . . to prevent his troops plundering and eating up all their provisions, yet he did not shew the least inclination to hinder them.

"The evening this Colonel and his officers spent in feasting and drinking . . . and although they were told how disagreeable it was to the sick woman, yet they did not appear to have the least tenderness or humanity in them, but used the most profane language, damning the rebels (as they called the Americans) for a pack of cowards, and wished they would make a stand and fight them, and they would be as willing their army might consist of a hundred thousand as ten thousand.

"They swore they would be in Philadelphia by Christmas or in Hell."

The plunderers, according to the published report, were members of "the light horse gentry [who] are said to be the best bred part of the army, and there were no others at this house. They neither offered to buy or pay for any thing."

General Washington's men, many of them, had been bad enough. Now the British were coming, along with the Hessian barbarians; they would reach Princeton any day now—the British with their hot-headed Highlanders, who went berserk in battle and hacked helpless victims to pieces with their long swords; the Hessians, who ran screaming into battle and bayoneted wounded soldiers begging for mercy. So it had been widely reported.

Off the battlefield the enemy soldiers were reported to be leaving a trail of rape, murder, and plunder. In the New York area shocking atrocities had been reported. "In many places," a typical account read, "the graves in the churchyards were opened and the bodies of the dead exposed on the ground for several days . . . coffins broken open, bones scattered around. At Delancey's farm the body of a beautiful young lady, which had been buried for two years, was taken out of the ground and exposed for five days in a most indecent manner."

In the atrocity reports American propagandists were stressing two points: that the British were every bit as bad as the Hessians, and that Tories as well as Whigs were being victimized; no one was safe. "They have treated all . . . without discrimination, the distinction of Whig and Tory has been lost in one general scene of ravage and desolation." So the *Pennsylvania Packet* reported on November 19, the day before the invasion of New Jersey began. The *Pennsylvania Evening Post* a few days later: "The English soldiers, it seems, were so jealous of the plunder the Hessians got that they likewise insisted upon the same privilege, which General Howe was obliged to allow in order to pacify them and prevent a mutiny. And now the devastation they make, wherever they come, is not to be equaled in history. They make no distinction, Whig or Tory is all one to them." The *Freeman's Journal:* "The Hessians plunder all indiscriminately, Tories as well as Whigs. If they see anything they want, they seize it and say, 'Rebel good for Hesse man.' A Tory complained to General Howe that he was plundered by the Hessians. The General said he could not help it—it was their way of making war."

A thirty-two-year-old Dutch clergyman, Domine Theodore Dirck Romeyn, was among the first of New Jersey's residents to be extensively plundered. A 1765 graduate of the College of New Jersey in Princeton and an outspoken Whig, Romeyn was the pastor of a church in Schraalenburgh, a village near Hackensack. He and his family were not at home when the British arrived there on November 23. As the British proceeded to sack Romeyn's house and outbuildings, local Tories gathered and cheered them on. In his journal that day Romeyn wrote: "The British Troops & followers plundered me of all my Furniture Cloathing Books Papers &c. to the amount of about £500 York currency, at the parsonage house . . . I being absent."

Another of the heavy losers was Adrian Post, who operated a gristmill and sawmill at Acquackanonck (Passaic). Before fording the Acquackanonck River near Post's mills the British demanded a guide to lead them safely across. Who could tell how deep the holes might be in the river bed? Post's twenty-one-year-old son was pressed into service. At the point of a bayonet the young man was forced to lead the troops through the frigid water. (The exposure would make him an invalid for the remaining twelve years of his life.) After camping on and around Post's farm overnight the British carted off, as Post would later swear, fifteen pairs of shoes, a felt hat, a new ax, a woman's silk hat, and, among other nonmilitary items, "six pair of pillow cases with lace." Two days later he lost again to enemy plunderers: "twelve women's caps faced with lace, £2, 7s; one black horse about 14 hand high, £18; a half-worn saddle worth three dollars or £1, 2s, 6d; six pair of pillow cases one third worn, £1, 10s; five check aprons one third worn, 16s."

From some of Post's neighbors the British carried off human beings along with the booty. Christopher Vanoorstand lost an almost new boat, four horses, a wagon, potatoes, turnips, and "2 Negro men valued at £90" and "2 Negro women" valued at £100. Losses sustained by John Sip, Sr., included 32 hives of bees, four horses, four cows, and "1 Negro man, £60, 1 Negro boy, £40, 3 Negro women, £30." In all, from just the Acquackanonck area the British took along sixteen black slaves, in addition to such other plunder as chintz gowns, a silver snuff box, rugs, aprons, silken handkerchiefs, infant apparel, a Latin Bible and "1 Dutch Testament & the Psalms."

The women traveling with the British army, in particular the wives of the Hessians, often assisted in the plundering. An eyewitness in Piscataway, about six miles north of Brunswick, gave this description of what was becoming a familiar scene: "I saw the soldiers plundering the houses, the women of the village trembling or weeping or flying with their children; the men had retired to await the day of retribution. In many houses helpless old men or widowed females anxiously awaited the soldiers of monarchy. A scene of promiscuous pillage was in full operation. Here a soldier was seen issuing from a house armed with a frying pan and gridiron, and hastening to deposit them with the stove over which his helpmate kept watch. The women who had followed the army assisted their husbands in bringing the furniture from the house, or stood sentinels to guard the pile of kitchen utensils and other articles already secured and claimed by right of war."

In Newark, it would be reported by a congressional committee, "three women were most horridly ravished by them, one of them an old woman near seventy years of age . . . another of them was a woman considerably advanced in her pregnancy, and the third was a young girl. . . . Yea, not only common soldiers but officers, even British officers, four or five, sometimes more, sometimes less in a gang, went about the town by night entering into houses and openly inquiring for women.

"There was one Nutman, who had always been a remarkable Tory, and who met the British with huzzas of joy, had his house plundered of almost everything. He himself had his shoes taken off his feet, and threatened to be hanged, so that with difficulty he escaped being murdered by them."

Thomas Hayes, who lived near Newark, "as peaceable and inoffensive a man as in the state of New Jersey, was unprovokedly murdered by one of their Negroes, who run him through the body with his sword. He also cut and slashed his aged uncle . . . [and] stabbed one Nathan Baldwin."

Farther on, near Woodbridge, "one of the most respectable gentlemen . . . was alarmed by the cries and shrieks of a most lovely daughter. He found an officer, a British officer, in the act of ravishing her. He instantly put him to death. Two other officers rushed in with fusées and fired two balls into the father, who is now languishing under his wounds." (In another version of this incident, the offending officers were Hessians.)

Were the reported offenses of the enemy troops any worse than the accustomed misbehavior of some of the American troops? Or was it just that the British and Hessians had greater opportunities and more time for misdeeds than the Americans, exhausted and on the run?

Whatever the answers, the clever and sometimes imaginative American propagandists continued to find a sufficiency of material as the war approached the Raritan River. A farmer living in Piscataway found the British soldiers to be "a set of blackguards" not to be outdone in atrocious behavior: "The last thing when they go to bed and the first in the morning is to remind God to damn their eyes, tongues, liver, pluck, heart and soul, and this they do more than a thousand times a day. They have stole the chief of my loose estate, all my meat and flour, hay, horses, a hundred and more bushels of wheat, two hogsheads of lampblack, beds and bedding. . . .

"I am not alone. All my neighborhood . . . fared the same fate. . . . Not a pannel of fence left standing in a mile, all the wheat fields open, some houses burnt down, some pulled down and burnt. They came into my room in the middle of the day and stole my watch. . . . If such people are to rule and reign on earth, then the Devil must be styled God of this world."

Such complaints were effectively publicized by American propagandists, who were assiduously inflating even the most minor infractions by the British and Hessians into "atrocities." The charges, however, were not baseless, as even the most ardent of British adherents entirely admitted. Joseph Galloway would three years later testify before a parliamentary committee that in New Jersey "by far too many were plundered of their property while they had their written protections in their hands, or in their houses. Friends of government and those disaffected to government shared the same fate in a great variety of instances." British troops as well as the Hessians were guilty, according to Galloway, who added: "The people plundered have come to me recently from the fact, with tears in their eyes, complaining that they were plundered of every-thing they had in the world, even of the pot to boil victuals."

A short time after the New Jersey campaign began, Major Ste-phen Kemble, a Loyalist from New Jersey serving in General Howe's headquarters in New York, had predicted: "His Lordship [Cornwallis] will not be able to restrain the troops from plundering the country; their excess in that respect carried to a most unjustifi-able length."

Charles Stedman, a captain with Cornwallis, would find Kemble's prediction to be accurate: "No sooner had the army entered the Jerseys than the business (we say business for it was a perfect trade) of plunder began. The friend and the foe from the hand of rapine shared alike." So would Judge Thomas Jones: "A licentious army was suffered to plunder and to commit every kind of rapine, injus-tice and violence indiscriminately upon the inhabitants, the conse-quence of which became dismal."

On November 20, the day the British army crossed the Hudson to New Jersey and captured Fort Lee, this reminder was issued to field officers: "As the inhabitants of this country [that is, New Jersey] are in general well effected to government, Earl Cornwallis expects the commanding officers of brigades and corps will exert themselves to prevent plundering amongst the troops." During the night of November 20–21, however, as Captain Ewald observed, "All the farms in the vicinity were plundered, and whatever the soldiers found in the houses was declared booty."

Like many another commanding officer of the time, Captain Ewald looked upon a certain amount of plundering as routine behavior and inevitable. "A good soldier," he had observed, "knows his way about." However, Ewald stayed within "the rules" and at several stops along the way he saw to it that "everything was left undisturbed, save for a few provisions." In a typical instance of staying within the rules he would use the flat of his sword to strike a soldier in the act of deliberately defacing furniture, even though it belonged to a rebel.

Not all officers were as concerned with the rules as Ewald and, as General Howe was aware, there were in many cases far too few officers to control the soldiers. On November 30, the day his amnesty proclamation was issued, Howe expressed fear that his soldiers would get out of control. In some British units, he wrote Lord Germain that day, there were as few as two officers to three hundred men, "and altho' the men behave with great spirit, yet the temptations for plunder are so great that it is now not in the power of a few officers to keep the men under proper restraint."

One of the factors in the widespread plundering was the bottom-of-the-barrel condition of many of Howe's troops from England. There had been great resistance to recruiting for this unpopular war and rosters were often filled with convicted criminals ordered to serve their terms in America rather than in a prison. The resistance was the main reason the Hessians had been hired, and why England had tried in vain to sign up some 20,000 Russian mercenaries. That was why, in a marked departure from custom, Roman Catholics—most of them from Connaught and Munster in Ireland—were welcomed to the service, if not by General Howe himself. The British army, he had lamented late in 1775, "must have between 6,000 and 7,000 recruits and of the worst kind if chiefly composed of Roman Catholics, certain to desert if put to hard work, and from their ignorance of arms are not entitled to the smallest confidence as soldiers."

Some British apologists—not including Howe, who knew better—blamed the Hessians entirely for the massive plundering. "They were led to believe before they left Hesse-Cassel," a British officer, not identified, declared, "that they were to come to America to establish private fortunes, and hitherto they have certainly acted on that principle." Another such officer charged: "It is a misfortune we ever had such a dirty, cowardly set of contemptible miscreants. The Hessians are more infamous and cruel than any." Looking back on the New Jersey campaign, Sir Henry Clinton, second in command to General Howe, would have this comment: "Unless we would refrain from plundering, we had no business to take up winter quarters in a district we wished to preserve loyal. The Hessians introduced it."

Captain Stedman agreed, but only up to a point: "The odium began with the Hessians . . . though the British troops were far from escaping a share of the imputation." Captain Hall bemoaned "the licentious ravages of our licentious soldiery (both British and foreign) who were shamefully permitted, with unrelenting hand, to pillage friend and foe."

CHAPTER 17

We Sustained an Orderly Retreat

"Trenton," Thomas Paine observed upon arriving in the town, "is situated on a rising ground, about three-quarters of a mile distant from the Delaware . . . and is cut into two divisions by a small creek or rivulet sufficient to turn a mill which is on it." General Washington's 3,000 troops remained in and around Trenton and Princeton until Saturday, December 7, when, Paine noted, "on the approach of the enemy, it was thought proper to pass the Delaware."

Washington had reached Trenton with about half of his force around noon on December 2, having left some 1,400 men at Princeton, twelve miles back, as a rear guard. During the next three days the Americans moved most of their baggage and stores across the river to Bucks County, Pennsylvania, crossing at both Beatty's Ferry, above "the falls" of the Delaware opposite Trenton, and at Trenton Ferry, below the falls. The job was accomplished with the help of a hastily formed flotilla of vessels ranging in size from rowboats to ferryboats. Commodore Thomas Seymour was there in command of galleys of the fledgling Pennsylvania Navy, flat-bottomed boats forty to fifty feet long, painted black and yellow and bearing such names as *Burke, Camden, Chatham, Congress, Experiment, Franklin, Ranger,* and *Washington.* Before being ordered to Trenton by the Pennsylvania Council of Safety, Seymour's galleys had been patrolling the Delaware above and below Philadelphia, on the alert for spies attempting to cross the river and for possible British naval activity. The galleys were manned by crews of some thirty men and were powered by two lateen sails and by twenty oars, twenty-two feet long and double banked. The galleys were armed with cannon ranging in firepower from howitzers to eighteen-pounders to thirty-two-pounders. In addition to getting the stores and baggage across the river, the men of the Pennsylvania Navy helped to clear the New Jersey shore of anything that would float. Captain Thomas Houston was on the scene in command of the galley *Warren,* having been ordered on December 2 by the Pennsylvania Council of Safety to "immediately proceed up the River

Delaware as far as Trenton to remove all the river craft, vessels and boats from the Jersey to the Pennsylvania side of the Delaware in order to prevent their being serviceable to the enemy in their attempts to cross said river." The council's order coincided with General Washington's order of December 1 placing Colonel Richard Humpton in charge of the mission, in which about forty miles of riverbank were cleared. The job included the removal of all boats from streams feeding the river as well as the river itself. Among those taking part were men of the Second Militia Regiment of Hunterdon County, New Jersey, led by Captains Daniel Bray, Jacob Gearhart, and Thomas Jones.

The clearing of the New Jersey riverbank had been completed when, early in the morning of Saturday, December 7, General Washington set out from Trenton for Princeton with a small party of troops. Near Maidenhead (Lawrenceville) he encountered General Greene, retreating with his troops from Princeton. The British, it had been learned, had finally left Brunswick and were on the march toward Princeton, hoping no doubt to catch the Americans before they could reach the Delaware. Within a few hours, on Washington's order, his troops began crossing the river at Trenton. John Bayard, a prominent Philadelphia merchant serving as a militia colonel, had arrived in Trenton around eleven in the morning and learned "by express, from the General at Princeton" that further retreat was necessary: "The enemy are advancing and it is expected they will be there tonight. . . . They are coming in two columns. We are removing the stores across the river and purposing making a stand there." So Bayard wrote at two p.m. to a friend in Philadelphia. Fearing that the enemy might soon reach Philadelphia, he added: "Pray send for Lank immediately and remove the goods from my house to the country."

By the light of bonfires and torches, the crossings that had begun in the afternoon continued far into the night of December 7. "All the shores were lighted up with large fires, boats continually passing and repassing, full of men, horses, artillery and camp equipage. The sick and half naked veterans of the long retreat streamed past. I thought it the most hellish scene I have ever beheld."

That is how Charles Willson Peale would recall the night. At the age of thirty-five, Peale was one of the most popular painters in America. Lanky, pale, and fragile-looking, he was also perhaps America's most unlikely soldier. But here he was, at Trenton, on the frosty bank of the Delaware, waiting with his men for the boats that would carry them across the river. A lieutenant of militia and second in command, Peale had helped to round up eighty-one of his Philadelphia neighbors and marched off with them as a company to reinforce the retreating Continentals. They had left Philadelphia two days earlier as part of the Second Battalion, Pennsylvania Militia, and sailed up the Delaware toward Trenton.

"He is ingenious," John Adams had observed of Peale. "He has vanity, loves finery, wears a sword, gold lace, speaks French, is capable of friendship and strong family attachment and natural affections." Peale described himself as "totally unfit to endure the fatigues of long marches and lying on the cold wet ground." And yet he was a resourceful man, who knew how to endure the rigors of combat, as he said, "better than many others whose appearance was more robust." How? "By temperance and by forethought in providing for the worst that might happen." The forethought included a chunk of dried beef and a pocketful of hard biscuits plus a canteen filled with water, a drink "better than rum."

Peale had learned to cope at an early age. Growing up in Queen Anne's County, Maryland, he was indentured as an apprentice to a saddler from the age of twelve to twenty. He got into art by trading a saddle for a series of lessons from a painter named John Hesselius. Within a short time he showed such promise that in 1766, when he was twenty-five, a group of Maryland patrons sent him to England to study for almost three years under the celebrated Benjamin West. Peale worked hard, socialized seldom,* and perfected his style. He was less than enamored of life in London and, reacting to Britain's ongoing repression of the colonies, he resolved never to raise his hat when George III's carriage passed by. On leaving England he carried out another resolve: to take no English clothes back with him.

Back home in Maryland, he began to make a reputation as a portrait painter. In 1772, on one of his commissioned projects, he went to Mount Vernon in Virginia to do a three-quarter-length portrait of George Washington, Esq., a forty-year-old colonel in

---

*An exception was the day he dropped in unannounced on Benjamin Franklin, who "showed me his experiments . . . and desired me to call on him any of my leisure moments." Approaching the apartment, Peale found Franklin "sitting with a young Lady on his knee"—a scene he sketched for posterity.

the Virginia militia, the first of many portraits of Washington he would eventually do. On that occasion, Peale later recalled, he came upon some young men pitching an iron bar on the lawn, a sport of the day. Washington came on the scene, picked up the bar and heaved it well beyond the mark of the others. "When you beat my pitch, young gentleman," he said, "I'll try again."

Early in 1776, Peale moved his family from Maryland to Philadelphia and established a salon on Arch Street. There he did portraits of numerous congressmen and others. He also routinely joined the Philadelphia militia and, to his surprise, since he was "but a stranger to them," he was elected a lieutenant. As the war moved closer to Philadelphia, Peale's mother raised objections to his enlistment. What if he were killed? What would happen to the household? In addition to his wife and mother, it comprised a son, Raphael, a daughter, Angelica, and Peale's sister, whose husband was a captain serving in the Maryland line. What would they do without Peale?

Mrs. Peale decided to call on an old friend from Maryland to talk some sense into her son: Charles Carroll, a lawyer who was serving in the Continental Congress. A meeting was arranged and Mrs. Peale stated her case. "After the first civilities were made," Peale would report in his autobiography, "she began to talk on the subject, expressing her fears for the life of her son and the situation he must leave his family in a strange place without friends to assist them." But Peale's mind was made up; he interrupted to remind her that he had promised to serve in the common cause and, when called on, he would respond. This declaration, "was spoken in such an emphatic manner that the barrister did not say anything in favor of his mother's wishes." End of visit.

Lieutenant Peale was second to Captain Beeman (first name not known) in command of the company, and he proved to be a mother hen of an officer. He recruited most of the company and did not have to go far in doing so; the company members were all from the city block formed by Arch Street, where he lived, and Market, Front, and Second streets. When the company was alerted to leave the city, Peale visited the home of each man and listed the needs of each family. He had promised the men that in return for enlisting for six weeks they would "get everything they should want, and told their wives that they would be supplied with necessaries while their husbands were doing their duty in the field." Peale saw to it that the families would receive sufficient firewood and food. For some of them he arranged cash loans from the Council of Safety. On Tuesday, December 3, he collected blankets, cartouche boxes, belts, canteens, and other items his men would need in the field, including thirty guns and fifty-five haversacks. The next day he rounded up fifteen more guns, thirty knapsacks, and some bayonets. There were also arrangements to be made for his wife, daughter, son, and sister. Because of what appeared to be the impending invasion of Philadelphia by the British army, some families had already left the city and many more were planning to leave. Peale succeeded in arranging for accommodations for his family in Abington, about fifteen miles directly north of Philadelphia. A friend agreed to help the family move there.

In the small journal he had just started keeping, Peale noted that on December 5 he bought a cot for 55 shillings and borrowed a frame for it. He also bought a pair of fur gloves for three dollars. That evening, with his company, he went aboard a sail-powered shallop in the Delaware River, and presently the vessel set sail upstream: "We do not get more than about ten miles from the city. We make use of the tents for lying, and have a very tolerable night.

December 6: "Very little wind . . . At sunrise we weigh anchor, and get as high as Bristol with the first tide. The wind now coming fair, we are able to stem the tide by making use of the tents as helping sails. We got a little beyond Bordentown this night."

December 7: "Go with Mr. Barker on shore and buy some milk. Settle our expenses; I pay 1s, 3d. We arrived at Trenton about one o'clock. Have just rested and eaten when Major Bradford says we must cross the river. Each man having received his complement of cartridges, we are ordered to prepare to march, and send our heavy baggage across the river. I expected we were to advance toward the enemy, but it was to retreat across the river."

As he and the rest of the company awaited their turn to cross the Delaware, Peale watched in empathetic wonder as Washington's ragged Continentals plodded past toward the boats. At one point he experienced the shock of his life: "Suddenly a man staggered out of the line and came toward me. He had lost all his clothes. He was in an old dirty blanket-jacket, his beard long and his face full of sores . . . which so disfigured him that he was not known by me on first sight. Only when he spoke did I recognize my brother James."

Ensign James Peale—Jemmy to the family—was twenty-seven, eight years younger than Charles. Having been tutored by Charles, he had shown promise as a painter of miniatures before enlisting in Brigadier General William Smallwood's Maryland Regiment. He and 1,100 other members of the regiment, "men of honor, family and fortune," had marched off in July to reinforce the Continental Army. They had distinguished themselves in combat on Long Island and at White Plains and they had lost heavily to enemy fire and such diseases as typhus and smallpox, for now they were down to about 100 men, many of them in no better shape than James Peale. Presently they would be across the Delaware and in Pennsylvania; there they would at least be able to stop running; the retreat would be over, though perhaps only temporarily. Presently, too, Charles Peale and his company would cross and "put a few tents for the night on the shore."

The militiamen from Philadelphia who made the crossing that afternoon and evening ranged in age from the early teens to the fifties. One of the oldest was a devout, Bible-quoting supply sergeant named William Young. He and no fewer than three of his sons were serving with the Third Battalion, Pennsylvania Militia.

Young's company, like Peale's, had left Philadelphia on December 5. As he noted in his journal, they "set out by water from Philadelphia in a schooner for Trenton in the Jerseys to oppose General Howe's march toward Philadelphia." The schooner reached Burlington, New Jersey, about fifteen miles up the Delaware, around two in the afternoon. Young and his company "went on shore and marched to Trenton. Got there by night. Met with some difficulty to get a lodging. Providence directed me to Mr. Brown's who kindly let us lodge in his stove room."

Young spent two nights in Trenton, one in Mr. Brown's stove room and the other in "a good lodging room, warm and comfortable." But then the British were really coming on and it was time for the exodus to Pennsylvania. "Orders to remove our quarters and retreat over Delaware on account of Howe's advance party was near at hand," Young noted on Saturday, December 7. "Got over after night, and lay on the shore very cold—and with much difficulty got some wood to make a fire. Renewed a cold I got coming up the river."

The next day, Sunday, December 8, Young and his unit marched about a mile into Pennsylvania and pitched their tents. "All pretty well. Our captain very kind to our men."

In the punishing days and nights that were to come, Sergeant Young would place his faith in Providence and even in the most trying of circumstances he would find a good word for the Lord: "I am much fatigued, yet have my health very well thanks be to thee, oh God!" He was dismayed, however, by the profanity and irreverence of the young men about him: "It is melancholy to think what looseness prevails among all our men . . . A great deal of swearing and taking the Holy Name of God in vain." Before long he would conclude that "if salvation comes to our guilty land it will be through the tender mercy of God, and not through the virtue of her people. So much swearing and profane living is nowhere else to be found."

The crossings were resumed with the first light of Sunday, December 8. "We paraded in Trenton at 4 a.m.," Sergeant James McMichael of the Pennsylvania Rifle Regiment noted, "and at dawn crossed the ferry into Pennsylvania." Captain Enoch Anderson did not cross until the afternoon, "and in two hours afterwards the British appeared on the opposite bank and cannonaded us. But we were in the woods and bushes and none were wounded that I heard of. This was the crisis of American danger."

The leading elements of the British, including the jagers or chasseurs in their forest-green uniforms, arrived at the New Jersey bank of the Delaware just before the last boat carrying Washington's troops reached the Pennsylvania shore. As more and more enemy troops, some of them British in bright scarlet, arrived at the river's edge, American cannoneers, who had been positioned and ready for several hours, opened fire on them, a concentrated, heavy fire. Many of the cannon balls and racks of grapeshot found their targets, scattering the enemy troops and forcing them to flee along the uphill paths leading back to Trenton.

For the weary Americans the retreat, at long last, was over—for a while at least. The Delaware, mightiest of the four rivers they had crossed since their arrival in New Jersey, was about a thousand feet wide here. Its strong current, running as deep as ten feet, prevented easy fording and there was no bridge here or anywhere else along its course. There were no ferries or boats of any kind either, thanks to Washington's foresight. "The enemy," a Connecticut officer observed, "came marching down with all the pomp of war, in great expectation of getting boats and immediately pursuing." But they found none; Washington's order of December 1 had been thoroughly carried out. Enemy contingents "made forced marches up and down the river in pursuit of boats but in vain."

Looking back on the nineteen days of the retreat from the

Hudson to the Delaware, Captain Henry Miller of the First Continental Pennsylvania Regiment observed that he had been "so harassed . . . by the pursuing enemy that I had not had time to change my clothes for two weeks." Perhaps now there would be time.

Safely across the Delaware, Thomas Paine, as usual, accented the positive: "With a handful of men we sustained an orderly retreat for near an hundred miles, brought off our ammunition, all our field pieces, the greatest part of our stores, and had four rivers to pass. None can say that our retreat was precipitate, for we were near three weeks in performing it, that the country might have time to come in. . . . The sign of fear was not seen in our camp, and had not some of the cowardly and disaffected inhabitants spread false alarms through the country, the Jerseys had never been ravaged. Once more we are again collected and collecting. . . . By perseverance and fortitude we have the prospect of a glorious issue; by cowardice and submission the sad choice of a variety of evils: a ravaged country—a depopulated city—our homes turned into barracks and bawdy-houses for Hessians, and a future race to provide for, whose fathers we shall doubt of. Look on this picture and weep over it! and if there yet remains one thoughtless wretch who believes it not, let him suffer it unlamented."

———— ◆◆ ————

CHAPTER 18

Neither Boats Nor a Ferry

"The Army marched in three divisions towards Prince Town in order to pass a place called Rocky Hill, 12 miles from Brunswick, where it was said the Rebels were posted." So Lieutenant Archibald Robertson noted in his journal on December 7. "The right column, consisting of [Colonel] Donop's corps, marched along the northwest side of the Millstone River by Hillsborough and Schencks Bridge, where we were joined by the centre column under General Grant, consisting of the 4th Brigade. The reserve and guards with the General kept the highway. We all got to Prince Town in the evening. The Rebels had gone a few hours before towards Trenton. I was with the Hessians."

Captain Muenchhausen was as usual at the side of Commander in Chief Howe on the march of sixteen miles from Brunswick. "In the evening we arrived at Princeton . . . a nice little town," he noted in his journal. He went on to describe the College of New Jersey's Nassau Hall: "Princeton . . . has a fine college. Its main building has 36 windows on its length and 24 on its width, and is four stories high. A remarkably excellent library has till now been spared by the war." (It was not to be spared for long; American troops had started the job of destruction and the British completed it. In his diary Sergeant Thomas Sullivan, of His Majesty's Forty-ninth Regiment, blamed it all on the British: "Our army when we lay there spoiled and plundered a good library that was in it.")

Captain Ewald's Second Jager Company marched through Princeton and on for about a mile on the road leading to Trenton. So did Captain Wreden's First Jager Company. In a wooded area there the two companies, as usual, occupied the most forward position of the army. There was to be little rest for the fatigued troops: "We were repeatedly alarmed during the night by enemy parties and remained under arms the whole night," Ewald noted. But no casualties were reported.

The British army strutted into Trenton to the accompaniment of a Hessian band in the afternoon of Sunday, December 8. They reached the Delaware, as General Howe would report, "soon after the enemy's rear guard had crossed." Charles Stedman, an officer in Howe's army, would put it another way, charging that the commander in chief had done it again: "General Howe appeared to have calculated with the greatest accuracy the exact time necessary for the enemy to make his escape."

It had been a twelve-mile march from Princeton, much of it over rough terrain. The army moved out early in the morning, as Captain Muenchhausen noted, "after the dismantled bridge over the Stony Brook had been repaired." The march proceeded "in a single column, the Hessian grenadiers having joined us last night after having marched as a second column yesterday. Again today, we had in front of us a vanguard in battle order, which followed closely on the heels of the retreating enemy.

". . . At two o'clock in the afternoon we reached Trenton outskirts. Some inhabitants came running toward us, urging us to march through the town in a hurry so we could capture many of the enemy who were just embarking in boats and were about to cross [the Delaware]. General Howe, who probably knew that the rebels had strong batteries on the other side of the Delaware, surmised that they hoped we would follow the straggling parties and become exposed to enemy fire as we reached the plain." (Muenchhausen described "the plain" beyond Trenton as being "more than 200 paces wide with the Delaware to the right and a wooded valley to the left.") Because of his suspicions, General Howe "ordered a halt of all troops except some light infantry and Jagers."

The jagers—who else?—led the way toward the Delaware. Their mission, Captain Ewald noted, was "to seize the rear guard of the enemy at the crossing . . . but the last boats were already leaving the shore when we were still about 300 paces away."

General Howe ordered the main body of his troops to remain on the north side of Trenton, away from the river. Then, accompanied by Captain Muenchhausen and other aides, he followed the route of the jagers and light infantrymen through the town and down to the open area along the riverbank. It was then that the rebels, across the river in Pennsylvania, "opened a terrific fire upon us," according to Muenchhausen, "with all their batteries, containing 37 cannon. The light infantry and the jagers were forced to retreat in the greatest hurry to the valley at the left. On their way, in the blink of an eye, they lost 13 men."

It was such a confused scene that there was little agreement among the participants on details of the cannonading. Lieutenant Henry Stirke of the British light infantry would report that "between the town and the ferry . . . just as we halted we received a very heavy cannonade from the opposite side of the river which (before we could get under cover of a hill, at the back of town) killed one of the dismounted dragoons, wounded a man of the 27th light company and (died soon after) an artillery man." Lieutenant Archibald Robertson "found the rebels had all crossed the Delaware River, and gave our advanced troops a very brisk cannonade across the river from eight or nine pieces. We had only three men wounded." Ewald noted far greater firepower: "The enemy . . . rendered us the honor of firing eighteen heavy guns at us until we were all dispersed; however, without great damage, for we lost only one jager in spite of the devastating fire."

Commander in Chief Howe himself barely escaped the cannonballs. Even though the heavy fire continued unabated, Howe, Muenchhausen, and the other aides, all on horseback, remained at the scene. "Howe," Muenchhausen observed, "rode with us all around, stopping from time to time. He stayed there with the greatest of coolness and calm for at least an hour, while the rebels kept their strongest fire going. Wherever we turned, the cannon balls hit the ground, and I can hardly understand, even now, why all five of us were not crushed by the many balls." At one point, "just as General Howe was about to move into the town, a ball landed so close to him in soft ground that dirt splattered his body and face."

Captain Muenchhausen had an even narrower escape: "I had the honor to receive a small contusion on my knee. We were just standing still when a ball took away the hind leg of my horse, and hit some stones on the ground, one of which hit me in the knee and caused my leg to swell up. I was lucky, for my horse fell to the ground with me, with great force, and feeling the blow on my knee just then, I believed that I was really seriously wounded. Afterwards General Howe gave me a superb English horse to replace mine."

After leaving the area under bombardment and returning to the other side of Trenton, General Howe ordered the main body of troops into the town. He settled in for the night in a house that would become a favorite target of the rebel artillerymen across the river. Fortunately for Howe during his stay there, the rebel fire would be ineffectual. As Muenchhausen would put it: "The rebels must know the house where our General is staying, for they have thrown several shells at our house. But so far none have come very close."

That evening, Sunday, December 8, Colonel Donop and his grenadier brigade found quarters in Trenton. One battalion of English light infantry bivouacked at the upper Trenton ferry, and another below Trenton, near the drawbridge over Crosswicks Creek, not far from its confluence with the Delaware River. Captain Ewald and his jagers "were assigned posts in a small wood near Falls Ferry to protect this crossing over the Delaware." Looking back on the advance from Brunswick, Ewald again made note of what in a later day would be called a "no win" policy: "On this two-day march, which could have been done in twelve hours by an army that carried so little artillery, it became clearly evident that the march took place so slowly for no other reason than to permit Washington to cross the Delaware safely and peacefully. I was assured that Lord

Cornwallis had orders from General Howe to proceed in such a way. The two Howe brothers belong to the Opposition Party. Therefore no more need be said. They will not and dare not act otherwise."

Even so, Ewald anticipated an early assault on Philadelphia that would end the rebellion. "As soon as the Delaware, which freezes almost every winter in this area, was covered over with ice, the army was to cross the river and capture Philadelphia, where it was expected to end the war, since Washington's army consisted of only three thousand men, of which a majority were dispirited." If the river did not freeze over, then, according to Ewald, "the army would cross the river in this vicinity with the aid of pontoons."

While the jagers and other units were settling into position in and around Trenton, Lord Cornwallis was making preparations for a more immediate crossing of the Delaware. Cornwallis and his British Regulars had halted in Maidenhead, about six miles north of Trenton, but they were not to remain there even overnight. Shortly after midnight the drums sounded and the weary Redcoats groaned as they received the order to prepare to march. This was to be, as they were about to learn the hard way, a march of about twenty miles.

Around one a.m. on Monday, December 9, the Regulars formed into a column and trudged out into the frigid night: the Forty-second Regiment, three battalions of light infantry, two battalions of grenadiers, and two battalions of foot—a formidable corps, all-British; no Hessians. Their destination: Coryell's Ferry on the Pennsylvania bank of the Delaware, sixteen miles up the river from Trenton. They would cross (from Lambertville, New Jersey, to New Hope, Pennsylvania, in later terms), and damn their eyes if they wouldn't be in Philadelphia before Christmas.

With Cornwallis in active command, the corps reached the Delaware, opposite Coryell's Ferry, around daybreak. Now, with a few boats, they would make the crossing to Pennsylvania. But where were the damned boats? Where was the ferry? The troops spent the morning scouring the riverbank and the nearby creeks. They were unable to find even one rowboat. For miles along the river the damned rebels had taken everything. Occasionally the British scouting parties were fired on by rebels from across the river. It was sporadic, harmless; nobody was hit.

A whole day's search turned up not a single vessel. There would be no crossing of the river today. Nor tomorrow either, since they had failed to bring along even a raft. Giving up the search, Cornwal-

lis and his troops headed south to bivouac in and around Pennington, a village about five miles northeast of Trenton.

Before the end of the day, Monday, December 9, the negative
report reached Howe in Trenton. "News was received from Lord
Cornwallis that a crossing was impossible," Captain Muenchhausen
reported, "because he could find neither boats nor a ferry. Besides,
the rebels had been informed of his intentions."

On the same day, Howe dispatched a detachment to reconnoiter
the Delaware closer to Trenton. "General Howe's First Adjutant
General received orders today to reconnoiter along the Delaware,"
Muenchhausen noted. "He asked me to accompany him. We returned unhurt, even though the rebels shot many cannon and even
more muskets at us." Like Cornwallis's troops, this party found no
boats.

On Tuesday, December 10, Muenchhausen reported that American raiding parties were making the British support line "very
unsafe." One party had on the previous night "captured a small
escort with eight baggage wagons." The next day he noted further
action to the rear: the enemy had "captured several patrols and
individual dragoons with letters" and had taken "700 oxen and
nearly 1,000 sheep and hogs from our commisariat." On the same
day, according to Muenchhausen, a detachment was sent "to the
left along the Delaware River to look for boats or to find any other
means of crossing this cursed river." But it was the same story: not a
vessel of any kind in sight.

Captain Hall, who had been critical of the delay at Brunswick,
bemoaned the lack of foresight: "Pontoons or boats on carriages,
essentially necessary for the service in this country, had been
neglected, the want of which at this time proved a capital oversight
in the ordnance department. It is true, an old boat or two were
found in the neighbourhood of Trenton, in which General Vaughan
offered to cross the river and continue the pursuit, but this proposal
was not approved of by the commanding officer."

Looking back on the march across New Jersey, Captain Hall
could hardly believe what had been allowed to happen: "Thus to
suffer the shattered remains of the rebel troops, a set of naked
dispirited fugitives encumbered with baggage, to run a race of
ninety miles and outstrip the flower of the British army, three times
their number, appears to be an omission, not to give it another
name, without example. . . .

"We had every thing to encourage our progress: the enemy were depressed, and drove from every quarter, their principal force was flying before us, the country-people eagerly assisting our advances by repairing the bridges and guiding the pursuit. Yet, for want of vigor and decisiveness, we flagged in the career of conquest and neglected to follow the blow, which would have finally crowned us with success and crushed the rebellion.

"In the catalogue of military errors and misconduct, I will venture to assert, this appears so singular that it almost stands without example. Yet this march was extolled in the publick papers, and drew applause from the deceived and credulous multitude."

In a report to London General Howe presented a different view: "I cannot too much commend Lord Cornwallis's good service during this campaign, and particularly the ability and conduct he displayed in the pursuit of the enemy from Fort Lee to Trenton, a distance exceeding 80 miles, in which he was well supported by the ardor of his troops, who cheerfully quitted their tents and heavy baggage as impediments to their march."

The weather by this time had, in Howe's opinion, "become too severe to keep the field, and the winter cantonments being arranged, the troops marched . . . to their respective stations." In the days that followed, the weather would become an increasingly important factor in the struggle.

Joseph Galloway, the Loyalist from Philadelphia who had accompanied the British from Brunswick to Trenton, was all for continuing pursuit of the rebels. "At Captain Montresor's request," he would later testify, "I did inquire whether there were any materials in or about Trenton with which pontoons, boats, or rafts might be constructed; and I found 48,000 feet of boards, a quantity of wire, and there was timber enough about Trenton for that purpose. No boats were brought from the Raritan River, as the Americans feared and anticipated. Nor does it appear that the work of building boats or rafts was ever begun."

There would be no crossing to Pennsylvania—not until the cursed Delaware froze over.

CHAPTER 19

A Neighborhood of Very Disaffected People

Most of the American troops spent their first night in Pennsylvania just as they had been spending their nights in New Jersey—out in the open. Thomas McCarty was not only without shelter but also without relief from the pain of a festering finger. "We lay in the woods all day," he noted in his journal after crossing the river, "and I had great pain with my finger as the nail came clean off." Lieutenant James McMichael and his company "remained in the woods, having neither blankets nor tents." Captain Enoch Anderson and his men "lay amongst the leaves without tents or blankets, laying down with our feet to the fire. We had nothing to cook with but our ramrods, which we run through a piece of meat and roasted it over the fire, and to hungry soldiers it tasted sweet." The anonymous and semiliterate Pennsylvania soldier keeping a "Gornall" made this note: "Then We Ware ordered over the river of Daluaware Whare We were forst to Ly ought in the Woods night and Day."

Sergeant Joseph White, the onetime "featherbed soldier" from Massachusetts now serving with an artillery unit, was among the fortunate, for a change, that first night in Bucks County, Pennsylvania. In retreating across New Jersey he and his fellow cannoneers had subsisted on little more than flour, but now there was welcome news: "After crossing the river, we were put into the back part of a tavern." They would be warm and dry—and perhaps even fed—for a change. There was also some bad news: the tavernkeeper had a plentiful supply of food and drink but he "refused to take rebel money, as he called it."

A few months earlier, near New York, White had encountered and overcome similar resistance while recuperating from "a dangerous sickness" in a barn that was being used as a hospital. A Quaker owned the barn and, "after some time," White "went into his house to buy some milk. The Quaker said, 'We can't sell thee any.' Then I told them I would milk the cows. The woman consented to let me have a pint every morning by paying her three coppers. My health gained fast."

But now, in the Bucks County tavern, the owner was adamant: no rebel money. No amount of persuasion was going to succeed this time, so White decided to apply some pressure. He hurried off to the house nearby where General Israel Putnam, "Old Put" of Bunker Hill fame, was spending the night. White told the general that the tavernkeeper had "everything we wanted, but he will not take paper money, he calls it rebel money."

Putnam was furious: "You go and tell him, from me, that if he refuses to take our money, take what you want, without any pay."

White returned "and told the man what the General said. 'Your Yankee general dare not give such orders,' says he. I placed two men at the cellar door as sentries. 'Let nobody whatever go down,' I said. I called for a light and two men to go down cellar with me. We found it full of good things: a large pile of cheeses, hams of bacon, a large tub of honey, barrels of cider and one barrel marked cider-royal, which was very strong; also all kinds of spirits.

"The owner went to the General to complain. 'The sergeant told me,' said the General, 'that you refused to take paper money.' 'So I did,' said he. 'I do not like your rebel money.' The General flew round like a top. He called for a file of men. A corporal and four men came. 'Take this Tory rascal to the main guard house!' "

Now it was time for a long overdue feast. There was plenty for all of the cannoneers, and some for Putnam: "a ham of bacon, one large cheese, and a bucket full of cider-royal." Who had sent all this? the general wanted to know. Informed that it was Sergeant White, he said, "Tell him I thank him."

New Jersey had been bad enough. Bucks County, predominantly populated by Quakers steadfastly opposed to the war, as Sergeant White and the rest of Washington's Continentals were about to learn, was going to be no better. Washington was dismayed by the cool reception his men were meeting. There was even a report that the millers here were refusing to grind grain for the soldiers. He would look into such matters as that, but first there was some high-priority business to attend to. After the crossings of the Delaware were completed and all available boats secured, he gave orders for precautionary measures against an attempted crossing by the enemy. He entrusted one order to Colonel John Cadwalader, thirty-four, a prominent Philadelphian who had been a member of the city's Committee of Safety and who had risen from captain of a "silk stocking" militia company to commanding officer of a Pennsylvania militia regiment. Soon he would be in command of all Pennsylvania militiamen on duty in the area. Cadwalader had been captured when the enemy stormed Fort Washington on November 16 but, as General Washington reported, he "was immediately released without parole by [General] Howe at the instance of General Prescott who, when a prisoner in Philadelphia, had received civilities from Colonel Cadwalader's father." General Washington, Cadwalader informed the Pennsylvania Council of Safety, "desires me to request that you will immediately dispatch a party of men from Philadelphia to cut down and destroy two bridges on the Burlington road, one of Pensawkin and the other on Coopers Creek, as he is apprehensive the enemy intend to pass to Philadelphia by that route." Cadwalader appended a plea for help: "Let me beg of you in my own name that you will alarm the whole country, south and west, nothing but their assistance can save us!"

A state of panic was by this time developing in Philadelphia. There were rumors that the Congress was about to flee to the south. In a diary note of December 8 an elderly Philadelphia resident wrote this of the city scene: "News brought of General Howe's intention of bringing his army by land through the Jerseys to this city. Martial law declared and General Putnam constituted chief ruler in this province." December 9: "All shops ordered to be shut; the militia to march into the Jerseys; all in hurry and confusion; news that General Howe is on his march . . . ."

General Washington had meanwhile settled in Colvin's Ferry (Morrisville), directly across the Delaware from Trenton, having set up headquarters in a commodious brick mansion there—"Summer Seat," the summer home of Thomas Barclay—on rising ground about a half mile from the river's edge. From this place, which was to be his headquarters for about a week, Washington issued orders for the defense of strategic points along the Delaware, from Dunk's Ferry, below Bristol, upstream to Coryell's Ferry (New Hope), a stretch of some forty miles. "You are to post your brigade at and near Bristol," he ordered Colonel Cadwalader. "Colonel Nixon's regiment to continue where it is at Dunk's Ferry. . . . You'll establish the necessary guards and throw up some little redoubts at Dunk's Ferry and the different passes in the Neshaminy.

"Pay particular attention to Dunk's Ferry as it's not improbable something may be attempted there. Spare no pains or expense to get intelligence of the enemy's motions and intentions. . . . Keep proper patrols going from guard to guard. Every piece of intelligence you obtain worthy notice, send it forward by express. If the enemy attempt a landing on this side, you'll give them all the opposition in your power. . . ."

To Brigadier General James Ewing, in command of a force of militiamen, Washington wrote: "Your brigade is to guard the river Delaware from the ferry opposite to Bordentown till you come within two miles or thereabouts of Yardley's Mill to which General Dickinson's command will extend. . . . You are . . . to give every possible opposition to the enemy, particularly at crossing the river. . . ."

To General Philemon Dickinson, in command of a few hundred New Jersey militiamen, Washington wrote: "You will post your troops at Yardley's Ferry or somewhere near it. Find out the fording place there and have a redoubt thrown up immediately. You and General Ewing must divide the ground between Trenton Falls and your post, and establish the proper guards and patrols to watch the enemy's motions. You will spare no pains or expense to obtain intelligence. . . ."

Troops under the command of Brigadier General Matthias Alexis de Roche Fermoy, a Frenchman of dubious merit, were posted farther up the Delaware, at Coryell's Ferry and other possible crossing points nearby. The rest of the troops were quartered in improvised camps a short distance inland from the river. Detachments of guards were stationed at every likely fording place for a stretch of about fifty miles.

Apparently convinced that the British would attempt to cross the Delaware, Washington repeatedly stressed the importance of gaining intelligence about the enemy. In messages to Stirling, Mercer, and other key officers he ordered them to select "some person who can be engaged to cross the river as a spy, that we may if possible obtain some knowledge of the enemy's situation, movements, and intention. Particular inquiry should be made by the person sent, if any preparations are making to cross the river; whether any boats are building and where; whether they are coming over land from Brunswick; whether any great collection of horses is made, and for what purpose. Expense must not be spared in procuring such intelligence, and it will readily be paid by me."

Then, mindful of the prevailing mood of the people of Bucks, he added: "We are in a neighbourhood of very disaffected people. Equal care therefore should be taken that one of these persons does not undertake the business in order to betray us."

Despite the fact that Trenton was being occupied by Hessian

troops, it was possible for someone, using one excuse or another, to get into and out of the village. The problem, as General Dickinson learned in attempting to recruit spies, was the fear of betrayal by Tories remaining in Trenton. "I have endeavoured to prevail with some intelligent person to go down into Trenton," he informed Washington, "but hitherto without success. If 'tis agreeable to your Excellency, I will offer fifteen or twenty dollars to a good hand, who will undertake it, if such a one can be found. People here are extremely fearful of the inhabitants of Trenton betraying them."

In the same message Dickinson reported this intelligence, for what it might be worth: "A negro fellow, whose master lives in Trenton, whom I have just seen, informs me they are building boats at Henry's Mills, a mile from town, and that he was told by soldiers there were many boats coming from Brunswick. What degree of credibility is to be given to this information I will not determine."

Colonel Reed, directing intelligence operations from Bristol, was convinced that the British army would soon attempt to cross the Delaware somewhere between Bristol and Trenton. On December 12 he informed Washington: "The gentlemen of the Light Horse who went into the Jerseys have returned safe. They proceeded into the country till they met an intelligent person directly from Trenton, who informed them that General Howe was then with the main body of his army . . . that they are certainly waiting for boats from Brunswick; that he believed they would attempt a landing in more places than one. . . . They are collecting horses from all parts of the country. Some movement was intended yesterday morning but was laid aside."

In setting up the defensive positions along the riverfront, Washington had to depend largely on militiamen and other troops with little or no combat experience. Thousands of Continentals, the regulars, needed now perhaps more than ever before, were gone. Three of the best-trained and most reliable regiments—troops who had marched proudly off to battle in the summer—had by this time all but vanished. Colonel George Weedon's Third Virginia Regiment of some 600 men, once "the strongest," in Washington's opinion, had plummeted to "between one hundred and thirty and one hundred and forty men fit for duty, the rest being in hospitals." So Washington would report. Brigadier General William Smallwood's Maryland Regiment had established an enviable reputation in combat but suffered so many casualties that only 100 or so remained from the original roster of about 1,100 men. Washington referred dolefully to "the shattered remains of Smallwood's regiment which by fatigue, want of clothes, etc., are reduced to nothing." General Smallwood, suffering extensive wounds, was at home in Maryland hoping to form a new regiment.

The Delaware Blues, as Colonel John Haslet's men were known, had been one of the proudest regiments in the Continental Army. On the parade ground they had precision to match that of a veteran European unit. They attracted admiring glances as early as the summer of '76, when they marched off to battle in their leather breeches, white waistcoats, blue outer coats lined with red, and their tall headgear of black leather inscribed with the words "Liberty and Independence. Delaware Regiment." Under Haslet's able leadership, the Blues served with conspicuous gallantry on Long Island and "fought like regulars" at White Plains and elsewhere. But along the way they suffered many casualties, some of them caused by American guns. On October 23 near White Plains one of the Delaware companies met with a scouting party of Pennsylvania riflemen. "Unfortunately," Lieutenant James McMichael, of the Pennsylvania unit, noted, "taking the Delaware Blues for the enemy, we fired on each other, in which six of our riflemen and nine of the Blues were killed."

"Putrid fever," smallpox, pneumonia, and other afflictions took a heavy toll among the Delaware Blues. So did desertion. During the retreat across New Jersey some of the troops went home, with permission, to join a new regiment being formed, and some departed without permission. Nine officers left and most of their men went along with them. As Christmas approached, the regiment that had numbered about 700 was down to six men. Colonel Haslet would report the bad news to his friend Caesar Rodney, the elder brother of Captain Thomas Rodney. Caesar Rodney, a brigadier general in the Delaware militia, had been a signer of the Declaration of Independence. In what was to be one of his last letters, Haslet wrote: "Captain Holland, Ensign Wilson, Dr. Gilder and myself are all who have followed the American cause to Trenton, two privates excepted. On General Washington being informed of this, he declared his intention of having officers and men bound neck and heels and brought back as an example to the army. I told the General the truth, but not the whole truth; the last I reserved for you, and you will blush with me." Colonel Haslet apparently kept some of the disheartening details from Washington.

With so many of such troops as Haslet's and Smallwood's gone, General Washington was sorely aware of the need for reinforcements if he was ever going to attempt a stroke against the enemy. He was counting heavily on the troops reported to be coming from the north with General Horatio Gates and those in New Jersey with General Charles Lee. With the help of these two forces Washington might be able to achieve some sort of bold stroke against the enemy. But time was running out. In message after message he had pleaded, begged, and urged Lee to hurry on through New Jersey with his badly needed troops. Thus far, Lee had chosen to ignore the messages.

———♦♦♦———

CHAPTER 20

Sad Work This Day

On Tuesday, December 10, his third day in overcrowded Trenton, Colonel Donop was ordered "to make an expedition to Burlington, a place 17 English miles from Trenton, with 100 jagers and 400 Hessian grenadiers and . . . to reconnoiter that neighborhood since the future winter quarters were to be in that area"—so an aide to Donop noted in the headquarters journal.

"Therefore," the aide continued, "he set out on the 11th in the morning at two hours before daylight, marching over the so-called drawbridge over Crosswicks Creek. . . . Along the way . . . they met with several parties of Rebels who hastily retired and destroyed several small bridges."* Near a hamlet called Bustleton, south of Bordentown, Donop's troops encountered a detachment of about a hundred rebels. There was a brief exchange of fire but presently the outnumbered Americans raced off in the direction of Burlington.

Captain Johann Ewald, in the forefront as usual with his jagers,

---

*One such was apparently a "strong scouting party" led by Captain Henry Miller of the Pennsylvania Rifle Regiment, quartered in Bucks County. Miller reported that he fell in with about 400 Hessian troops "marching to Burlington." On being fired upon, Miller's party recrossed the Delaware to Pennsylvania.

briefly noted the action: "Halfway, in the vicinity of Bustleton, we ran into an enemy detachment of about one hundred men who were attacked and partly killed or captured." From the prisoners taken, Ewald "learned that the town of Burlington was protected by six row galleys." The galleys, or gondolas as they were also known, were part of the recently formed Pennsylvania Navy and were patrolling the Delaware River under the command of Commodore Thomas Seymour. The heavy artillery pieces they carried were more than a match for Donop's firepower. On this mission the Hessian force had not brought along any artillery.

The detachment of rebels routed near Bustleton was under the command of the row-gallery officers, Ewald learned from further questioning of the men captured.

The fleeing American force reached Burlington around ten a.m. Earlier, some disturbing reports had reached the town. This is how a remarkable Quaker widow, Margaret Morris, would recall the scene: "After various reports from one hour to another, of light-horse approaching, the people in town had certain intelligence that a large body of Hessians were come to Bordentown, and we might expect to see them in a few hours.

"About 10 o'clock, a party of about sixty men marched down the main street. As they passed along the way they told our doctor and some other persons in the town that a large number of Hessians were advancing and would be in the town in less than an hour.

"This party were riflemen who, it seems, had crossed the river somewhere in the neighbourhood of Bordentown to reconnoitre and, meeting with a superior number of Hessians on the road, were then returning and took Burlington in their way back. From us they crossed to Bristol and by the time they were fairly embarked the Hessians, to the number, as we heard, of four or five hundred, had passed what we call York Bridge. On the first certainty of their approach, John Lawrence and two or three others thought best, for the safety of the town, to go out and meet the troops. He communicated his intention to one of the gondola captains, who approved of it and desired to be informed of the result."*

One of the townsmen who met with the Hessians at the eastern

---

*Lawrence's son James Lawrence, born five years later, grew up to become a famous naval officer. As commander of the frigate *Chesapeake* in 1813 he was mortally wounded during an encounter with the British frigate *Shannon* in Boston harbor. His final words on the day of the battle, said to be "Don't give up the ship!," became a motto of the U.S. Navy.

edge of town was the Reverend Jonathan Odell, pastor of St. Mary's, the Anglican church in Burlington. Known for both his high intelligence and his pro-British sentiments, Odell had been urged to take part in the negotiations. As he would later report, "Some of my neighbors thought it advisable to meet the [Hessian] Commandant on his approach to the town, and to request him to spare the inhabitants from insult and their property from pillage. They requested me to go with them and assist in that charitable address as an interpreter. I did so, and had the pleasure to find that I had a good prospect of being of real service to my peaceable neighbors."

Odell was fluent in the French language and, as he learned when the negotiations began, so was Colonel Donop, the commanding officer of the Hessians. Donop, as Odell would later confide to his friend Margaret Morris, "seemed highly pleased to find a person with whom he could converse with ease and precision." Donop assured Odell that Burlington would be spared if the inhabitants remained peaceable. He made clear that no one in the town was to have "any arms, ammunition or effects belonging to persons that were in arms against the king." Donop further assured Odell that, upon the honor of a soldier, he would be "answerable for every kind of disorder on the part of his troops." As the discussion continued, Odell noted, the troops "remained in profound silence in their ranks."

There appeared to be little likelihood of resistance from inhabitants of the town—especially with such a Hessian force at hand—but Commodore Thomas Seymour's fleet of heavily armed riverboats presented a clear and often present danger; it was known that they had orders to bombard the town if enemy troops entered.

According to his headquarters journal, Donop "required that a deputation of citizens should be sent off to the commodore of the enemy's boats in order that they might exact an agreement from him that he would not molest the town. Then, since the commodore's boat lay some miles down the river toward Philadelphia and communication with him could not be effected and his decision obtained quickly, Colonel von Donop, in company with several of his officers, enjoyed the hospitality of [John Lawrence] in his house and while waiting partook in all tranquility of the noonday meal which had been prepared."

Captain Ewald, as usual at the side of Donop, noted that Commodore Seymour "requested two hours time to consider." Everyone seemed to enjoy the meal, Ewald added, and, when it was over, all present "looked at the clock and noticed that the two hours had almost elapsed." As he waited anxiously at the same table, Odell observed in Colonel Donop "much of the gentleman . . . and the appearance, at least, of generosity and humanity." And so, as a man of honor, he decided to inform Donop about some possibly incriminating items that had been stored in his home. Esther de Berdt Reed, the wife of General Washington's adjutant general, Joseph Reed, had passed through Burlington with her mother and children a few days earlier. Before leaving the town and heading for a safer area, Mrs. Reed had begged Odell, as a longtime friend, to store in his house some of the things she was unable to take along. Odell assured Donop that he would submit an exact account of the items Mrs. Reed had left with him.

"Sir," Donop responded without a moment's hesitation, "you need not be at the trouble of giving any further account of those things you have so candidly mentioned. Be assured that whatever effects have been entrusted with you in this way I shall consider as your own and they shall not be touched." Impressed with the colonel's forthrightness, Odell was "encouraged to hope that . . . nothing would occur to disturb the peaceable disposition that was making." Perhaps he could be of still further service to his fellow townsmen.

By taking part in the negotiations, Odell was risking serious trouble. As a known British sympathizer, he had already been put on parole. Now, dealing with the Hessians along with other Loyalists, he might be making himself fair game for the Tory-hunters who had been coming into Burlington almost daily in search of "disaffected" persons.

About six months earlier, around the time of the adoption of the Declaration of Independence, Odell had closed down his church; at such a time one could hardly continue to offer prayers for the royal family as required by the Anglican liturgy. Odell remained in Burlington with his family, and, as he later explained, "made it a rule to myself . . . not to interfere directly or indirectly in public affairs. . . . I presumed it reasonable . . . to expect I should be indulged in the unmolested enjoyment of my private sentiments, so long as I did not attempt to influence the sentiments or conduct of other men, and that *private* sentiments ought not to be made matter of public notice, much less of public censure."

Now thirty-nine years old, Odell had served as pastor of the Burlington church for almost a decade. He was a grandson of the

Reverend Jonathan Dickinson, the first president of the College of New Jersey, and he had been graduated from that school in 1754 at the age of seventeen. He had gone on to study medicine and to serve as a surgeon in the British army during the French and Indian War. Later, he studied for the ministry in England and was ordained in 1767. In July of that year he was assigned to Burlington, and he had been there ever since. In 1772 he married Anne DeCou of Burlington. Within four years they produced two daughters and a son, William Franklin Odell, named for his godfather, the royal governor of New Jersey.

Jonathan Odell was one of Burlington's most respected and popular men. Many in the town, perhaps a majority, shared his affection for the mother country and his abhorrence of such an extreme measure as independence. Many sympathized with him in the predicament his Loyalism had got him into.

Odell's troubles could be traced to the first week of October 1775. At that time his friend Christopher Carter was about to leave Burlington for a trip to England. But before he could depart his papers were seized by the local committee of inspection and observation. Among them were two letters that Jonathan Odell had written to friends in England—letters critical of the movement for independence. The committee took Odell's parole not to leave the city, and "referred the matter to the Council of Safety, before whom he appeared October 8th." The letters were passed on to the Committee of Safety of New Jersey and finally to the Provincial Congress. Summoned before the Congress, Odell was "heard and then ordered to withdraw." After deliberating for a day, the Provincial Congress decided to "decline passing any public censure against him."

It was a couple of poems that eventually got Odell into further trouble. Some British officers captured in Canada were being held as prisoners in Burlington in the spring of 1776. Somehow, they arranged to have a party on Burlington Island in the Delaware near Burlington on June 4, the birthday of George III. They wined and dined under a tree and, to the accompaniment of their own band, sang a song that Odell had written for the occasion. It ended with these lines:

> *While thousands around us, misled by a few,*
> *The phantom of pride and ambition pursue,*
> *With pity their fatal delusion we see;*
> *And wish all the world were as happy as we!*

Odell, a prolific versifier (who in later years would become one of the most effective of British satirists), also wrote an "Ode for the King's Birthday" for the frolicsome prisoners:

> *O'er Britannia's happy land,*
> *Ruled by George's mild command,*
> *On this bright auspicious day*
> *Loyal hearts their tribute pay.*

And so forth for ten quatrains.

As a result of such outward signs of "disaffection," Odell was called in on July 20, 1776, and made to sign this parole: "I the subscriber do on my parole of honour and on the faith of a gentleman promise the Convention of the State of New Jersey that I will repair to the City of Burlington and there or within a circle of eight miles thereof, remain and not depart therefrom unless with leave of the Convention . . . that I will not carry on any political correspondence whatever on the subject of the dispute between Great Britain and the United States of North America. Neither will I furnish any provision or give any intelligence to the enemies of the State."

Since that time Odell had succeeded in keeping a low profile. But now, around midday of Wednesday, December 11, here he was, sitting with Colonel Donop and praying that the "river tyrants," as he privately described the men of Commodore Seymour's galleys, would spare the town by leaving peacefully.

But this was not to be, as Odell's friend Margaret Morris would report. In a daily record she was keeping, Mrs. Morris noted that John Lawrence, host of the midday meal, went down to the wharf with two other men, expecting to discuss Donop's proposal with the riverboat officers. One of the boat captains had set off earlier to inform Commodore Seymour of the situation. Lawrence and two other men, Mrs. Morris noted, "went down upon the wharf and waved a hat, the signal agreed on . . . for the boat to come ashore and give the commodore's answer in peace. To the astonishment of these gentlemen, all the answer they received was first a swivel shot. Not believing it possible this could be designedly done, they stood still and John Lawrence again waved his hat, and was answered with an eighteen-pounder."

A few minutes earlier, one of Captain Ewald's jagers had come running to the Lawrence home to report that the gunboats were approaching the town. Everyone sprang up from the table, according to Ewald. Now they would have the commodore's reply. "But instead of the reply, there was a rain of bullets from the topmasts." The galley men were cannonading the town.

Turning to Odell before leaving the Lawrence home, Donop said that he was going to take a look at the galleys and see what measures might be necessary on his part. He added that he would be sorry to be the occasion of any damage or distress to the inhabitants. After viewing the river scene, Donop returned to the main body of troops, who were still obediently waiting at the edge of town, and rode off with them, vowing to return with the necessary firepower. Presently, in a message to General Alexander Leslie in Princeton, he would write: "I am waiting with impatience the arrival of the Grenadier Battalion Koehler which will bring with them six eighteen-pounders, after which I will take possession of Burlington, where there are according to reports eight to ten gondolas. We will see what resistance they will make to our heavy artillery."

As the Hessians marched off, a boy who had been overcome with curiosity about the arrival of the soldiers almost became a casualty. He had gone off, without permission, to see these strange soldiers and, as he reported, "stayed later than prudent. . . . My father arrived in search of me just as the row galleys . . . began firing."

As the boy raced homeward, "an eighteen-pound, double-headed shot struck the back of a house within less than twenty yards of us. It broke a large hole through the wall and lodged in the fireplace, driving ashes out the front door which, my father observing, said he thought they were firing red-hot balls." Farther on: "We had to face the cannon as they fired up York Street. My father bade me watch the flash and immediately fall flat, which we both did, and were favored to arrive safe. We found the family had retired to the cellar, which was the retreat chosen by numbers."

A Burlington Quaker named James Craft summed up the day's doings in his diary: "Sad work this day . . . the Hessians came. The town fired on by the guns of the gondolas . . . Many people much troubled though nobody hurt although large and small shot was fired plenty and in every direction . . . Vast body of inhabitants left the town. Scattered about the neighborhood . . . here and there."

The riverboats continued to bombard the town for several hours after the Hessians departed, according to Margaret Morris. She and her children were living on Greenbank, overlooking the Delaware River, about a half mile from the center of Burlington, in a house that had once been the West Jersey residence of William Franklin, New Jersey's last royal governor.* At first, she and her neighbors on Greenbank had gone about their business despite the artillery fire: "While all this tumult was in town, we, on our peaceful bank, ignorant of the occasion of the firing, were wondering what it could mean, and unsuspecting the danger, were quietly pursuing our business in the family when a kind neighbor informed us of the occasion and urged us to go into the cellar as a place of safety. We were prevailed on by him to do so and remained there till it ceased."

Several houses in town were struck and slightly damaged, Mrs. Morris learned, "but not one living creature, either man or beast, killed or wounded. About dark the gondolas fell down a little way below the town and the night was passed in quiet."

But how long would the quiet last? How soon would the row galleys, with their Tory-hunters, return? For a neutral such as Mrs. Morris there were likely to be troubled days ahead. As a devout member of the Society of Friends she detested war and she deplored what it was bringing out in her countrymen: "Instead of good will, envy and hatred seem to be the ruling passions in the breasts of thousands." Mrs. Morris was concerned about the safety of her family and perhaps even more so about her friend Jonathan Odell— "the doctor," as she called him. Surely, now that he had met with the Hessians, he would be a prime target for the Tory-hunters.

At age thirty-nine, Margaret Morris was the head of a household that included two sons, fourteen and seventeen, and two daughters, ten and sixteen. She had been a widow ever since her husband, a Philadelphia merchant, had died suddenly a decade earlier. Three of the children were under seven years at that time and she was pregnant with the fourth. In 1770 she and her "flock," as she liked to call the children, moved from Philadelphia to Burlington.

Mrs. Morris had been visiting a friend in Haddonfield, about twenty miles south of Burlington, when, on Friday, December 6, she heard what everyone else was hearing: the British were coming,

---

*And who, in December 1776, was a prisoner in Connecticut, having been escorted there under guard after being arrested about six months earlier in his East Jersey home in Perth Amboy. On at least one occasion en route, Franklin complained, overzealous guards refused even to let him answer "nature's call."

and Philadelphia was their destination. Mrs. Morris's children, on the riverbank in Burlington, "without a father to guide them," were in danger. She hurried home, as usual putting her faith in God: "I felt a humble confidence that He who had been with me in six troubles would not forsake me now." Arriving at Greenbank, she "was favoured to find my family in good health . . . and my dear companion not greatly discomposed." Her companion was her sister, Sarah Dillwyn, whose husband was off serving as a Quaker missionary.

The Burlington area was brimming with rumors about the oncoming troops. In nearby Evesham a Quaker preacher named John Hunt observed: "About this time things did work together in a strange manner. . . . Great fear fell on our neighborhood, we being in full expectation of the English Army upon us so that there was great to do moving of goods and talk of hiding earthly treasure." Hetty Cox, Mrs. Morris's next-door neighbor at Greenbank, received a message from her husband, John Cox, who was in the field, serving as a militia colonel: "Begone in haste!"—advice that Mrs. Cox and her children promptly followed. Other families were packing up and departing. Mrs. Morris's brother, at her urging, left town. Mrs. Morris herself, however, was determined to stay: "Our trust in Providence still firm, and we dare not even talk of removing our family."

And so she was there on December 11, the day the Hessians arrived, and there the next day when word was received that the row galleys, with their Tory-hunters, were coming up the river again.

♦♦♦

CHAPTER 21

They Called Us Damned Rebels

The damned Tories were everywhere. Major General Charles Lee had never before encountered so many "strangely contaminated" people. Lee and his dwindling corps had, at long last, ferried across the Hudson River from New York to New Jersey on December 2 and 3. As Major General William Heath would later observe, Lee "took with him into the Jersies some as good troops as any in the service; but many of them were so destitute of shoes that the blood left on the rugged frozen ground, in many places, marked the route they had taken; and a considerable number, unable to march, were left at Peek's Kill."

A few weeks earlier, at White Plains, Lee had had some 7,000 troops; now he had fewer than 3,000. A whole brigade departed just before the corps crossed to New Jersey, according to General Heath: "The time of service for which General Scott's brigade was engaged to serve, expired, when the whole, except about 50, went home, notwithstanding the generous encouragement offered them by their State [New York] if they would continue one month longer."

Ever since arriving in New Jersey Lee had been grousing about the disaffected inhabitants met along the route of march to the Morristown area. He was also, as usual, continuing to ignore General Washington's repeated summonses to come on. Instead, he was running his own show, harassing the enemy's flank and rear, inflicting, as he thought, far more damage than he ever could as part of Washington's force. By way of such maneuvers Lee would perhaps be able to demonstrate something that he and numerous other high-ranking officers believed to be true: that he, a well-trained professional, ought to be commander in chief in place of the bumbling, unimaginative Virginian. Had not Lee been right and Washington egregiously wrong about the Fort Washington fiasco, among other things?

In crossing New Jersey, Lee was following a route to the north of the one Washington had taken. The lower route was now controlled by the enemy. Like Washington's soldiers, Lee's men were encountering stiff resistance to their Continental paper money and they were finding the progress slow. A few days into New Jersey, General Lee complained that his men were "so ill-shod that we have been obliged to halt these two days for want of shoes." As for sustenance, the men were lucky to get a little rum and firecakes. Except, that is, those—officers as well as enlisted men—who were supplementing their daily ration—and creating bitter and long-lasting resentment—by plundering the inhabitants, Whig and Tory alike.

Among the most energetic of the plunderers were the men of

Captain Loring Peck's company, one of the units on the march with Colonel Christopher Lippitt's Rhode Island State Regiment. A noncommissioned officer with that company, Sergeant John Smith, apparently did not take part in the looting but on many occasions he dined on the spoils: roasted geese, turkeys, chickens, pigs, and whatever other edibles were to be found during night raids on nearby farms. Some of the edibles served a double purpose. "Many of our soldiers," Smith noted, "had no shoes to wear, was obliged to lace on their feet the hide of the cattle we had killed the day before."

The night raiders—in the notebooks he had brought along Smith called them Pad Rounds (a spinoff perhaps from the term "Mud Rounds")—had resorted to plundering early on in their march from Rhode Island to join General Lee's corps. At the home of Deacon Lyman in New Haven, Connecticut, it had not been necessary: "The soldiers sleept in his great room and some in the stable. We was well treated at this house as any soldiers could expect from strangers, and they used him as well as could be expected from soldiers on their march.

"We arose early in the morning. After I had paid for my lodging and took a dram we marched . . . and eat breakfast at an house where the people was very kind and free to us. We had baked lamb and boiled ditto and good tea and plenty of butter and cheese."

In Norwalk, Connecticut, the night raiders went on the prowl: "The houses being much crowded, we was obliged to take up our quarters in an old shop amongst the rubbish and about midnight I was awaked by something pulling me and a voice crying, 'Turn out, damn you. Look here, see and behold!' I looked and saw five fat geese. Some was fit for the cook and others was a dressing by the fireside. I eat a hearty meal, asking no questions with the rest of my brother soldiers who seemed hearty in the cause of liberty of taking what came in the way first to their hand, being resolved to live by their industry. By the road in the morning we eat the fragments and rested in our hut, or Den of Th—fs."

One night later "our visiting rounds went out on a patrol again and took up a sheep and two large fat turkeys, not being able to give the countersign, and brought them to our castle where they was tried by fire and executed by the whole division of freebooters. Then whilst the feast was getting ready two of our party went out and found a boat and crossed over the river to the other side and found a boat afloat loaded with oysters." Presently Smith and company were consuming oysters on the half shell, followed by "an excellent meal of soup."

Farther on, at Peekskill, New York, Smith's company "stopt to refresh ourselves a little about noon and the inhabitants abused us, calling us Damned Rebels and would not sell us anything for money. The soldiers killed their fowls and one stole a hive of bees at noon day and carried it off with him."

At Pompton, one of the first stops in New Jersey, "all the inhabitants were Dutch and chiefly Tories." A day or two later there was a friendly reception: "We lodged on a very high hill. The people here and at Chatham are English and very kind in a general way as any strangers would be expected. At the next stop, near Morristown, however, "the inhabitants refused to give us straw to lie on but we took what we wanted from them."

General Lee was not one to condone the kind of plundering the night raiders carried out, but he was realistic about meeting the needs of his troops. In a dispatch written on December 7, he ordered the members of a foraging party "to proceed to Harrington Township, where they are to collect all the serviceable horses, all the spare blankets (that is to leave a sufficient number to cover the People), they are to collect any spare shoes, greatcoats, to serve as Watch Coats. The people from whom they are taken are not to be insulted; either by actions or language; but told that the urgent necessity of the Troop obliges us to the measure. That unless we adopt it, their liberties must perish. That they must make an estimate of what is taken and the Publick shall pay them."

Farther to the north and to the west of the route being followed by Lee's corps, a smaller body of Continentals—some 600 of them, including a boy named John Greenwood—was advancing toward General Washington's encampment in Bucks County, Pennsylvania. Greenwood was marching with the Massachusetts Fifteenth Regiment through the rolling hills of Sussex County, New Jersey— marching, but just barely because of the pain. Like many another soldier in the field, he was suffering from an inflammatory skin disease afflicting his groin and upper thighs and commonly called "the camp itch." Each day the itch and other afflictions were forcing troops to drop out of the line of march, but John Greenwood persisted, even when the itch became so widespread that his thighs adhered to his leather breeches, and he managed to keep up with the few troops remaining in the Massachusetts Fifteenth. These men, along with three other depleted regiments, had come from Ticonderoga, near the Canadian border, under the command of Major General Horatio Gates. Because he was ill, Gates had turned over active command of the corps to Brigadier General Benedict Arnold, who, despite the failure of the invasion of Canada, had proven himself to be an able and courageous leader while serving there.

John Greenwood was only sixteen years old but he had been in the army for eighteen months. For pragmatic as well as patriotic reasons he had enlisted during the period of anti-British fervor following the skirmishes at Lexington and Concord. He had grown up in Boston and, as he recalled in his memoirs (far more literate than most memoirs of the time), was "educated in the North School until thirteen years of age, but as children were not at that time taught what is called grammar, or even correct spelling, it must not be expected to find them in this relation. All that we learned was acquired by the mere dint of having it thumped in, for the two masters, who had to overlook and manage some 300 or 400 boys, could pay little attention to us except so far as flogging went, which right was rather freely indulged in.

"While I was at school the troubles commenced, and I recollect very well of hearing the superstitious accounts which were circulated around: people were certain a war was about to take place for a great blazing comet had appeared and armies of soldiery had been seen fighting in the clouds overhead; and it was said the day of judgment was at hand, when the moon would turn into blood and the world be set on fire. These dismal stories became so often repeated that the boys thought nothing of them, considering that such events must come in the course of nature. For my part, all I wished was that a church which stood by the side of my father's garden would fall on me at the time these terrible things happened, and crush me to death at once so as to be out of pain quick."

John Greenwood remembered the so-called Boston Massacre— "when the British troops fired upon the inhabitants and killed seven of them, one of whom was my father's apprentice, a lad eighteen years of age named Samuel Maverick.* I was his bedfellow, and

---

*Three people were killed that day and eight were wounded, two of them fatally. Greenwood's father carried on the business of ivory-turning and as an adjunct practiced dentistry, as did his friend Paul Revere, the goldsmith. Both of them had "learnt the method from Mr. John Baker," a surgeon dentist from London who had visited Boston in 1768.

after his death I used to go to bed in the dark on purpose to see his spirit, for I was so fond of him and he of me that I was sure it would not hurt me.

"About this period I commenced learning to play upon the fife, and, trifling as it may seem to mention the circumstance, it was, I believe, the sole cause of my travels and disasters. I was so fond of hearing the fife and drum played by the British that somehow or other I got possession of an old split fife and, having made it sound by puttying up the crack, learned to play several tunes on it sufficiently well to be the fifer in the militia company of Captain Gay. . . . I must have been about nine or ten years old. . . .

"I saw the tea when it was destroyed at Boston . . . and likewise beheld several persons tarred and feathered and carried through the town; they were tide-waiters, custom-house officers. I think they called them informers.

"At the age of thirteen I was sent eastward to a place called Falmouth [later Portland, Maine], 150 miles from Boston, to live with my father's only brother, whom I was named after. He was a cabinet-maker by trade but had concerns in the shipping business likewise, and was looked upon to be an able, or rich, man. His wife was dead, he had no children, and I was his favorite. The whole country at this time was in commotion and nothing was talked of but war, liberty, or death. Persons of all descriptions were embodying themselves into military companies, and every old drunken fellow they found who had been a soldier . . . was employed of evenings to drill them. My uncle was lieutenant of an independent company (the Cadets), and of course I was engaged to play the fife while they were learning to march, a pistareen an evening for my services keeping me in pocket money.* Being thus early thrown into the society of men and having, as it were, imbibed the ardor of a military spirit, being moreover the only boy who knew how to play the fife in the place, I was much caressed by them.

"I stayed with my uncle two years, until the time arrived when we had an account that the British troops had marched out of Boston, attacked the country people at a place called Lexington, and killed a number of them. I had frequently been inclined to return to Boston that I might see my father, mother, sister, and brothers, but as I was not permitted to do so, I took it into my head,

---

*A pistareen was a small coin of little value.

saying nothing to anyone about it, to go alone on foot in the beginning of May, 1775." This was a few days before his fifteenth birthday.

"I concluded to set out on a Sunday, for then they would not be so apt to miss me, and not having mentioned my determination of going, they would not think it possible so young a boy would, without any manner or cause, attempt such a journey. My reason for going was I wished to see my parents, who, I was afraid, would all be killed by the British. . . .

"Sunday morning, when in New England all is still and no persons are in the streets, having eaten my breakfast, I took a handkerchief and tied up in it two or three shirts and a pair or two of stockings, and with what clothes I had on my back and four and a half pistareens in my pocket, jumped over the fence in the back yard and set off. I walked rapidly through the town without meeting any one I knew, as it was breakfast-time, and when once beyond the outskirts, being a very strong-constitutioned boy, off I went with a light heart and a good pair of heels. Sometimes I ran and sometimes trotted like a horse, and I really believe I accomplished forty miles the first day. . . .

". . . As I traveled through the different towns the people were preparing to march toward Boston to fight, and as I had my fife with me—yes, and I was armed likewise with my sword—I was greatly caressed by them. Stopping at taverns where there was a muster, out came my fife and I played them a tune or two. They used to ask me where I came from and where I was going to, and when I told them I was going to fight for my country, they were astonished such a little boy, and alone, should have such courage.* Thus by the help of my fife I lived, as it were, on what is usually called free-quarters nearly upon the entire route."

The war fever was running high when Greenwood arrived in Boston—"nothing was talked of but murder and war." A few days after rejoining his family he enlisted as a fifer in a militia company, part of a regiment being raised under the leadership of Colonel John Paterson, a 1762 graduate of Yale College who was about to give up his law practice to go to war. After several months of garrison duty in

---

*Apparently Greenwood did not inform them of something he later admitted: that he planned to enlist not "for the purpose of remaining in the army, but only through necessity, as I could not [otherwise] get to my parents in Boston."

the Boston area and after being reorganized, expanded, and designated the Massachusetts Fifteenth Continental Regiment, the unit was ordered north to take part in the Canadian campaign.

Greenwood served for seven horrendous months in the north and took part in the equally horrendous retreat from Canada to Fort Ticonderoga. Along the way, "the sad sight of many a companion who had died from exposure met our gaze." The daily ration "consisted of a pint of flour and a quarter-pound of pork for every man." The flour was "mixed up with the water from the lake by fellows as lousy, itchy, and nasty as hogs. I have seen it, when made and baked upon a piece of bark, so black with dirt and smoke I do not think a dog would eat it. But with us it went down, lice, itch, and all, without any grumbling, while the pork was broiled on a wooden fork and the drippings caught by the beautiful flour cakes."

At Mount Independence, opposite Ticonderoga, "plenty of cattle were driven into the camp and, being fed constantly on fresh meat without a particle of salt to give it a relish, our soldiers at length got the flux (or camp distemper) and died like rotten sheep, so that out of the 500 men we had in our regiment upon entering Canada, but 100 were left when orders came, toward the close of November, for marching to Albany. I had the fever and ague . . . and what I suffered on the march cannot be described. With no tents to shelter us from the snow and rain, we were obliged to get through it as well as we could."

Another member of the Massachusetts Fifteenth who, with some difficulty, was managing to keep up with the march toward Pennsylvania was a thirty-year-old Congregational minister named David Avery. A 1769 graduate of Yale College, he had been ordained at Dartmouth College in 1771. At the outbreak of the revolution he had been serving as pastor of a small church in western Massachusetts and as a missionary to Indians near the frontier. In the revolution he saw an opportunity for "a revival of true religion" (not to mention a chance for him to escape a congregation less than enraptured with his performance), and he was confident that the outcome was safely in God's hands.

Chaplain Avery had been ill, off and on, ever since the past summer, when he was serving in the Canadian campaign. On the march now he was concerned about the state of his health and, like Sergeant William Young, he was dismayed by the misbehavior of the soldiers. "My heart trembles," he wrote one day in his diary, "on account of the sin, vanity and almost every vice which is rampant through the camp. Jehovah's name is daily, hourly . . . profaned by most all characters among us—even the poor sick soldiers."

During the past August, Avery had suffered an attack while visiting the sick and wounded: "Visited three wards. Find the men extremely dirty, and a few of the new recruits are here with the small pox. . . . Exercised with a severe pain in my head and eyes and much disorder at my stomach." The next day he made some early visits but then experienced "a fit of fever and ague . . . which continued about 12 hours." His condition worsened eventually to the point where he was forced to take a leave of about two months. Although still suffering an occasional fit of fever and ague and depending on such medications as "a preparation of bitters," he set off on horseback in mid-November to rejoin the Fifteenth Regiment in Ticonderoga. But after traveling in that direction for a week he learned that the regiment "had marcht for Albany." He rejoined his unit there and headed south with his "waiter" and the others remaining in the regiment. First, two days on a sloop, from Albany down the Hudson River to Esopus. Then they were marching again. Avery no longer had a horse, and the marching quickly took its toll. After seven or eight miles on the road, "a blister on each little toe and a corn on the joint of the great toe of my right foot made it very tedious for me to march. . . . A few of our men were left sick at Esopus."

The next day, Sunday, December 8, Avery "had an opportunity of riding in a wagon. Have been much unwell, sick at my stomack. Took cold and was much fatigued yesterday." A day later, he bought a pony for fourteen dollars and proceeded to ride instead of walk. But even the ride had its hazards. On Wednesday, December 11, the day when the regiment crossed the New York borderline and entered New Jersey, Avery "had the misfortune to bruise my left great toe and foot by my pony's falling thro' a pole bridge." Food was becoming scarce around this time: "We are put to much difficulty for flour." More men were dropping out: "Left Goodrich and Reynolds dangerously unwell." A day later: "Left Drummer Twiggle, disabled for the march by the camp itch." And Tories, it seemed, were everywhere.

Two days of marching, through "snow about $1\frac{1}{2}$ inch deep" and "over the mountains thro' Sussex," brought the men of the Fifteenth to the county seat, Sussex Courthouse (Newton). Along the way there was news "that the enemy have got to Trenton, within about thirty miles of Philadelphia." And reports of Tory activity: "Last night," Avery noted after arriving at Sussex Courthouse on Friday, December 13, "one Smith, a Tory, was apprehended in this place and carried to General Gates. This evening is under our guard. He was out buying provisions for the enemy. We hear the enemy are in three grand divisions, at Princeton, Trenton and Burlington."

Sussex Courthouse, Avery discovered, was not unlike enemy territory: "This town we are now in is noted for the number of Tories it contains. Some of them treat certain of the army with rudeness and indecency; and we are put to much difficulty in getting accommodations for the troops. We have marched over a very rough mountain and both the road and the country thro' which we passed are very poor." Farther on: "We find the Tories abound in this State of New Jersey."

Thanks in large measure to the popularity of spruce beer, twenty-one-year-old Private William Chamberlin was still on the march with the remains of another unit in General Gates's corps: the Fifth New Hampshire Continental Regiment, commanded by Colonel John Stark.* There had been seventy-nine serving in Chamberlin's company in the previous spring when they were on duty in Canada, but smallpox and other diseases had taken a heavy toll. Chamberlin, his friend Sergeant Seth Spring, and four or five others were the only company members remaining by the time Stark's regiment reached Sussex County, New Jersey.

Spring and Chamberlin had, so to speak, gone into the beer business the previous summer in the Fort Ticonderoga area. "Sergeant Spring . . . procured some boughs of spruce. . . . We gathered a quantity of indianroot . . . and with two quarts of molasses made a barrel of beer which proved to be very good. . . . We made another and we sold the second barrel by the mug. . . . Finding it to be in good demand, we concluded to pursue the business. . . .

"We made and sold from three to five barrels per diem and at the end of six or seven weeks Spring and myself divided 300 dollars, which we had cleared by the business."

Early in the autumn of 1776 Chamberlin began to anticipate a reunion with his family in Loudon, New Hampshire; his enlistment was almost up. Then, as it often does in the army, the bad news arrived: instead of going home for the first time in two years, he and

---

*Chamberlin would one day be a general and for a time a member of Congress.

his company were ordered to join General Gates's corps on its southward march. It was tough going most of the way—"our shoes scarcely sufficient to keep our feet from the frozen ground without wrapping them in rags, the allowance of provision being poor, fresh beef without salt to season it." Thanks, however, to the spruce-beer profits, Chamberlin "had money and I lived upon it without tasting the government allowance."

Chamberlin and others in General Gates's corps remained on duty beyond their enlistment terms, but other troops Gates had been counting on decided not to march. As his unit approached the New York–New Jersey border, Gates learned that some 1,500 New York militiamen due to join his corps had opted for home. Like many other militiamen, they were not willing to leave their home state.

Entering Sussex County, New Jersey, with his dwindling force, Gates could only guess as to where he would be able to come together, as he had been ordered, with General Washington's army. By way of express messages he knew that Fort Washington on the Hudson River had fallen to the British and that Washington's force had begun to retreat across New Jersey.

A dispatch recently received from one of Washington's aides mentioned New Brunswick as a likely meeting place, but how could one be sure the British weren't there already? On December 12, a day after entering New Jersey, General Gates composed a message to Washington; he could wait no longer for orders. He recounted his recent movements and added: "I send the bearer, Brigade-major Wilkinson, for your excellency's orders in respect to the route you would have me take at present. I propose to march by that delivered to Major Wilkinson."

Major James Wilkinson was a nineteen-year-old member of a well-to-do Maryland family. He had given up the study of medicine to join the army about a year earlier and had served ably under General Arnold in the Canadian campaign.* "In this sequestered valley," Wilkinson would recall in his memoirs, "we were thrown

---

*Wilkinson's *Memoirs of My Own Times* is considered to be unreliable and self-serving in part by some historians. Following the Revolution he earned the reputation of scoundrel and double-dealer. However, as of December 1776, he had performed creditably as an officer and somehow had the knack of being on the scene when history was being made. Before publishing his memoirs in 1816 he visited many of the battle areas where he had served.

out of the ordinary current of intelligence, and cut off from all authentic information respecting the adverse armies. The winter had set in with severity: our troops were bare of clothing: numbers barefoot, and without tents, provisions, or transport of any kind. The men and officers sought shelter wherever they could find it in that thinly settled tract. We were halted on the 11th [of December] by a heavy fall of snow, which increased the General's anxiety for information from General Washington, and to relieve his solicitude, I volunteered my services to find him."

The next day, after a ride of several hours, Wilkinson reached Sussex Courthouse and there learned that Washington had already crossed the Delaware to Pennsylvania and that the enemy had reached Trenton. Before the day was done, Wilkinson wrote a report of his findings and sent it off, via an express rider, to General Gates: "The information of a person who has escaped from the enemy, corroborated by an inhabitant . . . just from Philadelphia, obliges me to inform you that the enemy arrived at Trent-Town on Saturday or Sunday last [December 7 or 8] and that General Washington was on the opposite shore. The numbers of either army I have not been able to collect, and I am in equal uncertainty respecting General Lee's present situation or force. . . .

"Pursuant to your orders I shall proceed to General Washington with all possible speed by the most convenient route . . . and flatter myself that I shall be able to meet you at Bethlehem, Pennsylvania, or East-town, Pennsylvania."

Wilkinson hired a guide and continued to ride southward. Along the way he met an officer he knew and learned from him that it was all but impossible to get across the Delaware to Washington's headquarters in Pennsylvania; all the boats had been removed from the New Jersey shore. He also learned that General Lee was in the vicinity of Morristown, leading his corps across New Jersey. Wilkinson decided to deliver Gates's message to Lee: "Finding such obstacles in my way to the commander in chief, I determined to seek his second, and to ask orders from him for General Gates, and, although dark, I continued my journey without halt."

Accompanied by his guide, Wilkinson rode far into the night of December 12–13. "Around midnight," he would recall, "passing a house by the wayside, I discovered a glimmering light." What was this? A tavern, the guide said.

Wilkinson dismounted and, "after a short parley at the door, gained admittance and found the women on the watch over the embers of an expiring fire; for I perceived the whole country to be in terror and alarm. These women knew nothing of General Lee; but after some whispering, informed me that two strange officers were in bed above me, on which I desired one of the party to awaken and inform them an express desire to speak with them. The maid proceeded with a candle to execute my orders, and soon after I heard a loud shriek."

One of the officers the maid had awakened apparently thought she was offering more than news of a visitor's arrival and shocked her with his reaction. Hearing the maid shriek, Wilkinson "instantly mounted the stairs and, guided by the light, entered the chamber, when a momentary scene of some interest took place. Two gentlemen were sitting up in the same bed, and the maid standing at a distance from them, in an apparent agony, with the candle in her hand. The shriek had been caused by the conduct of one of the gentlemen whom the girl had awoke.

"But this wanton levity was in a moment changed into painful apprehension," and little wonder: wearing a "Canadian capot, a scarlet under coat and a gold laced hat, with a pistol in each hand," Wilkinson just about scared the two officers out of their wits, and, as he noted, his sudden arrival "was sufficient to dissipate all sense of an amorous nature. . . .

"For a moment the gentlemen were struck dumb with alarm; literally naked and defenseless, and believing me to be a British officer, their situation appeared hopeless, and it was several seconds before they demanded, 'Who are you?' " They asked the question several times before Wilkinson, "reflecting on the circumstance of my appearance with arms," identified himself. "By God!" said one of the officers, "you have almost scared me out of a year's growth."

The two officers had been with General Lee the previous evening, before departing on furlough, Wilkinson learned. One of them was Lee's private secretary. They informed Wilkinson that he would find Lee, not at corps headquarters in Vealtown (Bernardsville), but at Mrs. White's tavern in a place called Basking Ridge.* A long ride, but Wilkinson decided to continue. He reached Mrs. White's around four o'clock in the morning of Friday, December 13.

---

*According to unconfirmed gossip of the time, Lee had left his headquarters and gone there for an assignation.

Even at that hour he was promptly escorted to Lee's room: "I was presented to the General as he lay in bed and delivered into his hands the letter of General Gates. He examined the superscription, and observed it was addressed to General Washington, and declined opening it, until I apprised him of the contents and the motives of my visit. He then broke the seal and read it, after which he desired me to take repose.

"I lay down on my blanket before a comfortable fire, amidst the officers of his suite; for we were not . . . encumbered with beds or baggage. I arose at dawn, but could not see the General . . . before eight o'clock."

General Lee, it quickly became clear, was in a sour mood and, as usual, openly critical of Washington as commander: "After some inquiries respecting the conduct of the campaign on the northern frontier, he gave me a brief account of the operations of the grand army, which he condemned in strong terms." He observed that "Sir William Howe could have given us checkmate at his discretion and that we owed our salvation to his indolence, or disinclination to terminate the war." And so forth.

Lee went on to comment on, among other things, the disastrous loss of Fort Washington. If only his advice had been taken. He had been right, and Washington wrong, time after time. Lee, Wilkinson observed, had been "opposed to the occupancy of Fort Washington, and the fall of that place enhanced his military reputation, while unavoidable misfortunes and the unfortunate issue of the campaign, originating in causes beyond the control of the commander in chief, had quickened the discontent generated at Cambridge, and raised a party against him in Congress, and it was confidently asserted . . . that a motion had been made in that body tending to supercede him in command of the army." If Lee should now succeed in making some sort of spectacular raid on the rear guard of the British in New Jersey, he might well replace Washington as commander in chief. So it seemed to Wilkinson.

In recent letters and conversations Lee had made it clear that he considered himself far better qualified than Washington to be commander in chief. In view of Washington's record as a loser, from Long Island to Fort Washington, many high-ranking officers agreed with Lee. One of them was Colonel Joseph Reed, Washington's highly regarded adjutant general. On November 21, the day after the loss of Fort Lee, Reed had made his feelings clear in a letter to Lee: "I do not mean to flatter or praise you at the expense of any other, but I confess I do think it is entirely owing to you that this army, and the liberties of America, so far as they are dependent on it, are not totally cut off. You have decision, a quality often wanted in minds otherwise valuable, and I ascribe to this our escape from York Island, from Kingsbridge, and the [White] Plains, and have no doubt had you been here the garrison of Mount [Fort] Washington would now have composed part of this army."

Lee, of course, agreed, and in answering Reed, observed that "eternal defeat and miscarriage must attend the man of the best parts if curs'd with indecision."* Confident of his own judgment, Lee felt free to act on his own even in defiance of the commander in chief's orders. Despite a series of increasingly urgent requests from Washington to hurry his corps on to Pennsylvania, Lee had been advancing across New Jersey at a snail's pace. On the morning of Friday, December 13, it appeared to Wilkinson that Lee had decided to abandon even his desultory advance toward Pennsylvania. Instead, he would stage a bold raid on the British army at Princeton, or perhaps at Brunswick. Lee apparently made this decision, Wilkinson would report, while conferring with Colonel Alexander Scammell, his adjutant general. Scammell had just left General John Sullivan, who was with the main body of Lee's troops in and around Vealtown, waiting there for Lee's orders.

After "musing a minute or two," Lee called for a map and, as Wilkinson and Scammell looked on, he traced with his finger a route from Vealtown to Pluckamin to Somerset Courthouse to Rocky Hill to Princeton. Then he traced the route from Vealtown to Bound Brook to New Brunswick. Apparently deciding upon Princeton as the target of an attack, Lee turned to Scammell and, according to Wilkinson, said, "Tell General Sullivan to move down towards Pluckamin, that I will soon be with him."

A few days earlier, Lee had apparently had such an attack in mind when he made this comment in a letter to the president of the Council of Massachusetts: "There are times when we must commit treason against the laws of the state, and the present crisis demands this brave, virtuous kind of treason." And now, it appeared to

---

*Washington's friendship with Reed survived a nasty episode involving this exchange of letters. In Reed's absence from headquarters, Washington opened and read Lee's letter, which was clearly a response to Reed's comments. Though stung by the criticism from his friend and closest adviser, Washington apparently chose to overlook the matter for the sake of the cause.

Wilkinson, Lee "had reduced himself to the dilemma of abiding the sentence of a general court martial, for disobedience of peremptory orders, or of exciting, by some coup, at once brilliant and solid, a blaze of popular applause, which might not only justify his offence but give him the chief command."

Lee wasted much of the morning of December 13, according to Wilkinson, "in altercation with certain militia corps of his command." Among the victims of his black mood were four bumbling members of the Connecticut light horse. Each of them presented a problem that was hardly of concern to a busy general. One "wanted forage, and to have his horse shod, another his pay, a fourth provisions, etc." Lee finally exploded: "Your wants are numerous, but you have not mentioned the last—you want to go home, and shall be indulged, for, damn you, you do no good here!" Out they went.

Because of this and other interruptions, it was around ten o'clock when Lee sat down for breakfast. Afterward, he took pen and paper and proceeded to write a letter to General Gates, one in which he gave vent once more to his feelings about General Washington:

Basking Ridge, Dec. 13th, 1776

My dear Gates,

   The ingenious manoeuvre of Fort Washington has unhinged the goodly fabric we had been building. *Entre nous*, a certain great man is most damnably deficient. He has thrown me into a situation where I have my choice of difficulties; if I stay in this province, I risk myself and army; and if I do not stay, the province is lost forever. I have neither guides, cavalry, medicines, money, shoes or stockings. . . .

   In short, unless something, which I do not expect, turns up we are lost; our counsels have been weak to the last degree. As to what relates to yourself, if you think you can be in time to aid the General, I would have you by all means go; you will at least save your army. It is said that the Whigs are determined to set fire to Philadelphia. If they strike this decisive stroke, the day will be our own. But unless it is done, all chance of liberty in any part of the globe is forever vanished. Adieu my dear friend! God bless you!

Charles Lee

As Lee finished the letter, Wilkinson got up from the breakfast table "and was looking out of an end window, down a lane about one hundred yards in length . . . when I discovered a party of

British dragoons turn a corner of the avenue at a full charge. Startled at this unexpected spectacle, I exclaimed, 'Here, sir, are the British cavalry!'

" 'Where?' replied the general, who had signed his letter in the instant.

" 'Around the house;' for they had opened files and encompassed the building."

———— •••• ————

CHAPTER 22

Tell Them General Lee Submitted

The cavalry advance on Mrs. White's tavern was led by Cornet Banastre Tarleton, a twenty-two-year-old Oxford-educated aristocrat known for his derring-do.* Shouting and brandishing long sabers, Tarleton and six other green-coated horsemen of the British Sixteenth Regiment of Light Dragoons appeared as if out of nowhere.† "I went on at full speed," Tarleton would write home a few days later, "when perceiving two sentries at a door and a loaded wagon, I pushed at them, making all the noise I could. The sentries were struck with a panic, dropped their arms and fled. I ordered my men to fire into the house thro' every window and door, and cut up as many of the guard as they could. An old woman upon her knees begged for life and told me General Lee was in the house."

Assured now that Lee was really there, Tarleton and his men—the advanced guard of a mounted raiding party—circled the house and continued to use their muskets and sabers. In the action that ensued they shot several of the guards, and, following Tarleton's

---

*And for his boasts. Passing through London early in 1776 on his way to Portsmouth and service in America, he had stopped at the Cocoa Tree, a fashionable club in St. James's Street, and, between drinks, announced: "With this sword I will cut off General Lee's head!"

†As an officer in the British army, Lee had led the Sixteenth in action in Portugal in 1762.

order to cut up as many as possible, they severed the arms of at least two of the Americans.

Tarleton and the rest of the raiders—about thirty in all—had set out from Pennington, above Trenton, early in the morning of the previous day, December 12. They were under the command of Lieutenant Colonel William Harcourt and the mission they had been given by Lord Cornwallis was to gather intelligence about General Lee's "motions and situation." The idea of attempting to capture Lee had evolved along the way.

"Our first day's march was 18 miles, but barren of incidents," Tarleton would report. "We took up our quarters at night at Hillsborough upon the River Millstone. . . . Our house caught fire at 1 o'clock in the morning and burnt to the ground. We escaped without loss or damage. We bedded ourselves in straw till 5 o'clock. We then received orders to march. Colonel Harcourt gave me the advanced guard, consisting of six men: a circumstance I ever shall esteem as one of the most fortunate of my life."

After riding about fourteen miles in the direction of Morristown, Cornet Tarleton and his men encountered some rebels and captured one of them. Two miles farther on, they "found by some people that General Lee was not above four or five miles distant. . . .

"We trotted on about 3 miles when my advanced guard seized 2 sentries without firing a gun. The dread of instant death obliged these fellows to inform me . . . of the situation of General Lee. They told us he was about a mile off, that his guard was not very large."

Farther on, Tarleton "observed a Yankee light-horseman, at whom I rushed and made prisoner. I brought him in to Colonel Harcourt; the fear of the sabre extorted great intelligence, and he told us he had just left General Lee from whom he had an express to carry to General Sullivan in Pluckamin."

The quaking express rider pointed out the tavern where General Lee was staying, and Tarleton and his men raced off, flashing their sabers. As they approached the tavern a few rebel guards raced forward but offered little resistance as the raiders slashed away furiously with their sabers. On high ground nearby, Colonel Harcourt and the rest of the horsemen were on guard against a surprise attack by the rebels. "I carried on my attack with all possible spirit," Tarleton would report, "and surrounded the house, tho' fired upon in front, flank and rear. General Lee's aide de camp, two

French colonels* and some of the guard kept up a fire for about eight minutes, which we silenced." Tarleton fired twice through the front door of the house and then shouted that he "knew General Lee was in the house, that if he would surrender himself, he and his attendants should be safe, but if my summons was not complied with immediately, the house should be burnt and every person without exception should be put to the sword."

According to another version, which would appear in the *Freeman's Journal*: "Intelligence of General Lee's unguarded situation was given to the enemy . . . by an inhabitant of Baskenridge, personally known to the general, and who had made great pretensions of friendship for the American cause, though at heart the greatest villain that ever existed. This Judas rode all the preceding night to carry the intelligence and served as a pilot to conduct the enemy, and came personally with them to the house where the general was taken."

The sentry on duty at the front door of Mrs. White's tavern, according to the *Freeman's Journal* account, "saw the troopers coming on the run, and at first supposed them to be ours; but soon perceived his mistake by their swords, which are more crooked than ours. His piece not being loaded, he charged. They rode up to him and said, 'Don't shoot; if you fire we will blow your brains out.' "

Inside the tavern, "General Lee cried out, 'For God's sake, what shall I do?' The lady of the house took him upstairs in order to hide him between the chimney and the breastwork over the fireplace, but he could not, the place being so small.

"The enemy at this time firing in at the windows, the captain gave orders to set fire to the house."

Realizing by this time that he would have to surrender, Lee "sent down he would resign himself." Perhaps the other officers would be captured as well. There were three in addition to Major Wilkinson: Lee's aide-de-camp, Captain William Bradford of Rhode Island; Lieutenant Colonel Gaiault de Boisbertrand, who had recently arrived from Paris with dispatches to be delivered to the Continental Congress; and another Frenchman, Captain Jean Louis de Virnejoux, on duty with Lee's corps.

According to a third account, that of Captain Bradford, Lee had "dressed and sent for his horses, was ready to mount, and would

*Actually a colonel and a captain.

have been gone in five or ten minutes when, about 10 o'clock," the British raiding party suddenly appeared. "About fifty horse . . . came on the house from the wood and orchard at once and, surrounding, fired upon it."*

Where the hell were the guards? General Lee ran to the window just in time to see "the enemy twice with his hanger cut off the arm of one of the guards crying for quarter. The guard behaved well, fired at first, but were rushed upon and subdued.

"The General [saw] then that they must submit, and after walking the chamber perhaps ten or fifteen minutes" told Bradford "to go down and tell them General Lee submitted." Bradford "went to the door and, on opening it, a whole volley of shot came in the door." He "spoke loud and opened again and delivered his orders.

"General Lee came forward and surrendered himself a prisoner of war, saying he trusted they would use him like a gentleman. Of this one of them gave assurance and ordered him instantly to mount." There was no time to lose.

Looking disheveled as usual, and shivering against the cold morning, Lee asked for his hat and cloak. The British granted the request and Captain Bradford, sensing an opportunity to escape capture, volunteered to get them. Inside the house he quickly threw off his uniform coat and put on a servant's garment luckily at hand. He hurried back and found to his relief that the British "did not know him from a servant." After handing over Lee's hat and cloak, Bradford "escaped back into the house." The cavalrymen "immediately rode back in triumph with the General," leaving Bradford at liberty.

Colonel de Boisbertrand had tried to make his getaway during the confusion of the raid but "was pursued and overtaken." The whole strike had lasted only about fifteen minutes and the raiding party had executed it without suffering a casualty.†

In a minute or two after the British rode off, Major Wilkinson was

---

*About thirty horse, according to Tarleton.

†"One horse's leg was slightly grazed," Tarleton would report, "and one saddle which was shot through the pommel were the only damages we sustained. We retreated afterwards 13 miles . . . without any accident. We then forded a river, approached Hillsborough and gave each other congratulations with every symptom of joy. . . . This is a most miraculous event. It appears like a dream. We conducted General Lee and the French colonel to Lord Cornwallis at Pennington. Our day's march . . . exceeded sixty miles."

on his way to rejoin General Gates and his force. As usual, Wilkinson had been lucky. After spotting the cavalrymen charging down the lane, he had picked up his two pistols from a table, stuffed General Lee's letter to Gates into a pocket, and raced to "a room in the opposite end of the house where I had seen the guard in the morning. Here I discovered their arms, but the men were absent."

With a loaded pistol in each hand, he put his back against a wall and "awaited the expected search, resolved to shoot the first and second person who might appear, and then to appeal to my sword." But no one appeared, and presently the British rode off with their two prisoners.

Wilkinson thereupon "repaired to the stable, mounted the first horse I could find, and rode full speed to General Sullivan, whom I found under march towards Pluckamin. I had not examined General Lee's letter, but believing a knowledge of the contents might be useful to General Sullivan, who succeeded him in command, I handed it to him, who after the perusal, returned it with his thanks, and advised me to rejoin General Gates without delay." With that, Wilkinson set off on what was to be another long ride. He could only guess how far the Gates corps had advanced in his absence.

---•♦•---

CHAPTER 23

Our Army Forms a Chain

During what turned out to be a week-long stay in Trenton—Sunday, December 8, to Saturday, December 14—General Howe decided it was time to end the 1776 campaign. He would not, after all, make the attempt on Philadelphia. Not now, at least. Winter was almost here, a time for settling in, not for fighting. Here, as they would have been in Europe, the soldiers were ordered into winter quarters. Spring, Howe decided, would be soon enough to put an end to the whole unpleasantness. And who could be sure that Washington would be able to pull together an army even by that time?

To Joseph Galloway, as to many others siding with the British, it appeared that one final blow now would be sufficient. Why wait until spring? "At this time," Galloway would later testify, "the panic arising from the several defeats of the rebel force at Long Island, New York, the White Plains, and the progress of the army through New Jersey had extended itself from the military to all the civil departments of the New States, and particularly in the Middle Colonies. . . . The rebel state in Philadelphia had dispersed, and the Congress themselves giving up all as lost, fled with great precipitation into Maryland. General Mifflin and others attempted in vain to raise the militia of Pennsylvania. Three of the principal citizens of Philadelphia, in behalf of the rest, waited on Congress before their flight and boldly informed them that they intended to meet Sir William Howe and implore his protection—to which the Congress did not object. And all the Middle Colonies were ready to submit, the Loyalists from principle and the rebels from an opinion that the British troops hitherto victorious, were invincible."

It would be a simple matter, Galloway thought, to build the necessary vessels "in a few days," cross the Delaware and rout the enemy. "But," he added, "this great opportunity of giving a fatal blow to the rebellion was neglected, without the least apparent necessity or reason."

On Friday, the thirteenth, Howe's next-to-last day in Trenton, there arrived a report that set off celebrations and caused many, even on the rebel side, to surmise that not just the campaign but also the whole rebellion might be over. General Charles Lee had been captured! Lee, the only real military man in the whole rebel army. "Victoria!" Captain Muenchhausen wrote in his journal. "We have captured General Lee, the only rebel general whom we had cause to fear." There were many who, like Muenchhausen, shared the view of Lieutenant Tarleton. "This coup de main," Tarleton exulted in a letter home, "has put an end to the campaign."

Before leaving Trenton for the journey back to New York, General Howe prepared several orders. One of them was aimed at troublemakers among the rebel civilians: "Small straggling parties not dressed like soldiers . . . who presume to molest or fire upon soldiers or peaceable inhabitants of the country will be immediately hanged without trial, as assassins." Some rebels in the area, damn them, were already making sneak attacks on small British detachments and on the homes of "Tories." As Captain Muenchhausen put it: "It is now very unsafe for us to travel in New Jersey. The rascal peasants meet our men alone or in small unarmed groups.

They have their rifles hidden in the bushes, or ditches, and the like. When they believe they are sure of success and they see one or several men belonging to our army, they shoot them in the head, then quickly hide their rifles and pretend they know nothing."

Another of Howe's orders concerned the occupation of Trenton, Bordentown, and other areas near the Delaware: "Headquarters, December 14, 1776. The campaign having closed with the pursuit of the enemies army near ninety miles by Lieut. Gen. Cornwallis's Corps, much to the honor of his Lordship and the officers and soldiers under his command, the approach of winter putting a stop to any futher progress, the troops will immediately march into quarters and hold themselves in readiness on the shortest notice.

"The Commander-in-Chief calls upon the commanding officers of corps to exert themselves preserving the greatest regularity and strictest discipline in their respective quarters, particularly attending to the protection of inhabitants and their property in their several districts." Like other such orders this one would prove to be ineffective.

At breakfast with Colonel Rall one morning shortly before leaving Trenton, Howe was persuaded to make a decision he would come to regret. He had designated Colonel Donop as commanding officer of the troops—some 3,000—who were to occupy Trenton, Bordentown, six miles down the Delaware, and perhaps Burlington. Because it was easily approached from the river and surrounded mostly by open country, Trenton was obviously vulnerable to an attack. "It would not be suitable to leave complete regiments there," Donop contended, "because they would become too fatigued by continuous disturbances." Colonel Rall, however, in a display of what Donop called "improper ambition," asked for the Trenton command, and not merely his own regiment but also the Lossberg and Knyphausen regiments. Disagreeing, Donop said that Trenton should be manned as an outpost, with contingents of about 150 troops each taking turns on the strenuous duty in the town.

General Howe agreed; this made sense; but at the fateful breakfast with Rall he allowed himself to be persuaded to let Rall have his way. After all, did not Rall deserve a reward of some kind for his gallant leadership at White Plains and Fort Washington?

Disappointed, Donop gave Rall orders to build redoubts—artillery emplacements—at the northern and southern edges of the town, and rode off to his new headquarters in Bordentown.

On Thursday, December 12, Rall rode into Trenton on horse-back with his regiment of about 500 grenadiers—an awesome if colorful sight for the few inhabitants on hand for the occasion. Here, looking fierce with their darkened mustaches and towering brass headgear and strutting to the music of Rall's beloved band, were the mercenaries who, it was said, had killed more Americans than any other unit of the British army. They were wearing the usual Hessian blue coats, with red collars, cuffs, and lapels, and contrasting with straw-colored vests and breeches. Many of the uniforms were rag-ged and muddied. The grenadiers settled in and around the French and Indian War barracks near the southwestern edge of town.

On the same day the Knyphausen Regiment marched into the center of Trenton and took quarters in and near the Presbyterian Church. They were wearing brass headgear and straw-colored vests and breeches similar to those worn by Rall's troops, but their blue coats were accented by black collars, cuffs, and lapels. The Loss-berg Regiment arrived two days later, on the fourteenth, and found quarters in houses and shops in the western section of town. They, too, wore towering brass headgear and blue coats. Their collars, cuffs, and lapels were orange and their vests and breeches were white, or once had been. A detachment of about fifty jagers, in forest-green attire and dark tricornes, occupied The Hermitage, the home of a rebel general (Philemon Dickinson), about a mile up the Delaware from Trenton. In all, Rall was now in command of about 1,400 crack troops—not just a regiment but a brigade. He had had his way and he was exuberant.

If the Knyphausen Regiment's Company Five was typical, the Hessians were not the gigantic figures that widespread reports had pictured. Perhaps it was the towering headgear that enhanced their stature. Of Company Five's 110 members, 87 stood less than five feet seven, the shortest being listed at five two, the tallest at five ten and a quarter. In age they ranged from the teens to the high forties.

There were two Catholics and six Lutherans in the company and all the rest, except one, were members of the (Calvinist) Reformed Church.* The exception, Corporal Christoph Lampertus, a former linen weaver (five feet eight inches, nineteen, and married), report-

---

*Many of the most active in behalf of the rebels' cause were also, as Presbyteri-ans, adherents of John Calvin.

ed his religion as "none." He was one of six linen weavers in the company. The roster also listed six tailors, four shoemakers, three millers, and two carpenters. Now they were all soldiers and all in crowded little Trenton.

An officer in the Lossberg Regiment, unidentified, complained in his journal: "We marched to Trenton and joined our two regiments of Rall and Knyphausen in order to take up a sort of winter quarters here, which are wretched enough.

"This town consists of about one hundred houses, of which many are mean and little, and it is easy to conceive how ill it must accommodate three regiments. The inhabitants, like those at Princeton, have almost all fled, so that we occupy bare walls. The Delaware, which is extremely rapid here and in general about two ells [90 inches] deep, separates us and the rebels. We are obliged to be constantly on our guard, and do very severe duty, though our people begin to grow ragged and our baggage is left at New York.

"Notwithstanding, we have marched across this extremely fine province of New Jersey, which may justly be called the garden of America, yet it is by no means freed from the enemy, and we are insecure both in flank and rear. This brigade has incontestably suffered the most of any, and we now lie at the advanced point, and thus as soon as the Delaware freezes we may march over and attack Philadelphia, which is about thirty miles distant." (General Howe's decision to postpone such a move was apparently not general knowledge.)

"My friend Sheffer and I lodge in a fine house belonging to a merchant, and we have empty rooms enough. Some of the servants of the inhabitants remain here. Last evening I gave one of them a box on the ear for his sauciness. I bid him bring me a candle, and he replied that if I wanted candles I should have brought them with me. I was furnished with a candle, but nothing else. There is no wine here except Madeira at three shillings and sixpence a bottle."

Although, as the Lossberg officer observed, Colonel Rall's brigade was insecure both in flank and rear, Rall failed to take some of the necessary precautions. On the day before marching into town with his men, he had received some routine orders from Colonel Donop, one of which was a reminder to see to the construction of redoubts—artillery emplacements—at the upper and lower edges of the village for protection against surprise attack by the rebels. Donop had emphasized the importance of this order before leaving

Trenton to take up his post at Bordentown, about six miles down the Delaware. Rall, however, chose to ignore it. He would run his own show. Who needed redoubts for protection from those damned rebel wretches across the river? Certainly not his brave grenadiers.

In Trenton, meanwhile, as in New Brunswick a short time earlier, many of the area's inhabitants were already coming in to take the oath of allegiance to the king and receive Protection papers. As many as fifty or sixty rebels a day were signing up, according to one of Rall's officers. Rall himself deigned to countersign some of the papers.

Pleased to see his proclamation working, General Howe set off with his small party from Trenton on Saturday, December 14. "At eleven o'clock this morning," Captain Muenchhausen noted, "General Howe started to ride back to New York, taking us with him. We rode to Princeton where I saw [General] Lee who has behaved very impudently until now, but has suddenly lost heart. The reasons are as follows: (1) He has repeatedly asked to see General Howe, but Howe will not see him nor speak to him. (2) He has begged to be paroled and vouches that he would not attempt to escape, so that it would not be necessary to keep a strong guard over him. The answer to all this was that a man such as he, whose life was in danger because he could be considered a British deserter, as well as a rebel, could not possibly be trusted to keep his parole.

"As a result he is not allowed to write letters, and one officer and two sentries are continuously in the room with him, in addition to many other sentries being posted around the house in which he is being kept.* This is very annoying to Lee."

Muenchhausen recognized the importance of the capture: "Lee . . . is the second-ranking general, with only Washington his senior. As to his ability and knowledge of the art of warfare, he is undoubtedly the first general."

Lord Cornwallis joined General Howe's party for the journey to New York. The campaign "having closed," he had been granted leave to return to England and spend the winter with Jemima, his beautiful but ailing wife, and his two-year-old son. He had left England for America in the previous spring over the protests of his wife, who, in tears, begged him not to go. Reluctantly, good soldier Cornwallis opted for duty. But having done his duty, he had earned

---

*Lee would be escorted under guard to Brunswick a few days later. British soldiers on duty there would mark the occasion by getting his horse drunk.

a trip home. He made plans (which were soon to be suddenly interrupted) to sail on December 27 aboard the *Bristol*, a sixty-four-gun ship of the line, and to deliver to George III the heartening news of the rebellion's collapse. Perhaps he would not have to return to the colonies. As Captain Muenchhausen observed, Cornwallis would return in the spring—"that is, if there is to be another campaign, which we doubt."

There was good news awaiting General Howe on his arrival in New York: as a reward for his outstanding generalship, he had been honored by the king. Howe and his party arrived in New York around two o'clock in the morning of December 17. "We met Major Cuyler, adjutant to our General," Muenchhausen would report. "He had gone from here to England on September 6 to bring the King news of the first successful feat of our campaign, the affair at Flatbush, etc. He brought back with him the Baronet or Sir William title and the Order of the Bath for our General."

Shortly after returning to New York, Howe would report to Lord Germain in London on the success of the New Jersey campaign and on the chain of outposts in New Jersey: "The chain, I own is rather too extensive, but I was induced to occupy Burlington to cover the county of Monmouth, in which there are many loyal inhabitants, and trusting to the almost general submission of the country to the southward of this chain, and to the strength of the corps placed in the advanced posts, I conclude the troops will be in perfect security."

Howe's "rather too extensive" chain stretched from Staten Island to Perth Amboy to Newark to New Brunswick to Princeton and on to Trenton and the other outposts near the Delaware River. With Cornwallis homeward bound, Major General Sir James Grant, fifty-six, a bumbling nobleman with a low opinion of the rebels as fighting men, took over the New Jersey command. Ensconced in his headquarters in New Brunswick, Grant let it be known that he "would undertake to keep the peace in New Jersey with a corporal's guard."

Brigadier General Alexander Leslie, stationed in Princeton with a brigade of British foot, and Colonel Donop, in Bordentown, were next in command to Grant. And Rall, except in such matters as redoubts, took his orders from Donop.

"Winter quarters are now fixed," a British officer wrote home from Brunswick on December 16. "Our army forms a chain of about ninety miles in length from Fort Lee, where our baggage crossed, to Trenton on the Delaware, which river, I believe, we shall not cross till next campaign, as General Howe is returning to New York. I understand we are to winter at a small village near the Raritan River, and are to form a sort of advanced picket. There is mountainous ground very near this post where the rebels are still in arms, and are expected to be troublesome."

———— ◆◆◆ ————

CHAPTER 24

Are Our People Fast Asleep?

Captain John Lacey, Jr., twenty-one, who had been serving with the army in the north, came home to Bucks County early in December 1776 and was so dismayed by what he found that, as he put it, "I almost begun to doubt whether I had mistaken my native country for that of an enemy's." He found his friends and relatives all siding with the British and he learned that many from his neighborhood had gone off to fight for the enemy.

Lacey was one of the few birthright Quakers who defied family and fellow members of the Society of Friends by joining the army. He was "born in Bucks County in the Province of Pennsylvania on the 4th day of February in the year 1755 of very reputable parents, John and Jane Lacey. . . . My great-grandfather was among the first settlers under Willian Penn and emigrated from the Isle of Wight in England. My grandmother was a Heston. Her family came from New England and settled in Bucks County, were reputable farmers and owned considerable landed property. My grandfather possessed two plantations and a share in a grist mill, one of which, at his death descended to my father with his part of the mill. The other part was purchased by my father and to which he added a saw mill on the same stream running through the plantation."

John Lacey was, in other words, the scion of a well-to-do family— a solidly Quaker family in a solidly Quaker area: "None but Quaker families resided in the neighbourhood where I grew up." That neighborhood was Buckingham, a village situated about three miles east of the county seat, Doylestown, and about five miles to the west of the Delaware River.

Lacey was one of the first young men in Bucks County to become an Associator and to join the militia. He took these steps early in the summer of 1775, the time of war fever brought on by the widely publicized skirmishes at Concord and Lexington. In Bucks County, as in most other American communities, the people were dividing in 1775 into Associators and Non-Associators (that is, those willing to join the local militia and those not willing to do so), and anyone suspected of outright "Toryism" was to be reported to the local committee. John Lacey was among those who righteously turned in their "disaffected" neighbors. In midsummer 1775 he informed the Committee of Safety that Thomas Smith of Upper Makefield, a fellow Quaker, "had uttered expressions derogatory to the Continental Congress and inimicable to the liberties of America." After hearing such testimony, the committee found Smith guilty of having "uttered expression to the following purport, viz.: That the measures of Congress had already enslaved America and done more damage than all the Acts of Parliament ever intended to lay upon us, that the whole was nothing but a scheme of a parcel of hot-headed Presbyterians and that he believed the Devil was at the bottom of the whole." The committee resolved that Smith "be considered as an enemy to the rights of British America and that all persons break off every kind of dealing with him until he shall make proper satisfaction to this committee for his misconduct." (Smith eventually got off the hook, as many of his neighbors in Bucks did, by declaring himself "heartily sorry for my imprudent expressions" and promising "for the future to coincide with every measure prosecuted for the redress of American grievances so far as is consistent with the religious principles of the society to which I belong.")

In July 1775 John Lacey was chosen to be standard bearer of the Second Battalion of the Bucks County militia. A short time later, the young men of his neighborhood, many of them fellow Quakers, organized a volunteer company and chose him as their captain. When this news reached the local Quaker congregation, Lacey and the other young Quakers in the militia were called in and had the error of their ways pointed out to them. If they persisted, they were told, they would be read out of the meeting. This was enough of a warning for the others; they quit the militia company. But not Lacey: "I alone stood the ordeal of the Quaker Society, of which I was then a member."

And so, a few days before Lacey marched off to war in February

1776, the following was inscribed in the minutes of the Buckingham meeting: "Whereas John Lacey Junior hath had his birth and education amongst Friends; but hath so far deviated from the principles of Friends as to learn the art of War; and having been treated with on that account, but not coming to a sence of this error, we give forth this our Testimony against such practices and can have no further Unity with him as a Member of our Society untill he comes to a sence of his Misconduct, and condems the same to the satisfaction of Friends, which he may do is our desire for him. —Joseph Chapman, Clerk."

Lacey was commissioned a Continental Army captain on January 5, 1776, and received his recruiting orders two weeks later. He rounded up a company of eighty-five young men, farm boys, mostly, and apparently not a Quaker in the group. As members of the Fourth Pennsylvania Regiment of the Continental Army, they marched off from Bucks County in style: "Our regimental coats were deep blue, faced with white, white vests and overalls, edged with blue cloth; a very beautiful uniform, but . . . much better adapted for parade than utility in the hardship of a camp, as it too easily became soiled and was hard to clean."

Lacey served with distinction but under what he considered to be intolerable circumstances near the Canadian border in the disastrous northern campaign of the summer and autumn of 1776. The most intolerable of the circumstances was the "tyranical and haughty treatment" he received from his commanding officer, Colonel Anthony Wayne. At the campaign's end in mid-November Lacey decided not only to return home but also to resign his commission temporarily.

On returning to the family homestead in Buckingham early in December, Lacey was "greatly alarmed on finding the enemy had pursued General Washington to Trentown in the state of New Jersey, where they had gone into winter quarters. The General with the remnant of his troops had crossed the Delaware, and were encampt along the western border of that river from Bristol to Coryell's Ferry [New Hope], & scattered all through the country."

He found "the family all well" but learned to his dismay that "a sullen, vindictive and malignant spirit seemed to have taken hold of a large portion of the people in this County, whose hostility to the Revolution was too apparent not to be noticed, and seemed only waiting a good opportunity to brake forth openly in favour of England, and against their own country. . . . A radical change had taken place in the political sentiments of my neighbours and acquaintances during my absence."

In February 1776, when Lacey had marched off with his company, "all was peace and harmony among the people in the neighbourhood." But now, in December 1776, "they appeared all hostile to each other, Whig and Tory in a state little better than open enemies. They were worse, especially the Tories, for they were secretly doing the Whigs all the harm they could possibly do—traducing, villifying, and in all ways and means committing hidden acts to weaken the Americans cause, and applauding the British, representing the power of Great Britton to be omnipotent, and that it was the height of madness and folly to oppose her."

Everywhere Lacey turned there were Tories, and all of them talking of giving up the rebellion: "The hostility of the Tories was so great to Independence that nothing but cowardice alone prevented their taking up arms and openly declaring themselves in favour of and joining the British army. They actually did every thing they dare do, by encouraging the youth to go over and join the British, and actually did send many to them."

Lacey's own people were the biggest disappointment: "My friends and relatives," he would recall in his memoirs, "being all disaffected to the American cause, and friendly to the British, laboured with me to abandon the American Army. My uncles assured me they would procure me a commission of a field officer— that is a Major or Colonel if I would go over to the Enemy and join their Army. Four of my cousins, the Chapmans, had already gone." (If Lacey's uncles actually did urge him to serve in *any* army they were not typical members of the Society of Friends.)

These, according to Lacey, were some of the points made by the uncles:

—"that it was impossible to oppose the prowess of British arms;
—"that America would be conquered by them;
—"that every one found in arms would be hung or banished from this country;
—"that now was my time to come off safe, which if I neglected to do or refused to do, I never would have another opertunity.

"My uncles argued that I had nothing to expect from such hotheaded men as composed the American Army officers, and having learned the ill treatment of Colonel Wayne to me, pressed me hard to follow their advice.

"But their entreaties were all in vain. I had entered into the

American Cause on principle, was a patriot from motives of the purest kind, my integrity not to be shaken. I remained firm and told my Uncle Abraham, who said he was authorized by my other uncles to advise with me, that I was determined to pursue the cause I had embarked in, and from which nothing but death could detach me, firmly determined to rise or fall with the liberty and independence of my country.*

"My uncle dispaired of gaining me over to his cause, made me promise not to betray him, and keep what he had said to me a perfect secret, as he had been induced to do it from motives of the purest affection, of love & friendship.

"Here ended all treaty of the kind between us forever."

Lacey's relatives were typical of many families in the area in their reaction to what they considered to be an invasion of their home territory by a pack of rebels, for just as the troops at times felt as if they were in enemy territory, many inhabitants of Bucks felt as if their land were being occupied by enemy soldiers. Abraham Shoemaker would later recall what it was like when American "press" contingents came to his village, Gwynedd, near Doylestown: "Soon after the army arrived in our neighbourhood we suffered very much from the depredations of foraging parties who carted away our hay and drove off all our cattle for the subsistence of the army, not leaving us a cow to give milk for the support of a family of small children, and if we brought a fresh one she was immediately driven off again."

Like many another wealthy family in the county, the Merricks suffered heavy losses to the officers and enlisted men who moved into their home, one of the finest in Buckingham. It was commandeered as headquarters for General Nathanael Greene and treated with something less than loving care. But there was little the Merricks could do but look on as Greene and his men disposed of a flock of turkeys as well as a calf, and drank almost all of the daily output of the family's only milk cow. Before long Greene, finding the cupboard bare, would be complaining: "No butter, no cheese, no cider." For years thereafter the Merricks would tell how Greene, a mere blacksmith from Rhode Island, lived the good life at their expense.

---

*Lacey would rejoin the army within three months and in ensuing years of service would rise to the rank of brigadier general.

Greene, himself a birthright Quaker, was one of the Quakers' severest critics. In September 1773 he had been "put from under the care of the meeting" back home in Rhode Island for attending a military parade. A few days after arriving in Bucks County he wrote to his friend, Governor Cooke of Rhode Island: "You think you are greatly infested with the Tories and disaffected, but there is but a shadow of disaffection with you to what there is here. The Friends, or Quakers, are almost to a man disaffected. Many have the effrontery to refuse the Continental currency. This line of conduct cannot fail of drawing down the resentment of the people upon them."

In refusing to join the militia, in refusing to recognize Continental money, in refusing even to grind corn for the troops, the Quakers were merely adhering to the tenets of the Society of Friends. They were forbidden to have anything to do with "the Commotions." Diplomacy was the answer, they felt, not warfare. They wanted to stay out of the whole business, to give aid and comfort to neither side. Many Quakers suffered property loss and verbal abuse for their neutrality. John Adams called them hypocrites—people "who love money and land better than liberty or religion."

It was largely because of the heavy concentration of Quakers in Bucks County that the response to Washington's call for reinforcements was so feeble. Even in the summer of 1775, a time of growing sentiment for armed rebellion in most communities, roughly half of the eligible men of the county had refused to become Associators. Newtown, the county seat of Bucks, was one of several communities in which Non-Associators outnumbered Associators. The roster of Captain Francis Murray's Newtown militia company on August 21, 1775, included fifty-one men; as of that date no fewer than seventy-one men refused to bear arms. A month later, Henry Winkoop, clerk of the Bucks County Committee, reported: "I have received the returns of the Associators and the Non-Associators, except three townships and one company lately raised, and the number stands: Associators 1688, Non-Associators 1613." Some of the non-associating Quakers refused even to give up a weapon to be used by an Associator. In John Lacey's largely Quaker village, Buckingham, no fewer than eighty-four men—well over half of those eligible—refused to sign up.

A year later, it became clear that many who had signed up were not really willing to serve. "This minute," Colonel Joseph Hart reported from Perth Amboy, New Jersey, on September 2, 1776, to

Pennsylvania's Council of Safety, "I received information . . . that there was two or three companies of the Third Battalion in said county [Bucks] commanded by Colonel Kichline who do not intend to march forward in defence of their country."

Now, in December 1776, with the enemy just across the Delaware River, a great many of the county's Associators were choosing not to associate. Twenty-two militiamen in Warrington Township refused to march. So did thirty-two in Solebury, thirty-nine in Buckingham, forty-nine in Warwick Township. Perhaps the worst turnout in all of Bucks was that of Plumstead Township: of seventy-three members of Captain William McCalla's militia company, only six agreed to march.

Apprised of the lack of response, General Washington petitioned the Pennsylvania Council of Safety for help: "The spirit of disaffection that appears in this country, I think, deserves your serious attention. Instead of giving any assistance in repelling the enemy, the militia have not only refused to obey your general summons and that of their commanding officers but, I am told, exult at the approach of the enemy and our late misfortunes."

In a message to Congress, Washington wrote: "Our little handful is daily decreasing by sickness and other causes and without aid, without considerable succours and exertions on the part of the people, what can we reasonably look for or expect but an event that will be severely felt by the common cause and that will wound the heart of every virtuous American, the loss of Philadelphia?"

The reports from other Pennsylvania counties were no more encouraging than those from the various townships of Bucks County. "No militia has joined us yet from the back counties of Pennsylvania," an officer reported, "and I am afraid but very few will. A strange consternation seems to have seized everybody in this country. A universal dissatisfaction prevails, and everybody is furnished with an excuse for declining the public service." Typical of the bad news being received by the Pennsylvania Council of Safety was the report made by Colonel William Dewees, Jr., from French Creek Powder Mill, outside Philadelphia: "With unfeigned sorrow I think you have not much assistance to expect from the Mallitia in these parts. . . . I went to two of our captains and several of the men who promis'd they would march on Thursday morning early. I went to meet them, but they did not come untill afternoon. . . . I proposed marching to Philadella . . . but the men & officers utterly refused going, as they said they were ill-used and behaved in such a manner as convinced me there could be no good done with them, some of whom I had advanc'd money to, out of my own pocket, who neither would or did return it."

In a letter to his wife, General Greene made an interesting distinction: "We have been endeavoring to draw a force together to check General Howe's progress but the militia of New Jersey have been so frightened and Pennsylvania so disaffected that our endeavors have been ineffectual."

John Bayard, the prominent Philadelphia merchant serving as a militia colonel, was incensed at what he considered to be a poor turnout of Pennsylvania's militiamen. Bayard was thirty-eight, the father of eight children and the adoptive father of the three children of his twin brother, now deceased. Despite these responsibilities he had gone off to war during the past summer and he couldn't understand why so many others were refusing to turn out now for only a few days. In camp at Bristol on December 13 he decided to give the Council of Safety in Philadelphia a piece of his mind. "We are greatly distressed," he wrote, "to find no more of the militia of our state joining General Washington at this time. For God's sake what shall we do? Is the cause deserted by our state, and shall a few brave men offer their lives a sacrifice against treble their number without assistance?

"For my own part, I came cheerfully out, not doubting we should be joined by a number sufficient to drive our enemy back, with shame, disgrace and loss. But, alas, here we are, about 4 or 5000 men, to oppose a regular army, well disciplined and flushed with success, said to consist of 15,000, headed by able generals and encouraged by the inhabitants of the country through which they march. We now ought to have at least 10,000 militia from our state. Instead of that we have about 1200 from Philadelphia and 200 from Bucks County.

"Are our people fast asleep, or have they determined basely to give up the cause of their country?

". . . You cannot expect that our few citizens, join'd to the small remains of General Washington's army, will offer up their lives without a prospect of success, unless joined by a proper force.

"For God's sake, exert yourselves."

Captain Samuel Morris, in command of the crack First Philadelphia Troop of Light Horse on duty in Bucks, wrote a similar complaint to Philadelphia's Committee of Safety: "Those who have nobly appeared on the field in this inclement season think it hard that others equally able should be suffered to stay at home." Morris went on to list the names of thirty-two men from one light infantry company—one of them a captain—who had "not turned out with us at this time of imminent danger, and I think it highly proper they should be called upon for their reasons for not taking share with us in our distresses." These missing men were "almost all young and hearty.

"The fate of our city still depends on the militia marching forward. For God's sake strain every nerve to urge them on. Everything dear and valuable depends on the exertion of a few days."

In a postscript addressed to Samuel Howell, a member of the Committee of Safety, Morris again referred to the thirty-two men who were absent without leave: "You know the names of the above, and I believe know where they all live. Do think of us who are in the field."

Every day express riders were carrying urgent messages from the encampments in Bucks County to Philadelphia:

—"Captain Philip Albright and . . . the Quartermaster have been absent without leave these two days. I am informed they are in Philadelphia. It is such a precedent at a time when we may expect an attack hourly."

—"There no doubt are many of our soldiers straggling in Philadelphia and . . . it perhaps would be very well that [someone] should collect and march the stragglers to the regiment."

Major Ennion Williams, in command of the Pennsylvania Rifle Regiment and stationed at Thompson's Mill, below Coryell's Ferry, reported the disappearance of an entire battalion: "There is not now either officer or soldier of the late Col. Atlee's battalion with me. They are either in or near Philadelphia. . . . Adjutant Wallace has not been with the regiment since we left Trenton Ferry and if he joins the regiment again, he will be tried for his conduct; his absenting himself thus without leave, at a time when we heard the enemy were landed on this shore, and expected to go immediately to action, is too gross behaviour to pass unnoticed. Captain Farmer and Lieutenant Maise are gone to Philadelphia with a complaint of the rheumatism. Perhaps by this time they may be recovered and may collect a number of our men that are strolling in Philadelphia."

Many of the riflemen in Major Williams's regiment were, he

reported, "barefooted and very thinly clad and have not received any pay these three months." The quartermaster, Colonel Owen Biddle, had turned down Williams's request for shoes and stockings; these were only for soldiers enlisting for the duration of the war or three years. "Therefore," Williams complained to the Council of Safety, "unless you provide shoes and stockings on purpose for our bare-footed men, and direct them to me . . . it will be impossible for the regiment to do duty here much longer. Our regiment have undergone as much hardship and fatigue as any in the army since July, and it is not unreasonable to request that they will be well provided."

Despite the ragged condition of many of the troops and despite the discouraging reports arriving at headquarters, Lieutenant Samuel Blachley Webb, Washington's private secretary, was among those officers who remained optimistic. "You ask me our situation," he wrote on December 16 to his friend, Colonel Joseph Trumbull.* "It has been the devil, but is to appearance better. About 2,000 of us have been obliged to run damn'd hard before about 10,000 of the enemy. Never was finer lads at a retreat than we are. . . . No fun for us that I can see; however, I cannot but think we shall drub the dogs." Webb expressed the hope that "the lads" of his home state, Connecticut, would "not behave in the dam'd cowardly, rascally manner the people of this country have." Even so, he ended on a hopeful note: "Never mind, all will come right one of these days."

———— ♦♦♦ ————

CHAPTER 25

Some Winter Quarters Indeed!

In crowded and vulnerable little Trenton there was less than unanimous agreement among the officers and enlisted men with General Howe's judgment that they would be "in perfect security." The town was the closest to the rebel encampment across the Delaware

---

*Who by this time was with General Gates, only a few days from Washington's headquarters.

and was particularly vulnerable to hit-and-run attacks. The troops grumbled about the exposure to attack, the constant guard duty, and the crowded quarters. They had for a long time looked forward to celebrating Christmas in the biggest city in America, Philadelphia. There had been talk of three days of roistering and plunder there. And did they not deserve it after all they had done for the British king? Would this not be a fitting reward for Long Island, for White Plains, for Fort Washington, where they had left so many of their dead?

Now, however, they were being forced to settle for cramped quarters in a miserable little village. Officers as well as enlisted men openly wondered if *this* was their reward for leaving their loved ones, for crossing an ocean at great peril, for risking their lives in combat. And to think that their commanding officer, the great Colonel Rall, had actually asked for this place!

"When we arrived in Trenton with our regiments torn apart and fatigued," Colonel Francis Scheffer would recall, "Major Ludwig von Hanstein asked Rall if these were the good winter quarters they had been promised."

Oh, no, said Rall. They would soon be enjoying fine quarters in Philadelphia.* Rall "would march ahead of us across the ice of the river Delaware and straight into Philadelphia. He told Major [Friedrich] von Dechow to stay behind if he didn't want to win any honors. Colonel Rall's behavior was inexcusable; it made me sick."

Scheffer, in command of the Lossberg Regiment, and Dechow, in command of the Knyphausen Regiment, had asked Rall to send to headquarters in New York for more winter clothing for their troops, but Rall had scoffed at the request, just as he had at other requests and even orders. Fearful that Rall's negligence might lead to disaster, they spelled out their complaints in a letter addressed to Lieutenant General Heister at headquarters in New York. They entrusted the letter to a Hessian captain passing through Trenton en route to New York and hoped it would bring results in time.

Rall was fifty years old. The Lion, some called him, because of his aggressiveness and durability in battle. He had joined his father's regiment thirty-six years earlier, in 1740, had worked his way through the ranks, and had been a colonel for more than five years.

---

*Despite General Howe's closing of the campaign, Rall apparently still considered an advance to Philadelphia in the near future a likelihood.

He had performed with distinction since arriving in America the past summer, serving with particular brilliance and audacity at Fort Washington, and now, by God, he had his own separate command and was luxuriating in its perquisites, pomp, and ceremony. Ah, those musicians! How he loved to hear the brass and drums of his bandsmen as they strutted about the headquarters area. Formations, parades, patrol missions, sentry duty—Rall loved the hustle and bustle, all of it.

A fellow officer provided this description: "Colonel Rall was made for a soldier but not for a general. . . . He had courage enough to undergo the most daring tasks but he lacked a cool presence of mind. . . . He was flighty. One idea replaced another, and so he could never make a decision. . . . He was generous and liberal, hospitable and courteous to everyone. To his servants he was more a friend than a master. . . . He was a very sociable man who knew how to give a party and make it a nice one."

On December 14 Rall set up his headquarters in the home of a wealthy Trentonian named Stacy Potts. This was a spacious white frame dwelling on King (later North Warren) Street, almost directly across from the English Church.* (The pastor of that church, the Reverend George Pantin, had closed it during the past summer, around the time of the adoption of the Declaration of Independence, and had fled north to join the British army.)

Like Colonel Scheffer and Major von Dechow, Lieutenant Andreas Wiederholdt was highly critical of Rall's insistence on Trenton as winter quarters. With the rest of the Knyphausen Regiment he had reached Kingston, "a miserable place" about three miles northwest of Princeton, on December 9. Around ten o'clock that night, just as he and his weary company were settling in, they "had to set out in haste." The night march ended in Maidenhead, a village situated about halfway between Princeton and Trenton, "and there we stayed in bivouac for a day and a night. The houses had been abandoned by their owners. I wanted to make my winter quarters here because I had a good house and my whole company with me, all of us being comfortable."

But, of course, it was too good to last; Rall wanted all his troops quartered in Trenton. "On December 14," Wiederholdt noted, "we marched to fabulous Trenton, a place I'll remember as long as I

---

*Today it is the site of the rectory of St. Mary's Roman Catholic Cathedral.

live—the place to which our strange Brigadier is said to have brought us by his special request. How much better had he not asked for it! Maybe he would have kept the undeserved acclaim that had been unwittingly given to him." (Wiederholdt apparently did not think much of Rall's combat heroics.) But in Trenton, "all that acclaim fell into the dung. Some winter quarters indeed!"

Instead of seeing to the setting up of artillery redoubts at the upper and lower edges of the town, as he had been ordered to do by Colonel Donop, Colonel Rall had the cannon "all drawn up in front of his quarters, and every morning two of the guns had to be dragged to the upper part of the town for no other reason than to cause noise and turmoil."

Rall "enjoyed himself into the small hours of the night, went to bed, and slept until 9 o'clock in the morning. There were times when we would go to his quarters for the morning formation between 10 and 11 o'clock and he would still be sitting in his bath, something he had become accustomed to. As a result the men had to stand waiting a half hour for the changing of the guard."

Even worse, Lieutenant Wiederholdt felt, was Rall's refusal to take the rebels seriously: "Not the slightest precaution was taken. No rendezvous place or alarm was ordered in case of an attack. There was no consideration that such an attack might be made."

Colonel Rall had a way of overreacting that irritated and sometimes amused both his superior officers and his subordinates. One day he sent off some letters to General Leslie in Princeton by way of two mounted dragoons. About three miles outside of Trenton the dragoons rode into an ambush, and one was killed. The other galloped back to Trenton. On hearing what had happened, Colonel Rall exploded. Those damned rebels! He'd show them. And so, for the task of delivering a few letters, he put together a force that no rebel party would dare attack: a hundred soldiers led by a captain and three other officers, plus a cannon and a crew of artillerymen.

Lieutenant Wiederholdt, the officer in charge of the artillerymen, would never forget this mission: "It was exceedingly bad weather. We delivered the letter and, after sleeping that night on the bare ground, returned the next morning without having seen or heard anything." Except some laughter: "The English laughed at us and really it was ridiculous; one non-commissioned officer and fifteen men would have been enough to complete the errand."

Rall's refusal to establish redoubts in such an open town as Trenton resulted in a tremendous amount of extra guard duty. "Our poor, worn-out soldiers," Wiederholdt complained, "lacking proper clothing and equipment, were less able to recover their strength in this place than in the field. The demands on the soldiers were extraordinary: sentry duty, commands, picket duty, all without end, and all of no use, just a lot of restless commotion around the Brigadier's headquarters all day long. It was of no concern whatever to him whether the off-duty soldiers were sloppily dressed or not, and it was of little moment whether or not they kept their muskets cleaned, polished and in good repair, and kept their ammunition ready. He never even asked about things like that. But the music, the band! That was his affair!" Since the guardhouse was only six or eight houses down the street from Rall's quarters, Wiederholdt reported, the musicians got very little rest; the colonel couldn't get enough of their music. The English Church, surrounded by a picket fence, was the scene of a daily ritual: "The officer in charge of the guard had to march around the church with his guards and musicians. It looked just like a Roman Catholic procession, lacking only the banner with the crucifix and some little boys and girls marching in front and singing. The colonel would always follow the parade as far as the guard house just to hear the music during the changing of the guard.

"Any other commander during this period would have discussed the security and welfare of the garrison and other such things with his staff officers and others on duty." But not Rall: "Around 2 in the afternoon the guards were relieved and at 4 o'clock the pickets. All the commissioned officers and non-commissioned officers had to participate and to be around his quarters so that it might look grand and like a real headquarters."

Such criticism to the contrary, the valiant Colonel Rall was idolized by the enlisted men of his regiment—seventeen-year-old Johannes Reuber, for example. Reuber would never forget Rall's daring in battle, especially during the attack on Fort Washington. What a day that had been! And now, in Trenton after advancing across New Jersey with the rest of Rall's grenadiers, Reuber anticipated another big day—the day when they would march into Philadelphia under the leadership of Colonel Rall. (Enlisted men such as Reuber were apparently not informed of Commander in Chief Howe's decision to end the campaign.) As he did guard duty near the edge of the Delaware, Reuber made note in his diary of his impatience. If only it would freeze over, they would march straight to Philadelphia.

◆◆◆

CHAPTER 26

The Worthy Inhabitants Were Seized Upon

Early on December 12, the day after the Hessians' visit, which had provoked the bombardment of Burlington by Commodore Seymour's fleet, the men from the riverboats were back again—on the prowl, looking for "damned Tories," and, according to Margaret Morris, "suspecting that some troops were . . . yet concealed in the town" and warning inhabitants that "it was their settled purpose to set fire to the town." Mrs. Morris had been up during much of the previous night. Her children had been sick and she had kept a lamp burning through the night. A risky business, as she was to learn from the sailors. "This morning," she would note, "a galley with a great many men, and a number of boats, came ashore at our wharf. I ordered the children to keep within doors and went myself down to the shore, and asked what they were going to do. They said to fire the town if the [British] Regulars entered. I told them I hoped they would not set fire to my house.

" 'Which is your house, and who are you?'

"I told them I was a widow with only children in the house, and they called to others and bid them mark that house, there was a widow and children and no men in it.

" 'But,' said they, 'it is a mercy we had not fired on it last night. Seeing a light there, we several times pointed the guns at it, thinking there were Hessians or Tories in it. But a hair of your head shall not be hurt by us.'

"See how Providence looks on us. Then they offered to move my valuable goods over the river. But I pointed to the children at the door and said, 'See, there is all my treasure, those children are mine.' And one who seemed of consequence said, 'Good woman, make yourself easy; we will protect you.' "

In her journal Mrs. Morris had a ready explanation for being spared: "Though they did not know what hindered them from firing on us, I did; it was the Guardian of the widow and the orphan, who took us into His safe keeping, and preserved us from danger. Oh, that I may keep humble, and be thankful for this, as well as other favours vouchsafed to my little flock."

In the ensuing days, as Mrs. Morris put it, "the spirit of the devil continued to rove through the town in the shape of Tory hunters." As she was well aware, her good friend, the Reverend Jonathan Odell, was in great danger. The men from the galleys had been searching for him in particular ever since December 11, the day he had participated in negotiations with the Hessians. Odell had somehow managed to elude them for a time, but on Saturday, December 14, it appeared that his time was up. He was conversing with Mrs. Morris and some other friends when the dread word came. "A message was delivered to our intimate friend," Mrs. Morris noted, "informing him a party of armed men were on the search for him. His horse was brought and he retired to a place of safety." Other suspected Tories were less lucky that day: "Some of the gentlemen who entertained the foreigners were pointed out to the gondola men. The worthy inhabitants were seized upon and dragged on board."

Odell's hideout for the next three days was a secret room in the home of the John Cox family, which adjoined Mrs. Morris's. Colonel Cox was serving with the Americans. His wife, Hetty, had left the house keys with Mrs. Morris the day she departed for safer quarters with her children. The secret room—an "auger hole," Mrs. Morris called it—was a slant-roofed, windowless attic area at the rear of the second floor. Its only furnishings were a box of sawdust and a pile of straw. To enter the hideaway one raised the stationary-looking but movable backboard of a closet, then crawled through and lowered the backboard into place.

While hiding out, Odell spent most of his time in the bedroom adjoining the secret chamber. Mrs. Morris remained on the alert for Tory-hunters around the clock and kept him supplied with food. They had agreed on a danger signal: if the men from the galleys came to search the house, Mrs. Morris would warn him by ringing a bell vigorously. At the sound of the bell Odell would crawl into the secret room and there be safe from the Tory-hunters. So they hoped.

On Monday, December 16, Odell's third day in hiding, the hunters arrived at her door. Around noon, according to Mrs. Morris, there was "a very terrible account of thousands of Hessians coming into town, and now actually to be seen on Gallows Hill." It turned out to be just another scary rumor, but it piqued the curiosity of her seventeen-year-old son, Dick: "My incautious son caught up the spy-glass and was running towards the mill to look at them. I told him it would be liable to misconstruction but he prevailed on me to allow him to gratify his curiosity. He went, but returned much dissatisfied, for no troops could he see. As he came back, poor Dick took the glass and, resting it against a tree, took a view of the fleet."

The "fleet" was made up of four or five gunboats, still busily patrolling the Delaware River. The sailors aboard, it presently became clear, did not like to be spied upon. According to Mrs. Morris, they "suspected it was an enemy that was watching their motions. They manned a boat and sent her on shore; a loud knocking at my door brought me to it. I was a little fluttered and kept locking and unlocking that I might get my ruffled face a little composed. At last I opened it and half a dozen men, all armed, demanded the key to the empty house.

"I asked them what they wanted there. They said to search for a damned Tory who had been spying at them from the mill."

A Tory so close! It was time for Mrs. Morris to go into her act. First, she rang the bell "violently." Then, to give Odell more time to crawl into the secret room, she put on "a very simple look" and dissembled a bit.

"Bless me," she said, "I hope you are not Hessians."

"Do we look like Hessians?" one of the sailors grumbled.

"Indeed, I don't know."

"Did you never see a Hessian?"

"No, never in my life. But they are *men* and you are men, and may be Hessians for anything I know."

Continuing to stall, she explained that the person at the mill with the spyglass was not a spy but her son: "He is but a boy and meant no harm, he wanted to see the troops."

If the sailors insisted, however, she would take them through the adjoining house. The sailors, no doubt rolling their eyes heavenward, proceeded to follow their apparently harebrained hostess through the house. The party "searched every place but we could find no Tory; strange where he could be. We returned—they greatly disappointed—I, pleased to think my house was not suspected."

The men went on to search James Veree's house, on the other side of Mrs. Morris's, and two other houses on Greenbank, "but no Tory could they find." Arriving back at the riverbank, the sailors were confronted by an angry Colonel John Cox. He upbraided them for searching the houses—one of them his own—and, as Mrs. Morris would later learn, ordered them back to their gunboats.

That evening she and Odell decided it was time for him to seek another hideout. She went into town with him and placed him "in other lodgings." Before returning home she passed on a warning to another likely target of the Tory-hunters. She had been told that day "of a design to seize upon a young man in town as he was esteemed a Tory. I thought a hint would be kindly received and, as I came back, called upon a friend of his and told him. Next day he was out of the reach of the gondolas."

Early in the morning of Tuesday, December 17, next-door neighbor James Veree, the quidnunc of Greenbank, dropped in on Mrs. Morris with great news. "The British troops actually at Mount Holly! Guards of militia placed at London and York bridges. Gondola men patrolling the street . . ." And the plunderers had been at it again: "Another attempt last night to enter Richard Smith's house." Smith, a neighbor on Greenbank, was a prisoner of the gunboat men.

Neighbor Veree had a request: would Mrs. Morris let her son Dick go a few miles out of town to do a little business errand for him? Mrs. Morris consented, "not knowing the formidable doings up town." After the boy left on the errand she had some second thoughts. There were reports of Hessians acting up in the area, "playing the very mischief," demanding free liquor, and so forth. Mrs. Morris felt "a mother's pangs for her son all the day. But when night came and he did not appear, I made no doubt of his being taken by the Hessians."

There was, the next day, the eighteenth, "hope of a quiet day but my mind still anxious for my son, not yet returned."

While Margaret Hill Morris was parrying Tory-hunters and agonizing over what her son might be suffering at the hands of the Hessians, another widow with young children and a home on the east bank of the Delaware River was playing hostess to Hessian officers and making the most of it. Her name was Mary Peale Field. In days to come she would be paid a formal visit by Colonel Donop himself, and her guests for afternoon tea would include Joseph Galloway, the prominent Philadelphia lawyer who had joined the British, and the Reverend Jonathan Odell, only a few days out of Mrs. Morris's auger-hole hideout down on Greenbank.

Mary Field owned a spacious brick tavern building situated on the river about ten miles upstream from Mrs. Morris's place in

Burlington and about seven miles below Trenton. It was a well-known landmark, called Whitehill because it was surrounded by apple and cherry trees that came alive with white blossoms in the spring.*

Like many another "neutral" in the area, Mrs. Field was playing a waiting game, accommodating either side in the ongoing war as occasion demanded and accepting help wherever she found it. Like Mrs. Morris, she was anxious to maintain at least the semblance of neutrality out of concern for her children. She was a woman of some social standing. The Fields hobnobbed with the likes of the Richard Stocktons of Princeton. (Both of her children would grow up and marry into the Richard Stockton family.) Whitehill stood on land that ancestor John Field received as a grant in 1674; the original house built there had been known as Field's Hope. It had a large basement, which could be reached by way of a tunnel from the river's edge, a tavern on the first floor, and on the second, spacious living quarters. Mrs. Field lived there with her mother, her infant son, Robert, and her toddler daughter, Molly. Also living at Whitehill at this time was a longtime friend from Philadelphia, Sally Redman. Mrs. Field had been raising her family and overseeing the operation of the tavern alone, but with the help of a staff of servants, ever since the summer day in 1775 when her husband drowned in the Delaware River after his boat capsized.

Mrs. Field was "confined with a sore throat and fever" on Sunday, December 8. On this day she heard that the British army had just reached Trenton and on this day, while she remained upstairs, Whitehill was visited by a contingent of men from the river boats (whom she described privately as "the violent people" or simply rebels). "Captain Tom Houston with the captain of the Province ship and several other officers and about fifty sailors came ashore to seize a quantity of flour that was put in my stores, and came up to the house to dine. Immediately after dinner all went away.

"Nothing more did I hear from either army till Thursday [December 12] when in the afternoon of that day some of the British Light Horse came to the house and demanded the rebels that was secreted there. I had yet never been downstairs, but being in our

---

*The area is now known as Fieldsboro. A restaurant occupies the site of Whitehill.

dear Mother's room I could hear and see everything that passed. I threw up the window and assured them I had no rebels in nor to my knowledge about my house.

"They went away up the lane where was their captain and took my poor old Dick [a servant or slave] with them who they put many questions to and received the same answers they had from me."

The captain was not satisfied. He sent two of his horsemen back to the house with orders to bring Mrs. Field back to him. "This," as Mrs. Field later noted, "was a message I did not much like and I ventured to tell them I had been unwell and did not think it safe to go so far. They then rode off, and presently return'd with the Captain's compliments to beg it as a favor I would endeavour to reach to the [fence] pails as he dare not venture nearer the house.

"Upon this polite request I ventur'd alone for none of my family dare go with me. Upon my going up to him he behaved with the utmost politeness, declared his uneasiness at being obliged to ask me out of my house, begged to know (as it could answer no good to deny it) whether I had any rebels secreted in my house.

"I assured him I had not, upon which he discharged Dick and urged me going to the house as he was fearful I might take cold and begged a thousand pardons for compelling me to come out of it.

"I now began to think we might sit down easy for this night. Candles being lighted, I went up to my dear mother."

But there was to be no sitting down easy. Within a few minutes another party of British horsemen arrived. A servant came upstairs with their message. They wanted to talk to Mrs. Field. Downstairs. "With fear and trembling," she descended, to find a happy surprise. Her good friend William Imlay was the first person she met. He had left Whitehill only a short time earlier, after having a cup of tea with her. He explained that he had just met the British visitors as they were approaching Whitehill and decided to return with them, since he was apprehensive about her being alarmed by the visit.

The British entered the room, each of them holding a cocked pistol! They explained why they had come: Mrs. Field's neighbors were watching Whitehill carefully. Rebels were in hiding here; that was what the neighbors were saying. Just within the past hour there had been five reports that rebel soldiers were being sheltered here—a great number of men.

This intelligence, Mary Field said, was absolutely false. She was firm about it, and they took her word for it. Without searching the building, they assured her they meant no mischief and off they rode.

Mrs. Field returned to the second floor and looked in on her little daughter, Molly, who lay "at this time as we all thought at the point of death and no doctor to be got, Doctor Moore being gone to Cranbury to see his family where they were fled for fear." Sally Redman, the visitor from Philadelphia, was sitting with Molly. A quiet scene, but soon to be invaded.

First came Nurse, Mrs. Field noted, bursting into the room with the breathless report that a British officer had come into the house! He had to speak to Mrs. Field. But while Nurse was delivering this message, Mrs. Field looked beyond her and saw for herself the intruder, who had "whipt up after Nurse through the back stairs" and entered her mother's room. "The dear old lady had no time to be frightened before he begged pardon and desired to know if this was Mrs. Field's room as he had a message to deliver to that lady. My Mama told him in the next room he might find her, upon which in he came."

As he entered, Sally Redman—"frightened almost to death"—ran screaming from the room. That left Mrs. Field, at the side of her ailing daughter, to face the intruder alone. But only for a few moments. Jacob, a young servant, suddenly appeared; he had been sent up by "poor old" Dick.

The young British officer, it immediately became clear, was just as distressed as Mrs. Field. This, he said, all apologies, was the most difficult duty he had ever done. He assured her she would not be harmed in any way by him or any of his soldiers waiting downstairs.

But he had to talk to Mrs. Field alone. At his request, she told Jacob to leave the room. As the boy left, the officer walked to the door and shut it. What next? "Judge you my feelings," Mrs. Field would later note. "A fixt bayonet, loaded gun and a young officer in a bedroom alone or at least with nobody but a sick baby." But her fears were groundless. "The poor gentleman (for such I may justly style him) discovering my fright, in a few words told me the commanding officer had been assured I expected a number of Rebels from over the river that night." The officer asked her, as a favor, to send a servant to him as soon as the rebels arrived.

This was too much. Mrs. Field told him that the Light Horse had already made the same request and she had assured them she knew nothing about rebels coming across the river. Besides, if they were so fearful of the rebels crossing, why didn't they leave soldiers to watch? "For my part," Mrs. Field said, "I don't look upon it as an incumbent duty upon me to look out for the motion of the American army for them." And now, "if General Howe's troops would give us leave I should endeavor to compose the family to rest."

The officer "begged my pardon and declared me right, and said if I pleased he would call in my servant, which he did immediately. I told him I had treated the British troops with great respect, but I began now to lose patience, and his commanding officer could be no gentleman or devoid of common sense to suppose a lady without protection as I was should secrete thirty of the American Army or even encourage them to come over when she knew the British army was at their heels.

"He agreed it looked unlikely, took leave begging his compliments to Mama with an apology for rushing into her room, declaring it to be his express orders, and said he could not be happy to leave the house till I had assured him I would pardon his seeming rudeness though in reality in their situation it was not so.

"It was now 10 o'clock, and as I did not know what time they might make another visit, Sally Redman and I lay in our clothes all that night."

That, it turned out, was to be the last of the British visits. The British troops were being removed from the area of Whitehill. But this was no cause for joy: they were being replaced by Hessians.

On Friday, December 13, the day following the British officer's visit, all was quiet. That night Mrs. Field and Sally Redman changed into their nightgowns and tried to catch up on their sleep. But early the next morning, very early, they were awakened by word that a Hessian captain was downstairs and asking for Mrs. Field. Sally Redman, "who is soon frightened," tried to persuade Mrs. Field not to go down. But Mrs. Field, sure that she had no choice, put on a dress, prepared herself for another crisis, and hurried downstairs.

There were two Hessians awaiting her, a captain and an enlisted man. She was "much alarmed," and it showed. The captain rushed up to her. What was this? He kissed both of her hands. She flinched. He tried to calm her but he didn't have the words. For help he turned to the soldier, who, it turned out, spoke some English. Through the soldier the captain apologized for coming so early. He explained that he merely wanted to be the first to request quarters in her place. Hessian officers were allowed to make their own arrangements for quarters and several of them already had their eyes on Whitehill. Would it be all right if he made his quarters here? He would be most grateful.

But, Mrs. Field asked, would she be *obliged* to take an officer? Well, the captain said, Colonel Donop, the commanding officer, would not require a lady to do anything really disagreeable. But her lot would be either officers or soldiers, one or the other. He recommended an officer; soldiers would be quite troublesome, especially out of the sight of their officers.

Ah! This had a look that pleased Mrs. Field. She asked his rank. He told her he was a captain, that he commanded a company of jagers, and that he received colonel's pay. (She checked on this later, and found it to be true.)

The visitor, she learned, was Captain Carl August von Wreden, commanding officer of the by now somewhat renowned First Jager Company. The company was posted along the road between Black Horse (Columbus) and Mrs. Field's neighborhood (Fieldsboro). (The Second Jager company, commanded by Wreden's friend Captain Johann Ewald, was posted along the road leading south from Bordentown.)

Mrs. Field cheerfully agreed to Captain Wreden's proposal. As he prepared to leave she mustered enough courage to tell him she was fearful that the Hessian soldiers would come plundering in the night. The captain admitted the Hessian soldiers had a very bad name—but worse than they deserved, he hoped. They were indeed bad enough when their officers were not watching them. But he had a suggestion: to make sure nothing happened to her he would send out a detachment to guard her house.

That night a twelve-member guard arrived, and they stayed on duty until Captain Wreden appeared with his entourage. He did indeed have the privileges of a colonel. He was attended by a cook, a footman, a waiter, a butler, and a hostler to take charge of his eight horses. He proceeded to prove himself an ideal guest— provided his own food, put Mrs. Field to no trouble at all, and, as she was to say before long, he was "the sweetest little Dutchman you ever see, the politest, obliging creature in the world."

By Monday, December 16, Whitehill had become all but unique in the area. The atmosphere was gay. Everything intact, even the fences. Elsewhere, fences, trees, outbuildings—anything that would burn—had been carried off for firewood. At Whitehill not a thing had been touched. And Colonel Donop himself was about to make a visit. A Hessian captain and a lieutenant arrived, bearing Donop's compliments and word that he would at the first opportunity call on Mrs. Field and present her with a Protection paper.

Mrs. Field said she would be happy to see him.

And how, one of the officers asked, had the soldiers been behaving?

Oh, very well, she replied.

The next day, the seventeenth, Mrs. Field and her guest, Sally Redman, were at the breakfast table when a Hessian captain named Georg Heinrich Pauli dropped in. Would it be convenient, he asked, for Mrs. Field to receive Colonel Donop at eleven o'clock? It would indeed. Before departing with his answer, Pauli had a cup of tea with the women.

The count himself coming! Mrs. Field hustled about. Summoned her servants. Ordered a fire made in the parlor. Tea. Her best dishes.

Promptly at eleven Colonel Carl Emil von Donop arrived in his customary high style, his entourage mounted on sleek, well-groomed steeds. First in the prancing line, "a flying mercury dressed beyond your conception. Elegant. Next . . . four grenadiers, the Colonel and his two aides de camp, then twelve officers, then four grenadiers more."

It turned out to be a long and largely formal visit. After coming in and graciously paying his respects to Mrs. Field, Donop introduced his aides, both of whom, he informed her, were his nephews: Ernst Friedrich Wilhelm von Donop and Carl Levin von Heister, son of Lieutenant General von Heister, commander of all the Hessian troops in America. He also introduced Captain Pauli, but not any of the other officers. Those introduced took their seats. Mrs. Field indicated chairs for the others but they remained standing until Donop deigned to signal that they could sit.

Donop presented Mrs. Field with a Protection paper. She would be safe from harm. He assured her that the first one of his Hessians who offended her or robbed any of her property would be shot. He told of the great number of New Jersey people "going over to General Howe" and in return receiving Protection papers. The reports were true, he said; great numbers were coming in every day and those who had taken an active part in the rebellion had to take the oath of allegiance to the King; those who had not taken part, such as Mrs. Field, were not obliged to take the oath.

So it went, for more than an hour, Donop, the perfect gentleman, turning on his considerable charm. Then, begging Mrs. Field to "command freely anything in his power to grant," he said farewell and rode off with his colorful entourage.

In the halcyon days that ensued—war or no war—Mrs. Field maintained the best of relations with the Hessians and continued to receive preferred treatment. She was presented with a dozen Protection papers. So she would report. Whitehill remained unpillaged, untouched, an oasis in a desert of devastation. And Captain von Wreden, her "sweetest little Dutchman you ever see," was not her only beneficent guest. A "very gentlemanly" Hessian physician bearing the rank of captain moved in for several days and made himself more than welcome. "To him am I greatly indebted for the particular attention he paid Molly," Mrs. Field would later note. "When it was not in my power to be with her he never left the room, which was often many hours, having at that time 27 prisoners in my house for four days on their way to be exchanged. The doctor was here but a little time, being obliged to attend some sick soldiers who was at a distance."

As Christmas 1776 approached, Mary Field's Whitehill suite became an ever more popular gathering place for her new friends. English as well as Hessian officers dropped in for afternoon tea. So did the Reverend Jonathan Odell, who had fled Burlington, and Joseph Galloway. At this time Galloway was lodging in Bordentown with Captain Thomas Gambell, a quartermaster officer, and assisting in the cause. "I drew, at his request," Galloway would later report, "invitations to the people of the country to bring in their provisions towards forming a magazine at Bordentown, and . . . a very considerable magazine was formed and great quantities of provisions brought in." Both Galloway and Odell, according to Mrs. Field, "stuck close to Count Donop. They came almost every day to see me."

There would soon be an abrupt halt to these visits.

———— ◆◆◆ ————

CHAPTER 27

Our Worst Fears Were Soon Fulfilled

In Trenton, as the Reeds—mother, ten-year-old daughter and eight-year-old son—could testify, Commander in Chief Howe's order concerning protection of the inhabitants' property was not being strictly followed. The Reeds were among the few families, mostly Quakers, who had decided to remain in town as the foreign troops came on. Mrs. Reed's husband was off serving as a lieutenant in the Continental Army.

Years later, Martha Reed, the lieutenant's daughter, would recall the grim December days: "I remember well seeing my mother and the neighbors scraping lint to send to the suffering soldiers. I was about ten years old and had one little brother, two years younger. Our house was one of the largest and best situated in the town and to this we owed the trouble that befell us.

"We had heard a great deal about the Hessians, who were objects of dread on account of their lawless brutality. The state was overrun by the enemy, whose army was largely composed of this hired soldiery, scarcely one remove from brutes. From every side came accounts of their savagery. No house nor home, no woman nor child was safe from their wanton cruelty. They pillaged and destroyed as they chose, only stopping short of absolute murder. We lived in momentary dread of their appearance, and our worst fears were soon fulfilled."

It happened one frigid night in mid-December: "Mother and we two children were gathered in the family room; a great fire blazed in the chimney place, and mother sat with her feet on the low fender talking to us about father who was away with the army. Suddenly there was a noise outside, and the sound of many feet. The room door opened and in stalked several strange men and a couple of women who looked like giants and giantesses to us they were so tall. These were the dreaded Hessians surely come. They jabbered away in harsh gutteral tones and, coming to the fire, spread out their hands to the blaze.

"We children jumped up screaming and clung to our mother. She was a brave little woman and, standing up, pointed to the door, telling them to go out. They understood the gesture, if not the words, and shook their heads doggedly. As they crouched about the fire, one of the women caught sight of the large silver buckles which mother wore in her shoes . . . and made signs for her to take off the shoes. Seeing her hesitate, the woman snatched at the buckle and, pulling off the shoe, rapped my mother in the face with the heel.

"Among the men there was one who seemed a captain and who managed to make himself understood a little. He rebuked the buckle-snatcher and explained to my mother that they had been sent to secure quarters for the British commander and his suite [and] as our house seemed suitable they had taken possession.

"My mother realized how completely we were at their mercy, and with great tact followed them from room to room with apparent willingness. She made them believe by signs, and what few words they could understand, that father was an officer in the British army, and when they learned this they treated us with rough kindness and permitted us to go to our beds in safety.

"But there was little sleep for us as we heard them rummaging in the closets, and finding what they could to eat.

"The next morning mother was obliged to open her store room and they helped themselves liberally to its contents. Nothing was sacred to these marauders. They killed a hog and cut it up on the mahogany dining table; pickles and preserves and our winter stores vanished away as they devoured our substance like a pest of locusts. We looked on in fear and trembling, thankful that our lives were spared and that we were permitted to remain in our own house."

In the perilous days and nights that ensued Mrs. Reed and her children were permitted to remain in a small area of the house, but their presence did little to inhibit the Hessians. The "giants and giantesses" smashed precious glass and china, defaced or shattered chairs and tables, carried off the household linen, most of which Mrs. Reed had spun herself, and one day carted off her feather bed.

Ten-year-old Martha tussled one day with a woman who was making off with a prized possession: a sugar bowl with a handle on top shaped like a little lamb. "Springing up, I caught her arm and . . . wrenched away the bowl, but in the struggle the cover was broken. I ran away and hid the bowl but cried long for the loss of the little lamb."

The Hessian women later discovered an item that led to far more serious trouble: "To please my little brother, my mother had made for him an officer's coat of the rebel buff and blue, in which he delighted to strut and fight imaginary battles. This coat was carefully folded away in the linen chest, and one day when the women were tossing about its contents, they came across the rebel coat. It was a revelation; they found they had been deceived and instead of being the family of an English officer, we belonged to the hated patriot rebels. What a storm broke around us! They shook the little coat in our faces, jabbering and threatening, and we understood by their gestures that they only awaited the orders of their captain to punish us."

Apparently taking the threat seriously, Mrs. Reed decided that she and her children would risk a night in the cold rather than face the Hessians' retribution: "Mother hurried us into our room but we were all too much frightened to feel any longer safe. We kept out of sight until the angry hubbub died away and when it grew dark we crept softly down the stairs and out of the back door to the hen house where our poultry was sheltered in the winter. Here was a ladder, and in the loft the corn was kept to feed the fowls. There were no cackling hens to betray us for our enemies had killed them all. We ascended the ladder, which mother pulled up after us, and here in this loft we remained all night, trembling with cold and fear. We did not know whether our persecutors had missed us or whether they would trouble themselves to look for us if they did. We were too thoroughly frightened to reason.

"The Hessians built fires in the barnyard, and cooked in large pots, in the manner of gypsies. In the cold grey of the morning, mother crept down the ladder and brought up her apron full of warm ashes to try and warm our numbed feet and hands. That was a night I can never forget."

The next day, apparently having decided to risk Hessian retribution rather than endure another such frigid night, the Reeds slipped back into the single room where they had been confined. The Hessian ransacking of the house continued, but the Reeds did not suffer any special punishment as a result of the discovery of the rebel coat of buff and blue.

Families who had fled their Trenton homes sustained even greater losses than the Reeds did. The Presbyterian minister Elihu Spencer's church, home, and barns were stripped of everything portable, combustible, or edible. Absent Tories suffered as well as

Whigs. Perhaps the man most severely victimized was Daniel Coxe, a wealthy and staunch supporter of the British cause. Writing in the third person, he would later declare to claims commissioners in England that "his houses, offices and estate were seized up as quarters for Hessian troops under the command of Colonel Rhode [Rall], and notwithstanding his well known public and loyal character and every remonstrance of his friends and servants to the contrary, his rooms, closets, stores and cellars were all broken up, ransacked and pillaged and every species of furniture, china, glass, liquors, etc. plundered, destroyed or taken away, his servants compelled to fly for safety elsewhere, and most wanton desolation committed on his property and estate."

In and around Princeton, Tory and Quaker families as well as Whig families were being similarly victimized by occupation troops. Many of the soldiers' misdeeds were being recorded by eighty-four-year-old Robert Lawrence, a retired lawyer who had served in New Jersey's General Assembly for many years, for a time as Speaker of the House. Instead of fleeing, he had decided to remain and take his chances with the oncoming enemy troops. He was living in the home of the David Oldens, situated on high ground overlooking the Post (Princeton–Trenton) Road, about a mile to the west of the center of Princeton.* There he was making note of every enemy offense he heard of, ranging from petty thievery to rape. Like many another in occupied New Jersey, Lawrence was outraged by what, in many instances, was no more than routine behavior of European soldiers at war and no worse than what some American troops had done in New Jersey and were continuing to do in Bucks County, Pennsylvania.

"The Regulars," as Lawrence (like most others) called the British, had marched into an all-but-deserted Princeton in the afternoon of Saturday, December 7. "Most of the inhabitants," he observed, "a day or two before that and some on that day, others after, left their dwelling houses and went where they could go with their familys to escape from the Regular Army and left a great part of their goods behind them in their houses for want of carriages to take them away, a great part of which fell into the Regulars' hands. They not only burnt up all the firewood that the inhabitants had provided

---

*The Oldens were apparently his daughter and son-in-law; David Olden was the husband of Elizabeth Lawrence.

for winter but stript shops, out houses and some dwelling houses of the boards that covered them and all the loose boards and timber that the joiners and carpenters had in store to work up. They burnt all their fences and garden inclosures within the town and after sent their carriages and drew away the farmers' fences adjoining within a mile, and laid all in common. They also cut down apple trees and other fruit-bearing trees and burnt them, and either by accident or wilfully burnt a large house lately finisht belonging to Jonathan Sergeant, Esquire, in Princetown."*

On December 8, the second day of occupation, according to Lawrence, "there followed the Regular Army a Parcel of Hessians and took away four horses from the people to the westward of the town. One of them was said to be valued at 100 pound." The Hessians "committed several other outrages the same day in pulling of men's hats from their heads, though the Regular officers had given them Protections as they went before. . . . Yet these men had no regard to it but directly to the contrary injured the Protected Men both in their persons and propertys by insulting their persons and by robbing them of their propertys.

"Another officer," he went on, "went to another farmer's house and imperiously demanded two of the first rooms in his house each with a good bed in it for him to lodge in and another to receive in which he accordingly took and the owner with his family was obliged to live in his kitchen, while their horses were eating and destroying the very best of his provender and hay for which the owner never was paid a farthing."

Another farmer in the area suffered a far greater loss when his home was taken over by a British captain "of an overgrown size and terrifying countenance." The captain "demanded a room with a bed and fireplace in it for him to lodge in. The man of the house not being within, the woman told him that they had none but that her husband and she lodged in and that they could not spare.

"Upon that, he swore and curst that he must and would have it, and this Monstrous Destroyer of human race before they are born went on so horribly with his threats, oaths and curses that he so affrighted the poor woman that she fell into a violent disorder and soon after miscarried."

---

*This was the home of Jonathan Dickinson Sergeant, then serving as a member of the Continental Congress. The Nassau Club now stands on the site.

Lawrence was particularly affronted by the fact that many of the enemy's victims were Quakers—"a people that never bore arms against them which they knew well and therefore had some right to their favour and yet used them in that manner." He was more than affronted by those of his neighbors who, for the special attention of the plunderers, went out of their way to point out the homes belonging to men serving in the American army: "There was a wicked company of talebearers that informed the Regular Officers of their names that had born arms against them, and also of their names that was chosen officers by the people. This gave them an advantage to call them Rebels and to say that their estates were forfeited to the King and that those that were missing (as many of them was) was gone to the Rebel army."

Guided by "those wretched informers," the foragers and outright plunderers took from the property of the absent men "most (if not all) of their cattle, horses, sheep, swine, and poultry besides ravage-ing their houses. . . . For after they had got what was needful to them they broke, destroyed and burnt tables, chairs, looking glasses and picture frames that they could find. Hiding will not protect where there is wicked informers."

Lawrence alluded to reports of rape in Pennington, a village about five miles distant, and added, "Another Treacherous Villainy: There was two of General Howe's light horsemen quartered at Penn's Neck, about two miles from Princetown, who pretended to a young woman that they was searching for rebels, and had been informed that some of them were secreted in the barn and desired her to go with them and show them the most secret places there, and she (knowing that nobody was there) to convince them went to the barn with them. . . . When they had got her there, one of them laid hold on her and strangled her to prevent her crying out while the other villain ravisht her. When he had done, he strangled her again while the other brute repeated the horrid crime upon her again. She is a farmer's daughter but her name, with her father's, must be kept secret to avoid the reproach above mentioned."

In Pennington it was not the Hessians but the British troops who were creating new enemies for their king. "An officer of distinction in the American Army" would make this report of the incidents there: "Besides the sixteen young women who had fled to the woods to avoid their brutality, and were there seized and carried off, one man had the cruel mortification to have his wife and only daughter (a child of ten years of age) ravished. This, he himself, almost choked with grief uttered in lamentations to his friend, who told me of it and also informed me that another girl of thirteen years of age was taken from her father's house, carried to a barn about a mile, ravished, and afterwards made use of by five more of these brutes."

Wartime propaganda? Some said so, but there were some women in the Pennington area who, at a time when it was considered shameful to disclose such things, would swear under oath that they had been raped by British soldiers. One justice of the peace took depositions from six of the victims. The youngest, aged thirteen, swore "on the Holy Evangelists of Almighty God" to details of what occurred at her grandfather's house near Pennington: "A great number of soldiers belonging to the British Army came there. One of them said, 'I want to speak with you in the next room,' and she told him she would not go with him. . . . He seized hold of her and dragged her into a back room, and she screamed and begged of him to let her alone. But some of said soldiers said they would knock her eyes out if she did not hold her tongue. Her grandfather also and aunt entreated and pleaded for her, telling them how cruel and what a shame it was to use a girl of that age after that manner. But they were deaf to their entreaties. Finally, three of said soldiers ravished her and likewise the next day and so on for three days successively divers soldiers would come to the house and treat her in the same manner."

Another of the six who were later willing to testify swore that she had been raped by two British soldiers and that, after escaping from her house, she found her ten-year-old daughter in the barn with five or six other British soldiers.

Such reports, along with other, sometimes exaggerated, accounts of misbehavior, spread through New Jersey and beyond. Many a "neutral" and Tory, having been victimized by the king's troops, came to view the foreigners in a new light. The British and Hessians found themselves in increasingly hostile territory. Even in "friendly" New Jersey more and more militiamen were becoming active and snipers and ambuscades were beginning to take a heavy toll among the occupation troops.

Meanwhile, thousands of captured Americans were dying of disease and maltreatment in New York prisons, and word of the shocking conditions was spreading through New Jersey and the rest of the states. In mid-December a soldier named William Darlington, who had escaped one of the hellholes in New York, passed through New Jersey and reached the American encampment in Bucks County. The horror stories that he and others were telling—actual atrocities, not creations of propagandists—served to inflame further the feelings of many against the king's soldiers.

---◆◆---

CHAPTER 28

Philadelphia Made a Horrid Appearance

In and around Bristol, Pennsylvania, a town directly across the Delaware River from Burlington, New Jersey, large numbers of militiamen were, for a welcome change, coming in. In Philadelphia on December 4, Congressman Robert Morris had observed: "Our Associators had been much disgusted with their service in the Flying Camp and their spirit had gone to sleep. They were called upon but did not rouse until . . . they began to conceive their danger was real and they are now turning out with a Spirit becoming Free Men. This day and tomorrow the whole militia of this city and suburbs march to join General Washington. The Country will follow the example of the City."

By the middle of December almost a thousand militiamen, most of them from the Philadelphia area, had reached the Bristol area. Each day there were new arrivals—"companies" ranging from a handful of men to more than eighty. They were being formed into units under the command of John Cadwalader. As the senior colonel of the Philadelphia battalions of Associators, Cadwalader had been given command of the Bristol encampment and had been designated acting brigadier general at General Washington's request. Even so, he continued to sign his letters and messages as a colonel.

In addition to the Philadelphia companies, militiamen were reporting in from Northampton and other rural counties of Pennsylvania, from New Jersey, and from elsewhere in the middle states. One company came on from Dover, Delaware, some eighty miles south of Philadelphia. It was commanded by thirty-one-year-old Captain Thomas Rodney, the younger brother of Caesar Rodney, a general of militia. (It was Caesar Rodney who, though ill, made a dramatic eleventh-hour appearance at the Continental Congress on July 2, 1776, and thereby enabled the Delaware delegation to vote 2–1 in favor of the resolution for independence.) Thomas had lived with his brother for many years and assisted him on his farm and in his official county duties. In 1772 Thomas had gone to Philadelphia and opened a shop. He returned to Delaware in 1774 and served as a justice of the peace and as a member of the Council of Safety.

In setting off with his company, Thomas Rodney believed—so he would later claim—that he was acting on orders from above. A short time earlier he had been visited by an angel sent by God to show him how to stop the British army. So he said. Along the route of march to Philadelphia, he heard a surfeit of defeatist talk: the rebellion was all but over; the British army was unstoppable; perhaps it was time to sue for peace. But Rodney knew better; things would turn out all right; a messenger from God had told him that as well.

In December 1776 Delaware's ruling council, instead of authorizing reinforcements for Washington's army, "met twice," as Rodney noted in his journal, "and separated without doing anything, and a general dismay seemed to spread over the country." Caesar Rodney, now confined to his home by illness, was, according to his brother, "much concerned; said everything appeared gloomy and unfortunate, that he was very apprehensive for the safety of our cause."

As the council members stalled, Thomas Rodney decided it was time to take action. He called for volunteers from the Dover Light Infantry Company, the militia unit he had been trying to whip into shape for about a year. Originally there had been sixty-eight men in the company and they had a long-standing reputation as hell-raisers. On one occasion, in March 1776, they had surrounded and pounced on a couple of assemblymen passing through Dover on their way to serve in the legislature. Against Rodney's orders, the militiamen put the legislators in jail as suspected Tories. On another occasion four of Rodney's militiamen manhandled a suspected Tory with such brutality that they were threatened with hanging by their victim's supporters.

Though often spoiling for a fight on home territory, most of the

Dover militiamen, in December 1776, had no desire at all to fight the enemy. Of the sixty-eight militiamen, thirty-nine decided they did not want to march. Of the twenty-nine willing to go, only sixteen had guns, and nine of the sixteen guns were not in working condition. This was not going to deter Rodney; he collected enough weapons to arm all of his men.

Outfitted in their green uniforms faced with red, those willing to march set off around three p.m. on December 14: Lieutenant Mark McCall, Ensign Simon Eillson, two sergeants, two corporals, and twenty-three privates including Boice Emery, a fifer, and Phillip Wheeler, a drummer. Six other men, not members of the company, volunteered to go along, bringing the total to thirty-five. Rodney closed his shop, wound up his affairs, and caught up with the company the following day on the road. "This morning," he noted in his journal, "I took leave of a loving wife pregnant with woe as well as child, one lovely boy five years old and as lovely a girl but two; which nothing could have separated me from in so dangerous a character but the bleeding cries of my country. But my dependence is in God that he will enlist the just cause, and disappoint the cruel end of tyranny." On joining the men, Rodney found them to be a "little uneasy about their blankets but . . . in high spirits."

In Wilmington, Delaware, reached on December 16 after a march of about forty-five miles, the company came upon a disheartening sight: hundreds of frightened people fleeing southward from Philadelphia with all the goods their carts and wagons could carry. "We saw," Rodney noted in his journal, "the road full of the citizens of Philadelphia who had fled with their families and effects, expecting the British army would be there in a few days."

Also on the road, Rodney noted, were several members of Congress: "At Christiana Bridge [below Wilmington] I met with Mr. Thomas McKean . . . and several other members of Congress on their way from Philadelphia to Baltimore."

Captain Rodney stayed up late that night and listened to a disheartening recital of the facts: "Mr. McKean . . . gave me an account of all the information Congress had received, and observed that everything was very gloomy and doubtful and that the chief hope that remained was that General Lee, who was in the mountains in the rear of the enemy, would be able to effect some lucky stroke that would prevent the enemy's crossing the Delaware." (They were not aware that Lee had been captured by the British, three days earlier.)

But, if no such lucky stroke was made, McKean continued, "Congress would be obliged to authorize the Commander in Chief to obtain the best terms that could be had from the enemy." In other words, barring a miracle, the revolution was over.

This from Thomas McKean, one of the most steadfast patriots in the Congress! Here was a prominent lawyer, forty-two years old, who had openly criticized British rule more than a decade earlier when he was a member of the Stamp Act Congress. As a judge, McKean had defied the British by ordering the use of unstamped legal papers; as speaker of Delaware's assembly, he had used his political power to help create a colonial congress in 1772; and as an influential member of Congress he had worked to sway opinion toward independence from Great Britain. On July 2, 1776, he had voted Yes on Richard Henry Lee's resolution calling for independence. (George Read, Delaware's only other representative present, had voted against it, creating the deadlock broken by Caesar Rodney's eleventh-hour vote.)

But now, less than seven months after making his stand for the Declaration, Thomas McKean was admitting that the costly struggle with Great Britain might soon be lost.

Nothing, however, according to his own testimony, was going to daunt Thomas Rodney: "I desired him not to dispair, and urged that the members of Congress might not say anything on their way that would discourage the people, but would endeavor by all means in their power to animate them to make use of what we were doing as an example;—that the spirited exertion of a few men at such a time would have great weight, and assured him that he would soon hear of a favorable turn in our affairs."

Resuming the march, Rodney and his men "had the pleasure of receiving the good wishes of thousands on our way and of seeing our example enspirit the people to follow it." On December 17 they marched into Chester, about twenty miles below Philadelphia, and heard conflicting reports on the progress of the war. "I have a great number of officers from camp, no two of which tell the same story about any one fact," Rodney wrote his brother Caesar. "I have heard that Lee has found Washington—again that Washington has crossed into Jersey—again that none of these things have happened—again that Lee has given the enemy a drubbing—again that Lee is taken prisoner—and again that the enemy has retreated before him, etc.

"And the news of this day is that Lee is actually taken . . . That

70 Light Horse . . . took him prisoner and rode off with him without giving him time to get his hat; that General Washington received this account from General Sullivan by express. . . . But I believe none of all this, nor any thing I have heard since I left Kent. Nobody knows any thing about the designs or actions of the Generals and yet every body seems to know everything. It was reported as a fact at New Castle [Delaware] that I was taken very sick at Cross Roads and turned back. And a few hours before we arrived at Wilmington it was affirmed that all the company had got discouraged and gone home again. Judge of the rest by this."

Despite the perplexing reports, Rodney remained optimistic, exceedingly so, about the way things were going: "We are all at Chester now in very good health and the highest of spirits, and we have had the pleasure on our way of receiving the prayers and blessings of men, women and children—the Whigs sincere and the Tories dissembling—and the country seems inspired with new spirit as we come. New Castle County is rousing fast. Three companies have marched already. . . . Pennsylvania is marching in by hundreds and 1000's."

Below Philadelphia Rodney's men "met the Philadelphia Tories and other prisoners under guard . . . going to Baltimore." In Philadelphia, reached on December 18: "All the company in good health and spirits but some have blistered feet." As for the capital city, Rodney was shocked by what he saw: "When we arrived in Philadelphia it made a horrid appearance,* more than half the houses appeared deserted, and the families that remained were shut up in their houses and nobody appeared in the streets. There was no military of any kind in the city, only General Putnam who was there to give orders to any militia that might come in."

In his accustomed take-charge manner, Rodney surveyed the scene and, seeing the need for security, had his men mount guard over the city. Everywhere he went he assured people that all would be well: "I asked them where all the Whigs were, and they said

---

*On the day of Rodney's arrival in Philadelphia, Henry Melchior Muhlenberg, a Lutheran clergyman living near the city, made the following notes in his diary: "It is said, to the joy of many and the terror of many more, that the British armies will eat their Christmas dinners in Philadelphia and that for their encouragement they have been promised three days of liberty to plunder, etc. Men, women and children are still fleeing the city for the country daily, under unusually hard circumstances."

there were but few in town, and they expected the British in town every moment and were afraid to be out. I told them again they need not be afraid."

On the morning of his second day in Philadelphia, Thursday, December 19, Rodney went to see some of his in-laws, the family of Joshua Fisher, "who is uncle to my wife but are Quakers and very great Tories. They seemed glad to see me and were all extremely cheerful. Said that the contest would soon be over now; that the British would be in town in a day or two."

That evening Rodney encountered more of such talk in the company of some more of his wife's relatives, the Thomas Fishers. Following supper and some good Madeira wine, three of the Fishers—Thomas, Samuel, and Miers—"began on the times. They informed me, I believe very truly, of the situation of the British and American armies; told me General Lee was certainly taken prisoner; that there was no prospect that America could make any further exertions."

Sarah Logan Fisher, the twenty-five-year-old wife of Thomas, apparently did not take part in the discussion. "Dined at Mammy's on venison," she confided to her diary that night, making no mention of Rodney's visit. Amidst the small talk of the day, she did, however, observe that "the smallpox was broken out" among the soldiers in town, "many of them not having a bed to lie on or a blanket to cover them." Three days earlier, her bias had been evident: "Heard this evening that . . . General Lee was taken by Howe, which was a great damp to the spirits of some of our violent people."

Sarah's husband and the others went on far into the night of the nineteenth: Washington was ready to give up, had asked for terms. The rebellion was about to be crushed. Why not make peace now while there was still time?*

Rodney "answered them by pointing out those circumstances that were still favorable to America, and concluded by assuring them

*On December 20, the day following Rodney's visit, Thomas, Samuel, and Miers Fisher were among those who took part in promulgating a Quaker paper that urged members of the Society of Friends not to submit to "the arbitrary injunctions and ordinances of men who assume to themselves the power of compelling others . . . to join in carrying on war." Because of their part in this "seditious publication," the three Fishers and seventeen others were some months later arrested and exiled to Virginia.

that I should not change my determination, that I knew my business and should not return until the British were beaten. But they treated this as levity and concluded that I was an obstinate man, and must be left to take my own way. I told them I was perhaps better informed than they were, and should most certainly proceed in my enterprise."

Earlier that day Rodney had been depressed by what he saw. Philadelphia was all but deserted and appeared "as if it had been plundered." No chairs in the public houses, no food available, no one in the streets. Late in the day, however, "to our great joy we saw streets full of militia and hundreds pouring in every hour."

The next morning the Dover militiamen set off for the growing American encampment in the Bristol area, their captain vowing not to return "until we have recovered all Jersey from Brunswick to the Delaware."

CHAPTER 29

A Country Filled with Tories and Informers

General Lee's corps, now down to about 2,000 troops, had meanwhile, as General Washington had hoped, increased the pace of its advance toward Bucks County under the leadership of General John Sullivan of New Hampshire, an officer with a less than distinguished record. Described as an "able if somewhat litigious lawyer" in civilian life, he was the son of a couple who had come to America from Ireland in the 1720's as redemptioners.* He had been captured in the Battle of Long Island on August 27, 1776, and, after being exchanged a month later, he had rejoined the army. While a prisoner in New York he agreed one day to deliver to the Congress in Philadelphia a message dealing with possible reconciliation, one that led to the abortive "peace conference" of September 11. As

---

*Emigrants who received passage to America on the condition that their services there would be disposed of by the master of the vessel until the passage-money and other expenses were repaid out of their earnings.

Sullivan gave the message, John Adams whispered to Dr. Benjamin Rush, a fellow Congressman, "a wish 'that the first ball that had been fired on the day of the defeat of our army [on Long Island] had gone through his [Sullivan's] head.' " Adams took the floor later that day to denounce Sullivan as "a decoy duck whom Lord Howe has sent among us to seduce us into a renunciation of our independence."

On December 11, two days before General Lee was captured, Sullivan, second in command, had issued orders for the march to Vealtown: "The whole army to strike their tents tomorrow morning at half past seven and to parade in order to march at eight." Apprised of Lee's capture on December 13, Sullivan sent a dispatch to Washington describing "the sad stroke" and promising to get the troops to Washington's encampment as quickly as possible. On the same day the corps proceeded toward the ferry crossing of the Delaware from Phillipsburg, New Jersey, to Easton, Pennsylvania, some forty miles upstream from Hessian-occupied Trenton. Along the route of march the troops, as before, were experiencing mixed receptions, and some, such as the Pad Rounds in Sergeant John Smith's Rhode Island company, were continuing their nightly raids. On occasion, in addition to the pilfered fowl, there was something sweet for dessert: "Honey was brought to our tent by one or two of our company that was out on a patrol for something to eat. One of them went to take a piece of the comb out of the hive [and] was stung in the eye and to be revenged took the whole family of them and put them to death and shared the spoil amongst us. In the morning the neighbors came all to see us, bringing their wifes and children with them who never saw so many men before together."

That was on Saturday morning, December 14, and shortly thereafter, Smith noted, "the whole division paraded for a march with all our baggage teams and waited till about 10 o'clock when Mr. William Bradford* came to us . . . and informed that General Lee and a French colonel was taken prisoner . . . and carried off. Then the whole division marched forward to Germantown and lodged in the woods. This day's march was exceeding tiresome as the road was full of stones and very muddy. . . . Here the inhabitants refused to give us straw to lie on but we took what we wanted from them."

A day's march later, the reception was friendly. A family "gave

*Who had barely escaped being captured along with General Lee.

vittles to near 70 men, officers and soldiers, saying they had rather we should have it than the enemy who was expected there as soon as we had crossed over the Delaware. They gave us cyder and apples as long as they had any left. Tho' they appeared to be but poor people they refused to take any pay for what we had." At another stop that day the soldiers "got two barrels of salt pork . . . from the Tories."

Smith's company and most of the rest of General Sullivan's troops crossed the Delaware to Easton, Pennsylvania, on Monday, December 16. Others crossed a day later. "I crossed over the ferry to Easton in the evening," Sergeant Smith noted, "and went to several houses to get liberty to lay by the fire but could not and so was obliged to lay myself down on the frozen ground and snow for we could not pitch our tent the ground was froze so hard. We made a little fire with some rails that we took for there was no other wood hereabout to be had. The ferry men was obliged to work all night to get our baggage over the Delaware and all the next day."

In Easton, "the inhabitants," according to Smith, "were all Dutch and not the kindest in the world." Moreover, the town was already crowded with soldiers. As the British hounded Washington's force across New Jersey, many of the sick and wounded Americans had been carried in wagons to Easton, Bethlehem, and other places in Northampton County. Easton's churches and other improvised hospitals bulged with diseased and disabled soldiers. Private householders took in some of the casualties. The town's standing committee appealed to the Council of Safety in Philadelphia for emergency funds to provide for the hospital cases. Now came Sullivan's troops, no doubt with more hospital cases. Where to put them all?

As had been true in many a town in New Jersey, the ablebodied men of Easton willing to fight were already in the army; the rest, by and large, were having no part of the war. Most of those who were neutral or opposed to the war held their tongues but the more aggressively "disaffected" openly damned the cause and tried to persuade young men not to enlist. In the course of recruiting expeditions, militia officers were sometimes assaulted and, in Easton as elsewhere, the soldiers were encountering resistance to their Continental paper money.

Yost Dreisbach, a colonel of militia, was among the recruiters who had suffered for their efforts. One day, in company with a fellow officer, he encountered a Non-Associator named Frederick Beck who "assaulted him . . . and caught him at the throat, having a stick in his hand, lifted up threatening to strike." Presently, another member of the Beck family, William, got into the fray and warned Colonel Dreisbach that "if he resisted against Frederick Beck, he, the Colonel, should be a dead man." Before the ruckus ended, five members of the Beck family joined in the attack on the colonel, pummeling him and dragging him about by the neck.

What had brought all this on? The Standing Committee's investigation would find that Colonel Dreisbach had enraged the Becks by sending to William Beck's house for a drum that belonged to the local militia battalion. William Beck's son Leonard, a company drummer in the battalion, insisted on keeping the drum even though he refused at this critical time to serve with his company. Leonard's father not only backed him up but also threatened "that if the whole battalion were to come they should not have [the drum] for he had powder and lead in his house . . . and would defend himself."

Easton's jail was filling up with "disaffected" citizens early in the final month of 1776. On December 9 three more suspected Tories had been brought to trial before the Standing Committee. The three men, it was testified, had, on December 6, "behaved in a very rude and indiscreet manner by damning Congress, Convention and Committee, saying they were all a parcel of damned rascals and were selling the people's liberties, or words to that effect." Found guilty, the men were jailed, then released within a few days after "setting forth that they were heartily sorry for their past conduct."

Among those in the Easton area who refused to march were the 107 members of a militia company recruited by Captain Christopher Fisher. The Standing Committee of the county issued to Fisher "bounty and advance" money—a total of 588 pounds and ten shillings—for distribution to the militiamen and ordered the company to set off for the American encampment in Bucks County. The bounty amounted to three pounds per enlisted man, a substantial sum for a few weeks' service, but the men—all 107 of them—refused to budge, despite repeated orders from the committee. Captain Fisher would eventually inform the committee that his men insisted on being paid immediately, not only for the forthcoming time of active service but also for the nonactive period beginning with the time of their enlistment. Informed that this was impossible, they refused to march. Thus was lost another company of men at a crucial time, and there was little or nothing the Standing Committee could do about it.

Before pushing on toward Bethlehem, Sergeant John Smith and most of the rest of Sullivan's corps spent a second night in Easton. For a change, Smith was in luck: "I had a fine warm room with a stove in it where our company all stoed in this night. This was the first house I sleept in since I left Connecticut. . . . Some two or three of the company sleept in the kitchen, there being no room in the stove rooms. After the Dutchman and his frau had gone to sleep, went down in the cellar and got some cyder and apples and potatoes and held a feast this night.

"In the morning the old woman having occasion to draw cyder, missing the apples and cyder, made a great gabber about it but got no satisfaction for it. Some other of her neighbours lost their bees that made the honey but could not tell where to find them for they swarm in the night and flew from their quarters to ours where they had care taken of them." The night raiders had been at it again.

As they made their way toward the encampments in Bucks County, Pennsylvania, the men of Sullivan's corps occasionally got word from home. It was usually long delayed and sometimes, as in the case of young John Howland, it was the kind of news that made one yearn to be back home. Howland was a private marching with Captain David Dexter's company in the depleted ranks of Colonel Christopher Lippitt's Rhode Island regiment. On the day when Howland and the other Rhode Islanders crossed the Delaware to Easton with General Sullivan's corps they received a report that was to cause them many a restless night: General Henry Clinton's British force, about 6,000 strong, had invaded their home state. And here they were, marching through what at times appeared to be enemy territory, on their way to risk their necks in behalf of people who wouldn't accept their Continental money or readily take them in for a night. Meanwhile they could only guess at what a reportedly rapacious enemy was up to in their beloved Rhode Island. "This," as John Howland would later observe, "was reason sufficient, without taking into account the sufferings of the season, for us to wish to return home." Nevertheless, they kept on marching to join Washington's troops some thirty miles down the Delaware.

The members of Captain Dexter's Rhode Island company, like most of the veteran Continentals on the march, had more than enough to complain about. "The men had no bounty when they enlisted," according to Howland, "and were not furnished with any clothes. We found our own clothes, and we had the promise of forty shillings per month." The promise and little else, through the disastrous Canadian campaign and all the way from Ticonderoga to Bucks County, Pennsylvania. During the long marches, Howland was afflicted with a common problem: sore, bleeding feet. For a long time his feet were protected only by pieces of raw beefhide— "moccasins," he called them—and the pain grew worse each day. Along the way, "many of our men . . . whose shoes were worn out, repaired to the butcher's yard, and cut out a piece of raw hide, which they laced with strips of the same skin about their feet. This, when the weather was moist, was not so utterly bad, but I recollect, as soon as my moccasins became frozen, they chafed my toes till they bled."

One day at a farmhouse along the route of march the footsore Howland tried to bargain with the woman of the house. Her husband, "a Dutchman," was off at work in the field. "I proposed . . . to buy an old pair of shoes which I saw at the head of a bed. She said her husband would not sell his shoes."

By this time Howland was desperate. "I showed her the situation of my feet, and offered in haste what ought to have been the price of a new pair." Apparently the price was right: "She took the money and I carried off the shoes."

Even in these circumstances, John Howland experienced a twinge of conscience and a concern about the woman's feelings: "She may have been induced to close the bargain from apprehension that I would take them at all events, though I hope this did not influence her decision." In any case, Howland had the shoes; now he would be able to make it through the winter.

A thirty-one-year-old shoemaker from Ipswich, Massachusetts, Lieutenant Joseph Hodgkins, had no serious physical afflictions as he led one of the companies under General Sullivan's command. But along the way he had suffered something far worse: news from home that his infant son, whom he had never seen, had died. "I received your letter . . . by which I was informed of the death of my little son," he wrote to his wife. "It is heavy news to me but it is God that had dun it therefore what can I say? I hope it will please God to santifie all these outward afflictions to us for our best good."

During the previous March, while stationed in camp at Boston, Hodgkins had attempted to alleviate his wife's concern about his safety and to explain his own mixed feelings: "I would not have you Be uneasy about me for I am willing to sarve my Contery in the Best way & mannar that I am capeble of and as our Enemy are gone from us I expect we must follow them. . . . I would not be understood that I should Chuse to March But as I am engaged in this glories cause I am willing to go Whare I am Called. . . . I am sensible that the feteugues of marching will be grate But I hope if we are Called to it we shall March with Chearfullness.''

Hodgkins had enlisted as a Minute Man in January 1775, had served in a "verry hot engagement" at Bunker Hill, had barely escaped enemy fire and capture on Long Island, and now, his enlistment about up, he was hoping to return home soon. The news of his son's death reinforced his determination not to be talked into reenlisting. In their exchange of letters Hodgkins and his wife impatiently anticipated seeing each other again but faced up to the possibility that he might never return. Throughout, they put their trust in God.

Lieutenant Hodgkins: "My dear, I want to see you very much but when I shall I cannot tell but I hope I shall be presarved from all the evils & dangers that we are surrounded with & returned home in safety in God's good time.

"Give my love to my two children and tell them to be good galls and that Daddy whants to see them.''

Mrs. Hodgkins: ". . . at all times my heart akes for you to think of the dificultys & fateagues you have to undergo but all that I can do for you is to commit you to God who has hitherto preserved you and beg of him to be with you. . . . I think things look very dark on our side but it has been observed that mans extremity was Gods oppertunity and I think it seems to be a time of grate extremity now and I hope God will apear for us & send salvation and deliverance to us in due time and if you should be called to battle again may he be with you. . . .

"May we have oppertunity to praise his holy name together again but if it be Gods will that we are not to meet again in this world may we be prepared for a better where we shall have no more troble nor sorrow.''

Lieutenant Hodgkins: "I want to see you very much but I cant.''

Mrs. Hodgkins: "I hope if we live to see this campaign out we shall have the happiness of living together again. I dont know what you think about staying again but I think it cant be inconsistent with your duty to come home to your family. It would trouble me very much if you should ingage again.''

Lieutenant Hodgkins: "I have no thoughts of ingaging again . . . neither due I desire it as there is officers enough that are fond of the sarvis & perhap more caperble of sarving the cause than I am. . . . I think you hopt that I would excuse your freedom in expressing your desire of have me come home. My dear, you are very excusable for I am sensible that My being absent must of necesity create a great deal of troble for you and if you will belive me my being absent from my famely is I think the gratest troble I have met with sence I have been absent therefrom."

A few days after crossing the Delaware to Easton with the rest of General Sullivan's corps, Hodgkins brought his wife up to date: "we are vary much fatagued with a long march. We have ben on the march ever sence ye 29 of last month and we are now within 10 or 12 miles of general Washingtons Army. We expect to be there tonight but how long we shall stay there I cant tell, neither can I tell you much about the enemy, only they are on one side of the Dilleway River and our army on the other about 20 miles from Philadelphia. . . .

"We have marched sence we came from Phillips Manner [Phillips Manor, N.Y.] . . . about 200 miles. The greatest part of the way was dangrus by reason the enemy being near & not only so but the contry is full of them cursed creaters called Torys."

Later: "My dear I hope I shall live to get home but I due not know when. . . . But I expect to lay my head to the eastward in about fortanate. We have had extraordnary pleasant weather but now it is a snow storm. . . .

"Jonathan Wells is with us. He desires that if you see his wife to let her know that he is well & expects to get home by the last of January."

He signed it, as usual, "Your most affectionate companion till death."

About a day behind Sullivan's corps came the troops from the north—some 600 of them—under the command of Horatio Gates. After traversing the hilly northwest corner of New Jersey, they reached and crossed the Delaware River at a point about twenty miles above Easton on Sunday, December 15.

A day before taking part in the crossing, Chaplain David Avery made this note in his diary: "This morning Major Wilkinson returned from General Lee's army, and brings tidings that yesterday morning about 70 of the light horse came upon General Lee and took him prisoner and a French colonel."

Wilkinson had caught up with General Gates the day following Lee's capture and handed over the letter Lee had written to Gates. "Lee's misfortune afflicted Gates profoundly; they had been long acquainted, had served together in the British army, and were personally attached; their politics and political connexions were in unison, and their sympathies and antipathies ran in the same current," Avery continued. "The troops were soon put in motion." But, a short distance from the river, Gates suddenly changed his mind: he would not accompany his men in crossing to Pennsylvania. He was "in very feeble health," as Wilkinson had noted earlier, and not inclined to explain the abrupt change in plans. Gates ordered General Arnold to lead the troops directly across the river. With a few aides and a small mounted guard, he then rode off to the north. Among those with him, in addition to Wilkinson, was his deputy adjutant general, twenty-two-year-old Colonel John Trumbull.* Gates and his party, according to Wilkinson, proceeded on "a devious route and by a rapid march reached the Delaware" at a point where it was fordable. It was about eight in the evening when the party halted there for the night at an inn operated by a man named Levy.

A safe man, Levy, General Gates seemed to think at first, "observing that the Jews were Whigs." But then, Wilkinson noted, Levy started to make "certain inquiries . . . which the General considered a little mysterious." Gates called his party together and ordered them not to reveal his right name, nor Colonel Trumbull's either. Talking later with Levy, Gates identified himself as "Captain Smith of Berkley, Virginia." Apparently looking somewhat dubious, Levy turned to Colonel Trumbull and asked if he hadn't seen Trumbull some time ago up in Connecticut.

"No!" Gates cut in. "He is a neighbor's son in Berkley."

More than suspicious now about what the innkeeper might be up to, Gates decided this was no place to spend the night. Levy's inquisitiveness "so sensibly alarmed him that although the night was very inclement, he ordered the horses to be saddled, and we made a perilous passage of the river, through floating ice, and

---

*The youngest of the six children of Governor Jonathan Trumbull of Connecticut, Colonel Trumbull would in later years become celebrated as "the Painter of the Revolution."

marched until midnight before we lay down in a dirty stove room which almost suffocated me."

Chaplain Avery had meanwhile crossed the Delaware with the main body of Gates's troops. He made the passage in a ferry and noted that "the ice was considerable thick on the edges of the Delaware." The first stop in Pennsylvania was Mount Bethel, Northampton County, a place where, as in New Jersey, Tories abounded, and some were reported to be ready to come out and openly oppose the revolution. "Many disaffected men in and bordering the Township of Mount Bethel have, of late, by intelligence received, formed themselves in companies in order to repear to the King's standert, wherefore we have the greatest reason to believe that an attempt is by them in agitation to be made against the associators of said county, and in particular against the Township of Mount Bethel, as it lays most exposed, and being stript of men, almost void of arms and ammunition." That is what John Scott and Benjamin Depui, in behalf of the Mount Bethel Associators, reported to the Northampton County Committee on December 13, two days before Avery arrived in Mount Bethel.

Avery stayed there overnight and confined his remarks to the weather: "clear and more moderate than yesterday." The following day, Monday, December 16, he made more than twenty miles, presumably still riding his pony. "Marched to Nazareth, about 13 miles, a town of Moravians."

The soldiers passing through Nazareth were well behaved, according to the Moravian church journal kept there. "In the afternoon," it was recorded on December 16, "the New England troops arrived and were distributed in the town. In the Hall, 60 were lodged in three vacant rooms.* They were quiet and orderly, having received strict orders to that effect."

The next day Avery, accompanied by a doctor named Lee, "proceeded, and came to Bethlehem, about nine miles and put up on the west side of the Lahi [Lehigh], a river which forms the west branch of the Delaware."

Bethlehem, a quiet town of about 600 inhabitants, now became as overcrowded as Easton had been, perhaps more so. The town had

---

*Nazareth Hall was a boarding school attended by about 100 boys. The journal noted further arrivals of troops and on December 22 recorded the presence of a leader who had had to flee his state: "This afternoon Gov. Livingston visited the Hall and was quite friendly."

been settled in the 1730s by members of an evangelical Protestant sect known as Moravians. They had come from Germany to preach the gospel to Indians as well as whites in the area. Like the Quakers, the Moravians were refusing on religious grounds to bear arms but, as it was noted in a diary kept by Bethlehem's Moravian congregation, they were willing to bear their share of "the burdens of the country."

Dr. William Shippen, who had been in charge of the improvised hospitals in New Jersey, arrived in Bethlehem on December 12, accompanied by his wife and some of their children. Carrying out General Washington's orders, he promptly organized the setting up of hospitals in Easton and Allentown as well as in Bethlehem. The largest was in Bethlehem: a three-story, 83-by-50-foot building that had formerly served as the Single Brethren's House of the Moravian Order. In addition to the sick and wounded under care in that building, others were housed in shops and other buildings in the town.

The Moravian congregation's diary briefly sketched the scene as the patients began to arrive: "Many wagons with sick from the Jerseys arrived today." The next day: "Their sufferings and lack of proper care made them a pitiable spectacle." Later: "Two of the sick died today." The death rate increased in the days that ensued, and Moravian carpenters busied themselves in the making of coffins. The single brethren dug graves and helped in caring for the patients. The women made lint bandages and the Reverend John Ettwein, a Moravian minister, visited the patients daily.

From Bethlehem on December 17, Dr. Shippen wrote to his wife's brother, Colonel Richard Henry Lee, on duty in the Continental Congress: "After much difficulty and expense, I have removed all the sick to Easton, Bethlehem and Allentown. Their number is now much reduced, and all in a good way. I send twenty or thirty weekly to join the army. . . . I am almost out of cash; I must, therefore, beg the favour of you to procure me five thousand dollars and send them by the bearer, Dr. Halling, for the use of the hospitals. . . .

"I have not heard of my clothes and old wine: fear the varlets have them as secure as poor General Lee. Oh! what a damned sneaking way of being kidnapped. I can't bear to think of it. I saw all his troops, about four thousand, this morning, marching from Easton, about two days' march from Washington, in good spirits and much pleased with their General Sullivan. General Gates, with nine hundred men, marches from this place this afternoon and tomorrow. . . .* God send that all joined may save Philadelphia and disappoint the cursed Tories this winter."

Around this time Dr. Shippen also wrote a letter that was likely to be long delayed. It was addressed to his thirteen-year-old daughter, Nancy, who was attending Mistress Roger's School for Young Ladies in enemy-occupied Trenton: "My dear Nancy: I was pleased with your French letter which was much better spelt than your English one, in which I was sorry to see four or five words wrong. . . .

"Take care, my dear girl, of your spelling and your teeth. Present my compliments to Mrs. Roger and Miss Jones. Your loving father." He would later learn that despite the presence of the Hessians in Trenton Nancy was continuing with her studies, making a map "with the towns worked in marking stitch," and embroidering a pair of "ruffles" to be presented to General Washington.

Major Wilkinson reached Bethlehem on December 17 and "found General Arnold and the rest of our own corps, and also that of General Sullivan." He was happy to observe that Sullivan "had changed his route the moment he had found himself in command, and pressed forward to join the Commander-in-Chief."

Around noon that day, it was noted in the Moravian diary, "we heard that several thousand New Englanders under General Sullivan would reach here today, and that we should bake bread for them. . . . Towards evening some three or four thousand men arrived and went into camp." Soon the usual night fires were blazing: "As the night was cold, our fences . . . on both sides of the river suffered."

To protect a group of Moravian women, precautionary measures were taken: "General Gates set a guard . . . at each door of the Sisters' House until the soldiers withdrew. The New England officers politely asked for quarters and most of the houses took some in. In the Congregation House, ten or twelve of the higher officers were lodged; and in town between 500 and 600 men."

From some of the officers passing through, the Moravians learned that General Lee, before his capture by the British a few days earlier, had something unpleasant in mind for them: "We were told

*Shippen overestimated the size of both Sullivan's and Gates's forces.

that Bethlehem had been represented to the army as a nest of Tories and that General Lee had said that in a few hours he would make an end of Bethlehem.''

Except for the hospital cases and the usual stragglers, Sullivan's troops began to leave Bethlehem the next day, the eighteenth, for the final stretch of their march to Washington's Bucks County encampment.

Gates's troops left Bethlehem a day later, December 19. Setting off with them, Chaplain Avery observed that several fellow members of the Massachusetts Fifteenth and others had to be left behind in the Single Brethren's House. Outside Bethlehem he encountered many other sick soldiers making their way toward that house. Some would never leave Bethlehem. Moravian carpenters were continuing to hammer out coffins and the single brethren were digging graves. Dr. Shippen's optimistic reports notwithstanding, within the next three months 110 of the soldier-patients would be buried in Bethlehem.

A day beyond Bethlehem, Chaplain Avery got to wondering about his own physical condition: was he facing another long bout of illness? "Snow this morning which prevented the soldiers marching far. My cough was so heavy and severe last night that I judged it entirely unsafe to proceed. Therefore lay by all day." While recuperating, he heard some of the latest complaints about the plundering by men on the march: "Am informed by the inhabitants that General Sullivan's men have stole most all the bees in this neighbourhood, besides many fowls." The next day Avery recovered enough to advance to Buckingham, about fourteen miles. Here he learned that the plunderers had been at it again. "Sullivan's division went from here this day. The people inform us that those men have done them great damage by stealing their bees &c &c." Coming along in the rear, Avery noted, was a supply of meat requisitioned, stolen, or otherwise obtained along the way: "We now have 500 head of fat cattle in the rear, this side Bethlehem, which have followed Sullivan's division." Some of the cattle, he added, had come all the way from Connecticut.

Sergeant John Smith continued to record details of the ongoing battles between the Pad Rounds and the plundered civilians. At a village south of Bethlehem, some men in Smith's company learned that "a rich Tory" lived nearby. "They went to him to get something to eat. He refused to give them anything to eat, where upon they took what they could find in his house to eat & drink & went their way, he having plenty of cyder & other sort of liquor & honey & butter which they took away & destroyed several hives of bees for him before his face."

Farther on, they pitched tents in the woods "where two of the Pad Rounds went on patrole & took 2 hives of bees & two geese & brought to our tents. I was called up to eat some honey with them for my cold, it being verey toothsom for that, and then turned in again." In the nights to come, the plunderers would continue to supplement the army's menu at the expense of Bucks County farmers.

Chaplain Avery, fifer Greenwood, and the others remaining with the Massachusetts Fifteenth reached Newtown, the county seat of Bucks, about five miles west of the Delaware, on Sunday, December 22. For Avery there was a pleasant surprise: here he met his brother Jabez, who was serving as a sutler (a sort of one-man general store) for one of the Continental regiments. In Newtown, as elsewhere along the route of march, Avery observed that the weary soldiers with him were not befriended by the people they were told they were fighting for: "We find the people cold and indisposed to show kindness to the army. The Quaker conscience will not allow of their treating those well who are engaged in war."

Newtown proved to be the end of the line for General Benedict Arnold, who had been in active command throughout most of the corps' march from the north. He and Colonel John Trumbull were given new orders. Both of them, Avery noted in his diary, "set off for Rhode Island." General Gates had meanwhile rejoined his troops and was now in active command.

Upon arriving in Newtown, young Greenwood discovered how serious his skin affliction, the itch that had made marching painful, really was: "I had the itch then so bad that my breeches stuck to my thighs, all the skin being off, and there were hundreds of vermin upon me, owing to a whole month's march and having been obliged, for the sake of keeping warm, to lie down at night among the soldiers who were huddled close together like hogs." In the days to come Greenwood would learn how widespread the civilian disenchantment with the war effort was: "Our country was filled with timid, designing Tories and informers of all descriptions."

Among those meanwhile, as Christmas drew near, marching to join Washington's force were numerous small contingents of volunteers. One of them was being led by a sixty-two-year-old clergyman named John Rosbrugh. He was pastor of the Allen Township Presbyterian Church in Northampton County, Pennsylvania, some fifty miles northwest of Philadelphia.

Rosbrugh had been serving at the Allen Township church since 1769 and living with his wife and children in a nearby hamlet called the Irish Settlement. It was one of several such places in the area inhabited largely by families from Scotland or Northern Ireland. Rosbrugh had been born in 1714, either just before the family left Scotland or just after they arrived in Northern Ireland en route to America, the exact date of his birth not being known. Several years after the death of his first wife, he married Jean Ralston, some twenty years his junior, and with her had had five children, the oldest nine and the youngest less than a year at the time when he set off for the war.

Small as it was, the Irish Settlement was abundantly represented in the struggle for independence. The community had, the previous summer, contributed its quota of young men to the reserve force known as the Flying Camp. Several members of Rosbrugh's parish were prisoners in New York, having been captured by the British during the attack on Fort Washington on November 16. One of those captured was Captain Benjamin Wallace, a brother-in-law of Mrs. Rosbrugh. And Mrs. Rosbrugh's brother, John Ralston, was serving in the Continental Congress.

One of the form letters sent to militia commanders apparently prompted John Rosbrugh, despite his age, to leave his family and go off to the battlefront. In a letter to Colonel John Siegfried of Allen Township, General Washington urged the militia to come "to the assistance of the Continental army, that by our joint endeavors, we may put a stop to the progress of the enemy, who are making preparations to advance to Philadelphia as soon as they cross the Delaware, either by boats or on the ice."

Rosbrugh called together the members of his congregation, read the appeal for help, and urged the men present to volunteer for action. If they would go, Rosbrugh said, he would accompany them as chaplain.

The men would go, it presently became clear, but they wanted Rosbrugh to be not just chaplain but their commanding officer. This would mean more danger, a greater chance that he would not return. Rosbrugh would have to get the consent of his wife. What would become of her and the five children if . . . ?

The next day, December 18, Rosbrugh made out his will, "calling to mind that my dissolution may be near at hand, and that it is appointed for all men once to die." In addition to his worldly goods, he bequeathed to his wife and children "the protection, mercy and grace of God, from whom I have received them, being encouraged thereto by God's gracious direction and faithful promise, Jer. 49:11 'Leave the fatherless children, I will preserve them alive; and let the widows trust in me.' "

He had already talked it over with his wife. His country was calling for help. How could he refuse? And if he went, the men would follow him. "Then go," Jean Rosbrugh had said, and it was settled.

Rosbrugh's congregation assembled in church again the following day. Some had "counted the cost" of leaving their families unprotected and hesitated to go. Rosbrugh told them he would accept their offer and become their commanding officer. Those who felt it was their duty not to enlist, he said, were free to go home, but they would be expected to take care not only of their own families but also those of the men enlisting. Those willing to go were to follow him.

Rosbrugh shouldered his musket, a French fusée, and walked out to the roadway. Four brothers—John, Robert, James, and Francis Hays—fell in with him, and so did all of the men of age who were present, the total number unspecified. Rosbrugh's nine-year-old son, James, rode the family's big gray horse by his father's side for a short distance. Then, as James would recall in later years, his father took him from the horse, kissed him and told him to go home to his mother and be a good boy until his father's return.

John Rosbrugh mounted the horse and rode off with his company. They crossed the Lehigh River and followed the old "Bethlehem Road" to Philadelphia, where they arrived on December 24. There Rosbrugh stayed overnight with his wife's brother, Congressman John Ralston, and wrote to his wife:

My Dearest Companion:

I gladly embrace the opportunity of telling you that I am still yours, and also in a tolerable state of health, through the tender mercy of our dear Lord. The important crisis seems to draw near, which I trust may decide the query whether Americans shall be slaves or free men. May God grant the latter, however dear it may cost.

All our company are in Philadelphia in health and in good spirits. They are under the command of General Putnam, and it is expected they will be ordered to the Jerseys tomorrow or next day. . . .

Farewell for a while. Please to present my compliments to Stephen and Nancy [the family servants] and to all the children. Praying that God may pour out his blessing upon you all, this from your truly affectionate husband:

Jno. Rosbrugh.

Still in Philadelphia on Christmas Day, Rosbrugh would miss participation in some of the forthcoming action, but, unfortunately for him and his family, not all of it.

When the anxiously awaited troops of Sullivan and Gates finally arrived, General Washington at last had, or so he hoped, enough of a force to make some sort of move against the enemy—a bold stroke that might turn things around, one that might save the collapsing revolution. He had been thinking about such a strike ever since getting his retreating troops across the Delaware to Pennsylvania during the weekend of December 7–8. After maintaining headquarters for about a week at "Summerseat," across the Delaware from Trenton, Washington and his aides had moved upstream about fourteen miles to the home of William Keith. But by December 20, when the troops from the north began to arrive, Washington was "at Camp above Trenton Falls," apparently the headquarters of Lord Stirling (Brigadier General William Alexander), four miles below Keith's. From that camp Washington reported that Sullivan's newly arrived men were "in a miserable plight; destitute of almost everything, many of them fit only for the hospital." Gates's were no better off. Moreover, very few of the men in either unit were willing to reenlist. They had had enough. By the end of the year therefore, and that was little more than a week off, Washington's force would be all but nonexistent. Would he ever be able to raise another army?

If anything was to be done against the enemy troops on the other side of the Delaware, it would have to be done within a few days. On paper, Washington now had more than 10,000 men. But of that number, largely because of disease and desertion, he could count on no more than about 6,000. Moreover, this total included many militiamen, weekend soldiers accustomed to home duty. In striking contrast to the ragged and fatigued Continentals, the militiamen, by and large, were outfitted in clean and intact uniforms. They had shoes—shoes without holes. Their muskets gleamed in the December sun. Their faces showed none of the wear and tear of serving in the field. But how they would perform in combat was anyone's guess.

Despite his reservations about his troops, Washington knew he had to act. His first plan was for an attack on enemy positions in the Mount Holly area, to take place on December 23. During the second week of December, Major General Israel Putnam, on duty as military officer in control of Philadelphia, had rounded up a force of 500 to 600 men—militiamen from southern Jersey, many of them mere boys, plus a few Virginians—and dispatched them across the Delaware to New Jersey under the command of Colonel Samuel Griffin, formerly of the inglorious Flying Camp. These troops marched out of Haddonfield, about thirty miles south of Trenton, on December 14 and advanced toward Mount Holly. They were to be reinforced for the attack by some 700 of Colonel Cadwalader's troops, who had been alerted to cross the Delaware from Bristol to Burlington, New Jersey, early in the morning of December 23.

On Friday, December 20, Colonel Joseph Reed left Colonel Cadwalader's headquarters in Bristol to get a first-hand report on Griffin's progress. He crossed the Delaware to Burlington and that night rode six miles southeastward to Mount Holly "to see what force Col. Griffin had & what assistance the attack then meditated on the enemy's cantonments could derive from him." At Mount Holly, Reed was disappointed to find Griffin "in bad health" and to learn "that his force was too weak to be depended on either in numbers or discipline, that all he expected was to make a division [a diversion?] and draw the notice of the enemy before whom he proposed to retire if they should advance in any force." After offering Griffin what encouragement he could, Reed "returned that night to Bristol and informed General Washington by letter of these circumstances." In the same letter Reed passed on some valuable intelligence picked up by a spy called Pomroy. The spy had just returned to Burlington, having crossed New Jersey by way of South Amboy, Brunswick, Princeton, and Cranbury. He estimated that there were 600 to 800 enemy troops in Brunswick and "a very considerable body of troops" in Princeton. Pomroy "understood they were settled in their winter quarters, and had given over further operations till the spring." In Burlington County he found enemy troops "scattered through all the farmers' houses, eight, ten, twelve and fifteen in a house, and rambling over the whole country."

Then on Saturday, December 21, General Washington received a piece of intelligence indicating that the enemy had *not* abandoned operations until spring. According to an intercepted letter written by a Loyalist serving with the British, the enemy was planning to take Philadelphia by December 26, or "as soon as ice is made." Commenting on this in a message to Congress, Washington wrote: "Had I entertained a doubt of General Howe's intentions to pass the Delaware . . . it would now be done away." The weather had turned colder and, near the shores of the Delaware, ice was beginning to form. During the winter the river usually froze over, permitting passage by foot.

On Monday, December 23, Washington made known his decision to make the "bold strike" he had for several days been planning and secretly discussing with his leading officers; it was now or never. Possibly because of the reported weakness of Colonel Griffin's force in the Mount Holly area, Washington had already abandoned the plan to send some of Colonel Cadwalader's troops against enemy positions below Trenton on December 23. Instead, on that day he sent a rider off with a message for Colonel Reed, on duty with Colonel Cadwalader in Bristol, informing him that one hour before daylight on Thursday, December 26, was "the time fixed for our attempt upon Trenton." Washington had hoped to make the attempt earlier but, he explained, "we could not ripen matters for our attack . . . so much out of sorts and so much in want of everything [were] the troops under Sullivan, etc."

The plan was to attack the enemy from four directions. While Washington and his Continental veterans marched on Trenton from the north, three other units would strike from points farther down the Delaware. Brigadier General James Ewing and a force of about 600 militiamen would cross the river to Trenton and secure the Assunpink bridge at the southern end of the town, thus preventing the enemy from escaping along the route to Bordentown. In the Bristol area, Colonel Cadwalader would cross with his troops and attack Hessian posts below Trenton. General Putnam, on duty in Philadelphia, was to send additional reinforcements to join with General Griffin's troops for an attack in the Mount Holly area. On Christmas Eve, however, Colonel Reed, having ridden from Bristol to Philadelphia, learned from Putnam that because of "the short-ness of time and the unprovided state of the militia," no reinforce-ments were available.

Thus, the most General Washington could hope for as he made final plans was help from Ewing's and Cadwalader's mostly untried troops. As the time for the strike drew near, the stress was visible in the commander in chief's countenance and behavior. On the day before Christmas he had a distinguished visitor, Benjamin Rush, the congressman and Philadelphia physician. During an hour's visit Dr. Rush found Washington to be "much depressed." He "lament-ed the ragged and dissolving state of his army in affecting terms." Rush assured him that Congress was firmly behind him despite "present difficulties and distresses." As they talked on, a preoccu-pied Washington from time to time scribbled on pieces of paper. One piece fell to the floor. In retrieving it, Rush noted what the general had been writing: "Victory or Death."

These words, as Rush would learn, were to be the password designated for the night of December 25–26 as Washington's troops advanced toward Trenton.

———— ◆◆◆ ————

CHAPTER 30

What Was There to Fear from the Rebels?

At Colonel Donop's headquarters in Bordentown on Sunday, De-cember 22, one of his aides noted, "there came news that there were about 800 rebels in Mount Holly . . . under the command of Colonel Griffin. They had two three-pounders with them and were posted in front of the church at Mount Holly." Some of the intelli-gence Donop received was from Lieutenant Colonel Thomas Ster-ling, in command of a regiment of Highlanders a few miles above Mount Holly. "A gentleman of credit," Sterling wrote, "has just come who informs me that 1000 of the rebels were certainly at Mount Holly and they were to be at one o'clock at Slabtown [Jacksonville] and that 2000 more were in the rear to support them which he heard came in to Mount Holly this morning. He likewise heard that Washington proposed to send over 1000 to 1500 men to Dunk's Ferry which is 3 miles from Burlington . . . to make a conjunction with the above." (Apparently a spy had heard of the rebels' plan for a two-pronged attack on December 23.)

In a second message, dispatched the same day, Sterling called for an attack: "The Rebels without doubt mean to beat up our quarters and drive us from hence from their approaching so near to us. I am therefore of the opinion . . . that we should not wait to be attacked . . . but that you Sir with the troops at Bordentown should come here and attack them before they have time to extend themselves so as to surround us or to form a plan to drive us from hence."

Late in the morning of the twenty-second, Donop, as he would recall, "went personally to Blackhorse [Columbus] but found that the enemy had not advanced any further than to the Meeting House this side of Mount Holly, except for some patrols. Hardly had I returned at 3 o'clock in the afternoon to Bordentown when the alarm-shots, for which I had arranged, were fired by the two battalions at Blackhorse. . . .

"I then returned as fast as possible to Blackhorse and there I found every man under arms, since as soon as I had left there 400 to 500 rebels had attacked the outpost at Petticoat Bridge.* They succeeded in nothing more than forcing the outpost troops, consisting of one under-officer and twelve Scottish Highlanders, to retire. Captain [Ernst] von Eschwege's [Hessian grenadier] company, stationed in a house nearby, came to their assistance as did the troops of the Scottish outpost and the grenadier post behind them, and this made it impossible for the rebels to advance one step further." In this skirmish "Captain von Eschwege's company had two wounded and the Scottish command had two slightly wounded."

The next day, December 23, Donop went into action: "In order to get rid of these troublesome guests I marched early . . . in the morning toward Mount Holly with the 42nd [Scottish] Regiment and the [Hessian] Block and Linsing battalions. I met several hundred rebels in front near the Meeting House. They took to flight after firing a few shots and retired with the others toward Moorestown. Their strength was about 1,000 men and they were commanded by Colonel Griffin.

"It was the fault of one of my patrols, who had advanced too far

*This bridge crossed the Petticoat Branch of Assiscunk Creek east of Blackhorse.

against my will, that I could not go after the enemy as effectively as I wished. There were no casualties and the rebels were said to have lost only three men by my cannonade which consisted of only a few shots."

In this action, as usual, Captain Johann Ewald and his jagers formed the advanced guard. "At Mount Holly," he noted, "the rebels were posted on a hill near the church with some 100 men but retired quickly . . . so that there was no fire except some cannon shots. We had no one wounded on our side. The colonel let the battalions bivouac at Mount Holly."

That night the Hessians went on a spree, finding large supplies of liquor, according to Ewald, and plundering almost every house in town. Ewald had great difficulty in trying to keep his jagers together. The grenadiers, who found most of the liquor, were even worse. For a long time to come, shocking stories would be reported: drunken Hessians roaring with laughter as they kicked a family Bible down the street . . . drunken Hessians smashing furniture . . . drunken Hessians carting off anything portable, even a pair of andirons.

Colonel Donop took quarters that night in one of Mount Holly's finest homes and there, unfortunately for the British cause, he met a comely young widow, who was said to be the only woman remaining in the town. In Burlington Mrs. Margaret Morris heard a day earlier that "all the women removed from [Mount Holly] except one widow of our acquaintance." Unfortunately, she did not identify the widow.

Although Colonel Griffin's skittish troops did little more than fire a few rounds and retreat in the skirmishes of December 22–23, they accomplished something that turned out to be of great tactical importance: drawing Colonel Donop and a large number of his troops from the Bordentown area all the way down to Mount Holly, eighteen miles south of Trenton. Moreover, in the eyes of American propagandists the ragged retreat of Griffin's men was virtually a victory. According to a report in the *Pennsylvania Evening Post* a few days later, on December 22 (when, according to Captain Ewald, the Americans were "driven back by the grenadiers with heavy losses"), the Hessians "were forced to retreat with precipitation, having some killed, and leaving behind them many knapsacks and other necessaries, amongst which was a hat shot through the crown."

The action of the next day, when the Americans were soundly

defeated and forced to flee from the area, was described thus: "The enemy advancing with a considerable reinforcement, supposed to be about two thousand men with seven or eight field pieces, our little army was obliged to retreat (which they performed with great regularity) to prevent their being outflanked by superior numbers; and in the evening they had another skirmish at Mount Holly, in which the enemy, as an intelligent person informs, had several killed and wounded. In both skirmishes our people had only two killed and seven or eight wounded. Our army is at Moorestown [about thirty miles south of Trenton] and that of the enemy is at Mount Holly."

Casualty statistics were anyone's guess. Robert McCallen, a soldier from Lancaster County, Pennsylvania, described the action in a few brief and not necessarily accurate lines: "There was a scrimedy at Mount Holly," he wrote his wife. "There were sixteen of the enemy killed. We had but one wounded."

George Ewing, who had joined Griffin's force as a volunteer, was probably no more accurate in the notes he wrote in his journal. Ewing had come home to Cohansey, in southwestern New Jersey, having completed his enlistment period with the Third New Jersey Regiment in the Canadian campaign. "The militia of these parts were up in arms," he had found on arriving home, "and I, more regardless of my own ease that my country's safety, joined them and marched to oppose the unjust invaders of our rights!"

Of the December 23 retreat he wrote: "The enemy came down to attack us, drove and followed our sentries in so quick that before we could parade they were upon us. However, we kept up a brisk fire upon them as we retired and, from the best account we could get, killed seven on the spot."

Colonel Joseph Reed, though not on the scene, made what was probably a more accurate report: "Colonel Griffin retired skirmishing with the enemy a few miles with little loss on either side & bringing off his artillery with him." Reed also noted the decoy effect of Griffin's mission: "This manouver, though perfectly accidental, had a happy effect as it drew off Count Donop who then commanded at Bordentown, with his whole force to Mount Holly."

Joseph Galloway agreed with Reed's observation. A few years later he would report: "In order to draw Colonel de Donop from his post at Bordentown, and to prevent his supporting Colonel Rall . . . he [General Washington] sent a corps of 450 militia, many of whom were boys picked up in Philadelphia and the counties of Gloucester and Salem, to Mount Holly, with orders not to fight, but fly as soon as the effect of the manoeuvre had taken place. The plan succeeded. Colonel de Donop marched against the insignificant part of the rebel force with his whole corps of 2,000 men (eighty left at Bordentown excepted), down to Mount Holly, twelve miles from his post and eighteen from Trenton, the post he ought to have been at hand to support. The rebel corps immediately fled, and dispersed on his approach; and yet, instead of immediately returning to Bordentown to support Colonel Rall, he remained loitering . . . without having a single enemy to oppose."

Donop's prolonged stay in Mount Holly was explained in these words in the journal of the Hessian Linsing Battalion: "On the 24th [of December] . . . Colonel von Donop remained in Mount Holly with the two other battalions and the jager company, first, to let the people longing for protection take an oath of allegiance to the King and, second, to collect forage and food in the neighborhood."

Captain Ewald, as one of Donop's closest subordinates, was in a position to know a third reason: Donop, a man "extremely devoted to the fair sex," had "found in his quarters an exceedingly beautiful young widow of a doctor." In Ewald's opinion, Donop's dalliance, now in its third day, helped to bring about what was to be one of the most disastrous events in Hessian military history.

Had this young woman been purposely placed in Mount Holly to attract the attention of Donop, who was known to be a ladies' man? Was she there as a spy? Both perhaps? So far, history has not provided the answers, but whoever and whatever she was, the widow made a major contribution, perhaps unintentionally, to the American cause.

The day before Christmas, Colonel Donop's second day in Mount Holly, was a blissful time in company with the comely widow. Donop sent parties out early to collect forage and cattle for slaughter. All was quiet. Not a rebel in sight. Then a reassuring message arrived from the quartermaster, Captain Thomas Gamble. It included a list of "prices fixed by General Grant for the different articles furnished the troops by the inhabitants of this province. . . . The inhabitants begin to bring in supplies and our magazine fills so that I hope we shall not be reduced to the disagreeable necessity of sending out forage parties." The inhabitants were to be paid in gold and silver for their hay, oats, Indian corn, wheat, flour, bran, pork, and beef. None of that paper money the rebels used.

A rebel trumpeter on horseback arrived under a white flag. He presented Donop with a proposal from the rebel general, Washington, for exchange of some Hessian officers recently captured. Was this a way of confirming the report that Donop was still in Mount Holly, still too far removed to support Colonel Rall at Trenton? Definitely so, according to Captain Ewald: "The next two days would show that this was a ruse to find out whether the colonel was still in Mount Holly or was already marching back to Bordentown, which every reasonable man desired, since Trenton as well as Mount Holly was without any further support."

In Burlington on the twenty-fourth all was quiet, and, Margaret Morris noted, the sailors who had threatened to bombard the town were gone with their galleys. She had meanwhile been relieved of an even greater fear: her son Dick was back home, his dreams of high adventure unfulfilled. Don Quixote, Jr., as she now called him, "to his mortification saw not one Hessian, light horse, or anything else worth seeing."

A few miles up the river, at Whitehill, her tavern and residence, Mary Field was continuing to play the bountiful hostess. Friendly Hessian officers dropped in as usual for afternoon tea. So did Jonathan Odell and Joseph Galloway. A quiet day. No sign of rebel activity across the river.

Farther up the Delaware, in Trenton, where 1,400 of Colonel Rall's troops were living in crowded quarters, Mrs. Reed, her ten-year-old daughter, and eight-year-old son were living in dread of what the Hessians occupying their house would do next. The Reeds were still confined to one room of the house, and lucky to be there; it was far better than the loft of the hen house, where they had been forced to spend some bone-chilling hours a few nights earlier. From their room Mrs. Reed and the children could hear the movements of the Hessians and their women, who were, as usual, ransacking the house.

With Christmas almost there, it was becoming clear, even to Colonel Rall, that Colonel Donop had been right in warning that troops stationed without relief in Trenton would become fatigued by constant alarms. Colonel Donop was also right, some of Rall's subordinate officers felt, in ordering redoubts built at the northern and southern edges of town. Donop had in recent days reiterated that order, but Rall continued to ignore it.

Nevertheless, he complained about being in a very exposed position—"liable to be attacked at any moment." And who cared about his predicament? Nobody! That letter of December 21 from General James Grant in Brunswick, for example: "I am sorry to hear your brigade has been fatigued or alarmed. You may be assured that the rebel army in Pennsylvania . . . does not exceed eight thousand men who have neither shoes nor stockings, are in fact almost naked, dying of cold, without blankets, and very ill supplied with provisions. On this side of the Delaware they have not three hundred men. These stroll about in small parties under the command of subaltern officers none of them above the rank of captain, and their principal object is to pick up some of our Light Dragoons." Ha! Rall fumed in a message to Colonel Donop, General Grant "knows the strength of the enemy thirty miles off better than we do here."

Colonel Rall's contradictory protestations and actions must have confused some of his fellow officers. One day he would express the need for reinforcements, the next he would reject reinforcement by a large contingent of British troops, sending them back to Princeton, whence they had come. One day he would complain about the imminence of a rebel attack; the next he would minimize the danger: Let the rebels come! Concerned as he obviously was about the debilitating effect the rebels' sporadic, hit-and-run strikes were having on his men, he acted as if he believed the rebels would not actually dare to attack his vaunted grenadiers, fusiliers, and jagers— would not dare to fight like men.

As for the troops, some of them at least were still hopeful that they could winter in Philadelphia. One of Rall's grenadiers, Johannes Reuber, noted in his diary on December 19 that the Delaware River "started to freeze and this made us happy." Apparently unaware of General Howe's official closing of the campaign five days earlier, Reuber went on: "We were hoping to cross the river and take Philadelphia."

On duty at the river's edge the next day, Reuber noted: "The ice was becoming rather thick on the Delaware but it was not strong enough to cross. We had to be patient. Some inhabitants of the town passed on a report that the rebels were about to make a surprise attack on us. We discounted this since we were sure the rebels could not do so."

On December 21, according to Reuber, Colonel Rall decided to have a look himself at what the rebels were up to along the Delaware: "Early in the morning Commander Rall selected a strong force from his brigade and also a cannon and we were ordered to march in two divisions along the Delaware to see about the Americans attempting to cross the river to make an attack. There was no sign of it. We could see the Americans on the other side of the river." Back in Trenton, "all was quiet. An order was given that every night . . . all soldiers must be fully dressed just as if they were on watch duty. The officers and sergeants were ordered to see that this order was carried out."

The next day, the twenty-second, "we watched the Delaware again." The area was "completely quiet." At a point out of their visual range, however, a small party of rebels rowed across the river, apparently undetected by any of the troops on sentry duty. "They set fire to several houses and as the houses were burning they crossed back to their side of the river."

Such raids as these, Lieutenant Colonel Francis Scheffer warned, were part of a scheme to divert Colonel Rall's attention from the ferry crossings above Trenton. Scheffer, commanding officer of the Lossberg Regiment, had already joined in a formal complaint about Rall's handling of the brigade. Now, he complained, there was too much attention given to doings in the Trenton area and not enough to the ferry crossings a few miles up the Delaware. This, said Scheffer, at age fifty-four a veteran of thirty-five years of service, could be a costly mistake.

In recent days Colonel Rall had rejected this and other warnings that the rebels were about to make a full-scale attack on Trenton. Rall brushed aside such reports as "old women's talk." Among those who passed on such a warning was Dr. William Bryant, a British sympathizer who lived at the Bloomsbury Farm (now the Trent House), an extensive estate near the Delaware (where Johannes Reuber's company was doing guard duty). A Negro had just crossed the river from Pennsylvania, Bryant informed Rall a few days before Christmas, and reported that the rebels had drawn extra rations and were preparing to attack Trenton. Two deserters from the rebel army told Rall the same thing in the presence of two other Hessian officers.

On Christmas morning Colonel Rall received a warning from General Grant. It was datelined "Brunswick 24th Dec. 1776 past eleven at night." Grant had dispatched it to Colonel Donop, with a copy to Rall. "Washington," Grant wrote, "has been informed that our troops have marched into winter quarters and has been told that we are weak at Trenton and Princeton and Lord Stirling expressed a wish to make an attack on these two places. I don't believe he will attempt it, but be assured that my information is undoubtedly true, so I need not advise you to be upon your guard against an unexpected attack at Trenton. I think I have got into a good line of intelligence which will be of use to us all."*

On Christmas Day, Major von Dechow, it would later be testified, "made the proposition . . . to send away the baggage as it was only an encumbrance in case of an attack." But "Colonel Rall replied ridiculing and belittling the suggestion." This is how Rall's reply would later be recalled: "Fiddlesticks! These clod-hoppers will not attack us, and should they do so, we will simply fall on them and rout them!" Rall did, however, respond that day to still another warning: a party of rebels was on the prowl near Trenton. Rall rode around the outer limits of the town with a contingent of troops. He checked the guard and picket stations, found all to be quiet, and, late in the afternoon, returned to his headquarters, the home of Stacy Potts on King Street.

Rall was playing checkers with Potts when, around 7:30 p.m., he heard the sounds of small arms fire coming from the northwest sector of the town. The picket house on the Pennington Road! Rall dashed out of the house, mounted his horse, and in short order was leading some quickly alerted troops up King Street toward the high ground where the Pennington and Maidenhead roads came together. Presently he heard the bad news: a band of rebels, forty or fifty of them, had attacked the men on picket duty—a corporal and fifteen men—wounded six of them, and disappeared.

"The entire garrison was aroused and ordered under arms and a detachment of Rall's Regiment was sent out to see what was going on," Lieutenant Andreas Wiederholdt would report. "But that was all he did, outside of sending me with nine more men and one non-commissioned officer as a reinforcement of this post. The [Rall] detachment had already returned before I reached the post. Obvi-

---

*A spy or spies apparently close to the doings at Washington's headquarters reported to Grant that an attack on Trenton was discussed two days earlier at a meeting attended by Washington, Stirling, and other leading officers.

ously it had not been very far out. A vigilant commanding officer would have sent out reconnoitering parties to search all the roads as far as the river as well as the ferries in order to find them all quiet and peaceful or discover the enemy and not to come home before this was accomplished."

Upon reaching his post, Wiederholdt "ordered seven sentries. . . . I sent out patrol after patrol and warned them to be on their guard for any surprise." Finding nothing to report, the patrols eventually returned to take shelter in the picket house. "The night passed quietly."

Major Dechow had meanwhile—here again the weather was a deciding factor—issued orders canceling the next morning's predawn patrol because of the heavy storm. It had been his daily practice to go out the river road about two hours before daylight with a strong patrol accompanied by two cannon. Had he not neglected his duty, a major Hessian defeat might have been averted. Ironically, Dechow had joined Lieutenant Colonel Scheffer a few days earlier in complaining to General Heister about Rall's negligence. Heister, in New York, had received the letter of complaint on Christmas Eve, too late, as things were about to turn out, to do anything about it even if he had been so inclined.

After dismissing his troops, Rall dropped in on Abraham Hunt, a well-to-do merchant and the town postmaster, whose home stood at the northwest corner of Second and King streets (State and Warren), a short distance from brigade headquarters. There he would spend most of the night, supping, drinking his bottle, and playing cards. So *this* was the attack that Grant and the others had warned about. Ha! The crisis was over. What was there to fear from soldiers who were "nothing but a lot of farmers"?

An officer in the Lossberg Regiment, never identified, agreed with Rall's opinion of the rebels as soldiers but he was concerned about the effect these raids were having on his men. "We have not slept one night in peace since we came to this place," he confided to his diary (which was found a few days later by an American). "The troops have lain on their arms every night and they can endure it no longer."

However, like Colonel Rall, he minimized the possibility of a full-scale attack by the rebels. "We give ourselves more trouble and uneasiness than is necessary. For it is certainly not to be supposed that men who will not fight without some defense before them, who have neither coat, shoe nor stocking, nor scarce anything else to cover their bodies, and who for a long time past have not received a farthing of pay, would dare to attack regular troops in the open country—something they could not withstand even when they were posted amongst rocks and in the strongest entrenchments." What was there to fear from such a force?

PART FOUR

Some Lucky Chance May Turn Up

CHAPTER 31

Boats Were in Readiness

It was Christmas afternoon and the Continentals under General Washington's direct command in Bucks County—many of whom indeed had neither coat, shoe, nor stocking, nor scarce anything else to cover their bodies—were either preparing to march or already on the move. An hour or so before the sun would set at 4:35 o'clock,* John Greenwood, the sixteen-year-old fifer from Massachusetts, trudged out of Newtown in formation with his company and headed eastward, toward the Delaware River. He was still suffering from "the camp itch" and it showed in the way he gimped along. It was not as painful as it had been on the march from Ticonderoga—ointment had eased the pain considerably—but his thighs were still raw and scabbed. Greenwood was not just a fifer now; he was carrying a musket and about sixty rounds of ammunition stuffed into various pockets. And three days' cooked rations (heavily salted meat and hard bread). This, he figured, must be it, the marching order they had been expecting. But where were they going? Faithful to the enlisted man's long-standing credo, he was certain that anywhere at all would be better than where he had been. But where was it to be this time?

"None but the first officers knew where we were going or what we were going about," Greenwood would later recall, "for it was a secret expedition, and we, the bulk of the men coming from Canada, knew not the disposition of the army we were then in, nor anything about the country. This was not unusual, however, as I never heard soldiers say anything, nor ever saw them trouble them-

*The time of sunset, according to Timothy Trueman's *Burlington Almanac*.

selves, as to where they were or where they were led. It was enough for them to know that wherever the officers commanded they must go, be it through fire and water, for it was all the same owing to the impossibility of being in a worse condition than their present one, and therefore the men always liked to be kept moving in expectation of bettering themselves."

In all, some 2,400 Continentals were on their way to the assembly area centering on Samuel McKonkey's ferry, eight miles up the Delaware from Trenton (and thus also known as Eight-Mile Ferry).* "The regiments have had their evening parade," one of Washington's aides noted,† "but instead of returning to their quarters are marching toward the ferry. It is fearfully cold and raw and a snowstorm settling in. The wind is northeast and beats in the faces of the men. It will be a terrible night for the soldiers who have no shoes. Some of them have tied old rags around their feet; others are barefoot but I have not heard a man complain." It had been a mostly sunny day, with the thermometer around 32 degrees and the wind light out of the north. In the afternoon, however, there had been a shift of the wind and a falling barometer; a heavy storm of snow and sleet from the south was on its way. Although "settling in," it would not arrive until about an hour before midnight.

Under orders, the Continentals marched in silence toward the ferry house. "A profound silence to be enjoined," Washington had ordered, "and no man to quit his ranks on the pain of death." Earlier in the day, each regimental commander had received such an order as this: "You are to see that your men have three days' provisions ready cooked before 12 o'clock this forenoon—the whole fit for duty except a Serjeant and six men to be left with the baggage, and to parade precisely at four in the afternoon with their arms, accoutrements and ammunition in the best order, with their provisions and blankets. You will have them told off in divisions in which order they are to march—eight men abreast, with the officers fixed to their divisions from which they are on no account to separate. No man is to quit his division on pain of instant punishment. Each officer is to provide himself with a piece of white paper stuck in his hat for a field mark. You will order your men to

---

*Now Washington Crossing, Pennsylvania.

†Not definitely identified but believed by many to be Lieutenant Colonel John Fitzgerald. The diary is apparently a reconstruction of events.

assemble and parade them in the valley immediately over the hill on the back of McKonkey's Ferry, to remain there for farther orders."

John Greenwood was marching, as he had marched from the north, with the remains of Colonel John Paterson's Fifteenth Massachusetts Regiment, now part of General Arthur St. Clair's brigade. So was Chaplain David Avery, having recovered from the fits of illness that afflicted him during the march from the north to Bucks County.

Avery had anticipated today's alert. Two days earlier, like many others, including some enemy spies, he had heard something was up. "General orders for the army to be equipt for battle on a moment's notice," he noted in his diary, "as the General expects to attack soon."

On Christmas morning Avery left his horse with a new friend, Christian Van Horn, in Newtown, "as we expect to be gone upon an expedition, some time." He also "left a shirt and tenting irons in a white holland handkerchief in the care of Mr. William Ashburn in Newtown, a little more than half quarter mile north of the Presbyterian Church."

With the rest of St. Clair's brigade, Chaplain Avery and young Greenwood reached the ferry area about two hours after dark. It was a confused and crowded scene, and becoming more so as more units arrived. The men of the Fifteenth took off their packs and waited, and waited some more.

General St. Clair's aide, Major James Wilkinson, was among those missing at McKonkey's Ferry, absent not without leave, but not with St. Clair's blessing either. This was the second time he had taken leave recently. Back in Sussex County, New Jersey, about two weeks earlier, he had left St. Clair to deliver the message that General Horatio Gates had written Washington—the mission that ended with Wilkinson's being on the scene when General Lee was captured.

Now Wilkinson, as usual, was taking part in some unusual doings. This time, he was off to Philadelphia with General Gates. On the day before Christmas, Wilkinson would report in his memoirs, General Gates pressed him to come along on a ride to Philadelphia. Gates, the recipient of that *"Entre nous, a certain great man is most damnably deficient"* letter from General Lee, was ailing, or so he had indicated. Like Lee and many another high-ranking officer, he had lost faith in Washington as a military man. He felt an attack on the enemy at this time would be a mistake and wanted no part of it. Washington had appealed to him to take over for Colonel John Cadwalader as commander of the troops down in the Bristol area. "If you could only stay there two or three days," Washington had pleaded, "I should be glad." But Gates had begged off, and soon he would be on his way not only to Philadelphia but on to Baltimore, where the Congress now had its headquarters. There he would give a disparaging report on Washington as leader and present his own views on winning the war.

Wilkinson had asked General St. Clair for permission to accompany Gates to Philadelphia. In granting permission, St. Clair "observed that he should have no objection if he did not think it interested my honour, at that time, to remain with the brigade." *At that time*—the eve of Washington's planned movement against the enemy. Stunned by St. Clair's implication, Wilkinson decided not to go off with Gates. St. Clair's response "was incomprehensible to me and, not understanding it, I laid less stress upon it than I ought to have done. I, however, determined to abandon all thoughts of the ride to Philadelphia." But not for long. When he rode into Newtown on the morning of December 24 to take leave of General Gates he was prevailed on to change his mind, "and we set out for the city the same day.

"On the road the General appeared much depressed in mind, and frequently expressed the opinion that while General Washington was watching the enemy above Trenton, they would privately construct batteaux, pass the Delaware in his rear, and take possession of Philadelphia before he was aware of the movement." Instead of attempting in vain to stop the British army at the Delaware River, Gates added, "General Washington ought to retire to the south of the Susquehanna and there form an army." It was General Gates's intention, according to Wilkinson, "to propose this measure to Congress at Baltimore and [he] urged me to accompany him to that place."

Wilkinson was tempted; Baltimore was only a short distance from his home. But, perhaps mindful of St. Clair's implication about his honor, he decided not to go on with Gates. "The proposition, after eighteen months' absence from home, was tempting, but my duties forbade the thought."

He and Gates found Philadelphia a gloomy, silent place: "It was dark when we entered Front Street, and it appeared as if we had

penetrated a wilderness of houses. Such was the silence and still-
ness which prevailed that the dropping of a stone would have been
heard several squares, and the hoofs of our horses resounded in all
directions." At the City Tavern they encountered, among others,
some adherents of Joseph Galloway and the Allen brothers who had
recently gone over to the British. An "unpleasant altercation" between them and Gates ensued. Later, Gates "wrote a letter to the
commander in chief, with which he charged me and I took leave of
him."

Early the next morning, Christmas, Wilkinson was on his way
back to Newtown: "On my arrival there I discovered, to my surprise,
that General Washington had transferred his headquarters to that
place* and had himself marched with the troops in that neighbourhood. From Colonel Harrison, the General's secretary, who had
been left in charge of his papers, I received the necessary directions, and proceeded in quest of the troops." It was a ride of about
six and a half miles to McKonkey's Ferry on the Delaware, where
the troops were assembling, and it proved to be an easy route to
follow: "There was a little snow on the ground, which was tinged
here and there with blood from the feet of the men who wore
broken shoes."

At McKonkey's Ferry, now bustling with activity, Wilkinson
sought out Washington: "I found him alone with his whip in his
hand, prepared to mount his horse." Wilkinson handed the commander in chief the letter from Gates. Washington, furious, asked:
"What a time is this to hand me letters!" Wilkinson replied that he
had been ordered by Gates to deliver it.

"By General Gates! Where is he?"

"I left him this morning in Philadelphia."

"What was he doing there?"

"I understood him that he was on his way to Congress."

Exasperated, Washington could only repeat: "On his way to
Congress!"

As the general quickly broke the seal to read the letter (whose
contents are not known), Wilkinson made his bow and rode off to

---

*On Christmas Eve, while Washington was meeting with his leading officers at
Samuel Merrick's house in Buckingham, General Greene's headquarters, his own
headquarters papers and equipment were transferred from the Keith house, below
Coryell's Ferry, to Newtown. Washington himself apparently spent the night of
December 24–25 at the Keith house instead of coming on to Newtown.

join his commanding officer, General St. Clair, on the bank of the Delaware.

"Boats were in readiness," Wilkinson found, "and troops began to cross about sunset, but the force of the current, the sharpness of the frost, the darkness of the night, the ice which made during the operation, and a high wind rendered the passage of the river extremely difficult. And but for the stentorian lungs of and extraordinary exertions of Colonel [Henry] Knox, it could not have been effected."

Colonel Henry Knox's voice was, as one soldier would recall, "a deep bass," and at McKonkey's Ferry it was "heard above the crash of the ice which filled the river." Knox—six feet three and 280 pounds—was using his deep bass to direct the river crossings, across and back, across and back . . .

Lucy Flucker Knox, back home in Fairfield, Massachusetts, would have been proud of her Harry, as she called him. She would be with the army now if she had had her way; she had begged in her letters for permission to be with him. A member of a prominent Tory family, Lucy had married Knox, a struggling bookseller and supporter of the rebellion, over her parents' objections. Harry Knox was not what they had had in mind for their girl.

He was a son of an Irish immigrant who failed in business and ran off to the West Indies. Harry was nine years old when his father abandoned the family. He left school early and got a job in a bookstore to support his mother and younger brother, Billy. By the age of twenty-one he had his own little place, the London Book Store, in Boston. In June 1775, at the age of twenty-five, he turned the store over to Billy and set off for the war, leaving his beloved Lucy and their newborn child behind. Before long, even though he was lacking in experience, he was given command of the Continental Artillery Regiment, a unit very short of artillery. Late in 1775 he headed an expedition to Fort Ticonderoga to get some big guns needed in the Boston siege. He rounded up some fifty cannon, howitzers and mortars. He put them on ox-drawn sledges and led what he liked to call his "noble train of artillery" three hundred difficult miles to Boston. Emplaced on Dorchester Heights, these heavy guns enabled the Americans to end the siege successfully in March 1776. A short time later the British evacuated Boston.

Knox and his artillery regiment rendered valuable service in the fighting around New York and in the retreat across New Jersey. Along the way, whenever possible, he wrote letters to his Lucy, whom he addressed as "My Dearly Beloved Friend." Of the Christmas-night crossing of the Delaware he would inform her that it was done "with almost infinite difficulty, with eighteen field pieces. The floating ice in the river made the labor almost incredible. However, perseverance accomplished what at first seemed impossible."

Much of the perseverance was exhibited by a remarkably resourceful and uncommonly integrated unit, Colonel John Glover's Fourteenth Massachusetts Continental Regiment—the Marbleheaders. This regiment, unusual for its time in that it included black as well as white men, was accustomed to accomplishing the impossible. It was these men who had helped to rescue Washington's army following the disastrous Battle of Long Island.

From sundown on Christmas Day until around three the following morning, Colonel Knox rounded up the boatloads of men and horses and artillery, and the Marbleheaders got them through the ice-choked river to the New Jersey shore. Over and back they went, over and back, in a great variety of vessels, including McKonkey's ferry boat and that of Johnson, whose ferry house was on the New Jersey side of the river. The Marbleheaders relied heavily on Durham boats, which, along with other types of vessels, had been secured behind Malta Island, situated near the western bank of the Delaware a short distance above McKonkey's Ferry. Boats had also been kept in readiness nearby in Knowles Creek, which flowed into the river a short distance above the island. The Durham boats, black as tar, forty or more feet long, and about eight feet wide, carried loads up to fifteen tons and drew less than two feet of water. They were customarily used to carry iron ore, grain, and other freight from upstream to Philadelphia. Although unaccustomed to such boats, the Marblehead men, using poles as well as oars, got them across without losing a man or a horse or an artillery piece. The nearest thing to a casualty would be reported by Colonel John Haslet of Delaware: "I fell into the water and I have been suffering from piles ever since."

"There was an appearance of discipline in this corps," Captain Alexander Graydon said of the Marbleheaders. "The officers seemed to have mixed with the world, and to understand what belonged to their stations. Though deficient in polish, [the corps] possessed an apparent aptitude for the purpose of its institution, and gave confidence that myriads of its meek and lowly brethren were incompetent to inspire."

But the admiring captain, like many another accustomed to all-white units, found the Marbleheaders' integrated condition distasteful: "Even in this regiment there were a number of negroes, which, to persons unaccustomed to such associations, had a disagreeable, degrading effect."

Colonel Glover, the Marbleheaders' forty-four-year-old commanding officer, was, like Knox, anything but a career soldier. He had served in the militia before the war and he had risen from apprentice shoemaker to liquor salesman to wealthy shipowner and merchant. But he had developed into an able officer and earned the respect of his men. One of them was his son John, a company commander.

Glover's men and Knox's collaborated in the crossings of the night in a herculean task that was to pay great dividends: transporting eighteen artillery pieces across the river. This was an exceptional number of big guns for the size of the force, about three times the usual ratio. There were two six-pounder guns and two 5.5-inch howitzers of the Second Company of the Pennsylvania State Artillery, commanded by Captain Thomas Forrest; two six-pounder guns of the New York State Artillery Company, commanded by Captain Alexander Hamilton; and three three-pounder guns of the New York Company of the Continental Artillery, commanded by Captain Sebastian Bauman. There were two six-pounder guns of the Massachusetts Company of Continental Artillery, commanded by Captain-Lieutenant Winthrop Sargent; two three-pounder guns of the Eastern Company of New Jersey State Artillery, commanded by Captain Daniel Neil; two three-pounder guns of the Western Company of New Jersey State Artillery, commanded by Captain Samuel Hugg; and three four-pounder guns of the Second Artillery Company of Philadelphia Associators, commanded by Captain Joseph Moulder.

Not one of these field guns had been lost in the retreat across New Jersey, or in the crossing of the Delaware to Pennsylvania on the weekend of December 7–8, and not one would be lost in tonight's crossing back to New Jersey. These were the bad-weather weapons of the army and their payloads were capable of tearing apart humans and horses and demolishing buildings. Unlike muskets and other hand weapons that were unreliable in rain or snow, the artillery pieces could, with care on the part of the cannoneers, be kept in firing condition even in a heavy storm. The vents and muzzles could be plugged so that the interiors of the weapons were kept dry. Tonight the guns were being handled with all possible care. Washington was relying heavily on their firepower; they had figured prominently in his planning. So had the reliability and leadership qualities of Colonels Glover and Knox.

Like Glover and Knox, the rest of the American field officers came from backgrounds more civilian than military. Even His Excellency, the commander in chief, was just a country squire and farmer who, in the opinion of even some of his closest associates, was hardly qualified to command an army. Motions in Congress to replace him, frequently made since the Fort Washington disaster, were still being heard. As for the two men now next in command, Generals Sullivan and Greene, what did they know about fighting a war against experienced military professionals? Sullivan, thirty-six, knew more about the law than about soldiering and thus far had shown no exceptional qualities as a leader. Greene, thirty-four, had toiled in the family iron foundry in Rhode Island before setting up a forge of his own. He was the son of a Quaker clergyman but he had been read out of the local Friends' meeting because of his support of the rebellion. Then in 1774 he was denied the rank of lieutenant in the Kentish Guards, a unit he had helped to organize, because he limped as a result of a knee injury suffered in childhood, and what company wanted to be led on the parade ground by a cripple? He joined the guards anyway, as a private. But in 1775, when Rhode Island raised three regiments, the command was given to Greene and he was made a brigadier general. Now he was a major general but—like Sullivan—not without his critics. He was perhaps best known for his role in the disaster at Fort Washington in which some 2,800 sorely needed troops had been captured.

Brigadier General Hugh Mercer, fifty-one, a native of Scotland, had been a physician and proprietor of an apothecary shop in Fredericksburg, Virginia, when, in 1775, he informed the Virginia House of Burgesses that he would "serve his adopted country and the cause of liberty in any rank or station" to which he might be appointed.

And what of the other leading officers who were about to take on a well-trained and disciplined force of troops commanded by career militarists? Brigadier General Adam Stephen, fifty-eight, had served in the French and Indian War, had been politically active in his native Virginia, and had fought against the Cherokees in 1761. A heavy drinker and a braggart, he was known for ordering spectacular but unauthorized and usually ineffective moves in combat. Brigadier General Fermoy, about forty, was, according to Major James Wilkinson, "a worthless drunkard." He had been recently commissioned on the strength of his claim to be a French colonel of engineers. Brigadier General Arthur St. Clair, forty-two, owned mills and a large estate in Pennsylvania's Ligonier Valley. He had served in recent years as a surveyor, a judge, and a county probate officer. Born in Scotland, he had come to America in 1757 and served in the French and Indian War.

Colonel George Weedon, forty-six, had been an innkeeper in his native Fredericksburg, Virginia, and had somehow earned the nickname "Joe Gourd." Colonel Edward Hand, thirty-two, had been practicing medicine in the Lancaster area at the outbreak of war. He had sailed from Ireland to America in 1774 as a surgeon's mate in the Eighteenth Royal Irish Regiment, a post he resigned shortly after arriving. Colonel John Haslet, also a native of Ireland, first studied for the ministry, then turned to medicine and was practicing in Delaware and serving in the Delaware assembly before the war. Colonel Charles Scott, about forty, had been active in Virginia politics and would one day be governor of Kentucky. Colonel John Stark, fifty-eight, had in recent years engaged in farming in his native New Hampshire. Brought up as a hunter and Indian fighter, he had served as a major in Robert Rogers's Rangers during the French and Indian War.

Colonel Paul Dudley Sargent, thirty-one, and his nephew, Captain-Lieutenant Winthrop Sargent, twenty-three, were both on the scene. Colonel Sargent was the son of a Massachusetts judge. He had studied law and following the war would himself become a judge. He had been wounded at Bunker Hill. Winthrop Sargent, a native of Gloucester, Massachusetts, and a graduate of Harvard, had been captaining one of his father's merchant ships before joining bookseller Knox's regiment of artillery. Colonel William Shepard, thirty-nine, was also from Massachusetts. He had enlisted at age seventeen to take part in the French and Indian War. Before enlisting for the Revolution he had been a farmer, a selectman, and a member of the Committee of Correspondence in Westfield, Massachusetts.

Colonel John Paterson, Colonel John Chester, and Lieutenant Colonel Samuel Blachley Webb were all natives of Wethersfield, Connecticut, and were all political activists. Paterson, thirty-two, was a 1762 graduate of Yale. He had taught school for a few years in Wethersfield, then had turned to the practice of law. After moving to Lenox, Massachusetts, he had been named to the Massachusetts Provincial Congress in 1774 and 1775. Chester, thirty-two, was also a lawyer and a graduate of Yale. He had served in the Connecticut legislature and one day would become speaker of the house. Webb, twenty-three, had worked as private secretary to his stepfather, Congressman Silas Deane, before enlisting. He had been wounded at both Bunker Hill and White Plains. At least one other Connecticut politician was on the march with Washington: Colonel Charles Webb, fifty-two, a native of Stamford. He had been chosen twenty-three consecutive times to serve in the Connecticut legislature.

General Stephen and his "brigade" (the remains of three Virginia regiments, about 500 officers and men in all) were the first troops to cross the Delaware. Upon landing on the New Jersey shore, he was under orders to select from his troops "a guard to form a chain of sentries round the landing-place at a sufficient distance from the river to permit the troops to form, this guard not to suffer any person to go in or come out, but to detain all persons who attempt either. This guard to join their brigade when the troops are all over."

General Mercer's depleted brigade was the next to cross and then came Lord Stirling's, followed by General Fermoy's and the rest. Over and back, over and back through the ice-choked river. So it went as the Marbleheaders carried the bulk of the Continental force across. It was tedious work and it was taking far longer than anticipated. They would never get to Trenton before daybreak. According to Washington's plan, his troops would all be across the Delaware by midnight. Then they would march nine miles through the darkness and reach Trenton before dawn.* Before midnight, however, it was clear that they would not be able to arrive at Trenton until well after daylight. How, at that hour, would they be able to take the enemy by surprise?

John Greenwood, the young fifer, was one of the Continentals standing near bonfires and waiting on the New Jersey bank. Greenwood and his company were among those who had crossed early in

---

*Although they crossed the Delaware eight miles above Trenton, the circuitous routes taken by both columns measured nine miles.

the evening in a Durham boat—"a flat-bottomed scow," he called it. "We had to wait for the rest and so began to pull down the fences and make fires to warm ourselves, for the storm was increasing rapidly. After a while it rained, hailed, snowed, and froze, and at the same time blew a perfect hurricane; so much so that . . . after putting the rail on to burn, the wind and the fire would cut them in two in a moment, and when I turned my face toward the fire my back would be freezing. However, as my usual acuteness had not forsaken me, by turning round and round I kept myself from perishing before a large bonfire.

"The noise of the soldiers coming over and clearing away the ice, the rattling of the cannon wheels on the frozen ground, and the cheerfulness of my fellow-comrades encouraged me beyond expression, and, big coward as I acknowledge myself to be, I felt great pleasure."

This was the scene around three a.m., as reported by the officer thought to be Colonel Fitzgerald: "I am writing from the ferry house. The troops are all over, and the boats have gone back for the artillery. We are three hours behind the set time. Glover's men have had a hard time to force the boats through the floating ice with the snow drifting in their faces.

"I never have seen Washington so determined as he is now. He stands on the bank of the river, wrapped in his cloak, superintending the landing of the troops. He is calm and collected, but very determined. The storm is changing to sleet, and cuts like a knife."

Three a.m., and it would be almost another hour before the troops would be ready for the nine-mile march to Trenton. Damn! Was this going to be another disaster? Fort Washington . . . Fort Lee . . . and now Trenton? It would be broad daylight by the time they arrived there. There were spies everywhere. The Hessians would be alerted.

Washington's plan to attack the enemy had not been a well-kept secret. Tory sympathizers in the area heard about it and passed the word on to the enemy. Robert Morris, still on duty in Philadelphia, mentioned it in a letter he wrote to Washington on December 21: "I have been told today that you are preparing to cross into the Jerseys. I hope it may be true, and promise myself joyful tidings from your expedition. You have my sincere prayers for success."

In a letter written to Robert Morris a few hours before crossing the Delaware, Washington was optimistic despite all the recent setbacks: "I agree with you that it is in vain to ruminate upon or even reflect upon the authors or causes of our present misfortunes; we should rather exert ourselves to look forward with hopes that some lucky chance may yet turn up in our favor."

It appeared he might be pushing his luck when, shortly before the crossing, Washington received some ominous news from Colonel Joseph Reed, who was with Colonel Cadwalader's 1,800 men in the Bristol area, about twenty miles downstream. Things were not going well down there, according to a message from Reed.* Around six p.m., from the Pennsylvania shore, Washington reacted in a hasty note to Cadwalader: "Notwithstanding the discouraging accounts I have received from Colonel Reed of what might be expected from our operations below, I am determined, as the night is favourable, to cross the river and make the attack upon Trenton in the morning. If you can do nothing real, at least create as great a diversion as possible."

The crossing at McKonkey's Ferry had started on schedule, and Washington had thought, as he later would report to Congress, that "we should be able to throw them all over, with the necessary artillery, by twelve o'clock, and that we might early arrive at Trenton by five in the morning, the distance being about nine miles. But the quantity of ice made that night impeded the passage of the boats so much that it was three o'clock before the artillery could all be got over, and near four before the troops took up their line of march.

"This made me despair of surprising the town as I well knew we could not reach it before the day was fairly broke. But as I was certain there was no making a retreat without being discovered and harrassed on repassing the river, I determined to push on at all events."

Three men familiar with the area—David Laning, John Guild, and John Muirhead—rode on horseback and "in plain farmer's habit"† in advance of the leading troops as the army set off from the riverbank for Birmingham, a march of about four and a half miles. Laning, according to his wife, had escaped from confinement the previous afternoon. A few days before that, according to her ac-

---

*Like many other such documents, Reed's message was apparently not preserved.

†As several eyewitnesses would report years later to the Reverend Eli F. Cooley, a local historian. Cooley got the story about Laning (also spelled Lanning) from Mrs. Laning.

count, he had been taken prisoner in "the Scudder neighborhood," above Trenton, by a Hessian scouting party and confined in a house in the town. He made his escape a day before Christmas, hid out in a friend's house overnight, and then, "dressed in an old ragged coat and flapped hat, put an axe under his arm and went with his head down, limping along, and so passed in safety the enemy's sentries in the character of a wood chopper." After assisting in ferrying the troops across the Delaware, Laning joined the two other volunteer "farmers."

Astride a chestnut sorrel horse, General Washington was being escorted by a personal bodyguard made up of young volunteers from some of Philadelphia's leading families, the First Troop Philadelphia Light Horse. "It should never be forgotten," James Wilkinson would later observe, "that Captain Samuel Morris, with twenty-one gentlemen of Philadelphia, most of them with families and all of them in independent circumstances, did in an inclement season, take leave of their domestic happiness and personal comforts to rally round the standard of their country, and furnished an example as rare as it was disinterested and patriotic."

After getting the last of the eighteen artillery pieces across the river, Colonel Glover's Marbleheaders took up their muskets and joined the line of march. It led along a snow-encrusted road for a distance of about four and a half miles to Birmingham (West Trenton), which was about halfway to Trenton. There, after a brief pause, the men were divided into two wings for the approach to Trenton. In Washington's words: "I formed my detachment into two divisions, one to march by the lower or river road, the other by the upper or Pennington road. As the divisions had nearly the same distance to march, I ordered each of them, immediately upon forcing the out-guards, to push directly into the town, that they might charge the enemy before they had time to form." But would this be possible now that it was almost daylight?

And what of the two other attempts to cross the river to New Jersey? Had General Ewing's militiamen been able to get across to Trenton? The river was about 1,000 feet wide there, about 200 feet wider than where Washington's troops had crossed. Was Ewing's force already in Trenton, perhaps having inadvertently put the Hessians on the alert to an attack? Washington had no way of knowing, but—and perhaps this was just as well—the attempt to cross at Trenton had failed; the Delaware there was too much for

Ewing's inexperienced troops. Not one man had been able to get across.

As for the crossing from the Bristol area, there had been no further word since Colonel Reed's discouraging report. Washington could only hope for the best, but with or without help from below, he was determined to attempt a stroke against the enemy. There would be no turning back.

At Dunk's Ferry, below Bristol, the attempt to cross the Delaware to New Jersey proceeded far into the frigid night. Lieutenant Charles Willson Peale, the artist-turned-soldier, and his eighty-one young Philadelphians were there with the rest of the militiamen under the command of Colonel John Cadwalader. Captain Thomas Rodney was there with his thirty-five militiamen from Delaware. The Reverend John Rosbrugh was there with the parishioners he had led down from Northampton County, Pennsylvania.

Colonel Daniel Hitchcock's New England troops, the only Continentals under Cadwalader's command, were also at Dunk's Ferry, awaiting their turn to cross the Delaware. Among them were Sergeant John Smith and his company of night plunderers and the Massachusetts company of Lieutenant Joseph Hodgkins, who had heard only recently about the death of his infant son and who was yearning to return to his bereaved wife.

Cadwalader's troops, about 1,800 in all, had answered the call to turn out late in the afternoon of Christmas Day. This was the second time within three days that they had been given cooked rations and alerted for action against the enemy. On the night of December 22 they had turned out and were about to march off for a crossing of the Delaware when word arrived that the mission was called off.

Now they were alerted once more. "With this force," Colonel Reed would report, "it was resolved to cross the river and attack Count Donop, then at Mount Holly with about the same number of men, and to make the attack as nearly as possible at the time of that on Trenton, viz. on the 26th December in the morning."

Instead of having their troops make the river crossing directly from Bristol to Burlington, Cadwalader and his officers had decided to make the attempt farther downstream. As Colonel Reed put it: "To prevent as much as possible any notice to the enemy, it was concluded to take a circuitous march by Dunk's Ferry rather than cross at Burlington where it was supposed the enemy had too many friends—besides which tho' the distance was about five miles farther the country thro' which we were to pass was woody and uninhabited. Accordingly, about sunset the boats moved down from Bristol and at dark the troops began their march, the light infantry and militia in front and the Continental troops in the rear when they arrived at the ferry."

Lieutenant Peale had encountered some resistance on the part of his militiamen. "We were ordered to join brigade," he noted. "Many of the men were unwilling to turn out as it was a day [Christmas] they wished to enjoy themselves. However, with small battalions, we went through several manoeuvres."

Later in the day, Peale himself came close to missing his company's departure for the riverbank. As usual, he had been out scrounging for provender for his men. "One of our men informed me that he had heard of a person about three miles out of town who had butter and cheese but would only sell for hard money. I set out on foot with some men, and got there just before dark. But on asking to buy with hard money, I found that the man had been slandered. I tempted as much as I thought was justifiable, and finding the man never expected to get any other than continental money, and constantly sold his butter for it, I engaged with his wife to send me three pounds on the morrow." Peale paid one shilling, eight pence for two quarts of milk and returned to his post. "I was instantly ordered to join in brigade for a march. The men were waiting, nearly ready, for me." Presently they were on their way: "I hurried them out to the parade ground and marched over Neshaminy Ferry, then down to Dunkin's Ferry, rather a roundabout way, nearly six miles." There they would cross the river to New Jersey and do battle with the Hessians. That was the plan.

Thomas Rodney arrived early at the ferry with his militiamen and some other troops. Since reaching Bristol a few days earlier, Rodney had spent a great deal of time with Colonel Cadwalader. When Cadwalader heard of the forthcoming venture into New Jersey he promptly passed on the word to Rodney. "I was rejoiced," Rodney noted in his diary, "and assured him we should certainly be successful."

Rodney and his men were quartered about two miles below Bristol with the Allens and the Coxes, "Tory families" whose men had gone over to the British. That, it seemed to some, made them fair game. But Rodney didn't see it that way. He came to their rescue on the day before Christmas: "The Quartermaster General, at Bristol, sent wagons down to Coxes and Allens to take all their grain and forage, but I would not permit them to touch it unless they bought it, so they left it and went away." On Christmas Day, "a brigade of New England Continental troops were sent down to quarter here, and the Quartermaster came down to turn out both families, but I would not allow them to be disturbed."

Around dusk Rodney received the word: "March immediately to Neshaminy Ferry and await orders." Rodney and his men departed without letting their host families, the Coxes and the Allens, know they were leaving. What Tory families did not know would not hurt them. From Neshaminy they were ordered to Dunk's Ferry, below Bristol, "and after we arrived there the whole brigade came up, and also Col. Hitchcock Brigade of New England Regulars."

Rodney and his Delaware company joined with four companies of militia from Philadelphia to act as advance guard in crossing the Delaware. Captain George Henry, a Philadelphian, was in command of this unit, Rodney second in command. The rest of Cadwalader's troops were to follow across the river and march on to attack Colonel Donop's force in the Mount Holly area.

The crossing proceeded fairly close to schedule early on, but the river here, 1,200 feet wide compared with 800 feet at the point of General Washington's crossing, proved to be too great an obstacle. A tidal estuary from Trenton southward, the Delaware was more heavily clogged with ice here than upstream, the flooding tide having helped to create a jam along the New Jersey side that was impenetrable to boats. None could get through. With the expert help of experienced Marblehead seamen, the operation might have been successful, but the only Marbleheaders available were with General Washington.

"We were obliged to land on the ice 150 yards from the [New Jersey] shore," Rodney would report. "The wind was blowing very hard and the night was very dark and cold."

The advance guard "landed with great difficulty through the ice and formed on the ferry shore, about two hundred yards from the river. It was as severe a night as ever I saw, and after two battalions were landed the storm increased so much and the river was so full of ice that it was impossible to get the artillery over. . . ." The landed troops "formed in four battalions of double files. About six hundred of the light horse got over, but the boats with the artillery were carried away in the ice and could not be got over."

Waiting on the Pennsylvania shore to cross, Colonel Joseph Reed was concerned about alerting the enemy: "It had been attempted to keep the troops from kindling any fires on the shores before they embarked but this was found impossible, and we were obliged to take our chance of giving the enemy the alarm."

Writing in the third person, Reed would report that he "and two or three field officers of the militia crossed over to forward the landing of the men, but to their great surprise and mortification they found the ice had drifted in such great quantities upon the Jersey shore that it was absolutely impossible to land the artillery. An attempt was made by them to land their horses which was effected with such difficulty as excluded all hope of debarking the field pieces. Advice of this being sent over to the other shore, the troops which by this time were nearly all transported were ordered to return."

Rodney's militiamen and the others who had made the crossing grumbled when this order arrived. This was the second damn time they had been called out for nothing at all. "After waiting about three hours," Rodney noted, "we were informed that Generals Cadwalader and Hitchcock had given up the expedition, and that the troops that were over were ordered back. This greatly irritated the troops that had crossed the river and they proposed making the attack without both the generals and the artillery. But it was urged that if General Washington should be unsuccessful and we also, the cause would be lost, but if our force remained intact it would still keep up the spirit of America. Therefore, this course was abandoned."

After spending about three hours covering the landings on the New Jersey shore, Rodney and the rest "had to wait about three hours more to cover the retreat, by which time the wind blew very hard and there was much rain and sleet, and there was so much floating ice in the river that we had the greatest difficulty to get over again, and some of our men did not get over that night. As soon as I reached the Pennsylvania shore I received orders to march to our quarters, where I arrived a little before daylight very wet and cold." Some of his young militiamen would not be back until the middle of the following day.

The troops made the return crossing "with great reluctance," according to Colonel Reed. "By this time the ice began to drive with such force and in such quantities as threatened many boats with absolute destruction. To add to the difficulty, about daybreak there came on a most violent storm of rain, hail and snow intermixed in which the troops marched back to Bristol except a part of the light infantry which remained till next day."

Reed and his small party decided to remain on the New Jersey side of the Delaware: "It being impossible for us to cross with our horses, we went up to Burlington where we were concealed in the house of a friend, that part of Jersey being then considered as entirely in the enemy's possession."

Sergeant William Young, still trusting in "the good providence of God" and still deploring the profanity of his men, was among those who suffered through the two crossings. "Set out about 9 to Dunk's Ferry, crossed over," he noted in his journal. "On account of the ice on the Jersey shore they could not land the great guns. Crossed back again, it came on to snow and rain. Wind E.N.E. Very cold. Our men come home very wet and cold."

Charles Willson Peale and his eighty-one young men, serving with the Second Battalion of Pennsylvania militiamen, waited long hours on the Pennsylvania shore as the First and Third battalions attempted to get across. "When the 1st and 3rd were nearly landed on the other side," he noted, "the wind began to blow, and the ice gathering so thick at a considerable distance from the shore, there was no possibility of landing, and they were ordered back."

Peale and his men were back in Bristol "just before day of the 26th, when the wind had increased, with rain and hail. Being very much fatigued, having walked since 4 yesterday, at least eighteen miles, eleven of them with heavy baggage. The storm continues, with hail and rain."

———— ♦♦♦ ————

CHAPTER 32

Take Care Now and Fire Low

It was about six a.m. and the snowstorm was continuing as General Washington's two columns of Continentals, after a brief rest, set off from Birmingham. For each column it would be a march of about four and a half miles to Trenton. The left wing, commanded by General Greene and accompanied by Washington, set off along the upper route, the Pennington road, which led to the northern edge of

Trenton. General Stephen's troops formed the vanguard and they were followed by the brigades of General Mercer, General Fermoy, and Lord Stirling. Each brigade was accompanied by detachments of Colonel Knox's cannoneers, who were having a devil of a time getting their heavy artillery pieces over the rough, snow-encrusted trails.

The right wing, commanded by General Sullivan, headed for the western edge of Trenton by way of the lower, or river, road. Colonel Stark and his First New Hampshire Regiment formed the advance party. After them came Colonel Glover's brigade, including Glover's own Marbleheaders and two other regiments, General St. Clair's brigade and Colonel Sargent's brigade. As in Greene's column, each brigade was accompanied by artillery batteries.

At the head of each column rode the "farmers" on horseback who had volunteered for this duty.* After leaving Birmingham, the advance parties of both columns met up with contingents of about forty men, who had crossed the Delaware and proceeded toward Trenton early in the night. One of these contingents, commanded by Captain John Flahaven of the First New Jersey Continentals, took over the leadership of Sullivan's column as it advanced along the river road. The other contingent, commanded by Captain William Washington, a distant relative of His Excellency's, joined the advance guard of Greene's column. Both of these forces had a few hours earlier succeeded in carrying out Washington's order to "post themselves on the road about three miles from Trenton and make prisoners of all going in or coming out of the town."

Captain Washington had been studying for the ministry at the outbreak of the revolution. He had interrupted his studies to join the Third Virginia Continentals and proceeded to make a name for himself as a daring and resourceful leader in combat. On August 27, during the disastrous Battle of Long Island, he had been seriously wounded. Although he was not yet fully recovered from the wounds, he was on the march and about to lead an audacious and crucial mission. His second in command was eighteen-year-old Lieutenant James Monroe.

---

*In addition to the aforementioned David Laning, John Guild, and John Muirhead, according to the "Notes" of Eli F. Cooley, these included the following residents of the area: John Mott, Joseph Inslee, Edon and Stephen Burroughs, Ephraim Woolsey, Henry Simonds, and Joseph, Philip, and Elias Philips.

After crossing the Delaware, Captain Washington, Monroe, and their men, as Monroe would later recall, had "hastened to a point . . . at which the road by which they descended intersected that which led from Trenton to Princeton, for the purpose, in obedience to orders, of cutting off all communication between them and from the country to Trenton. The night was tempestuous . . . and made more severe by a heavy fall of snow." Here they remained on guard duty until General Greene's troops caught up with them. Captain Flahaven's men did the same down on the river road until Sullivan's column arrived.

One of those slogging along in Sullivan's column was John Greenwood, the young fifer, who was somewhat confused. After he and the rest of his unit got across the Delaware, he would recall, "we began an apparently circuitous march, not advancing faster than a child ten years old could walk, and stopping frequently, though for what purpose I knew not. During the whole night it alternately hailed, rained, snowed, and blew tremendously. . . . At one time, when we were halted on the road, I sat down on the stump of a tree and was so benumbed with cold that I wanted to go to sleep. Had I been passed unnoticed I should have frozen to death without knowing it. But as good luck always attended me, Sergeant Madden came and, rousing me up, made me walk about. We then began to march again, just in the old slow way."

One of the Marblehead officers, Lieutenant Joshua Orne, dropped into a ditch exhausted and numbed during the march and might have died of the cold if some soldiers coming along hadn't pulled him out and revived him. Two enlisted men, it was reported, fell out of the line of march and froze to death.

Some soldiers used rum and other strong drink against the cold. But not Greenwood or the others in his company: "We were all sober to a man; not only sober but nearly half dead with cold for the want of clothing. . . . Many of our soldiers had not a shoe to their feet and their clothes were ragged as those of a beggar. . . . Not a drop of liquor was drunk during the whole night, nor, as I could see, even a piece of bread eaten."

Like John Greenwood, First Lieutenant Elisha Bostwick had already completed his enlistment term and had recently been ailing, but he was still on duty and marching. He and "the unfortunate Nathan Hale of Coventry" had been among those enlisting (for eight months) when the Seventh Connecticut Regiment was activated in the spring of 1775.* He had reenlisted for a year on January 1, 1776, in the newly formed Nineteenth Connecticut Regiment, commanded by Colonel Charles Webb, and now, on the march toward Trenton, he was within a few days of completing his enlistment.

Bostwick, twenty-seven, had been stricken about ten weeks earlier with "a course of sickness call'd billious fever. Was very sick. Took all the hair off from my head." Even now the hair had not grown back in full. Although he could have joined the large homeward exodus of the sick, he had opted to rejoin his regiment on October 27, just in time to face some devastating fire in the Battle of White Plains: "As we were on the declivity of the hill a cannon ball cut down Lieutenant Young's platoon which was next to that of mine. The ball first took the head of Smith, a stout heavy man, and dash't it open. Then it took off Chilson's arm which was amputated. It then took Taylor across the bowels. It then struck Sergeant Garret of our company on the hip and took off the point of the hip bone. Smith and Taylor were left on the spot. Sergeant Garret was carried but died the same day. Now to think, oh! what a sight that was to see within a distance of six rods, those men with their legs and arms and guns and pack all in a heap."

Now, two months later, he was approaching Trenton and perhaps more of the same kind of enemy fire. He and his platoon members were making their way with the help of improvised torch lights: "our march began with the torches of our field pieces stuck in the exhalters. They sparkled and blazed in the storm all night."

Farther on, during the brief pause at Birmingham, Bostwick got a closeup view of General Washington himself: "about day light a halt was made, at which time his Excellency and his aides came near to front on the side of the path where the soldiers stood. I heard his Excellency as he was coming on, speaking to and encouraging the soldiers. The words he spoke as he passed by where I stood and in my hearing were these: 'Soldiers, keep by your officers. For God's sake, keep by your officers!' Spoke in a deep and solemn voice."

Washington had a near-accident here: "While passing a slanting, slippery bank, his Excellency's horse's hind feet both slipped from under him, and he seized his horse's mane and the horse recovered."

---

*Hale had been hanged as a spy by the British on September 22, 1776.

Captain Alexander Hamilton, in command of the New York State company of artillery, was one of several officers who remarked upon a new spirit among the troops. Despite the horrendous conditions, the men, Hamilton found, were "ready, every devil of them . . . to storm hell's battlements in the night." Colonel Knox observed that "the troops marched with the most profound silence and good order" even though "it hailed with great violence." At Kip's Bay and a dozen other places many had panicked on the brink of battle and skulked off, officers as well as enlisted men. But not tonight. For the first time in many months these troops were on the attack, not on the run, and this appeared to have a salutary effect. Perhaps some of the new feeling could be traced to the just-published words of Thomas Paine: "These are the times that try men's souls. The summer soldier and the sunshine patriot will, in this crisis, shrink from the service of his country; but he that stands it *now* deserves the love and thanks of men and women."

An officer from Connecticut, unidentified, had noted a new esprit de corps a few days before Christmas. "Now is the time for us to be in earnest," he had written to a friend at home. "As for what few troops we have, you would be amazed to see what fine spirits they are in; and the Continental troops are really well disciplined, and you may depend will fight bravely, and doubt not before one week you will hear of an attack somewhere, when I trust we shall do honour to ourselves. I well know both officers and men are determined to check the pride of the red-coats. They at present are flushed with their successes, which perhaps may lull them into too much security for themselves."

Approaching Trenton around dawn, the van of General Greene's column came upon a new reason to fear the Hessians would be alerted and ready for battle by the time the Americans reached the town. A force of about thirty men suddenly came into view, marching in the opposite direction. They were Americans, it became clear after some anxious moments, Americans who had been on the prowl. Led by Captain Richard Clough Anderson, these men, it was learned, had suddenly struck the picket on the Pennington road, wounded six Hessians, and then, as previously ordered, fled into the night.* They were members of the Fifth Virginia Regiment,

---

*How they spent the intervening hours is still a mystery.

commanded by Colonel Charles Scott, one of three regiments in Brigadier General Adam Stephen's brigade. They had crossed the Delaware to New Jersey during the afternoon of Christmas Day, a move authorized, apparently, by General Stephen but not by General Washington. They had been ordered to reconnoiter enemy outposts and gather whatever intelligence was available but not to bring on an engagement.

Captain Anderson's version of the attack on the Hessian picket was recorded by his son Robert long after the war:* "Having gone to the places designated without finding the enemy, he advanced upon Trenton. The party came close upon the Hessian sentinel, who was marching on his post, bending his head down as he met the storm, which beat heavily in a driving snow in the faces of the patrol. He saw them about the same time he was seen, and as he brought his gun to a charge and challenged, he was shot down."

Captain Anderson "having now accomplished the object of his mission, and knowing that the enemy's forces would be promptly turned out . . . ordered his company to countermarch, and marched them back towards his camp. He had not gone far before he saw, very much to his surprise, Washington's army advancing toward him. As he was then in a narrow lane he ordered his company to withdraw one side to an adjoining field."

Greene's advance guard, "seeing a body of soldiers ahead, and supposing that they were the advance guard of the British forces, halted, and very soon an officer approached near enough to recognize them as American troops. General Washington approached and asked who was in command and where he had been."

Captain Anderson "never saw General Washington exhibit so much anger as he did when he told him where he had been and what he had done."

Washington turned to General Stephen and asked how he dared to authorize such a mission without his authority: "You, sir, may have ruined all my plans by having them put on their guard." In gentler tones Washington instructed Captain Anderson and his men to fall in and march with the vanguard.

A short time before eight a.m., just before the troops in the vanguard of General Greene's column reached the northern out-

*Robert Anderson was the federal general who defended Fort Sumter at the outset of the Civil War.

skirts of Trenton, Colonel Charles Scott shouted his usual final instructions to the men of his regiment: "Take care now and fire low. Bring down your pieces. Fire at their legs. One man wounded in the leg is better than a dead one for it takes two more to carry him off and there is three gone. Leg them, damn 'em. I say, leg them!"

Down on the river road, General Sullivan's troops were about to encounter their first opposition. Captain John Flahaven and his forty New Jersey recruits were out in the front, followed by Colonel John Stark and his New Hampshire troops. The first structure to come into sight was a small house, a picket post perhaps. A little farther on stood The Hermitage, a stately home set in a 200-acre tract overlooking the Delaware River—another likely enemy post. Philemon Dickinson, a militia general on duty almost directly across the river, had bought the estate six months earlier.

They slogged on, Flahaven's and Stark's men, primed to attack the two places. And as they advanced they heard a welcome sound: an outburst of firing from the direction of the Pennington road! General Greene's column was on the attack. It was about eight o'clock. A few minutes later, Sullivan's column was attacking, too. With Flahaven's and Stark's men in the van and three brigades coming on, the Americans made a charge on the small house and drove Hessian infantrymen from it. Then they routed a company of green-coated jagers from The Hermitage.

"Our horses were then unharnessed," Lieutenant Bostwick, advancing with Sullivan, would report, "and the artillerymen prepared. We marched on and it was not long before we heard the out sentries of the enemy both on the road we were in and the eastern road, and their out guards retreated firing, and our army, then with a quick step pushing on upon both roads, at the same time entered the town."

"It was now broad day," Major James Wilkinson would recall, "and the storm beat violently in our faces. . . . The attack . . . on the left . . . was immediately answered by Colonel Stark in our front, who forced the enemy's picket and pressed it into town, our column being close at his heels. The enemy made a momentary shew of resistance by a wild and undirected fire from the windows of their quarters, which they abandoned as we advanced." Sullivan's fired-up troops raced into the town as "the dauntless Stark . . . dealt death wherever he found resistance and broke down all the opposition before him."

General Greene's column was meanwhile proceeding toward high ground at the north end of Trenton. Washington and one of his aides had a short time earlier been among the first to discover the Hessians' outpost on the Pennington road. "It was broad daylight," according to the aide, "when we came to a house where a man was chopping wood. He was very much surprised when he saw us. 'Can you tell me where the Hessian picket is?' Washington asked. The man hesitated, but I said, 'You need not be frightened; it is General Washington who asks the question.' His face brightened and he pointed toward the house of Mr. Cowell. . . ."*

"Looking down the road I saw a Hessian running out from the house. He yelled in Dutch and swung his arms. Three or four others came out with their guns. Two of them fired at us, but the bullets whistled over our heads. Some of General Stephen's men rushed forward and captured two. The others took to their heels, running toward Mr. Calhoun's house,† where the [main] guard was stationed, about twenty men under Captain Altenbrockum. They came running out of the house. The captain flourished his sword and tried to form his men. Some of them fired at us, others ran toward the village."

Captain Samuel Morris, in command of the Philadelphia Troop of Light Horse, the unit escorting Washington, noted a pitiable sight as they entered the town: a young Hessian lieutenant bleeding profusely into the snow and groaning in agony. Morris dismounted and went to the Hessian's side to comfort him. But not for long. No time for that, General Greene indicated, ordering Morris back to the advancing column. (In a few hours the Hessian would be dead.)

The Continentals were still fired up—their adrenaline flowing—according to Captain William Hull: "The first sound of the musquetry and retreat of the guards animated the men and they pushed on with resolution and firmness."

Within a few minutes, there was a sound that Washington had been anxiously anticipating. "From the west," according to his aide, "came the boom of a cannon. General Washington's face lighted up instantly for he knew that it was one of Sullivan's guns."

Now, it was clear, both columns were on the attack. And with

---

*This house, the first on the left side of Pennington road, in the approach to Trenton, was occupied by Dr. David Cowell and his lawyer brother Ebenezer.

†Alexander Calhoun lived and kept a general store on the Pennington road, opposite today's Calhoun Street.

their spirit still intact. "Indeed I never could conceive," Colonel Clement Biddle noted, "that one spirit should so universally animate both officers and men to rush forward into action." Colonel Knox agreed: "It must give a sensible pleasure to every friend of the rights of man to think with how much intrepidity our people pushed the enemy and prevented their forming in the town."

The snow and sleet had made the night's march a horrendous experience, but the storm had masked and muffled the Americans' advance, helping to make the surprise attack possible, and now, as the assault began, the weather provided a great advantage. Colonel Knox was among those who recognized the foul weather as a blessing: "The storm continued with great violence, but was in our backs and consequently in the faces of our enemy."

Sullivan's big guns and those accompanying Greene's column were now about to prove their worth as foul-weather weapons, and as direct-fire weapons. Many of the muskets and rifles carried by the Continentals could not be fired because of dampened priming powder. The big guns, however—artillery pieces capable of bombarding the enemy with loads up to six pounds—were in working order. Plugs that had been placed in their vents and muzzles had kept them dry. There were big guns at the head of each of the two columns and before long all of them would be booming. Captain Thomas Forrest's two six-pounders and two 5.5-inch howitzers, just behind the vanguard of Greene's column, were the first to be unlimbered and dragged into position at the head of town, where King (Warren) and Queen (Broad) streets, almost parallel for most of their length, came together.*

Looking down into the town, according to Washington's aide, "we could see a great commotion . . . men running here and there, officers swinging their swords, artillerymen harnessing their horses. Captain Forrest unlimbered his guns. Washington gave the order to advance."

Now the cannon were blasting heavy fire at low angles of elevation into the center of the town: round shot, grape, and explosive shells. The shells bounced along, demolishing everything in their

---

*Today's "Five points," where Pennington, Princeton, and Brunswick avenues come together with Warren and Broad streets. This intersection, known as The Gateway in the eighteenth century, was to have been the site of a Hessian artillery emplacement but Colonel Rall had rejected it as unnecessary.

path, their fuses burning until they finally exploded. They were capable of tearing a man or horse apart. Forrest's guns were soon joined by Alexander Hamilton's two six-pounders. Now the fire down Queen and King streets increased in volume. A Hessian force attempting to form for a counterattack was broken up by a combination of artillery and small-arms fire. General Mercer's men had made their way into the town and now were firing small arms from positions both inside and between the houses on King Street. Three more field pieces—three-pounders belonging to Captain Bauman's New York Company—were dragged to the extreme left of the sector covered by the men of Greene's column. Stephen's and Fermoy's riflemen and musketeers had been dispatched to this area to cut off any attempt by the enemy to escape in the direction of Princeton. Soon Bauman's guns were adding their loads to the devastating fire. Trenton was now sealed off from the east and north.

Just the sight of the field pieces bombarding their position appeared to compound the confusion of the suddenly roused Hessians. They were accustomed to forming in solid ranks and advancing as a unit; unable to do this now because of the grape and shells and canister landing all about them, they found it impossible to put a counterattack together.

The Hessians did, however, manage to get two of their six brass artillery pieces into action. These three-pounders were lined up in front of Colonel Rall's headquarters on King Street. Hessian cannoneers got off a shot or two in response to the heavy incoming fire. Then about twenty of them, with the help of eight horses, moved up Queen Street with two of the guns. They advanced without any escort of foot soldiers and in the face of the fire coming from the head of town and the continuing rifle and musket crossfire. Even so, they reached a new position on Queen Street and got off a few shots before being overpowered by the return fire. Preparing to retreat, they tried to hitch their horses to the guns, but five of the horses were knocked out of action by the continuing fire. In this maneuver and the action that ensued, eight of the Hessian cannoneers were killed or wounded.

This is how Colonel Knox would recall the early stages of the strike: "We . . . entered the town with them pell-mell, and here succeeded a scene of war of which I had often conceived but never saw before. The hurry, fright, and confusion of the enemy was [not] unlike that which will be when the last trump shall sound. They endeavoured to form in the streets, the heads of which we had previously the possession of with cannon and howitzers. These, in the twinkling of an eye, cleared the streets. The backs of the houses were resorted to for shelter. These proved ineffectual: the musketry soon dislodged them."

Captain William Washington, Lieutenant James Monroe, and their forty scouts—the unit that had marched toward Trenton well in advance of the army—helped to rout the Hessian artillerymen in what was perhaps the most daring stroke of the day. After crossing the river, these troops had headed toward Trenton with great care, aware that they might encounter an enemy patrol anywhere along the way. But they reached their destination without incident. It was an intersection of roads situated, according to Monroe's recollections, a mile and a half above Trenton. There, for the rest of a long, frigid night, in Monroe's words, "Captain Washington executed his orders faithfully. He soon took possession of the point to which he was ordered, and, holding it through the night, intercepted and made prisoners of many who were passing in directions to and from Trenton." Except for one curious incident, a fortunate one for Monroe as things were to turn out, nothing unusual happened as they awaited Greene's oncoming left column. "Whilst occupying this position," Monroe would later recall, "the resident of a dwelling, some distance up a lane, had his attention directed to some unusual commotion by the barking of dogs. He came out in the dark to learn the cause, and encountered my command, and supposing we were from the British camp, ordered us off. He was violent and determined in his manner, and very profane and wanted to know what we were doing there on such a stormy night."

Monroe ordered the man to go back into his house and be quiet, or else be arrested. But presently the man somehow learned that this force was American, not British. He invited the men into his house, out of the storm, and offered to give them something to eat. Orders were orders, Monroe told him, and they could not leave their post. The man hurried back to his house and in a short time returned with some food for the men.

"I know something is to be done," he said to Monroe, "and I'm going with you. I'm a doctor and I may be of help to some poor fellow."

This was agreeable to Monroe and to Captain Washington. The

man—he really was a doctor, it turned out, Dr. John Riker—waited with the soldiers for the rest of Washington's Continentals to appear. When they did, about dawn, Dr. Riker joined the march along with Captain Washington's party.

As the brief artillery duel ensued between the Hessians on King Street and the Americans at the head of the town, Captain Washington's men were given the mission of knocking out the two Hessian guns that were firing. At the same time Colonel Knox, in overall command of American artillery, ordered Sergeant Joseph White and his cannoneers to join in the attack. They had marched to McKonkey's Ferry late on Christmas afternoon, crossed the river during the night, and then had joined Greene's column for the march to Trenton. Now, at the head of the town, White's men got off three shots, but the third one broke the cannon's axletree, putting it out of commission. "We stood there some time idle," White would recall, "they firing upon us." What were they to do? An officer on horseback rode up—Colonel Knox himself!

"My brave lads," Knox shouted, pointing with his sword, "take your swords and go up there and take those two pieces they're holding! There is a party going; you must go and join them."

Colonel Knox rode off. There was a moment of hesitation. "You heard what the Colonel said, Sergeant White," Captain John Allen shouted. "Now take your men and join the others in the attack!"

The others were Captain Washington, Lieutenant Monroe, and their men, who were about to charge down King Street. Following orders, Sergeant White and his artillery crew joined the attack. "I hallowed as loud as I could scream to the men to run for their lives right up to the pieces," White would recall.

Meanwhile, according to Monroe, "Captain Washington rushed forward, attacked and put the troops around the cannon to flight and took possession of them. Moving on afterwards, he received a severe wound and was taken from the field." Referring to himself in the third person, Monroe continued: "The command then devolved on Lieutenant Monroe, who advanced in like manner at the head of the corps, and was shot down by a musket ball which passed through his breast and shoulder. He also was carried from the field."

Sergeant White was the first of his party to reach the Hessian artillery pieces. By this time all of the Hessian cannoneers but one had either raced off or been shot. "Run, you dog!" White shouted, holding his sword over the man's head. The Hessian "looked up and saw it, then run. We put in a cannister of shot (they had put in the cartridge before they left it,) and fired."

Major Wilkinson was among those who would recognize the daring of Captain Washington and Lieutenant Monroe and the importance of their "acts of gallantry." These acts, according to Wilkinson, "could not have been too highly appreciated for if the enemy had got his artillery into operation in a narrow street, it might have checked our movement and given him time to reform and reflect; and if he had retired across the bridge in his rear and taken post, he would have placed a defile between us, which in our half naked, half frozen condition, he ought to have defended against our utmost efforts, and we in turn might have been compelled to retreat, which would have been fatal to us."

Even without the two artillery pieces—the only ones they had been able to get into action—the Hessians fought on. Hessian artillerymen had dragged their four other cannon away from the heavy fire on King Street.

General Sullivan's column, with Colonel Stark and his charged-up troops still leading the way, had meanwhile been advancing through the west end of the town. "We marched down the street from the River Road into the town to the corner where it crossed the street running up towards the Scotch Road and turned up that street." That would be the recollection of Private Jacob Francis, a twenty-two-year-old former slave who had been born to a black slave mother (and father unknown) in Amwell, not far from Trenton. Francis had served as a slave to a succession of five masters before earning his freedom at age twenty-one. He had enlisted as a Continental in Salem, Massachusetts, about fourteen months earlier, and now he was storming into Trenton with the rest of Colonel Paul Dudley Sargent's regiment in Sullivan's right wing. "General Washington," Francis would recall, "was at the head of that street coming down towards us and some of the Hessians between us and them. We had the fight."

Fifer-musketeer John Greenwood, one of the youngest in Sullivan's column, was finally finding out where he was going and what he was to do: "The first intimation I received of our going to fight was the firing of a six-pound cannon at us,* the ball from which

---

*Greenwood overestimated the firepower. The Hessians had only three-pounders.

struck the fore horse that was dragging our only piece of artillery, a three-pounder. The animal, which was near me as I was in the second division on the left, was struck in its belly and knocked over on its back. While it lay there kicking, the cannon was stopped and I did not see it again after we had passed on.

"As we advanced, it being dark and stormy so that we could not see very far ahead, we got within 200 yards of about 300 or 400 Hessians who were paraded, two deep in a straight line, with Colonel Rall, their commander, on horseback, to the right of them. They made a full fire at us, but I did not see that they killed anyone.

"Our brave Major Sherburne ordered us to fall back about 300 yards and pull off our packs, which we accordingly did and piled them by the roadside. 'Now, my boys,' says he, 'pass the word through the ranks that he who is afraid to follow me, let him stand behind and take care of the packs!' Not a man offered to leave the ranks. . . .

"As we had been in the storm all night we were not only wet through and through ourselves, but our guns and powder were wet also, so that I do not believe that one would go off, and I saw none fired by our party." They moved toward the Hessians anyway: "When we were all ready we advanced and, although there was not more than one bayonet to five men, orders were given to 'Charge bayonets and rush on!' and rush on we did."

At this point apparently many of the Hessians' weapons misfired, having been affected by the rain and snow. "Within pistol shot," Greenwood noted, "they again fired point-blank at us. We dodged and they did not hit a man. . . . Before they had time to reload we were within three feet of them, when they broke in an instant and ran like so many frightened devils into the town, which was at a short distance, we after them pell-mell."

Under the heavy artillery bombardment a Hessian force of about 600 men had retreated to an orchard near the eastern edge of the town. Now, led by officers on horseback, they came charging toward the Princeton road, a possible escape route. But they were too late. General Washington, seeing the danger of a breakout, as he would later describe it, ordered Colonel Hand's Pennsylvania rifle regiment and Colonel Nicholas Haussegger's German Battalion "to throw themselves before them; this they did with spirit and rapidity and immediately checked them."

Having failed to break through, the Hessians turned about and, with drums beating and mounted officers urging them onward, they charged back into the center of town. And into increasingly heavy fire. The American artillery pieces blasted them at close range. Marksmen firing dried weapons from inside the houses took a heavy toll. A few inhabitants, who had somehow managed to keep their weapons during the occupation period, were firing from their houses. One of them, a woman, mortally wounded a Hessian officer.* (Like just about every woman who contributed to the common cause, she would remain anonymous.)

The Hessians found their small arms too dampened to fire and all six of their artillery pieces were out of action. They had bayonets, but the enemy was out of reach. The Americans were all but invisible as, from windows, from behind fences and trees, they kept up their musket and rifle fire. The Hessians, easy targets as they milled about in confusion, were falling by the dozen. The officer who led the charge into town fell from his horse, severely wounded.

Unable to stand the fire any longer, the Hessians retreated toward their former position in the orchard. But here too they were surrounded. Some of the Americans were firing at the disorganized enemy from a distance of only fifty paces. Hemmed in from all sides, outgunned and outnumbered, the Hessians could do nothing but ground their weapons and surrender. For them it was all over.

"The only resource left," Major Apollos Morris observed, "was to force their way through numbers unknown to them. . . . They did not relish the project of forcing and were obliged to surrender on the spot." Some of the American soldiers, Morris added, ran forward and mixed with the captured Hessians "and after satisfying their curiosity a little, they began to converse familiarly in broken English and German." (Morris, briefly serving with Washington, had left the British army, come to America, and offered his services.)

Another Hessian force was meanwhile advancing toward the mill pond of the Assunpink Creek near the southern edge of the town.

---

*This would be reported a few days later by a Hessian officer captured in Trenton and escorted under guard to Philadelphia. The Hessian told the Reverend Henry Muhlenberg that when he and his troops arrived in Trenton they found the inhabitants to be friendly and cooperative—eager to swear allegiance to George III. But, he said, as soon as Washington's Continentals stormed into Trenton, the woman and other civilians started firing on the Hessians from their windows. Muhlenberg noted the report in his diary.

These troops—about 300 men with two artillery pieces—made a bold-spirited attempt to reach the road to Bordentown, but the Americans were everywhere. They were already in command of the area surrounding the bridge and had their artillery pieces in position. Other American units were sweeping around into positions overlooking the Assunpink. The Hessians gamely tried to break through, but their two three-pounders, laboriously drawn from the center of town, became mired in the marshy ground along the creek and they lost so much time in trying to dislodge the guns that their situation became hopeless. St. Clair's, Stirling's, Sargent's and other troops were firing effectively. As it had done earlier in the upper part of the town, American artillery was riddling the enemy ranks. The frenzied Hessians ran to their left, following the Assunpink in search of a place where it was fordable, but by the time they reached a ford they found it formidably covered by Colonel Glover and his men. As Private John Dewey would note in his journal, he and others in Glover's force, following orders, waded through the Assunpink "about mid-thigh [deep] in order to cut off the enemy's retreat." There was no choice for the Hessians but surrender, just as their comrades in the upper part of the town had done a few minutes earlier. It was all over.

At one point during the action at the lower end of town the troops of the Seventh Connecticut Regiment crossed the bridge over the Assunpink and proceeded toward the Delaware. Here, as it turned out, they were in more danger from American fire than from Hessian fire—American fire from across the river. "A regiment of soldiers appeared," Lieutenant Bostwick would recall, "and they supposed us to be the enemy, fired upon us across the river. Colonel [Charles] Webb, seeing their mistake, swang his hat and gave a shout and instantly every hat on both sides of the river was swinging."

Coming through the town, Private John Greenwood and company passed by two of the Hessians' brass cannon, "by the side of which lay seven dead Hessians and a brass drum." Aha! Greenwood paused to inspect the drum—"a great curiosity," and what a souvenir! But it wasn't to be his: "It was quickly taken possession of by one of our drummers, who threw away his own instrument." Before hurrying on, Greenwood opted for a souvenir of another kind: "I obtained a sword from one of the bodies, and we then ran on to join the regiment, which was marching down the main street toward the market. Just before we reached this building . . . General Washington, on horseback and alone came up to our major and said, 'March on, my brave fellows, after me!' and rode off.''

Greenwood and the rest of his regiment trudged on and soon came upon another grim scene: Hessian dead lying in the bloodied snow, Hessian wounded moaning, crying, grimacing. Farther on, there were more souvenirs: "We reached the other side of town and on our right beheld about 500 or 600 of the enemy paraded, two deep in a field. At the time we were marching in grand divisions which filled up the street, but as we got opposite the enemy we halted and, filing off two deep, marched right by them—yes, and as regular as a Prussian troop.

"When we had reached the end of their line we were ordered to wheel to the right, which brought us face to face six feet apart, at which time, though not before, I discovered they had no guns. They had been taken prisoners by another party and we had marched between them and their guns, which they had laid down.

"A few minutes afterward a number of wagons came behind us, into which the guns were placed, and the next thing ordered was to disarm the prisoners of their swords, with one of which every man was provided. These we also put in the wagons, but compelled the enemy to carry their cartridge boxes themselves."

Sergeant Joseph White was appalled by the post-battle scene: "I took a walk over the field of battle and my blood chilled to see such horrors and distress, blood mingling together—the dying groans and 'garments rolled in blood.' " Some eighty wounded Hessians were strewn over the battle area, their colorful uniforms standing out against the snow. Some would not last out the day. Three Hessian officers lay dead, two others were dying. Sixteen Hessian privates and one noncommissioned officer lay dead. Presently they would be buried in a large pit being dug by a detachment of Americans near the Presbyterian Church.

"The sight," Sergeant White would recall, "was too much to bear. I left it soon." Affected as he was by the gory scene, White managed to control his feelings when he came upon the body of one of the dead Hessian officers—and a glittering souvenir. "I saw a field officer laying dead on the ground and his sword by him. I took it up and, pulling the sheath out of the belt, I carried it off. It was an eligant sword." The souvenir secure, White returned to the northern end of town, where his damaged field piece had been left. Here he encountered the artillery chief himself, Colonel Knox. The piece was beyond repair, Knox said. Leave it there.

But this, thought White, was the best cannon in the whole regiment. "I was determined to get it off. I hired four of our men and one of them had been a mate of a vessel. He contrived it and off we moved."

Elsewhere in town, the Reeds—mother, ten-year-old daughter, and eight-year-old son—were happy to find that their ordeal, at last, was over. The plundering Hessians had "hastily decamped" from the Reed home upon word that the Americans had arrived and, as Martha Reed would recall, "all was uproar and confusion. My mother and we children hid in the cellar to evade the shots that fell about the house, and we remained there until quiet was restored and the voices of neighbors calling for us reassured us to venture out." Some of the townspeople had been hit by stray shots. The Reeds' next-door neighbor, a blacksmith, lay dead near his front doorstep. He had been struck by a stray shot "in the act of closing himself in his cellar."

For the first time since the night the Hessians suddenly burst into their lives, Mrs. Reed and her children were free to go through their home. They found it "ransacked and pillaged from garret to cellar." The household linen, mostly of Mrs. Reed's own spinning, was missing. Even her featherbed was gone and so was every piece of silver. "Tables and chairs were broken, furniture defaced, china and glass utterly ruined, while not a crumb remained of our winter stores."

Nevertheless, "joy at our deliverance and the success of our army lessened the sense of loss and discomfort."

Now it was time to clean up the mess: "With truly grateful hearts we all went cheerfully to work to restore our home to its usual orderly comfort. And how proud we children felt to help mother, and we worked like beavers and did our part; at least mother told us she could not get along without us, and I believed her."

Among the other Trenton residents who had suffered during the occupation period was a Quaker man who later told Thomas Paine that the Hessians "treated and plundered all alike; what could not be carried away has been destroyed, and mahogany furniture has been deliberately laid on fire for fuel, rather than the men should be fatigued with cutting wood."

There were some stories of close encounters. One of the near-casualties, according to one report, was a daughter of Stacy Potts, whose house had been used as Colonel Rall's headquarters. Miss Potts, it was said, suffered a slight injury when a musket ball struck a comb from her head as she was running home from a neighbor's house.

Rall himself, it was learned, was among the most seriously wounded. He had been shot twice while attempting, astride his horse, to lead a counterattack. He had first been carried into the Methodist Church on Queen Street and placed on a wooden bench. Then, still on the bench, he had been carried through an alley to King Street and into his quarters in the Stacy Potts house.

Shortly after the surrender, General St. Clair, in the lower part of the village, dispatched Major Wilkinson to get orders from General Washington. Wilkinson would recall that he rode up to Washington "at the moment Colonel Rall, supported by a file of sergeants, was presenting his sword. On my approach the commander in chief took me by the hand and observed, 'Major Wilkinson, this is a glorious day for our country,' his countenance beaming with complacency." Meanwhile "the unfortunate Rall . . . now pale, bleeding and covered with blood, in broken accents seemed to implore those attentions which the victor was well disposed to bestow on him."*

Within twenty-four hours Rall would be dead. So would the next ranking officer in Rall's brigade, Major Friedrich Ludwig von Dechow, who had commanded the Knyphausen Regiment. The other Hessian officers killed were two captains and the lieutenant who had been briefly comforted by Captain Samuel Morris: Georg Christian Kimm.

After visiting the dying Rall, taking his parole, and assuring him he would not be harsh with the captured Hessians, General Washington met with his chief officers to discuss the next move. Perhaps now was the time to push on and make another bold stroke against the enemy.

---

*According to legend, and nothing more, Colonel Rall learned as he lay dying that a Tory (one of the infamous Doane brothers, one version has it) had come to Abraham Hunt's house the previous night and attempted to warn him that Washington's army was on the march to Trenton. Rall was given the message, but he was so engrossed in a card game that he stuffed the paper unread into a pocket. In his final hours the message came to light. Apprised of its warning, he said, "If I had read this at Mr. Hunt's I would not be here." Interesting if true, but no documentation has ever been found.

―――― ◆◆◆ ――――

CHAPTER 33

Der Feind! Heraus!

For the 1,400 Hessians quartered in crowded Trenton, the night of December 25–26 passed quietly. So Lieutenant Andreas Wieder-holdt of the Knyphausen Regiment would recall. Wiederholdt was in command of a picket post on the Pennington road—the one that had been attacked early in the evening by General Stephen's thirty-member raiding party. A patrol returned shortly after dawn of the twenty-sixth to report to Wiederholdt that all was quiet—not a rebel in sight—and that the jagers under his command, down at The Hermitage near the river road, had withdrawn the men from their alarm house nearby. All was quiet there, too. Another day of wearying picket duty had begun.

But then, about an hour after sunup, it happened: "I was sudden-ly attacked from the side of the woods on the road to John's [Johnson's] Ferry. If I hadn't just stepped out of my little picket house and discovered the enemy coming they probably would have come upon me before I could reach my gun. My sentries were not sufficiently alert since it was broad daylight and we were expecting Captain Brubach's patrol to return from that direction, not the enemy's vanguard.

"Even so, we were quickly under arms and we waited to give the enemy a firm challenge, thinking they were merely a roaming party. They fired three volleys at me and my seventeen men, who held their fire. After the third volley I gave the order to fire and we fought with them until we were almost surrounded by several battalions. I therefore retreated, under constant fire, until I reached Captain Altenbockum's company. While we had been engaging the enemy, this company had formed a line in the street in front of the captain's quarters. I took a position at their right wing and together we fired at the enemy. But soon we were forced to retire in the same manner as before so that we would not be cut off from the garrison."

One of the eyewitnesses of this action was John Barnes, a Tren-ton resident and high sheriff of Hunterdon County, who had gone over to the British. "From the idea I have of military matters," he would later testify, "[I] am clearly of opinion that Captain Bockum [sic] behaved well, and made a retreat which redounds to his honour."

Here, according to Wiederholdt, precious time was lost: "Nobody came to see what was happening, nobody came to support us with reinforcements in spite of the fact that the Rall Regiment was still on watch duty. I took up a position in front of one of the first houses of the town and fired at the enemy who were forming in battle order on the upper side of the town. It was only at this point that the Brigadier [Rall] finally appeared and he seemed to be quite dazed. I considered it my duty to report what had happened outside the town. Since he knew nothing of what had happened I told him everything I knew and what I had seen. I said that the enemy were strong in numbers, that they were not only above the town but also on both sides of the town. I said this so that he would take the matter seriously and not consider it a mere trifle."

How strong was the enemy force? Rall wanted to know.

Wiederholdt couldn't tell exactly—after all, he had had to look out for his men—but he had seen at least four or five battalions move out of the woods and he had withstood fire from three of these before retreating back to town.

Thereupon, Rall, on horseback at the head of troops who had gathered, "shouted: 'Forward march! Advance! Advance!' and he tottered back and forth, not knowing what he was doing. Thus we lost the few favorable moments we might still have had to break through the enemy in one place or another with honor and without losses."

Having played cards and imbibed far into the night at the home of Abraham Hunt, Colonel Rall had been fast asleep when Lieutenant Wiederholdt's picket on the Pennington road was attacked. He remained in his bedroom even after being informed of the attack. On hearing the first of the rebels' firing, Lieutenant Jacob Piel had raced to Rall's headquarters in the Stacy Potts house and passed the alarm. *"Der Feind! Der Feind! Heraus! Heraus!"* ("The enemy! The enemy! Turn out! Turn out!") Coming back a second time, Piel had found Rall still not dressed. The picket house under attack was the same one that had been fired on the previous night by a roving band of rebels. Perhaps Rall took this to be just another skirmishing party that would soon disappear. In any case, according to Piel, the first two times he reported the enemy fire, Rall remained in his bedroom "and the third time he was in his night shirt and in the act of dressing." And shouting from a window: "What is the matter? What is the matter?"

Piel: "Have you not heard the firing?"

Rall: "I will be there directly."

And so he was. But a lot of time had been lost. The rebels were already approaching the high ground at the top of the town with their big guns. The grenadiers of Rall's own regiment, many of whom had been on alarm-house duty throughout the night, were attempting to get into formation. The Lossberg Regiment was beginning to turn out on King Street. The men of the Knyphausen Regiment were coming on, though in some disorder, from the lower part of the town.

Some troops were meanwhile fleeing the town. Among them were the fifty green-coated jagers commanded by Lieutenant Friedrich von Grothausen, who had been routed from The Hermitage. All of them except one escaped. They would be severely criticized by Captain Ewald for having "abandoned their post as soon as they caught sight of the enemy." Twenty troopers of the Sixteenth Light Dragoons, the only British soldiers in town, mounted their horses early on and raced off toward Princeton. During the action almost 400 Hessians would escape by way of the road leading south to Bordentown. These included a guard of nineteen men who had been stationed at the Assunpink bridge, near the southern end of the town, and an officer and twenty-seven men who had been on picket duty at Trenton landing, below the town. These men had been shelled by the rebels from the Pennsylvania shore of the Delaware.

In front of Rall's headquarters on King Street, Lieutenant Johann Englehard and his cannoneers, in blue coats trimmed with crimson and white, got two of the six artillery pieces into position and with one of them got off a shot or two at the rebel position at the head of King Street. As he prepared to mount his horse to lead a counterattack, Rall ordered Englehard and Lieutenant Friedrich Fischer and their crews to get the two guns up King Street, closer to the enemy. These pieces fired a few more shots before being knocked out of action by a contingent of rebels who raced down from the top of the town, screaming and either routing or killing the cannoneers.

On King Street, where Rall was attempting to get his men into formation, and on Queen Street, parallel to King, where more troops were responding to the alarm, the artillery fire from the rebel positions at the top of the village was devastating. In addition, rebel marksmen had reached the houses on King Street and from there were firing into Rall's left flank, and picking off Hessians in the side streets.

Rall's grenadiers responded eagerly under the leadership of the man who had inspired them to heroic action at White Plains and Fort Washington. Among them was Johannes Reuber, the dedicated seventeen-year-old who had been impatiently awaiting the freeze-over of the Delaware. Shortly after the first *"Heraus!"* Reuber and the rest of his company turned out, ready for action. "The rebels attacked us ferociously," he would note. "Near Oberst Rall's quarters there was a barricade of boards and in front of that stood our two company cannon. As the Americans were attempting to reach the cannon, we of Rall's Grenadier Regiment encountered them, directly in front of Rall's headquarters. The fight was furious. The rebels dismantled the barricade and now we lost the greater part of our artillery and the rebels were about to use them. Then Oberst Rall led a counterattack on the rebels and the situation was thrown into utter confusion." Soon Reuber and the rest were forced to retreat out of the village and into the orchard. "Here Oberst Rall gave the order: 'All who are my grenadiers, forward!' This rush carried us back into the town. But in the meantime American troops had marched into the main street in lines of three.

"The Americans had seven artillery pieces in position there. We had to get through. It was very hard for us, very costly until we surrendered to this fate." If only his idol, Colonel Rall, had been spared, the disaster would have been avoided: "If he had not been severely wounded they would not have been able to take us prisoners alive! . . . his three regiments of brave men would have disputed every foot of the land. But when he was shot there was not an officer who had the courage to take up the half-lost battle."

Like many another Hessian on the scene, Reuber had an exaggerated idea of the rebels' strength: "They were 15,000 men, we were only 1,600. When they attacked, we had to give way. We were too weak."

In another view of the battle, apparently written by Lieutenant Jacob Piel,* the rebel force was described as a "corps of six to seven thousand men," and the length of the battle was somewhat exagger-

---

*This view was part of the history of the Lossberg Regiment. In his diary Piel used similar language in describing the action at Trenton.

ated: "We were surrounded from all sides, but we defended ourselves for fully two hours. . . .

"Our muskets could not fire any more on account of the rain and
snow, and the rebels fired on us from within the houses. Nothing
therefore was left to us but to surrender as prisoners of war. The
regiment von Lossberg lost in this affair seventy men killed and
wounded. . . . Our whole disaster was entirely due to Colonel Rall.
He did not think it possible that the rebels would ever dare to attack
us. . . . I must confess that we thought too slightingly of the rebels,
who thus far had never been able to resist us."

Lieutenant Wiederholdt also had some harsh words for Rall:
"The Colonel moved with his regiment to the right of the town
under the apple trees, intending only to charge the enemy on the
Princeton road. But when he was reminded, I do not know by
whom, of the loss of the baggage left behind in the town, he
changed his mind and with his own regiment and that of Lossberg
he attacked the town he had just left. What madness this was! An
open town which was useless to us and which he had only ten or
fifteen minutes earlier left of his own free will and which was now
filled with three or four thousand of the enemy and then to attempt
to retake it with six to seven hundred men. . . . A man . . . even of
very small experience in the business can here see his weakness."

The Knyphausen Regiment presently also lost its leader, Major
Dechow, an experienced and courageous officer who had once
served in the Prussian army under Frederick the Great. He had
been seriously wounded at Fort Washington only six weeks earlier,
and now he was even more severely wounded in the left hip. In a
weakened and quickly worsening condition Dechow turned over
command of the regiment to Captain Bernhard von Biesenrodt, next
in command, advising him to surrender; the regiment was in an
untenable position.

Captain Biesenrodt, however, was not through. He was going to
fight his way out of this trap, he told Captain Jacob Baum. They
knew, by this time, according to Baum, that the other two regiments had been captured and that the Assunpink bridge was strongly held by the rebels and "we were the only ones left to fight."
Baum and some fifty others made their way through the marshy
ground near the bank of the Assunpink, seeking a place to cross.
They found what appeared to be an easy ford and started across.
Like the rest, Captain Baum found it hard going: "I was unlucky

enough to hit a deep spot where the water reached as high as my mouth and I was in danger of drowning." He finally made it to the other side and was helped up a steep bank by a soldier who had crossed ahead of him. Safely across, Baum and the others could see that the rebels with their big guns had arrived on the high ground facing the remains of the Knyphausen Regiment. "I would have tried to rejoin my regiment," Baum would report, "even under a hundred times greater danger to my life if I hadn't seen to my painful mortification that our regiment had been captured." Obviously there was no need "to cross the water again only to be captured," so Baum and his party made off into the fields. It would take them about ten hours of groping through unfamiliar territory, but that evening they would reach Princeton to report the unbelievable thing that had happened in Trenton.

Before being marched out of Trenton, the Hessian soldiers were told they could keep their knapsacks and other equipment, everything but their weapons. Private Reuber credited this to the dying Colonel Rall: "After it was all over, Oberst Rall, although he was in his last agony, thought of his grenadiers and appealed to General Washington that nothing be taken away from them but their weapons. A promise was given and it was kept."

Reuber and the rest of the Hessian enlisted men who crossed the Delaware to the McKonkey ferry house area spent the night in what he described as "a miserable prison." The captured Hessian officers were kept overnight in the ferry house and, as Lieutenant Wiederholdt would recall, found the place no less miserable: "26 men in a room so small that we could hardly stand upright, and without any food or drink."

December 26 simply had not been Lieutenant Wiederholdt's day. Following the humiliating defeat by the rebels, he had been escorted with the rest of the prisoners to what was to be a precarious crossing of the Delaware to Pennsylvania: "The river was full of heavy ice, so heavy that we had to risk dying miserably in trying to cross it. The wind blowing against us and the ice jams prevented the boat I was in from landing on the bank. As a result it drifted almost two miles down the Delaware.

"I resolved not to die gradually by spending a night on this river but instead to jump into the river and either die quickly or reach the shore. I made it easily and all the men in our boat followed me. We were happy to reach the bank but in getting there we had to walk seventy feet in water up to our chest and break through the ice in some places." An ironic thought occurred to Wiederholdt as he struggled toward the shore: "What a shame if one were to lose his health and return home with a sick body instead of a promotion and a full purse, and there to meet one's ungracious ruler."

Advancing relentlessly across New Jersey, the Hessians had eagerly anticipated spending Christmas Day in America's biggest city, Philadelphia. "We expected to end the war with the capture of Philadelphia," Captain Ewald observed. The captured Hessian officers and enlisted men would be in Philadelphia by New Year's Day but, far from capturing the city, they would find themselves being paraded for the edification of its citizens.

———— ◆◆◆ ————

CHAPTER 34

We Should Have Gone On

The unbelievable had happened: the bold stroke that had obsessed General Washington for the past fortnight had succeeded. In about ninety minutes the Americans had, at last, achieved a clear-cut major victory, had proven to themselves and to the world that the vaunted foreign soldiers were not invincible. Years later, George Otto Trevelyan, the distinguished English historian, would evaluate the importance of the coup: "It may be doubted whether so small a number of men ever employed so short a space of time with greater and more lasting results upon the history of the world."

Washington's Continentals had captured 868 Hessians, had killed or wounded 106, had captured six field pieces, a thousand muskets, and, among other items, a full set of band instruments including a dozen drums, and forty hogsheads of rum. Among those captured were twenty-five musicians—in Captain Thomas Forrest's words, "a compleat band of Musick."*

American casualties were almost unbelievably light but the re-

---

*This band would provide the music on July 4, 1777, as Philadelphians observed the first anniversary of independence.

ports varied somewhat.* Not even Washington had the statistics straight. In one letter he would report "only two officers and one or two privates wounded." In another: "No more than a private or two killed, one or two wounded and Captain Washington." (Apparently he was not aware that Lieutenant Monroe, Captain Washington's second in command, was also wounded.)

The forty hogsheads of rum figured in a council of war called by Washington a short time after the Hessians surrendered. Should this bold stroke be pursued? Should they push on and attempt a further strike against a shaken, off-balance enemy? Or should they recross the Delaware with their prisoners and thus not risk losing the advantage gained? The debate among the leading officers was heated at times but prudence prevailed: they would return to the Bucks County encampment without further ado. One factor in the decision, according to Colonel Joseph Reed, was the heavy drinking that ensued at the battle's end. Before Washington's order to stave in the forty hogsheads could be carried out, many soldiers imbibed the rum and other intoxicants they found. Although Reed was with Cadwalader's force in Bristol and thus not on the scene at Trenton, he reported on the post-battle situation, apparently after conferring with officers who had attended the council of war.

"There were," he wrote, "great quantities of spiritous liquors at Trenton of which the soldiers drank too freely to admit of discipline or defence in case of attack."† Another consideration in the decision was the fact "that the enemy was in force both above and below, viz. at Princeton and Bordentown. . . . The stroke being brilliant and successful, it was not prudent or politick even to risque the chance of losing the advantages to be derived from it."

Ensign Robert Beale of the Virginia Fifth Regiment would recall taking part in some of the post-battle antics: "Our men fell into the utmost confusion, every man shifting for himself. After I had gotten

---

*One casualty report would come from Richard Scudder, whose home was situated near the Delaware a few miles above Trenton. According to him, several fatigued and all-but-frozen soldiers took refuge at his home during the night of December 26–27. Some of them were "very sick in the night . . . and two or three died."

†One newspaper report saw the imbibing as beneficial: "Luckily they found some hogsheads of rum at Trenton, large draughts of which alone preserved the lives of many."

pretty well refreshed with good old Jamaica and excellent beef and biscuits, I asked Captain Fauntleroy and our adjutant, by name, Kelly, to go to the stable and get us a horse apiece. We did so and all mounted, but it was much colder on horseback than on foot, so, seeing Colonel Lawson of the [Virginia] Sixth Regiment in the street, asked him what would become of the property taken here. He told us it was for the general good and not individual advantage, upon which I dismounted and set my horse loose."

General Washington diplomatically overlooked the imbibing in reporting the decision to return to Pennsylvania: "The weather was so amazingly severe, our arms so wet, and the men so fatigued, it was judged prudent to come off immediately with our prisoners and plunder." Colonel John Haslet agreed: "We should have gone on and, panick struck, they would have fled before us, but the inclemency of the weather rendered it impossible."

Some of the captured Hessians were ferried directly across the Delaware from Trenton, according to Jacob Francis, the former slave from nearby Amwell, New Jersey. Following the surrender, he would recall, "some officers, among whom I recollect was General Lord Stirling, rode up to Colonel Sargent and conversed with him. Then we were ordered to follow them . . . and we marched down through the town toward the Assunpink." The prisoners were escorted "to the old ferry below the Assunpink." Presently, "a number of men from our regiment were detailed to go down and ferry the Hessians across to Pennsylvania. I went as one, and about noon it began to rain and rained very hard. We were engaged all the afternoon ferrying them across till it was quite dark, when we quit. I slept that night in an old millhouse above the ferry on the Pennsylvania side."

Some Hessian prisoners made the crossing to Pennsylvania at Beatty's Ferry, about five miles above Trenton. The main body of prisoners was escorted another three miles upstream to the area of Johnson's ferry house,* across the river from McKonkey's ferry house.

John Greenwood was among those acting as escort guards at Johnson's. He watched pityingly as the Hessians clambered into Durham boats, the "scows," as he called them, that had carried most of the Continentals in the opposite direction the previous

---

*For many years misidentified as McKonkey's.

night. "The scow, or flatbottomed boat, which was used in transporting them over the ferry, was half a leg deep with rain and snow
and some of the poor fellows were so cold that their underjaws
quivered like an aspen leaf."

Along the route of march the Hessian prisoners had appeared to
be terror-stricken about their possible fate. According to Greenwood, they had been told, among other things, that the American
rebels were "a race of cannibals who would not only tomahawk a
poor Hessian and haul off his hide for a drum's head, but would just
as leave barbecue and eat him as he would a pig."

On the way to the boats, Greenwood continued, "seeing some of
our men were much pleased with the brass caps which they had
taken from the dead Hessians, our prisoners, who were besides
exceedingly frightened, pulled off those they were wearing and,
giving them away, put on the hats which they carried tied behind
their packs. With these brass caps on, it was laughable to see how
our soldiers would strut—fellows with their elbows out and some
without a collar to their half-a-shirt, no shoes, etc."

It was also laughable, according to Lieutenant Elisha Bostwick, to
see some of the Hessians springing up and down in the boats with
their long plaits flying. The men poling the boats across the river
found the job difficult because of ice forming on the walkways. So,
Bostwick noted, "the boatmen, to clear off the ice, pounded the
boats and, stamping their feet, beckoned the prisoners to do the
same, and they all set to jumping at once with their cues flying up
and down . . . sticking straight back like the handle of an iron
skillet."

Greenwood and the rest of his company crossed the river themselves after the Hessians had all been carried over. Most of the
company flaunted Hessian swords, headgear, or other mementos of
battle, but all of them were without their packs—the ones they had
piled by a roadside before entering Trenton. "As we never went
back that way," Greenwood would recall, "we all lost our packs. At
least I never heard anything of mine, and I had in it a beautiful suit
of blue clothes, turned up with white and silver laced."

Greenwood and the others in his unit were back at the Newtown
encampment late in the afternoon, after being on the move for more
than twenty-four hours. Some of Washington's other Continentals
would not reach their encampments until late the following day,
having been gone for fifty hours or more. Some, upon their return,
took time to note the day's doings in a diary. David How, an

eighteen-year-old from Massachusetts, summed things up with his usual Yankee succinctness: "This morning at 4 o'clock we set off with our field pieces. Marched 8 miles to Trenton whare we ware atacked by a number of Hushing and we toock 1000 of them besides killed some. Then we marched back and got to the river at night and got over all the Hushing."

A remarkable New Jersey officer, Captain John Polhemus, thirty-eight, was considerably more literate, though no more explicit, in recalling the action: "We whipped them terribly and took a thousand Hessians prisoners, driving them into Newtown jail and yard like a pack of sheep, during a severe hailstorm. We allowed the officers to wear their side arms, also the privilege of occupying part of the house with General Patterson and myself."

Polhemus, a wealthy mill owner, had recruited a company of eighty-six men late in 1775 and mortgaged his home in Rocky Hill, near Princeton, to arm and equip them. His company served in the New York area and later as part of the northern army. The term of enlistment having expired in November 1776, Polhemus returned to the family home, which his wife and five children had abandoned. After finding them in a friend's nearby mountain retreat and seeing to their safety and comfort, he reported for duty at Newtown a few days before Christmas, in time to take part in the attack on Trenton.

Riding along the river road for the return crossing to Pennsylvania, General Washington, Colonel Knox, and a few other officers came upon Sergeant White and his cannoneers. With the help of their horses, they were lugging the damaged artillery piece, the one that Knox had told White to abandon. Pausing astride his horse, Knox tried again: "You had better leave that cannon. I will not take charge of it."

White, however, was determined to persevere, especially after having already brought the piece a good part of the way: "I told him I rather ran the risk of being taken than to leave now, we had got so far." Shrugging off the debate, Knox rode off with Washington and the others. White and his men resumed their lugging.

Returning by way of the river road, William Chamberlin, the private who had made a small fortune on spruce beer, became suddenly ill and had to seek refuge. At the end of the battle he had found himself within a short distance of General Washington: "I was near the general when he took possession of the standard of the enemy." Then, he would recall, "it began to rain. I had got thoroughly wet before we began our retrograde march, and the rain and half-melted snow and water was almost over shoes; our feet was drenched in water at every step. I was seized with a kind of ague fit which lasted for half an hour. I went into an house with my teeth chattering in my head, but though my kind host made a good fire and did everything to favor me, the fire failed to warm me for some time and I expected to have been taken down with a violent fever. After a while, however, I got warm and made shift to get back to the ferry. Here we had to stand by the river until the prisoners were first got over. The wind by this time had shifted and blew a keen northwestern blast which chilled me to the heart. I at length went into an house at some distance from the ferry where was a girl which was called Miss Chamberlin. On the score of namesake I ventured to scrape acquaintance with her, and by her assistance I got a bowl of warm, fresh meat broth, which was of great service to me. I then went down to the river to wait for the boats. The ice was so thick near the shore as to bear for a rod or two. I went on the ice with a view to jump in, but it broke and let me into the river up to my waist, and the boat was filled before I could recover myself. The next boat, however, that struck I waded into the river to meet it, threw my gun into it, made leap with all my strength. I got in and got over to a fire but almost dead with cold and fatigue."

Before reaching the Eight Mile Ferry crossing of the Delaware, Sergeant White and his men again met up with Colonel Knox, General Washington, and the other officers. Knox paused in his saddle to take a close look at the field piece. He asked White which one it was. It was now time for White to gloat: "I told him the piece that he ordered to be left. I wanted the victory to be complete."

Knox smiled. "You are a good fellow," he said before riding on. "I will remember you."

Finally reaching the ferry crossing, White opted for some time out before going across: "I, being weary, laid down upon the snow and took a knap."

In the glow of victory, Colonel George Weedon of Virginia exulted: "The behavior of our people in general far exceeded anything I ever saw. It was worth remarking that not one officer or private was known that day to turn his back." Captain William Hull of the Seventh Connecticut Regiment expressed the feelings of many who had been part of the strike on Trenton: "The resolution and bravery of our men gave me the highest sensation of pleasure. . . . What can't men do when engaged in so noble a cause?" Hull also noted that "General Washington highly congratulated the men the next day in general orders, and with pleasure observed that he had been in many actions before but always perceived some misbehaviour in some individuals, but in that action he saw none."

There were, to be sure, some quibbles about which troops had done what. One view was expressed by Colonel John Haslet of the all but extinct Delaware Regiment: "A party of Virginians formed the vanguard and did most of the fighting."

General Sullivan, a New Hampshire man and aggressively proud of it, saw in the attack on Trenton further proof that so-called "Yankee cowardice" was better than so-called "Southern valor." In a letter to his friend Meshech Weare, Sullivan would write: "Perhaps you may want to know how your men (the yankees) fight. I tell you exceeding well when they have proper officers. . . . All the general officers allowed and do allow that the yankee cowardice assumes the shape of true valor in the field and the Southern valor appears to be a composition of boasting and conceit. . . .

"Believe me, sir, the Yankees took Trent Town before the other troops knew anything of the matter more than that there was an engagement, and, what will still surprise you more, the line that attacked the town consisted of but eight hundred Yankees and there was 1600 Hessians to oppose them."

General Washington, as usual the diplomat, had high praise for all concerned. "In justice to the officers and men," he would report to Congress, "I must add that their behaviour upon this occasion reflects the highest honor upon them. . . . When they came to the charge, each seemed to vie with the other in pressing forward and were I to give a preference to any particular corps, I should do great injustice to the others."

---◆◆◆---

CHAPTER 35

All Our Hopes Were Blasted

Word of the astonishing defeat of the Hessians at Trenton spread quickly. Captain Muenchhausen, General Howe's German translator, heard of the loss late in the evening of December 26. In his

New York quarters he had just completed some six weeks' worth of diary entries and tucked them into an envelope to be sent to his brother in Germany. In the diary he had reported on the uninterrupted successes of the British army in New Jersey and described the occupation scene there. After making his final entry and sealing the envelope, he received the bad news, necessitating this postscript: "I have reopened this letter to report an unhappy affair. Colonel Rall, who was at Trenton with the Knyphausen, Lossberg, and Rall regiments and 50 Jagers, was compelled to surrender at dawn on the 26th, after a fight of one hour, owing partly to the suddenness of the surprise, and partly to their superior power. Two officers and 17 men, the only ones that saved themselves, brought the news to us. We know no further details at the moment."

In his next diary entry Muenchhausen would put the blame on Colonel Rall: "To his good fortune, Colonel Rall died the same day from his wounds. I say this because he would have lost his head if he had lived." Captain William Bamford, a British officer in New York, like many others, agreed: "The Hessian officers say his [Rall's] death's a lucky circumstance for him, for had he lived he must have been broke with infamy. At least."

"All agree," Colonel Donop reported ". . . that if Colonel Rall with his brigade had retreated over the bridge and then destroyed it he could have saved his command instead of fighting for an hour against such heavy odds." (Donop had been informed that 8,000 American troops had taken part in the attack at Trenton.) In a later comment, he would write: "There, then, is an eternal disgrace to our nation, and a clear proof that men are brave only when they are well led. For these were the same regiments which only a little while ago displayed such bravery in the capture of Fort Washington."

From his headquarters in New York, Lieutenant General Leopold Philip von Heister, in command of all Hessian troops in America, wrote an apologetic report of "the fatal affair at Trenton" to His Highness, the Prince of Hesse, the nobleman who was being paid by the English for the services of the Hessian troops. According to the troops who had escaped at Trenton, General Heister reported, Rall, "through his hot-headedness . . . was not willing to retreat and sacrificed his men . . . rather than use the bridge behind him which he could have held possession of with advantage."

From London the Earl of Suffolk would express his displeasure in a letter to General von Heister about "the disaster which happened to the Hessian brigade. . . . In deploring the death of Colonel Rall we are not able at the same time to avoid the fact that his great rashness interfered with him as the commander of a post where he should have tried to preserve the lives of his men." Suffolk could not resist a bit of sarcasm: "We will always continue to hope that the occasion will present itself that the troops of his Serene Highness may be able to give essential proof of their valour in the service of His Majesty, and that you will have to send us great accounts of their brave conduct."

Captain Johann Ewald was among the few who defended Rall; he placed some of the blame on Donop, who, he said, "was not able to tell a sham attack from a real one and foolishly took his force to Mount Holly out of supporting distance of Rall's command. As Colonel Rall lost his life in the fight and was therefore unable to defend himself in person, the blame will forever rest on him. His memory has been cursed by German and English soldiers, many of whom were not fit to carry his sword."

It would become General Howe's sad duty to inform Lord George Germain, in London, that "the unfortunate and untimely defeat at Trentown has thrown us farther back than was at first apprehended, from the great encouragement it has given to the rebels.

"I do not now see a prospect of terminating the war but by a general action, and I am aware of the difficulties in our way to obtain it as the enemy moves with so much more celerity than we possibly can with our foreign troops, who are too much attached to their baggage which they have in amazing quantities in the field."

The bad news spread through the colonies. From New York it would travel in letters to England: "The unfortunate affair at Trenton has thrown things for the present much back," Andrew Elliot reported to his brother, Sir Gilbert Elliot. The rebels' coup at Trenton, William Tryon, the Tory governor of New York, reported to Lord Germain, "has given me more real chagrin than any other circumstance this war; the moment was critical and I believe the Rebel Chiefs were conscious if some stroke was not struck that would give life to their sinking cause, they should not raise another army."

Lord Germain would soon find himself on the defensive in debates in Parliament. If only General Howe had "followed his advantages properly up" by crossing the Delaware and possessing

Philadelphia, Germain would declare, there would have been "a fair prospect of a successful campaign, and of the happy termination of the war in the course of it. But all our hopes were blasted by that unhappy affair at Trenton." In a message to Howe, Germain would complain: "The disagreeable occurrence at Trenton was extremely mortifying, especially as I fear that this affair will elate the enemy and encourage them to persevere in their rebellion. . . ."

In Leesburg, Virgina, an itinerant English journalist named Nicholas Cresswell found such a fear justified: "The minds of the people are much altered. A few days ago they had given up the cause for lost. Their late successes have turned the scale and now they are all liberty-mad again. Their recruiting parties could not get a man (except he bought him from his master) no longer since than last week, and now the men are coming in by companies."

In New York on Christmas Eve, Ambrose Serle, secretary to Admiral Richard Howe, had detected "the dying groans of rebellion" in a congressional declaration. Two days later, upon hearing of the loss at Trenton, he was "exceedingly concerned . . . as it will tend to revive the drooping spirits of the Rebels and increase their force."

———————♦♦♦———————

CHAPTER 36

Your Country Is at Stake

The big guns bombarding the Hessians in Trenton on December 26 were heard at least as far distant as Bristol, Pennsylvania, a dozen miles down the Delaware, where Colonel Joseph Reed was quartered with Colonel Cadwalader's force. Early in the morning, Reed would report, "the firing was heard at Trenton and we remained in great suspense and anxiety for the event of an enterprise on which the Fate of America then seemed to depend."

Later in the day, according to Reed, the report that General Washington's troops had made a successful attack on Trenton "so animated the troops at Bristol that it was concluded to cross the river again the next morning and proceed to Bordentown and from thence endeavor to join General Washington, then supposed to be at Trenton. Accordingly, orders were given for the troops to refresh and be in readiness to march next morning [the 27th].

"At sunrise the company of light infantry proceeded about two miles above Bristol and embarked. They were soon followed by the battalions, the Rhode Island troops being delayed to receive some clothing which had arrived from Philadelphia the preceding night.

"About 1 o'clock, when the militia had all landed and the Rhode Island troops were about to embark, a certain account arrived of the Success at Trenton and also that General Washington had recrossed the river with his prisoners. This unexpected circumstance threw us into the greater perplexity and occasioned a variety of opinions. It was contended by those who proposed returning that the motives which had caused this movement had now ceased; that there were no troops to support us; that Count Donop was equal if not superior in numbers and might soon march back from Mount Holly." Colonel Daniel Hitchcock, in command of the Rhode Islanders, was, according to Reed, among those who argued in favor of calling off the march.

"On the other hand it was urged that the militia being taken from their families and kept out a long time without action began to grow uneasy; that this was the third time they had been drawn out and if they should again return without attempting anything, a general desertion might be apprehended. That our affairs required enterprise and, though the Success at Trenton might be brilliant in its effects, its effects would depend upon being followed up. That the shock to the enemy must be very great and if they were attacked before they recovered the panick, no one could say to what extend the success might be pushed. The glory and honour of emulating the troops at Trenton was also urged and the necessity of recovering Jersey to save Philadelphia.

"Long and pretty warm debates ensued and, of those who were against returning, some were for proceeding to Mount Holly to attack the Hessians who were supposed to be there." General Cadwalader was all for marching on to Bordentown, "which might be expected to be weakly provided with troops in Donop's absence."

Finally, as a compromise, it was decided that "the troops should proceed to Burlington," which was still being protected by the galleys on patrol in the Delaware. At Burlington, Reed noted, the troops "could wait farther advice and proceed to Bordentown or

Mount Holly as the intelligence might direct. Or, if necessary, embark and return to Bristol."

Meanwhile, an officer who had ridden forward to reconnoiter the immediate area "returned with an account that he had seen some of the enemy's jagers. This was so important as well as surprising a piece of intelligence that it was necessary to ascertain it immediately. I proposed to Colonel [John] Cox and Colonel [Joseph] Copperthwaite to accompany me. We accordingly set out, reconnoitered the woods where it was expected they were and to our great satisfaction found the report was groundless."

Reed, Cox, Copperthwaite, and a few enlisted men "pushed on towards the enemy's outposts which were about four miles from Burlington. Halted at a small distance from the place where their pickets usually kept and, seeing no smoke or appearance of men, advanced to it and found it evacuated. Upon interrogating the neighbours, it appeared that, on the advice of the disaster at Trenton, Count Donop immediately began his retreat in the utmost panick and confusion, calling in his guards and parties as he proceeded and that the guards in this neighborhood had gone off precipitately the preceding evening. Advice of this evacuation was immediately sent to General Cadwalader."

Reed and his party rode on to Bordentown, where they learned "that upon the runaways from Trenton coming in the 26th, the Hessians and their followers the refugees, fled in the greatest confusion, leaving their sick behind them." Along the road to Bordentown, Reed observed that the local turncoats were becoming patriots again: "Almost every house along the road had a red rag nailed up on the door, which the inhabitants, upon this reverse of affairs, were now busily pulling down."

Bordentown was a mess, having suffered "all the marks of a savage enemy. The poor, terrified inhabitants effectually broken and hardly resembling what they had been a few months before. Colonel Copperthwaite returned from this place to Burlington to give General Cadwalader a state of affairs and urge him to push on the troops.

"After getting some refreshment, we pushed on to Trenton, which we found evacuated in like manner, not a single soldier of either army being there, and the town in a still more wretched condition than the other."

In Burlington, Colonel Copperthwaite found Cadwalader's troops settled in for the night. Captain Thomas Rodney, who had been in the vanguard as the troops advanced a few miles north of Bristol and crossed the Delaware to New Jersey, noted: "We reached Burlington about 9 o'clock [p.m.] and took possession of the town, and when we had done this we found that the enemy had fled from there and all the adjacent parts in great precipitation. . . . The troops were quartered in houses."

Some of them were quartered in the riverfront home of James Veree, the next-door neighbor of the widow Margaret Morris and her "flock." A guard was placed between Veree's house and Mrs. Morris's, but she was to be undisturbed: "We were so favoured as not to have any sent to our house. An officer spent the evening with us and appeared to be in high spirits, and talked of engaging the English as a very trifling affair—nothing so easy as to drive them over the North River, etc." (Captain Rodney, perhaps, but she didn't identify the officer in her journal.)

Earlier that day, the twenty-seventh, Mrs. Morris had heard of Washington's success against the Hessians at Trenton, "taking them by surprise; killed fifty and took nine hundred prisoners. The loss on our side not known, or, if known, not suffered to be public." (*Our* side. Though a devout Quaker and therefore "neutral," she did at times take sides in her mind.)

Early in the morning of December 28, Cadwalader's troops marched out of Burlington "in high spirits," Mrs. Morris observed. "My heart sinks when I think of the numbers unprepared for death who will probably be sent in a few days to appear before the Judge of Heaven." In the days to come her heart would continue to sink as additional troops passed her way.

Rodney's men, like the rest of Cadwalader's troops, had found quarters in Burlington, but for only a few hours. By four a.m. of December 28 they were marching on the Great Road toward Bordentown. "Along the road," Rodney noted, "we saw many Hessian posts at bridges and crossroads; they were chiefly made with rails and covered with straw, all deserted. The whole country as we passed appeared one scene of devastation and ruin. Neither hay, straw, grain or any livestock or poultry to be seen.

"We got to within half a mile of Bordentown about 9 o'clock and made a halt just at the foot of a bridge where we heard that the enemy had deserted the town and were about five miles off but were disposed to return and that some of their light horse were expected every minute.

"We then posted ourselves in a cornfield, so as to be convenient to surround the town, and set posts on all the roads, but after waiting thus about an hour were informed that the enemy were flying with all speed.

"We then marched into the town in several detachments and took possession of a large quantity of stores which the enemy had left, then went into quarters and refreshed ourselves and in about 2 hours the main body of the army came up.

"This little town is pleasantly situated on the River Delaware about 10 miles above Burlington, the houses are chiefly brick, and several of them large, elegant and neat, but they all look like barns and stables, full of hay, straw, dirt and nastiness, and everything valuable about them distroyed and carried off, and all the inhabitants fled. Here had been the headquarters of Lord or Count Donop, one of the Hessian Generals, but it looked more like the headquarters of a swine herd. Mr. Borden's house had some hundred pounds worth of goods and valuable furniture ruined and broken to pieces."

On the march along the river road to Bordentown, Cadwalader's troops passed by Whitehill, the domain of the widow Mary Peale Field, which had been spared on orders from Count Donop. And it was to be spared again, as Mrs. Field noted: "Every horse and wagon in my neighbourhood is gone away except mine, which the soldiers said General Mercer forbid their taking. This was very kind." Mary Peale Field led a charmed life.

On Christmas Day, she had served tea, as had become her custom, to the Reverend Jonathan Odell, Joseph Galloway, and her friends among the Hessian and British officers. But that was to be the last she would see of them: "In the night of the next day they with the army and several other followers of it took a precipitate flight at about one o'clock."

Charles Willson Peale and his eighty-one young Philadelphia militiamen reached Bordentown around noon on December 28 with the main body of troops and settled in temporarily: "My company got quartered where some King's troops had been and left them full of hay, and very dirty." Peale told his men to clean up the rooms and, as was his custom, went on the prowl in behalf of his charges: "Taking a walk, I found a storehouse with 'King's Stores' written on it, and provisions delivering out. I got a quarter of beef and some pork. I then heard of some flour. Went and got a barrel. . . . I went to desire a family to let a Negro girl make up some bread for us, but the lady told us she would do it herself and bake it in her oven. She said she was obliged to be a hypocrite, for she was a Whig in her heart, and was extremely kind to us."

A relatively pleasant evening was in prospect: plenty to eat and enough room for comfortable sleeping. But, true to military tradition, it couldn't last: "We were ordered immediately to march. Having no wagon belonging to the company, we could not take the flour. . . . It was dusk when we got into motion and the ground being very slippery, I lost my foothold on the rising side of the road and in my fall broke the stock of my gun.

"We got to Crosswicks, four miles from Bordentown, at early bedtime. But no bed for us, who think ourselves happy to get a plank by the fire." Eventually, however, "we got quarters with Mr. Cooke, who made us very welcome. The Hessians had taken every shirt he had, except the one on his back; which has been their general practice wherever they have been. They have taken hogs, sheep, horses and cows, everywhere. Even children have been stripped of their clothes—in which business the Hessian women are the most active. In short, the abuse of the inhabitants is beyond description."

On arriving in Crosswicks with the rest of Cadwalader's main body of troops, Thomas Rodney and his Delaware company learned that the enemy was now about eight miles off. "Some of the militia colonels applied to our infantry to make a forced march that night and overhaul them," Rodney noted, but he was against the plan. "We had then been on duty four days and nights, making forced marches without six hours sleep in the whole time. Whereupon the infantry officers of all the companies unanimously declared it was madness to attempt it; for it would use up all our brave men, not one of whom had yet given out but were dreadfully fatigued." Fortunately, there was to be some rest for the weary: "Here we got good comfortable quarters and something refreshing to eat and drink."

Troops bringing up the rear of Colonel Cadwalader's force crossed the Delaware to Burlington on Saturday, December 28. Among them was Sergeant William Young, still in good health, "thanks be to God," and accompanied by the eleven young men of his detachment. Young's son George was one of the eleven but another son, "exceeding unwell," had been allowed to go home. Still another son was serving elsewhere in Cadwalader's force.

While waiting near Bristol a day earlier, Young learned that it was not just another rumor that "General Washington had defeated Howe's men at Trenton." It had really happened; he "had it confirmed." He wrote a letter to his wife that day, just as he had done the day before. And, "thanks be to God," he got some mail only a few days old. "Received letters from home dated 23, 24." War or no war, the mail was at times getting through.

On the twenty-eighth, Young and his party, after a toilsome crossing, reached Greenbank, at the river's edge, where Mrs. Margaret Morris was still tending to her flock and, like Young, trusting that God would make everything come out all right.

Mrs. Morris was looking out over the Delaware from Greenbank as Sergeant Young and company and hundreds of others crossed from Bristol to Burlington. "Early this morning," she would report, "the troops marched out of town in high spirits. A flight of snow this morning drove the gondolas again down the river. . . .

"The weather clearing up this afternoon, we observed several boats with soldiers and baggage making up to our wharf."

After disembarking at the Greenbank wharf, Sergeant Young politely questioned her about quarters for his men: "A man who seemed to have command over the soldiers just landed civilly asked for the keys of Colonel Cox's house, in which they stowed their baggage and took up their quarters for the night, and were very quiet." This was the home of Colonel John Cox and family, next door to Mrs. Morris's, the place where she had successfully secreted her friend, the Reverend Jonathan Odell, in an "auger hole."

"This morning," Mrs. Morris noted the next day, December 29, "the soldiers at the next house prepared to depart and, as they passed my door, they stopped to bless me for the food I sent them, which I received, not as my due, but as belonging to my master who had reached a morsel to them by my hand."

Sergeant Young had risen early, as usual. He and his men would march on to rejoin their company. He made note of the encounter with Mrs. Morris: "The good woman next door sent us two mince pies last night, which I took very kind. May God bless all our friends and benefactors."

Around nine o'clock that morning Young and his men "set off for Bordentown. Got to it about 2. Saw a room full of wounded Hessians, one of them with his nose shot off. All of them in a wretched condition."

There was to be no rest here: "Set out immediately for Crosswicks, four miles from Trenton." It was rough going; the roads were a mess. Along the way they encountered a party of seven prisoners, who were being escorted by an armed detachment toward Bordentown. Among them were a civilian from Philadelphia, a merchant from Trenton, a British light infantryman, and Edward (Neddy) Shippen III, eighteen, the eldest son of Pennsylvania Chief Justice Edward Shippen, a man suspected of Tory sympathies. Earlier there had been eight prisoners in this group. One of them, an elderly man named Isaac Pearson, had attempted to escape along the way and had been fatally wounded by the guards.

Young Shippen had left his home in Philadelphia early in December and, with the Allen brothers and Joseph Galloway, joined the British at or near New Brunswick. For a time, it was reported, he acted as a scout for the enemy. He was captured along with the seven others shortly after the battle in Trenton on December 26.

Upon his son's return to Philadelphia, Justice Shippen would contrive a likely explanation of the venture. Neddy, he said, had been sent to New Jersey on an errand. He remained there "longer than his business required. In order to avoid being pressed in the militia service, when General Howe had advanced as far as Trenton and it was thought he was making his way to Philadelphia Neddy was prevailed upon by Johnny, Andrew and Billy Allen, to go with them to the British army, which he accordingly did, and was civilly received there by General Howe and the British officers.

"When the attack was made on the Hessians . . . he was accordingly taken prisoner by our army and carried, with others, to General Washington, who, after examining his case, and finding that he had taken no commission nor done any act that showed him inimical, very kindly discharged him." Colonel Tench Tilghman, an aide to Washington who knew the Shippen family well, would help to procure the boy's release and would make this comment: "I do not think the Mr. Allens used him kindly, if they carried him with them from home, they should not have left him at his time of life in Trenton."*

Sergeant Young and his men reached Crosswicks "at sunset very much tired, having marched fifteen miles, put our baggage into the

*Back home, Neddy was placed on parole and his movements were restricted. His father was later stripped of his judgeship and placed on parole. Neddy's sister Peggy in 1779 married General Benedict Arnold.

[Quaker] meeting house, where I shall lodge tonight and where I am writing this. . . . At this place the woods are quite alive with men, all are illuminated with large fires. Very bad traveling this day. I am very well though somewhat tired. Blessed be God in good health as are all our men."

Young was so cold that night that he was unable to sleep. He got up "a great while before day" and checked the condition of his men. Eight of them were "hearty," three of them ill. Later, things were looking better: "A fine day, all well. Still in the Quaker meeting house. All busy in dressing and packing provisions. Ready to march which I believe will be soon. . . . Saw my son William who is well."

At Crosswicks Sergeant Young would become increasingly disenchanted with the young Pennsylvania militiamen about him. But despite their misbehavior and his own weakened condition, he never blamed Providence: "I am much fatigued but have my health very well thanks be to thee oh God!"

Young found Colonel Hitchcock's Rhode Island and Massachusetts troops to be of a breed different from the Pennsylvanians: "It is melancholy to think what looseness prevails among all our men. There is among the New England men some seriousness." Later: "I am obliged to put up with the disagreeable company of a mixed multitude. Our own people are very loose in their conversation. The New England men are a quiet set of men."

Young recalled that on the previous New Year's Day he had had the pleasure of dining with all his family. "But now the Providence of God orders it other way." Not that he was complaining: "God in his good Providence has now brought me to the beginning of another year, and what shall I render to thee O my God, for all the blessings bestowed on me through the last year?"

Still in Crosswicks on Monday, December 30, Sergeant Young observed that "General Mifling came to camp . . . and addressed the New England forces, and [they] agreed to stay until this campaign is over."

Brigadier General Thomas Mifflin was perhaps the most eloquent of Washington's generals. During the retreat across New Jersey in November he had been dispatched to Philadelphia, where he urged the Congress to help in securing reinforcements. He "spoke animatedly pleasing, which gave satisfaction," and a congressional committee was formed to help him in recruiting. Mifflin had also appealed successfully for recruits in several areas outside Philadelphia. It was largely through his efforts that the militiamen now with Colonel Cadwalader in Crosswicks had answered General Washington's call for help.

In recent days Mifflin had been hard at it again. Around eight o'clock in the evening of Saturday, December 28, he wrote Washington from Bristol: "I came here at four o'clock this afternoon. Five hundred men, sent from Philadelphia, crossed to Burlington this morning. This evening I sent over near three hundred more. Tomorrow seven or eight hundred shall follow. I will cross in the morning, and endeavour to form them into regiments and a brigade. They consist of many different corps and want much regulation. . . . Pennsylvania is at length roused, and coming in great numbers to your Excellency's aid." Mifflin took command of this irregular force on Sunday, December 29, and set up temporary headquarters in Bordentown.

The next day he rode to Crosswicks to try to talk Colonel Daniel Hitchcock's fatigued New Englanders into serving a few weeks beyond their enlistment period. Lieutenant Charles Willson Peale noted General Mifflin's appearance on the thirtieth: "This morning General Mifflin came here and we are informed that our friends are coming in very fast to Philadelphia. General Mifflin had some regiments of New England troops paraded, whose service was just up. He harangued them on the necessity of their continuing in the service one month longer, promising them ten dollars gratuity for their past and present services—with which they showed their ready consent by three cheers."

Sergeant John Smith and his plunder-prone company of night raiders were among the Rhode Island troops called out to hear Mifflin's appeal. "On Sunday the 29th," Smith noted, "to Crosswicks, a small town about four miles from Bordentown. . . . The inhabitants chiefly Quakers who have a very beautiful meeting house built of brick in which was kept our picket guard."

At sunup the Rhode Islanders had drawn "a gill of rum per man and then marched" out of Bordentown. The road to Crosswicks was "exceeding slippery and sharp." After reaching Crosswicks when "the sun was about two hours high . . . we built some fires to warm us by, there being no room in the houses and the inhabitants acquainted us the enemy went through the town a day before about noon and that there were about 4000 or 5000 men, Hessians chiefly, and had with them a great deal of baggage. In this town they left in a store several hundred barrels of pork and beef salted in bulk.

"We lay on our arms all day and at night we had orders to seek us quarters and some went into houses and shops whilst others was obliged to lie out of doors and to build themselves sheds with boards and burn fences to make them fires to cook with this night. . . .

"Monday the 30th in the afternoon our brigade was sent for into the field where we paraded before the General who was present with all the field officers and after making many fair promises to them he begged them to tarry one month longer in the service and almost every man consented to stay longer who received 10 dollar bounty as soon as signed their names. Then the General with the soldiers gave three huzzas and was with clapping of hands for joy amongst the spectators and as soon as that was over the General ordered us to have a gill of rum per man and set out to Trenton to acquaint General Washington with his good success, as he termed it, to make his heart glad once more.

"We was dismissed to go to our quarters with great applause, the inhabitants and others saying we had done honour to our country, viz. New England. We received our rum and every man paraded with all his accoutrements. . . . After it grew dark having orders to lay our arms nigh for to be ready in a moment of alarm. We heard the enemy were advancing this way."

James Johnston, in Crosswicks with a militia company from Chester County, Pennsylvania, was impressed by Mifflin's persuasive efforts: "On beat to arms, the New England troops, whose turn had expired a few weeks before and who were almost destitute of clothing, declared that they would perform no further service. General Mifflin addressed them in a very animated strain and finally desired that all who were willing to march should step forward and give three cheers. Every man of them did so." Johnston particularly remembered "the delight of General Putnam at this result."

Private John Howland, the young Rhode Islander, was among those standing in that formation but his heart was back home. He and the others in Colonel Christopher Lippitt's Rhode Island regiment had learned about ten days earlier that their home state had been invaded by the enemy—reason enough for any soldier to yearn for home. "This was the time which tried both body and soul . . . ," Howland would recall. "We were standing on frozen ground, which was covered with snow. The hope of the Commander-in-Chief was sustained by the character of these half-frozen, half-starved men, that he could persuade them to volunteer for another month. He . . . directed or requested General Mifflin to address or harangue our brigade." Mifflin harangued the troops quite effectively, even promising that "all or every thing which should be taken from the enemy during the month should be the property of the men and the value of it divided among them." A ridiculous promise, Howland thought, since "no one could suppose it probable we could take stores or baggage from the enemy, who had *six* men to our *one* then in Jersey." When Mifflin finished, however, Howland and the others in his regiment indicated that they would stay on "by our unanimously poising the firelock as a signal."

Captain Stephen Olney, in the same lineup, would report the response as a bit less than unanimous: "General Mifflin made a harangue to the three regiments of Rhode Island. . . . Our regiment, with one accord, agreed to stay to a man, as did also the others, except a few who made their escape by the enemy at Trenton the next day and was not seen in the army afterwards."

Gentleman Johnny Stark, as the colonel from New Hampshire was known, persuaded his entire force to stay on, according to one of his officers. "Colonel Stark," the officer later reported, ". . . appealed to the patriotism of the men of the Granite hills who composed the New Hampshire regiments. He told them that if they left the army all was lost, reminded them of their deeds at Bunker's Hill and other occasions . . . [and] assured them that if Congress did not pay them their arrears, his own private property should make it up to them. He proposed a re-enlistment for six weeks, and such was his influence and popularity that not a man refused."

Chaplain David Avery, afflicted with a heavy cold but still on duty with the remains of Colonel John Paterson's Massachusetts Fifteenth Regiment, noted the pressure being applied to the troops: "Much pains taken to persuade the Continental troops to tarry six weeks after their enlistment shall be out. . . . Colonel Paterson's regiment agreed."

But not all of Paterson's troops. John Greenwood, the young fifer, was among those who decided that they had enough. A bounty to stay six weeks longer? Greenwood was not interested: "I was determined to quit as soon as my time was out. . . . I told my lieutenant I was going home. 'My God!' says he. 'You are not going to leave us, for you are the life and soul of us and are to be promoted to an ensign.'

"I told him I would not stay to be a colonel."

And off to Boston with another young man went fifer John Greenwood. Along the way he would sell the fancy Hessian sword he had picked up in Trenton.

David How, the laconic eighteen-year-old from Methuen, Massachusetts, was homeward bound, too. "The General," he noted, "ordered all to parade and see how many wood stay six weeks longer and a great part of the army stays for that time." But not David How: "This forenoon we have been drawing our wages. . . . This afternoon we set out for New England."

Jacob Francis, the former slave who had fought with a Massachusetts unit in the battle at Trenton, would recall going home only partially paid: "We lay there [in Trenton] a day or two, and then the time of the year's men was out, and our regiment received part of their pay and were permitted to return home. . . . At that time I had seven and a half months' pay due to me, and I believe others had the same. I received three months' pay, and all the rest of the regiment received the same."

Before returning home to Massachusetts (where he would go on to serve several more tours of duty) Francis "had permission to return to the place of my nativity in Amwell, about fifteen miles from Trenton. I immediately returned to Amwell and found my mother living but in ill health."

Some troops—Private William Chamberlin, the spruce beer brewer, and the few others remaining in his company, for example—appear to have been pretty much on their own following the battle at Trenton. "When we got back to Newtown to headquarters," Chamberlin would recall, "we had to shift for ourselves. The remains of our company, consisting of five or six besides myself, went back about a mile to a Dutch house and hired a room for a week and our board until the last day of December."

Before coming down from the north to join Washington's force, they had been due for discharge. Now they were determined to go home. Chamberlin went to Colonel Stark's headquarters "and requested a discharge for myself and men. He told me he had no orders to give a discharge. . . . He said we must wait a day or two as he could give no discharge until orders arrived."

Instead of heeding the colonel's word, they decided to go sightseeing: "Finding ourselves under the necessity of waiting, Spring and one or two others, with myself, took horses and rode to Philadelphia to see the famous city, thinking we should never have another opportunity. We were absent two or three days and when we returned the whole army had moved across the river, and left no one there that we knew, or that had any knowledge of us. We understood that guards were placed at all the ferrys on the river and no one was permitted to pass without orders."

A few days later, however, Chamberlin and Spring would find a way across the Delaware and head for Massachusetts and home. For them the New Jersey campaign was over.

Perhaps the greatest exodus following the Trenton battle was that of Colonel John Glover's Marbleheaders, the seamen who had made the December 25–26 crossing of the Delaware possible. Like many other New Englanders, they had caught privateering fever, a fast-spreading affliction, and they refused, almost to a man, to stay in service even for a week longer. There was big money to be made in privateering—far more than in soldiering—and the Marbleheaders set off to get some of it. They would not, as Washington put it, "by any endeavors of mine re-enlist."

On December 28, having dispatched about 900 Hessian prisoners to Philadelphia, and having learned that Colonel Cadwalader's corps had crossed the Delaware to New Jersey, General Washington began preparations to do the same with his Continentals, most of whose enlistments would be up in three days. As Sergeant Joseph White would put it: "Our whole army crossed over to Trenton again with about one half the number less than we had when we retreated over the river Delaware." Some troops crossed the Delaware direct-ly to Trenton on December 28. The next day, despite a heavy snowstorm, General Greene's division managed to get over the river at Yardley's Ferry, about four miles above Trenton. Accompanying General Sullivan's division, Washington noted that this force was unable to make the crossing on the twenty-ninth at McKonkey's Ferry, eight miles above Trenton, "on account of the ice, which will neither allow us to cross on foot or give us an easy passage for the boats." Washington and most of Sullivan's troops made it to Trenton the following day. The artillery crews and other troops reached Trenton on the thirty-first.

Buoyed by the victory of December 26, Washington sensed that "a fair opportunity is offered of driving the enemy entirely from, or at least to the extremity of, New Jersey," but he needed more than a handful of men to attempt it. His Continental force had been coming apart again. Of the 2,400 who had attacked the Hessians in Trenton almost a thousand were now no longer fit for duty. Many of the rest were within a few days of completing their enlistments. Painfully aware of this, Washington was determined to keep enough men long enough for one more bold stroke: "We are now making our arrangements and concerting a plan of operations which I shall attempt to execute as soon as possible, and which I hope will be attended with some success."

On arriving in Trenton, Washington proceeded to take part in some of the arm-twisting himself. Lieutenant Elisha Bostwick reported the effect of the commander in chief's words on the men of his unit, the Seventh Connecticut Regiment: "By the pressing solicitation of his Excellency a part of those whose time was out consented on a ten-dollar bounty to stay six weeks longer and, although desirous as others to return home, I engaged to stay that time and made every exertion in my power to make as many of the soldiers stay with me as I could, and quite a number did engage with me who otherwise would have went home."

A noncommissioned officer known to history only as Sergeant R would make this somewhat fanciful report on the reaction to the commander in chief's appeal: "At this trying time General Washington . . . ordered our regiment to be paraded, and personally addressed us, urging that we should stay a month longer. He alluded to our recent victory at Trenton; told us that our services were greatly needed, and that we could now do more for our country than we ever could at any future period; and in the most affectionate manner entreated us to stay.

"The drums beat for volunteers, but not a man turned out. The soldiers, worn down with fatigue and privations, had their hearts fixed on home and the comforts of the domestic circle, and it was hard to forego the anticipated pleasures of the society of our dearest friends.

"The General wheeled his horse about, rode in front of the regiment, and, addressing us again, said, 'My brave fellows, you have done all I have asked you to do, and more than could be reasonably expected. But your country is at stake, your wives, your houses and all that you hold dear. You have worn yourself out with fatigues and hardships, but we know not how to spare you. If you will consent to stay only one month longer, you will render that service to the cause of liberty and to your country which you probably never can do under any other circumstances. The present is emphatically the crisis which is to decide our destiny.'

"A few stepped forward, and their example was immediately followed by nearly all who were fit for duty in the regiment, amounting to about two hundred volunteers. . . . An officer inquired of the General if these men should be enrolled. He replied, 'No. Men who will volunteer in such a case as this need no enrollment to keep them to their duty.' "

Summing up the situation, James Wilkinson would write: "Great exertions had been made. . . . The men were addressed by companies, regiments, brigades and divisions, and finally after all the persuasive arts were exhausted, 1,200 or 1,400 consented to engage for an additional six weeks on the receipt of ten dollars bounty." Washington's "whole force then consisted of this number of Continental troops . . . and 3,500 or 3,600 Pennsylvania volunteer militia.* That of the enemy was estimated at 8,000 combatants, artillery, dragoons and infantry duly proportioned. How dreadful the odds."

On Wednesday, January 1, Washington reported from Trenton: "We have been parading the regiments whose time of service is now expired, in order to know what force we should have to depend on. . . . After much persuasion and the exertions of their officers, half or a greater proportion of those from the eastward [New England] have consented to stay six weeks on a bounty of ten dollars." The bounty was paid in hard money. "I feel the inconvenience of the advance, but what could be done? Pennsylvania had allowed the same to her militia. The troops felt their importance, and would have their price. Indeed, as their aid is so essential, and not to be dispensed with, it is to be wondered they had not estimated it at a higher rate."

Robert Morris gathered most of the necessary money, and did so on short notice. Hard money was what the troops wanted, none of that Continental paper. First, Morris had sent along enough for Washington to get the bounty business started: "four hundred and ten Spanish silver dollars, ½ French crown, 10½ English shillings in two canvas bags." Then he got to the serious fund-raising: "I mean to borrow silver and promise payment in gold, and will then collect the gold in the best manner I can." So he wrote Washington on

---

*Eighteen hundred, according to Colonel Cadwalader.

December 29, adding this postscript: "Hearing that you are in want of a quarter cask of wine, I have procured a good one, which Mr. Commissary Wharton will send up."

Morris was up well before dawn on January 1 "to dispatch a supply of fifty thousand dollars to your Excellency. You will receive that sum with this letter; but it will not be got away so early as I could wish, for none concerned in the movement, except myself, are up."

While waiting for his fellow financiers to get out of bed, Morris reflected on the year just ended: "The year 1776 is over. I am heartily glad of it, and hope you nor America will ever be plagued with such another. Let us accept the success at Trenton as a presage of future fortunate events."

Morris had apparently been too occupied with fund-raising to note that meanwhile hundreds of the Hessians captured at Trenton were now in Philadelphia. "Near eleven," Christopher Marshall noted in his diary, "the Hessian prisoners, to the amount of nine hundred, arrived in this City and made a poor, despicable appearance." On the same day, Sarah Fisher encountered "a multitide of people going to see the Hessian prisoners march to the barracks. Some people think about 700 marched, with some women and children. They looked poorly clad, were dressed in blue, and their outside clothes appeared to be dirty. What is remarkable, they say there is not among them one English or Scotch prisoner, but all Hessians." Prisoners, according to Marshall, continued to arrive in town for the next two days.

————— ♦♦♦ —————

CHAPTER 37

The Women Would Have Killed Us

After spending the night of December 26–27 in a crowded room of the McKonkey ferry house, the Hessian officers had been escorted to Newtown by a detachment commanded by Colonel George Weedon. Weedon's "visage," Lieutenant Piel observed during this six-and-a-half-mile march, "spoke but little in his favor, yet he won all our hearts by his kind and friendly conduct." In Newtown the officers were given comfortable quarters, some in a village inn and some in private homes. Lord Stirling was among those who invited them to be guests at his quarters. General von Heister, commander of all the Hessians in America, "treated me like a brother when I was a prisoner," Stirling explained, "and so, gentlemen, will you be treated by me."

So Lieutenant Piel would report. "We had scarce seated ourselves," Piel would continue, "when a long, meager, dark-looking man whom we took for the parson of the place stepped forth and held a discourse in German in which he endeavored to set forth the justice of the American side in this war. He told us he was born a Hanoverian; he called the King of England nothing but the Elector of Hanover, and he spoke of him so contemptuously that his garrulity became intolerable. We answered that we had not come to America to inquire which party was in the right but to fight for the king.

"Lord Stirling, seeing how little we were edified by the preacher, relieved us of him by proposing to take us with him to visit General Washington."

Piel, a fourteen-year veteran of army service, was less than overawed by the rebels' commander in chief: Washington "received us very courteously, though we understood very little of what he said, since he spoke nothing but English, a language in which none of us at that time were strong. Nothing in his aspect shines forth of the great man that he is universally considered. His eyes have scarce any fire. There is, however, a smiling expression on his countenance when he speaks that wins affection and respect. He invited four of our officers to dine with him. The rest dined with Lord Stirling."

Lieutenant Wiederholdt, one of Washington's four guests, was no less self-assured than Piel. His own testimony indicates that he did most of the talking and that Washington listened admiringly: "General Washington did me the honor of conversing a good deal with me about the unfortunate affair. I freely expressed my opinion that if our troop arrangements hadn't been bad we would not have fallen into his hands." Could Wiederholdt have made better arrangements? Washington asked, according to Wiederholdt. Yes, indeed: "I told him yes. I pointed out all the faults in our arrangements. I showed him how I would have done it and would have managed to come out of the affair with honor." Washington, according to Wiederholdt, was impressed. More so, apparently, than Wiederholdt was with him: "General Washington is a courteous and distinguished man, but he . . . speaks little and has a crafty physiognomy."

Before going on to Philadelphia with the rest of the captured officers, Wiederholdt received Washington's permission to return to Trenton and retrieve a trunkful of clothing he had had to leave behind. In Trenton he would find the trunk intact, thanks to the vigilance of the woman in whose house it had been stored.

While the Hessian officers were living in relative comfort (some were still accompanied by their servants), Johannes Reuber and the other captured enlisted men were grumbling about their situation. After enduring the night of December 26–27 in "a miserable prison," Reuber noted, "we next arrived in Newtown and a bigger prison, one that had a stone wall around it." Reuber was among those being held in the Bucks County jail; others were crowded into Newtown's Presbyterian Church. The rebel guards, according to him, "came to the courtyard and dumped bread out of baskets into the snow. This was terrible to see. Hardly anyone could imagine how miserable we felt, and how cold. It was said that we would leave this valley of tears and would have regular barracks when we reached Philadelphia and that there we would be in peace."

Before leaving for Philadelphia, the officers signed this parole: "We, the Subscribers, Hessian Officers, made prisoners of war by the American Army of his Excellency, George Washington, at Trenton, on December the 26th inst., being allowed Our Liberty, under such restrictions as to place as may be from time to time appointed, do give our Parole of Honour, that we will remain at the place and within the limits appointed for us by his Excellency, the General, the Honourable Congress, Council of Safety, or Commissary of Prisoners of War, Peaceably behaving ourselves and by no way Send or give Intelligence to the British or Hessian Army or speak or do anything disrespectful or Injurious to the American States while we remain Prisoners of War. We will also restrain our Servants and Attendants who are allowed to remain with us, as far as in our power, to the same conditions—Newtown, December 30, 1776."

Looking back on the busy day's doings, Johannes Reuber would jot these details in his diary: "Early in the morning we left Newtown and marched to the big and beautiful city of Philadelphia and eventually to a three-sided barracks. We arrived at the front entrance to the city at noon and as we marched through the city, many people, big and little, young and old, stood there watching sharply, seeing what kind of people we were. Some of them came up very close to us. The old women screamed fearfully and started to threaten us. They cried out that we ought to be hanged for coming to America to rob them of their freedom. Others, however, brought us liquor and bread but they were not allowed by the old women to give them to us. At one time the people pressed on us with such force as to nearly break the guard over us. The old women were the worst. If the American guards had not protected us, the women would have killed us."

During the march through the city, "the mob became so rough and threatening that the commander said, 'Dear Hessians, we will go to the barracks,' and then drove the mob off. . . . Along with some English prisoners, we were put in the barracks for safety sake because of the anger of the people.

"Later, General Washington of the Americans made a proclamation and it was posted all over the city: the Hessians were without blame and had been forced into this war. The Hessians had not come of their own free will. They should not be regarded as enemies but as friends of the American people and should be treated as such. Because General Washington had full authority and he gave his honest word, it became better for us. All day long, Americans big and little, rich and poor, came to the barracks and brought food to us and treated us with kindness and humanity."

A few days later the enlisted men would be marched off toward Lancaster County, Pennsylvania, where most of them would be put to work on farms. The officers would be escorted to Baltimore, then to Dumfries, Virginia. Before leaving Philadelphia, several of them would be the guests of General Putnam, fifty-eight-year-old "Old Put." One of the Hessians would report: "He gave each of us his hand and we must drink a glass of Madeira with him. He may be an honorable man, but only the rebels would have made him a general."

—◆◆◆—

CHAPTER 38

The Colonel Was Detained by Love

Most of the Hessians who had escaped from Trenton on December 26 were, a few days later, bivouacked in the Princeton area as part of the corps commanded by Colonel Donop. The rebels' strike at Trenton had intruded upon Donop's pleasant, four-day stay with the "exceedingly beautiful young widow" in Mount Holly and prompted a sudden change of plans. "Since it was to be assumed now," Captain Ewald observed, "that Washington would occupy the Crosswicks pass in the rear of the Donop Corps, which had always been neglected, and cut it off from Princetown, the colonel set out with his entire corps for Crosswicks with the firm resolve to cut his way through at all costs."

Donop issued marching orders for all of his troops, including those quartered in and around Bordentown. He also "collected 292 men of the Rall Brigade" who had fled Trenton and added them to his force. At the drawbridge near Crosswicks he picked up more troops, four officers and a hundred men who had been on guard duty there. Donop proceeded to Allentown, about thirteen miles south of Princeton, and there awaited orders. They were received on December 28 from Brigadier General Alexander Leslie, commander of the British force in Princeton. "General Leslie," Donop reported, "urged me insistently to join him at once because he expected to be attacked by enemy forces from different sides at any hour." Donop was on the march immediately and arrived in Princeton during the afternoon of December 28. His men were fatigued and many of them were ill. Moreover, the Princeton area was already crowded with troops. Donop remained in Princeton with one battalion and sent off the rest of his force to Kingston, three miles northeast of Princeton. For many of his troops it was to be a horrendous night: "During the night 400 of my brigade had to camp in the open, and it was so cold that two cows were frozen to death. There will be tragic consequences if we do not find accommodations in houses. It does not appear that we will, however, since General Leslie does not wish to give up the quarters he occupies here."

On Monday, December 30, Donop received reports that "great numbers of rebels were at Pennington, Maidenhead and Cranbury. I sent Captain von Wrumb, with 100 grenadiers to Pennington. He returned by way of Maidenhead without having seen one enemy soldier. Captain Lorey, with 14 jagers, proceeded to the town of Cranbury, but met none."

The next day there were further reports of a likely attack by the rebels. "Since five o'clock this morning," Donop reported, "we have been under arms, having received certain information last night. Strong patrols have been sent in all directions but as of now they have learned nothing of the approach of the enemy. . . . I had two redoubts built, facing Trenton, and on all other main roads defense works thrown up and manned."

If the rebels came, Donop was sure his Hessians would make them pay dearly. He was determined to avenge the humiliating defeat of the Hessians at Trenton. Washington's rebel army, he declared in a letter to General James Grant, "ought to be driven immediately to the other side of the Delaware River. I do not believe at all that they have more than 500 of our men as prisoners which number surely cannot weaken our army. I acknowledge, however, that the shame is none the less for our nation to have lost six cannon, with fifteen banners and three regiments at one attack and this in a section of the country greatly demoralized."

Donop went on to put the blame on Colonel Rall and his second in command, Major Friedrich Ludwig von Dechow, both fatally wounded on the twenty-sixth: "Colonel Rall was to have been buried with his [acting] lieutenant colonel [Dechow] yesterday. I am very well satisfied because they would have been compelled to appear before a court martial, the former to explain his general conduct and the latter why he did not go out in the morning with Rall's patrol."

Quartered with his jagers in Kingston, above Princeton, Captain Ewald noted the widespread effects of the defeat at Trenton: "The Americans had constantly run before us. Four weeks ago we expected to end the war with the capture of Philadelphia, and now we had to render Washington the honor of thinking about our defense. Because of this affair at Trenton, such a fright came over the army that if Washington had used the opportunity, we would have flown to our ships and let him have all of America. For, as we had thus far underestimated our enemy, from this unhappy day onward we saw everything through a magnifying glass." Again, Ewald referred to the charms of the mysterious widow: the debacle at Trenton was due "partly to the fault of Colonel Donop who was led by the nose to Mount Holly and detained there by love."

On the final day of 1776, about two hours before daylight, according to Ewald, the entire British and Hessian corps "stood to arms on the heights around Princeton, since the enemy had strengthened his position at Maidenhead and we had information that Washington would attack." There had been reports, almost hourly, of the approach of the rebel army. Roaming parties of rebels were reported to be in the vicinity of nearby Rocky Hill and Cranbury.

That morning, December 31, a force commanded by Lieutenant Colonel Robert Abercromby was ordered to advance to Five Mile Run (Little Shabakunk), a stream on the far side of Maidenhead, and dislodge a detachment of rebels in defensive positions there. Captain Wreden's First Jager Company, a contingent of Hessian grenadiers, and a strong force of English light infantry marched through Maidenhead and toward Five Mile Run without encountering any rebels. But as they approached the run, described as "a small brook with steep banks, over which is a bridge that is surrounded on both sides by hills," they met some stiff resistance. The rebels held out for a time but eventually had to give way when an attack by the grenadiers put an end to the action. It was a bloody skirmish; there were about 140 casualties in all, Captain Ewald was told, including seven of Wreden's jagers.

Around ten in the evening of the thirty-first, according to Ewald, an American officer was taken prisoner by a Scottish patrol. He had sneaked past the outpost and, posing as an English adjutant on a special mission, asked for the password since he had forgotten it. The Scots did not like his story and so they brought him in as a prisoner. Later, the rebel officer identified himself as a major in command of riflemen and admitted he had intended to make a surprise attack.

In one of the minor clashes that occurred in the Princeton area around this time, two rebel soldiers were killed. It happened on January 1 near the western bank of Stony Brook, about a mile to the west of Princeton. From his front door, Robert Lawrence could see some of the action. "When it was over," he noted, "two Americans lay dead in the field." Later, from a woman who was working in the kitchen of the British adjutant, Lawrence would learn some of the gory details: "The regular [British] soldiers came in from the guard and she heard one of them tell the servant that he could not do as Brown did today. The servant asked him what that was, and he said there was a wounded man that could not stand and prayed Brown not to kill him. Upon that Brown clapt the muzzle of his gun to his breast and shot him dead. The servant said it was murder and so they all said that was present except one and he said he would have done the same.

"This," Lawrence noted in the narrative he was keeping, "is verifyed by two dead men being found near Stony Brook. One of them was shot in his groin and again through his breast, very probable the man that Brown murdered. The other was shot in his hip and again through his head and the palm of his hand and the wristband of his shirt on the other arm very much burnt with gun powder. It is very probable that this man, seeing his murderer point his gun at his head, clapt up both his hands to defend it as it is natural to us to defend against a blow. The bullet entered his head a little above his eyebrow and dasht out his brains so that some of them lay on his face. This concerning these men was told to me by a very reputable gentleman who saw their dead bodys, took notice of their wounds, and helpt to bury them."

Later on New Year's Day, according to Lawrence, some British soldiers who had apparently taken part in the action "came along the main road from over Stony Brook. One of them was very strangely wounded for he was shot with an iron gun rammer rather than a bullet, which entered under his chin and came out again at his nose near his eyes. . . . He languished a few days and dyed. . . . It was said that the [British] Regulars said that the Rebels were so damned cowardly that they shot their gun sticks at them and run away. It is generally thought that this was done in the skirmish where the two men were murdered as above said."

CHAPTER 39

Haussegger Said It Was Mutiny

On Monday, December 30, the day he returned to Trenton, General Washington had to concern himself not only with holding his own force together but also with determining what the enemy was up to. How were the enemy troops now deployed? Were the British preparing to attack? Washington had to know, and his spy system was proving to be ineffective. For help he turned to his adjutant general, Colonel Joseph Reed, who had left Colonel Cadwalader's corps to lead a scouting party into Trenton a few days earlier. Reed knew the area well. He had been born and raised in Trenton, had studied at the College of New Jersey in Princeton (class of 1757), and practiced law in Trenton. His familiarity with the two towns and the roads between them would in the next few days prove to be of great importance.

This is how Reed, writing in the third person, would recall the situation: "In this pause, no plan of farther proceeding being settled and intelligence being very obscure and doubtful, the General observing to the Adjutant General, who was a native of that place and well acquainted with the inhabitants and country around, that some intelligence must be secured if possible and that the great vigilence of the enemy had deterred spies from venturing or at least they were of little service."

Reed volunteered to lead a reconnaissance mission to the Princeton area and asked to take along a few members of the First Troop Philadelphia Light Horse, who were serving as Washington's personal bodyguard. Washington assented and presently Reed rode off with seven of the young men "to the neighbourhood of Princeton where either by prisoners or otherwise the desired intelligence could be had. . . .

"They met with very little success. . . . The arms and ravages of the enemy had struck such terror that no rewards would tempt the inhabitants, tho' otherwise well disposed, to go into Princeton on this errand. But, it being fully resolved not to return while there was a chance of success, it was concluded to pass on and even go round Princeton, expecting that in the rear they would be less guarded."

Near Clarksburg (Clarksville), about four miles south of Princeton, Reed's party espied a British soldier passing from a barn to a stone house. A plunderer? Reed dispatched two men to bring him in. Another British soldier came into sight, and then a third. Reed and the rest of his men charged on and surrounded the house. Then the unthinkable happened: "Twelve British soldiers, equipped as dragoons and well armed, their pieces being all loaded and having the advantage of the house, surrendered to seven horsemen, of whom six had never before seen an enemy." A British sergeant succeeded in escaping out a back door, leaving Reed's party with eleven prisoners.

The eleven, Thomas Peters, one of the cavalrymen with Reed would recall, "came out of the house and formed in the yard with muskets in hand. We compelled them to surrender and lay down their arms. A prisoner was mounted behind a trooper whose horse would carry double and the rest were marched towards Trenton. . . . We found they were a party of the Queen's Light Dragoons, late from Ireland, fine looking fellows."

Peters, riding double with one of the prisoners, was one of the first to reach Trenton. "It gave General Washington considerable satisfaction," he would recall, "to obtain the information he wished."

Interrogation of the prisoners and "a Commissioner" also captured along the way, according to Colonel Reed, gave Washington "a very perfect account . . . that Lord Cornwallis, with a body of picked troops and well appointed, had the day before reinforced Grant at Princeton* and that this party was pressing wagons to begin their march the next morning in order to dislodge us from Trenton. That their whole force could not be less than 7,000 or 8,000 but if it had been less it was still much superior to our whole force."

The prisoners were "separately examined," according to Major James Wilkinson, and "the information received . . . left no doubt of the enemy's superiority and his intention to advance upon us, which would put General Washington in a critical situation."

At least one spy, described by Colonel John Cadwalader as "a very intelligent young gentleman," got into Princeton and returned

---

*Actually, Cornwallis did not arrive at Princeton until "the middle of the night [of January 1–2] . . . and superseded General Grant in his command," according to Lieutenant Archibald Robertson. Because of what had happened in Trenton on December 26, Cornwallis had canceled plans to sail for home on December 27.

with information generally corroborating the intelligence gleaned from the prisoners. From Crosswicks, Cadwalader reported to Washington that the young man had sneaked into Princeton around noon of December 30 but in the course of his reconnoitering was taken prisoner. He escaped the next morning and hastened to Crosswicks. There he reported to Cadwalader on the number of troops in Princeton ("about five thousand men, consisting of Hessian and British troops—about the same number of each") and other details, including "the situation of the cannon" and the fact that there were "no sentries on the back or east side of town."

Cadwalader drew a map incorporating the spy's many bits of information and forwarded it, along with an explanatory message, to Washington. Perhaps the most important information contained in this "spy map" was the existence of a little-known road that, Cadwalader noted, "leads to the back part of Prince Town which may be entered anywhere on this side . . . the country cleared chiefly for about two miles."

With this intelligence in hand, General Washington and his aides discussed the advisability of ordering Cadwalader's force, now about 3,500 men, to march in from Crosswicks to Trenton. This would bring the total of troops under Washington's direct command to about 6,000.

About a thousand of his men had meanwhile taken up a defensive position along Five Mile Run, a stream situated about a mile and a half south of Maidenhead. Brigadier General Fermoy was placed in charge of this detachment, which comprised the remains of Fermoy's own brigade, the remains of Colonel Edward Hand's First Pennsylvania Continental Regiment, of Colonel Charles Scott's Fifth Virginia Continental Regiment, and of Colonel Nicholas Haussegger's German Regiment. These troops were supported by two artillery pieces of Captain Thomas Forrest's battery. From Five Mile Run, Fermoy sent forward a small party which set up a picket post in Maidenhead.

A short time after reaching Five Mile Run, Colonel Haussegger, a mysterious figure from Lebanon, Pennsylvania, proceeded with his German Regiment even farther toward enemy lines than Maidenhead and took part in one of the Revolution's most bizarre events.*

Haussegger's regiment (or battalion; the terms were often used

*In letters, orders and other contemporary documents the colonel's name is spelled Hausiker, Hossicker, and more than a dozen other ways.

interchangeably), made up of about 400 men,* was possibly the largest unit under Fermoy's command. Raised under a congressional resolution about six months earlier, it originally comprised some 700 men, all from Pennsylvania or Maryland and all of them said to be of German descent, even those bearing such names as James Murphy, Timothy Cahill, and Michael Crowley. Before being given command of this regiment, Haussegger had served with the Fourth Pennsylvania Regiment in the disastrous Canadian campaign. He had commanded the German Regiment in and around New York and retreated with the rest of Washington's force across New Jersey. During the days immediately preceding the December 26 attack on Trenton, Haussegger and his troops were part of the guard force posted in and around Coryell's Ferry. On Christmas Day he had a visitor, Captain John Lacey of Buckingham, a village situated about six miles southwest of Coryell's Ferry. Haussegger and Lacey had served together in the Canadian campaign. Lacey had recently returned to his Buckingham home, disgruntled but still committed to the American cause and horrified by the number of Tories abounding in Buckingham, particularly among his own relatives.

Having learned that Haussegger was nearby, Lacey "hastened to see him." Haussegger, Lacey observed, "was much pleased, or appeared to be so, to see me." They commiserated with each other about their mutual troubles with Colonel Anthony Wayne while they were serving in the north. As the conversation progressed, Lacey was dismayed to learn that Haussegger was disenchanted not only with Wayne but also with the common cause. Haussegger said many things "derogatory of the American army and extolled that of the British. I found before I left him that he was disgusted, and determined to leave the Army himself before long. I left him the night before the capture of the Hessians at Trenton and never saw him afterwards. Unfortunate and unhappy man—"

In the December 26 attack on Trenton, Haussegger's troops served ably as part of General Fermoy's brigade. A few days later, after reaching Five Mile Run as part of Fermoy's defensive force, Haussegger set off with his regiment toward Princeton on what he

*The return-of-the-forces report of soldiers encamped near the Delaware River as of December 22, 1776, listed 374 officers and men of the German Regiment as present and fit for duty, 36 "present sick," 18 "absent sick," and 20 on "command" (furlough).

would describe as a reconnaissance mission. Conrad Housman, a young man from York, Pennsylvania, took part in the march and a few days later reported the whole story to John Adlum, an acquaintance from back home. This is how Adlum recorded it:

"The regiment was marched toward Princeton and not meeting with any enemy, they continued marching until they came within about a half a mile of Princeton. Major Weltner rode up to Col. Housacker [sic] and immediately a smart altercation took place between them. The Major ordered the regiment to halt. Housacker ordered them to march, when the Major said, 'The enemy are in the town.'

"Housacker said they were not. The regiment halted during the altercation and most of the officers of the regiment came to where the Colonel and Major were disputing at the head of the regiment. The Major said, 'They shall not march until the town is reconnoitered and then we can act according to circumstances.'

"The Colonel replied he would go and reconnoiter the town himself. He ordered out ten men and Lieutenant Bernard Hubley to go with him. The Major ordered the Lieutenant to stand by his platoon. Housacker said it was mutiny and that he would have him punished. The Major replied that prudence was not mutiny and that he knew the enemy were in the town and that the Colonel also knew it, and that it was highly improper to go into a place occupied by the enemy. Housacker said there was no enemy there and he set out for Princeton taking ten men with him and went direct to the Hessian general's quarters."*

At this point, Conrad Housman, one of the ten men with Haussegger, learned that the whole business had been prearranged. The Hessian officer "came to the door and took him by the hand and asked him where his regiment was. The Colonel replied that the Major mutinied and usurped the command and had even ordered an officer back to his place who he intended to have brought with him, and these ten men was all he could bring with him.

" ' Well,' says the General, 'I am sorry you did not bring in your regiment. I had ordered all the troops to keep close in their quarters. You see, I have not even a sentinel at my own door and if they

---

*There was no Hessian general in the area. Housman was perhaps referring to Colonel Donop or one of his aides. Donop was at this time in command of a large Hessian force bivouacked west of Princeton.

had come in we could have taken them with little or no bloodshed.'

"And then pulled out his purse and poured some gold into his own hand and told Housacker to take what he wanted of it. The General then ordered a guard to take the men into their care. The Colonel told the General he wished to have one of the men as a waiter. The General told him to call out one, and he called up Housman, and then the General and Colonel went into the house together and the next day they set out for N. York."

CHAPTER 40

All Was Now Hurry, Confusion, and Noise

Benjamin Rush, the congressman and physician, was among those who crossed the Delaware near Burlington with Cadwalader's troops and advanced to Crosswicks. He was elated by the recent turn of events: "There is no soil so dear to a soldier as that which is marked with the footsteps of a flying enemy—everything looks well. Our army increases daily, and our troops are impatient to avenge the injuries done to the state of New Jersey. The Tories fly with precipitation of guilty fear to General Howe."

On New Year's Day Rush decided to leave Crosswicks, where Cadwalader's troops were still quartered, and visit some army friends in Trenton, a jaunt of about eight miles. He alighted from his horse in front of General St. Clair's quarters in Trenton and there "dined and spent the afternoon with General Mercer and Colonel Clement Biddle. It was a day which I have ever since remembered with pleasure. Col. Biddle gave me the details of the victory at Trenton a few days before. The two generals, both Scotchmen, and men of highly cultivated minds, poured forth strains of noble sentiments in their conversation. General Mercer with great composure said he would not be conquered, but that he would cross the mountains and live among the Indians, rather than submit to the power of Great Britain in any of the civilized states."

Happy to be with such friends again, Rush decided to spend the night in St. Clair's quarters. After supping, they continued their discussion around the fireplace—Mercer, Biddle, Dr. John Cochran, St. Clair, and, among others, Major James Wilkinson, St. Clair's aide.

At one point, according to Wilkinson, who reconstructed the conversation years later, the talk turned to Captain William Washington, who had led the heroic attack on the Hessian cannoneers on December 26. For his gallantry he was to be promoted from captain of infantry to major of cavalry. A fitting and well-deserved reward, the men agreed—all except Mercer. His testy reaction surprised the others; surely the captain deserved the promotion, did he not?

But, Mercer felt, that was not the point. "We are not engaged in a war of ambition," he went on to say. "If it had been so, I should never have accepted a commission under a man who had not seen a day's service." (He was referring to fellow Virginian Patrick Henry, a distinguished spokesman for the patriot cause but not a military man.)

"We serve not for ourselves but for our country," Mercer continued, "and every man should be content to fill the place in which he can be most useful. I know Washington to be a good captain of infantry, but I know not what sort of a major of horse he may make; and I have seen good captains make indifferent majors. . . .

"For my own part, my views in this contest are confined to a single object, that is, the success of the cause, and God can witness how cheerfully I would lay down my life to secure it."

The fireside talk was interrupted, according to Dr. Rush, when "an account was received that the British army then at Princeton intended to attack our posts at Trenton and Crosswicks. A council of war was held at General Washington's quarters to determine what steps should be taken to oppose them. A division took place in the council upon the question whether the troops at Crosswicks should be drawn to Trenton, or left where they were to occasion a diversion of the British forces. General Knox proposed that as I was connected with Genl. Cadwalader's corps, I should be called into the council, to give an opinion upon the question. I was accordingly sent for, and heard from General Washington a brief state of the controversy. He then asked my advice. I said that I was not a judge of what was proper in the business before the council, but one thing I knew well, that all the Philadelphia militia would be very happy in being under his immediate command, and that I was sure they would instantly obey a summons to join his troops at Trenton. After this information I retired, and in a few minutes was called in again and requested by Genl. Washington to be the bearer of a letter to General Cadwalader. I readily consented and set off for Crosswicks at ten o'clock accompanied by Wm. Hall, one of the Philadelphia troop of horse. The weather was damp and cold, the roads muddy, and the night extremely dark. When we came within a mile of Crosswicks we met Colonel Sharp who had the command of the patroles. He rode up to me and presenting a cocked pistol to my breast, demanded who I was. I answered 'An old friend.' 'I don't know you, Sir (said he), tell me your name,' still holding his pistol to my breast. I then told my name and my business. He ordered us to be conducted to Genl. Cadwalader's quarters, to whom in his bed I delivered Genl. Washington's letter. It was then about 1 o'clock. He instantly rose, and set his brigade in motion."

With some 3,500 troops—his own militiamen and the New England Continentals plus those recently raised by General Mifflin—Colonel Cadwalader rode eight miry miles through the night from Crosswicks to Trenton. The vanguard arrived around seven in the morning of Thursday, January 2. Some of Cadwalader's troops—Sergeant William Young and two of his sons among them—marched through Trenton and up the river road about a mile to The Hermitage, the home of Philemon Dickinson, who was on duty as commanding officer of New Jersey militia. The stately home had been ransacked and badly used by some fifty jagers, who had occupied the place until forced to flee on December 26.

The night march from Crosswicks, Sergeant Young would recall, was rough going: "It rained when we set out. On account of the thaw the road was very muddy and deep. Though we had but eight miles to go it was 9 o'clock before we reached Trentown. I was a good deal fatigued on account of the deepness of the road, and its being night I could not see my way. The moon gave some light, but it being on my back I could not see so as to get the best road."

Sergeant Young offered his usual thanks to Providence: "Through the goodness of God I am very well and am at quarters at Mr. Dickinson's green house near a mile from Trentown on Delaware. Passing through Trentown, I saw the six pieces of artillery taken from the Hessians the other day. I called to see Mrs. Brown, the old lady at whose house I lodged when I first got to Trentown, December 5, 1776."

James Johnston, an eighteen-year-old militiaman from Chester

County, Pennsylvania, was among the troops at Dickinson's place when the alarm sounded: "After marching all night, Trenton was reached about daylight," and his company "was ordered to occupy the greenhouse of General Dickinson, about one mile from that place, but whilst preparing breakfast, the alarm was given of the approach of the enemy."

Lieutenant James McMichael fixed the time of the alarm at ten a.m., when "we received news that the enemy were advancing, when the drums beat to arms and we were all paraded on the south side of the bridge." Others said the alarm was sounded around nine a.m.

Captain Stephen Olney, who had marched in from Crosswicks with his company, "took quarters in the houses and began to prepare for breakfast. But before it was ready the drums beat to arms. The enemy, whom we supposed at Princeton, 12 miles off, or at Brunswick, 24 miles off, were near at hand and double our number. Our troops paraded on the south side of a small river [the Assunpink] that passes through the town into the Delaware."

Lieutenant Charles Willson Peale and his company of Philadelphia militiamen, after marching through the night from Crosswicks—"so many runs to cross and fences to remove"—were just settling in when the drums beat to arms: "The sun had risen more than an hour before we reached the town, and afterwards the difficulty of getting quarters kept us a long time under arms.

"At last we were provided and had made a fire. I took a short nap on a plank with my feet to the fire; but was suddenly awakened by a call to arms—the enemy approaching and at a small distance from the town. We soon paraded and joined a battalion and appeared on the alarm ground."

Dr. Benjamin Rush had returned to Trenton with the vanguard of Cadwalader's force, arriving around seven a.m. As he had done a day earlier, he went straight to the quarters of his friend, General St. Clair, "and begged the favor of his bed for a few hours." He was asleep there when the alarm was sounded. Presently a black woman came into the room, crying and wringing her hands. Just behind her came General St. Clair, "with a composed countenance."

Rush: "What is the matter?"

St. Clair: "The enemy are on their way here."

Rush: "What do you intend to do?"

St. Clair: "Why, fight them."

St. Clair took down his sword from the wall and girded it on his thigh with a calmness such as Rush "thought seldom took place at the expectation of a battle." Rush followed the general out of the room, mounted his horse, and set out to find the Philadelphia militia. He met some of them a short distance below Trenton and rode slowly along with them toward the Assunpink. "How do you feel?" he asked one of the militiamen, John Chaloner. "As if I were going to sit down to a good breakfast," Chaloner responded.

It was all a new experience for Dr. Rush—the alarm signals, the shouted commands, the hurry-scurry. "All was now hurry, confusion and noise. General Washington and his aides rode by the Philadelphia militia in all the terrible aspect of war. General Mifflin, in a blanket coat, galloped at the head of a body of Pennsylvania militia. He appeared to be all soul. I recollect the ardor with which he called to them to quicken their steps. His command was not without effect. They ran after him.

"General Knox was active and composed. In passing me, he cried out, 'Your opinion last night was very fortunate for us.' " Rush was unable to make out the rest of Knox's remark, or perhaps too modest to repeat it. Knox rode off to issue final instructions to his artillery batteries.

As things were to turn out, the British did not come as quickly as had been feared. It was not until noon that Cornwallis's troops reached Maidenhead, six miles north of Trenton, and it was here, in front of the Presbyterian church, that the day's first casualty occurred. In advance of the British troops, a small party of mounted soldiers entered the north end of the village and espied a man on horseback. It was farmer Elias Hunt, who a few minutes earlier had emerged from the home that he and his family had temporarily abandoned. Hunt was, according to another resident of the village, "about three-fourths of a mile in advance of the American picket, who was posted opposite the church." Hunt was "pursued by a party of horse in full speed" until he reached a point between the church and the picket post. One of the pursuing cavalrymen "was in advance of the rest with his sword ready to make the blow when the guard fired and wounded him, but he did not fall from his horse. At this time a bugle sounded in the rear and he attempted to return, but a second fire killed the horse and rider."

After getting their man, the marksmen in the picket post, aware that the British were coming on, retreated to Five Mile Run, below

Maidenhead. General Fermoy's 1,000-man defensive force had abandoned this position a day earlier after skirmishing with a British force that had come out from Princeton. The men from the picket joined the small force that had been left on duty there. The main body of the defensive force had retreated about two miles to Shabakunk Creek, about three miles above Trenton.* It was at the Shabakunk that a skirmish of great tactical importance was about to take place.

———— •••• ————

CHAPTER 41

They Were to Kill All the Rebels

The Hessians in the British column advancing toward Trenton were determined to avenge the defeat suffered there on December 26. In Princeton a day earlier, New Year's Day, Colonel Donop was "so exasperated against the enemy, especially for the Rall corps being taken prisoners by them, that he resolved to be revenged. He therefore went thro' the ranks and declared openly to his men that any of them who would take a Rebel prisoner would receive fifty stripes, signifying to them they were to kill all the Rebels they could without mercy." So it was noted in the diary of Sergeant Thomas Sullivan of the British Forty-ninth Regiment of Foot.

A British force of light infantrymen, accompanied by Captain Wreden's jagers, marched from Princeton to Maidenhead on New Year's Day without meeting any resistance. Advancing about a mile and a half beyond Maidenhead, they reached a bridge over Five Mile Run that was defended by a rebel force. In the skirmish that ensued, four rebels were killed, according to Lieutenant Archibald Robertson. Back in Princeton, the British reported the findings of this mission: all clear at least as far as Maidenhead.

Lord Cornwallis was back in Princeton late in the evening of January 1, his return trip to England having been canceled by the

*Near what is today the site of Notre Dame High School.

disaster of December 26. He had ridden all the way from New York, a distance of fifty miles, that day. Within minutes of reaching Princeton, he ordered preparations for an attack on Trenton by a force that now numbered some 8,000 men. "Lord Cornwallis," Sergeant Sullivan noted, "deferring his going to England . . . reached Princetown this night. The troops being ordered there by Major General Grant, upon getting intelligence that the enemy, on receiving reinforcements from Virginia, Maryland and the militia of Pennsylvania, had repassed the Delaware into Jersey."

Cornwallis spent the night of January 1–2—what was left of it—at Morven, Richard Stockton's abandoned estate at the western edge of Princeton. He was up early on Thursday, January 2, eager to be on his way. After receiving their biscuits and brandy, his troops set off for Trenton in a single column, Colonel Donop's brigade leading the way. Cornwallis, as Sergeant Sullivan observed, "having received accounts of the rebel army being posted at Trenton, advanced thither early in the morning, leaving the 4th Brigade British under command of Lieutenant Colonel Mawhood in Princetown." As Captain Ewald put it, "It was planned . . . to give the enemy a beating and thereby repair the damage done at Trenton." The British and Hessians marched off, as Thomas Dowdeswell, an English officer, said, "expecting either to engage the rebels or drive them over the Delaware with considerable loss to them."

Once more, however, as it had on the morning of December 26, the weather was favoring the Americans. An early thaw had set in a day earlier, New Year's Day, with afternoon temperatures soaring to around 50°. A drenching rainstorm during the night, melting snows, and continuing above-freezing temperatures had made the eastern roadway a quagmire.* For the attacking force it was to be slow going all the way, the mud in some stretches being nearly knee-deep.

The labored advance was being led, as usual, by Captain Ewald's and Captain Wreden's jagers. Behind them came a company of Hessian grenadiers and two troops of light dragoons. Next came the light infantry and several artillery pieces, then English and Hessian grenadiers, including the Koehler Grenadier Battalion, the one that

---

*Phineas Pemberton, a member of the American Philosophical Society and a diligent weather-watcher, recorded an afternoon high of 51° in Philadelphia on New Year's Day and noted typical post-frontal conditions on January 2: fair and windy in the morning, windy and cloudy with sunshine in the afternoon, the temperature not rising during the day, but remaining steady near 39°.

Colonel Donop had so eagerly awaited for use at Burlington. With that battalion's big guns he had planned to blow the rebel vessels from the Delaware. Bringing up the rear were the remains of the late Colonel Rall's brigade, two British brigades, and a contingent of dragoons. A formidable force, and certainly one that no damned rebels could stop, even in the mud.

During the march of about six miles to Maidenhead, the army, with Cornwallis and Donop riding close behind the vanguard, encountered no opposition at all. Even so, it was around noon by the time the main body reached Maidenhead. Near the church there a few minutes earlier a cavalryman in the vanguard had been shot and killed by a rebel on picket duty. Now the picket post was empty.

Beyond Maidenhead, at the bridge over Five Mile Run, a small rebel force gave token resistance before fleeing back toward Trenton. The rout, it appeared, was on. For the next two miles there was no resistance except an occasional stray shot. Approaching the Shabakunk, members of the British advanced guard noticed that the rebels had dismantled the bridge over the creek. Perhaps here they would attempt to make a stand.

———— ◆◆◆ ————

CHAPTER 42

This Was the Moment

A curious thing happened as the British, having routed the small force left at Five Mile Run, approached the Shabakunk. General Fermoy, the Frenchman in command of the Americans' 1,000-man defensive force there, suddenly wheeled about on his horse and galloped off in the direction of Trenton.* This action, for which no explanation is known, turned out to be fortunate, for the command

*The following July, during the abandonment of Ticonderoga, Fermoy disgraced himself by falling into a drunken sleep without giving the withdrawal order for his troops on Mount Independence. Later in the night he set fire to his quarters, thereby illuminating the scene for enemy marksmen. Fermoy was "a worthless drunkard," according to Major Wilkinson, who observed his performance at both Trenton and Ticonderoga. He "resigned" early in 1778 after Congress refused the last of his many requests for promotion.

at the Shabakunk then passed into the capable hands of Colonel Edward Hand, a seasoned veteran who commanded the First Pennsylvania Continental Regiment's sharpshooting riflemen.

Hand's force was advantageously positioned for a delaying action, occupying ground that was heavily forested and looking out on open fields to the north, from which direction the British were coming. A detachment had dismantled the wooden bridge over the creek after the retreating party from Five Mile Run had passed over it.

Colonel Hand, according to Major Wilkinson, "secreted his men some distance within the wood, on the flanks of the road, posting Major [Henry] Miller on the left and in person taking command on the right. In this position he waited for the flank and advanced guards of the enemy until they came within point-blank shot, and then he opened a deadly fire from his ambush, which broke and forced them back in great confusion on the main body, closely pursued by the riflemen. The boldness of this manoeuver menacing a general attack, induced the enemy to form in order of battle and bring up his artillery and open a battery, with which time the rifle corps took breath and were ready to renew the attack."

During this firefight, with Hand's riflemen at one point actually forcing the enemy into a brief retreat, General Washington, on horseback, arrived on the scene with Generals Greene and Knox. They had ridden forward from Trenton to offer encouragement to the defenders and to emphasize how important it was "to retard the march of the enemy until nightfall." Washington had a plan and it depended largely on this delaying action. He "gave orders," according to Wilkinson, "for as obstinate a stand as could be made on that ground, without hazarding the [artillery] pieces, and retired to marshal his troops for action, behind the Assunpink."

Under Colonel Hand's determined leadership, the outnumbered American detachment succeeded in holding off the enemy force for two hours. Then, under increasingly devastating fire, the defenders began their planned retreat, grudgingly giving up ground—firing, falling back, reloading, and firing again. One contingent of retreating Americans withdrew southeastward toward the Assunpink Creek to prevent a flanking movement by the enemy, now coming on in great force. The main body of the defenders, under Colonel Hand's command, retreated along the main road to an area known as Stockton Hollow.* On high ground overlooking a ravine, they

---

*Near today's Helene Fuld Medical Center.

established another holding position. Hand now had about 600 men, supported by Captain Forrest's two artillery pieces. Here, James Wilkinson would report, "our advanced party made their last stand, in which the Virginia troops, under Colonels Scott and Lawson and Majors Josiah and Richard Parker, with Forrest and his field pieces, distinguished themselves.

"The battery, covered by about six hundred men, opened on the column of the enemy and was presently answered by a counter-battery. The cannonade continued twenty or twenty-five minutes." The defenders had succeeded in carrying out the first part of General Washington's plan, for the daylight was already beginning to fade. Wilkinson had "a fair flank view of this little combat. . . . The sun had set and the evening was so far advanced that I could distinguish the flame from the muzzles of our muskets."

As Colonel Hand's troops backtracked into and through the town, another force—Colonel Hitchcock's Rhode Islanders—hurried forward to provide covering fire for their retreat. The Rhode Island troops, as one of them, John Howland, noted, opened ranks as Hand's men raced through toward the far side of the Assunpink in the southern end of the town. "We then closed in a compact and rather solid column as the street through which we were to retreat to the bridge was rather narrow."

Howland and the rest of Hitchcock's men were able to hold out only briefly against the oncoming enemy and soon they, too, were, with many others, retreating toward the Assunpink bridge: "The British made a quick advance in an oblique direction to cut us off from the bridge. In this they did not succeed as we had a shorter distance in a direct line to the bridge than they had, and our artillery, which was posted on the south side of the brook . . . played into the front and flank of their column, which induced them to fall back. The bridge was narrow and our platoons were, in passing it, crowded into a dense and solid mass, in the rear of which the enemy was making their best efforts."

In the rush at the little stone bridge Howland got a close view of the commander in chief under pressure: "The noble horse of General Washington stood with his breast pressed close against the end of the west rail of the bridge, and the firm, composed, and majestic countenance of the General inspired confidence and assurance in a moment so important and critical. In this passage across the bridge it was my fortune to be next to the west rail and, arriving at the end of the bridge rail, I pressed against the shoulder of the

General's horse and in contact with the boot of the General. The horse stood as firm as the rider, and seemed to understand that he must not quit his post and station.

"When I was about half way across the bridge, the General addressed himself to Colonel Hitchcock, the commander of the brigade, directing him to march his men to *that field* and form them immediately . . . at the same time extending his arm and pointing to a little meadow at a little distance, on the south side of the creek . . . and between the road and the Delaware. This order was promptly obeyed and then we advanced to the edge of the stream, facing the enemy, who soon found it prudent to fall back under the cover of the houses."

A small party of New Jersey militiamen, among the last to reach the Assunpink bridge, had been on the run for about three miles, all the way from the Shabakunk. "I, with several others," one of them said, "was detached under the command of Captain Longstreet with orders to collect as many men as we could in the country between Princeton, Cranbury and Rhode Hall, and then unite ourselves with the company of riflemen who had remained in that neighborhood. We left Trenton by the nearest road to Princeton and advanced nearly to the Shabakunk when we were met by a little negro on horseback, galloping down the hill, who called to us that the British army was before us. One of our party ran a little way up the hill and jumped upon the fence, from whence he beheld the British army within less than half a mile of us.

"And now commenced a race for Trenton. We fortunately escaped capture; yet the enemy were so near that before we crossed the bridge over the Assunpink, some of our troops on the Trenton side of the creek, with a field piece, motioned to us to get out of the street while they fired at the British at the upper end of it. . . .

"Washington's army was drawn up on the [far] side of the Assunpink, with its left on the Delaware River and its right extending a considerable way up the mill pond along the face of the hill. . . . The troops were placed one above the other so that they appeared to cover the whole slope from bottom to top, which brought a great many muskets within shot of the bridge. Within 70 or 80 yards of the bridge, and in front of and in the road, as many pieces of artillery as could be managed were stationed."

Racing toward the bridge with the rest of Colonel Scott's Virginians, young Ensign Robert Beale heard this advice from a superior officer: "Shift for yourselves, boys, get over the bridge as quick as you can." Beale continued: "There was running, followed by a tremendous fire from the British. There were but few lives lost in getting to the bridge. A Mr. [Robert] Livingston, a very clever young man who had but a few days before been made an ensign . . . carried the colors. He was shot down in the street with his thigh broken, but the colors were brought off."

Hessian troops were the first to enter the town, grenadiers and jagers, one judged from their uniforms. Behind them marched the British light infantrymen, hundreds of them, and they were followed by thousands more. The bridge over the Assunpink, it appeared, would be their main goal. Some five hundred yards from the bridge the British put artillery pieces into position, and soon the cannon were booming.

With the support of the big guns, the enemy began to advance in a solid column, with bayonets fixed. American musketmen and riflemen, row upon row on the high ground south of the Assunpink, had their weapons primed. They were, as one of them, James Johnston, would recall, "formed into three lines, front, center and rear," and they were supported by a tremendous concentration of artillery power—some thirty pieces positioned along the creek, twelve of them, according to Johnston, concentrated "behind the mill" and in easy range of the bridge. But would these men and boys be able to stand their ground under bombardment and attack by the world's best-trained army, now coming on against them?

In the dying light, with colors flying and bandsmen playing, the Hessians and British stormed through the town. It could all end here, according to Wilkinson: "Thirty minutes would have sufficed to bring the two armies into contact, and thirty more would have decided the combat; and, covered with woe, Columbia might have wept the loss of her beloved Chief and most valorous sons." On a lower level, John Howland, the young Rhode Islander who had brushed against Washington's horse, would put it this way: "On one hour, yes, on forty minutes, commencing at the moment when the British troops first saw the bridge and creek before them, depended the all-important, the all-absorbing question whether we should be independent states or conquered rebels!"

The Assunpink approached Trenton from the northeast and turned westward as it flowed through the southern part of the town on its way to the nearby Delaware. The bridge over the Assunpink was an arched span made of stone and barely wide enough for the passage of a horse and carriage. On one side of the bridge the

Assunpink formed an extensive millpond; on the other the stream ran its course of about a quarter of a mile to the Delaware.

This is how Henry Knox, a general now, in recognition of his astuteness on December 26, would describe the scene: "Nearly on the other side of Trenton, partly in the town, runs a brook [the Assunpink] which in most places is not fordable. . . . The ground on the other side is much higher than on this and may be said to command Trenton completely. Here it was our army drew up, with thirty or forty pieces of artillery in front." In three lengthy rows on high ground along the Assunpink, some 6,000 men had been positioned by General Washington.

Here it would all be decided. Had Washington, with the ice-choked Delaware River at his back, boxed himself into an untenable position? Was this to be another in a long series of disasters—another Fort Washington? Or did the commander in chief have a surprise move in mind?

"If ever there ever was a crisis in the affairs of the revolution," Wilkinson would report, "this was the moment."

Ensign Beale agreed: "This was a most awful crisis. No possible chance of crossing the river; ice as large as houses floating down, and no retreat to the mountains, the British between us and them. Our brigade, consisting of the Fourth, Fifth and Sixth Virginia Regiments, was ordered to form in column at the bridge and General Washington came and, in the presence of us all, told Colonel Scott to defend the bridge to the last extremity. Colonel Scott answered with an oath, 'Yes, General, as long as there is a man alive.' "

———— ◆◆◆ ————

CHAPTER 43

This May Be the Last Letter

Approaching the Shabakunk Creek, three miles from their destination, Trenton, the British knew they were in for a firefight. "By a prisoner taken," Lieutenant Robertson noted, "we learnt that there were two battalions in the wood, one on each hand of us. The Horse Guards and the Highlanders were formed and advanced on our left in front where they saw the Rebels as if they intended to form, but they retired into the woods on the other side of the . . . creek just opposite to us.* . . . In order to amuse us they manoeuvered two or three thousand man on their right, very well making a demonstration at passing the creek at two different places in their possession where it was fordable, so that by that means to turn our left flank if we advanced toward Trenton.

"However, the heights and woods on our right were soon forced with little loss and our troops followed them into Trenton where their main body was drawn up, about 6,000 or 7,000, with the [Assunpink] Creek and bridge in front and a number of field pieces."

For Lord Cornwallis's troops the afternoon had been rough going, but now they had the damned rebels on the run and entrapped. "The enemy," Captain Hall would report, "abandoned Trenton on our approach, after a faint resistance, in which a few were killed on both sides. This happened . . . late in the day when the rebels, on evacuating the town, withdrew their whole force over a rivulet, the Assunpink, which runs by the place, and took their position on some high ground near it, with a seeming determined countenance to defend them."

The retreating Americans, according to the journal of the Hessian Minnigerode Battalion, "withdrew in the most perfect order [after] being attacked by the Linsing and Block Battalions." Upon entering Trenton, according to the journal, Colonel Donop "found the wounded belonging to the Rall Brigade who had been treated very well there." The officer keeping the journal of the Knyphausen Regiment also commented on the manner of the rebels' retreat: "The rebel generals did their utmost and withdrew in fairly good order through Trentown, occupied the bridge and took up their position on the far side of the intrenchments, which they had thrown up during our absence." The journal added this comment on the defeat suffered here a week earlier: "If Colonel Rall had done this, the disaster most certainly would not have occurred."

As usual, it was the Hessians leading the way and bearing the

---

*Misidentified as the Assunpink by Robertson. He also overestimated the size of the American force.

brunt of the advance. "The jagers and light infantry, supported by the Hessian grenadiers, attacked the enemy at once," Captain Ewald noted. Thereupon, the enemy "withdrew . . . across the bridge. . . . But the rear guard was so hard pressed by the jagers and the light infantry that the majority were either killed or captured."

One of the Americans hard pressed by the oncoming Hessians was John Rosbrugh, the sixty-two-year-old Presbyterian minister from Northampton County, Pennsylvania, who had said goodbye to his young wife and five children and led a company of his parishioners down to Philadelphia and on to Bristol. Just before crossing the Delaware to New Jersey with the rest of General Cadwalader's force on December 27, Rosbrugh had written a letter to his wife. He was on horseback, awaiting his company's turn to cross the river, and the message was hurried:

> Friday morning, 10 o'clock at Bristol Ferry. . . . I am still yours but I haven't a minute to tell you that by God's grace our company are all well. We are going over to New Jersey. You would think [it] strange to see your husband, an old man, riding with a French fusée slung at his back.
>
> This may be the last letter ye shall receive from your husband. I have counted myself yours, and have been enlarged of our mutual love of God. As I am out of doors I cannot at present write more. I send my compliments to you, my dear, and children. Friends, pray for us. From your loving husband,
>
> Jno. Rosbrugh

Having ridden with Cadwalader's corps from Burlington to Crosswicks, and then to Trenton, Rosbrugh was refreshing himself in a public house on Queen Street when the alarm was sounded: the enemy was coming! He raced out of the place and found that his horse, the one he had ridden all the way from home, had been stolen. As the Hessians in the enemy's vanguard drew closer, he ran toward the bridge over the Assunpink but he was unable even to approach it. Artillery pieces positioned on the far side of the creek were already firing point-blank toward the northern end of town. He was too late; no one was now allowed to cross.

Rosbrugh hurried off in search of a place where he could ford the creek. Again he was too late: he fell into the hands of a small detachment of Hessians—fired-up troops who were apparently determined not to take prisoners. They surrounded the minister; they took his fusée, his gold watch, his money. They slashed at his head with sabers and bayoneted him in seventeen places. Three of the saber slashes, it would be found, cut through his horsehair wig and into his scalp. "After he was thus massacred," the *Pennsylvania Evening Post* would report, "he was stripped naked and . . . left lying in an open field."

Was such barbarous action explained by the fact that the enemy soldiers mistook John Rosbrugh for the Reverend John Witherspoon, the militant congressman and president of the College of New Jersey? One day during the previous summer Witherspoon had been burned in effigy by enemy troops on Staten Island. In a letter to his son David, Witherspoon would write: "I have been making inquiry into the conduct of the enemy, which has been dreadful. At Trenton, they killed Mr. Rosbrugh, Presbyterian minister at Forks of the Delaware. . . . Though he fell down on his knees and begged his life, yet they pierced him through and through with their bayonets, and mangled him in a most shocking manner. Some of the people at Princeton say they thought they were killing me, and boasted that they had done it when they came back. But this is uncertain. . . . The fact of his death and the manner of it is beyond doubt."

"The enemy, who was Hessians, entered the town pell-mell," General Knox would report. The Hessians "pushed our small party through the town with vigour, though not with much loss. Their retreat over the bridge was thoroughly secured by the artillery. After they had retired over the bridge, the enemy advanced within reach of our cannon, who saluted them with great vociferation and some execution."

The foreign troops, according to an American militiaman at the scene, "moved slowly down the street with their choicest troops in front. When within about sixty yards of the bridge they raised a shout and rushed to the charge. It was then that our men poured upon them from musketry and artillery a shower of bullets under which, however, they continued to advance, though their speed was diminished. And as the column reached the bridge it moved slower and slower until the head of it was gradually pressed nearly over, when our fire became so destructive that they broke their ranks and fled.

"It was then that our army raised a shout, and such a shout I never since heard; by what signal or word of command, I know not. The line [of men] was more than a mile in length and from the nature of the ground the extremes were not in sight of each other, yet they shouted as one man.

"The British column halted instantly. The officers restored the ranks and again they rushed the bridge, and again was the shower of bullets poured upon them with redoubled fury. This time the column broke before it reached the centre of the bridge, and their retreat was again followed by the same hearty shout from our line.

"They returned a third time to the charge but it was in vain. We shouted after them again but they had had enough of it."

The thirty or more of General Knox's artillery pieces had bombarded the charging enemy force with the heaviest fire ever delivered on any field in the Western Hemisphere up to this time. Sergeant Joseph White, the young artilleryman from Massachusetts, would recall some details of the cannonading: "The enemy came on in solid columns. We let them come on some ways. Then, by a signal given, we all fired together.

"The enemy retreated off the bridge and formed again, and we were ready for them. Our whole artillery was again discharged at them. They retreated again and formed. They came on a third time. We loaded with canister shot and let them come nearer. We fired all together again, and such destruction it made, you cannot conceive. The bridge looked red as blood, with their killed and wounded and their red coats."

An officer from Connecticut, unidentified, was among those who credited Knox's artillery with three repulses: "Not long before sunset [the enemy] marched into the town and, after reconnoitering our situation, drew up in a solid column in order to force the bridge, which they attempted to do with great vigor at *three* several times and were as often broken by our artillery." In these attempts, he added, some of the enemy officers found it necessary to drive their men forward by swatting them with the flat of their swords.

Lieutenant Charles Willson Peale, near the bridge with his Philadelphians, noted that "some of our artillery stood their ground till the enemy advanced within 40 yards, and they were very near losing the field piece."

The enemy's artillery was meanwhile also taking a heavy toll. Not far from Peale's position, "some unlucky shot from a cannon killed one or two of the 3rd Battalion of Philadelphia troops, and also some of the Cumberland County militia." Many other such shots were finding their marks.

Captain Thomas Rodney and his small company from Delaware, after helping to prevent a flanking action by the enemy, had been ordered to the bridge area: "In their third and final attempt, the British came down in a very heavy column to force the bridge. The fire was very heavy and the light troops were ordered to the support of that important post." With Rodney in the lead, the Delaware militiamen ran toward the bridge, all except one man: "As we drew near, I stepped out of the front to order my men to close up. At this time Martinas Sipple was about ten steps behind the man next in front of him. I at once drew my sword and threatened to cut his head off if he did not keep close. He then sprang forward and I returned to the front."

The exchange of artillery fire, as General Knox would report, "continued till dark, when of course it ceased, except for a few shells we now and then chucked into town to prevent their enjoying their new quarters securely." Lieutenant James McMichael, of the Pennsylvania Rifle Regiment, made this note in his diary: "We continued firing bombs up to seven o'clock, p.m., when we were ordered to rest, which we very commodiously did upon a number of rails for a bed."

Captain Stephen Olney and his men "were dismissed to get our breakfast, dinner and supper. As the night advanced it became extremely cold." As usual the men built huge bonfires, but even at such a time as this Olney found it difficult to justify the despoliation: "It seemed to me extravagant that our men should pull down such good cedar fences to augment our fires."

As Olney and his company awaited orders, he reflected on what might happen next: "It appeared to me then that our army was in the most desperate situation I had ever known it. We had no boats to carry us across the Delaware, and if we had, so powerful an enemy would certainly destroy the better half before we could embark. To cross the enemy's line of march between this and Princeton seemed impracticable; and when we thought of retreating into the south part of New Jersey, where there was no support for an army, that was discouraging. Notwithstanding all this, the men and officers seemed cheerful and in good spirits. I asked Lieutenant Bridges what he thought now of our independence. He answered cheerfully, 'I don't know; the Lord must help us.' "

When the firing ceased, Lieutenant Charles Willson Peale and his company "marched to the skirts of the field, ground our arms, made fires with the fence rails, and talked over the fatigues of the day; and some, after eating, laid themselves down to sleep."

At this point, Lieutenant Peale, usually second in command, took charge of the company. Captain Bernie had injured his leg so seriously that he could not "hold out, and desired me to take charge of the company, having told General Cadwalader that he is unable to serve. We took out some of our baggage from the wagons, and sent it away."

Waiting at a bonfire with his Delaware company, Captain Rodney "had the roll called to see if any of our men were missing and Martinas [Sipple] was not to be found." This was the soldier Rodney had threatened with his sword. "Lieutenant Mark McCall informed me that immediately on my returning to the head of the column after making him close up, he fled out of the field."

Not far from the field of battle, Dr. Benjamin Rush had converted a house into a hospital and it was filling steadily with wounded Americans. The first man to be brought in was a soldier from New England. His right hand was hanging "a little above the wrist by nothing but a piece of skin." He had been hit by a cannonball. Rush gave him emergency treatment. Another wounded man was brought in, and another. Before the night ended there would be more than a dozen others. In treating them, Rush had the assistance of Dr. John Cochran and some young surgeons. Amid the moans and screams of the wounded they worked past midnight. Then: "We all lay down with some straw in the same room with our wounded patients. It was now for the first time war appeared to me in its awful plenitude of horrors. I want words to describe the anguish of my soul, excited by the cries and groans and convulsions of the men who lay by my side. I slept two or three hours."

British surgeons and their aides were meanwhile ministering to an even greater number of men, most of whom had been wounded in the three unsuccessful attempts to cross the Assunpink bridge. In the Block Battalion alone six men were dead or dying and thirteen wounded. According to the journal of the Minnegerode Battalion, three soldiers in Colonel Donop's brigade were dead or dying and eleven wounded. Overall British losses were heavy and, possibly for that reason, never revealed. Estimates would range from 150 to 500 casualties. Captain Ewald observed that "many men were killed and wounded on both sides." Among the fatally wounded was

Lieutenant Frederich von Grothausen, who had been in command of fifty jagers at The Hermitage, above Trenton, a week earlier when the rebels suddenly appeared. Grothausen had fled with his men in the face of enemy fire, thus, in the opinion of Ewald, disgracing himself. Of his death Ewald said: "Lieutenant von Grothausen—fortunately for him—was shot dead along with several jagers."

After the cannonading duel ceased around seven o'clock, except for a few stray shots from rebel artillery, the main body of the British troops withdrew to the northern end of the town and out to the forested area near the Shabakunk Creek, where Cornwallis set up temporary headquarters. Early in the morning he would see to Mr. Washington and his rebels. As noted in the journal of the Block Battalion, "Washington . . . was in a dangerous situation because of his position since he could not retreat across the Delaware because of the heavy ice and . . . was to be attacked the next day."

In the town the British posted a line of sentries a short distance from the Assunpink, some of them only about 150 yards from the roaring bonfires in rebel territory across the creek. During the night there were scattered reports of troop movements by the rebels. "The sentries who were advanced," Captain Hall noted, "heard the rattling of carriages, and patrols, in going their rounds, made their reports of an uncommon hurry in the enemy's camp that indicated they were in motion, which was visible also at times thro' the glimmering of their fires. And though these reports were confirmed and carried to headquarters, where some officers had communicated their suspicions of the enemy's forming some design, yet both the one and the other were disregarded."

General William Erskine and Lieutenant Archibald Robertson were among the officers who observed movement behind the rebel line. They were, according to Robertson, "apprehensive [that the enemy] meditated a blow on Prince Town, which was but weak." Throughout the night, "our troops all lay out. Hard frost and 2 Battalions Light Infantry lay in Trenton without fires by way of piquets to watch the Rebels on the other side of the Creek." At least one other British officer, an ensign, suspected a rebel movement as "Washington . . . filed off before his fires and not behind them."* For some reason, no action was taken, not even a patrol

---

*So the ensign would later report to Sir Henry Clinton, an arch-critic of Cornwallis.

dispatched to investigate. Reconstructing the night's events years later, apparently with the help of British observers, James Wilkinson wrote that Cornwallis explained the situation to his leading officers in these words: "The men had been under arms the whole day; they were languid and required rest; he had the enemy safe enough and could dispose of them the next morning." For these reasons he "proposed that the troops should make fires, refresh themselves and take repose." General James Grant, among others, acquiesced, pointing out that the rebels would not be able to retreat across the Delaware, having left their boats above Trenton. Quartermaster Erskine, according to Wilkinson, begged to differ: "My lord, if you trust those people tonight, you will see nothing of them in the morning!"

Instead of heeding this admonition, Cornwallis continued with the details of his plan to overwhelm his trapped enemy—to "bag the fox." As a precaution and in preparation for an all-out attack on the rebels in the morning, Cornwallis had ordered a battalion of British grenadiers and a battalion of Hessian grenadiers into positions along the Assunpink, one at Henry's Mill ford, about a mile upstream from the Assunpink bridge, and the other at Phillips Mill ford, another mile up the Assunpink. Neither unit encountered any rebels.

In further preparation for the next morning's action, Cornwallis ordered his troops at Maidenhead and Princeton to reinforce his corps at Trenton early in the day. Thus strengthened, the Regulars and the Hessian troops, spoiling for revenge, would cross the Assunpink at Phillips Mill ford, turn Washington's flank, and put an end to the rebel army and the damned war.

---◆◆---

CHAPTER 44

A Profound Silence to Be Enjoined

As he trudged, and at times stumbled, along a dark and unfamiliar route, Sergeant Joseph White, the nineteen-year-old artilleryman from Massachusetts, was joined by his commanding officer, Captain

Benjamin Frothingham. "You and I must march together," said Frothingham, falling into step, and so they did. "We marched some ways, I being exceeding sleepy," White would recall. "I pitched forward several times and recovered myself. Well, the captain observed with a laugh, that was the first time he'd ever seen anyone sleep while marching."

Farther on, Frothingham got to the point. "Did you know," he said, "that you are to command that left piece tomorrow morning? I expect we shall have some hard fighting."

Oh, no, White said, he wasn't capable of commanding that cannon. That was a job for a commissioned officer. Where *were* all the officers? Whose orders *were* these?

General Knox's orders, Frothingham said.

But White still didn't think he was up to it: "The responsibility is too great for me. I cannot think why he should pitch upon me."

"Why," said Frothingham, "he remembers what you did at Trenton."

It worked.

"I began to feel my pride rising," White would recall, "and I said no more."

Sergeant White's artillery company was part of a long line of troops whose destination, though most of them did not know it, was Princeton, twelve miles northeast of Trenton. After skirting the left flank of the British they were following a circuitous route considerably longer than the main road between Trenton and Princeton. The march had started in strict silence around one a.m. There had been no roll of the drums, no call of the bugle, no outward signal of any kind. "Orders came by whispering (not a loud word must be spoken) to form the line and march," Sergeant White would recall.

Reconstructing the situation following the cannonading duel, General Henry Knox would write: "The creek was in our front, our left on the Delaware, our right in a wood, parallel to the creek. The situation was strong, to be sure, but hazardous on this account, that had our right wing been defeated, the defeat of the left would almost have been an inevitable consequence and the whole thrown into confusion or pushed into the Delaware, as it was impassable by boats. From these circumstances the general thought it best to attack Princeton, twelve miles in the rear of the enemy's grand army, and where they had the 17th, 40th and 55th regiments, with a number of draughts, altogether perhaps twelve hundred men."

(Although Washington was not yet aware of it, a skirmish between an American force of 120 or more and a band of Tories had been fought near Monmouth Court House [Freehold], about thirty miles east of Trenton, around the same time as the battle at the Assunpink. The Americans, led by Major John Mifflin, had marched north from Cumberland County and on January 2, "about a half hour before night," according to a participant. Apparently warned of the approach of Mifflin's troops, the Tory contingent, led by Lieutenant Colonel John Morris, "accordingly pushed off from town, and got away about half a mile. We immediately pushed after them and they halted. We came up about a quarter of an hour before night and engaged them. A very heavy fire was kept up on both sides, and the enemy stood us about eight minutes, then gave way. . . . The next morning we sent out a party [and] . . . they brought four dead bodies which we buried. We took . . . twenty-three prisoners and brought them to this place [Bordentown].")

In preparation for the march to Princeton, General Washington had called his leading officers together for a council of war in the home of Alexander Douglass on Queen Street (South Broad Street), below the Assunpink. This was the house that General St. Clair had been occupying. As temporary headquarters Washington had been using the home of John Barnes, the high sheriff of Hunterdon County, now serving with the British. Washington had abandoned that house, since it was situated north of the Assunpink,* an area eventually occupied by the oncoming enemy.

At the Douglass house plans were made for a maneuver that Washington had apparently been thinking about throughout the day: instead of digging in and awaiting a confrontation with an obviously superior British force in the morning, his troops would set off in silence around the enemy's left flank and attack the depleted British garrison at Princeton around dawn. A force of some 400 militiamen, mostly from New Jersey and commanded by Colonel Silas Newcomb, would be left behind to deceive the enemy. They would keep the campfires blazing and, with pick and shovel, keep digging through the night. Because some of these troops might be captured and interrogated, they were not informed of the planned strike on Princeton. In the morning they would be on their own, free to follow the tracks of Washington's force or to set off for home.

"We were dismissed for an hour or two," Sergeant White later

---

*At the southwest corner of today's Lafayette and South Broad streets.

recalled, "to pull down all the fences we could find, to build fires with them, and get some refreshment. The fires were made to deceive the enemy; to make them suppose that we were there encamped." Ensign Beale, the young Virginian, noted that "every endeavor was made to convince the enemy we occupied our ground by making an immense number of fires and throwing ourselves before first one and then the other to make them believe we were very numerous."

"The more effectually to mask the movement," Major Wilkinson would report, Washington "ordered the guards to be doubled, a strong fatigue party to be set to work on an intrenchment across the road near the mill, within distinct hearing of the sentinels of the enemy, the baggage to be sent to Burlington, the troops to be silently filed off by detachments, and the neighbouring fences to be used for fuel to our guards, to keep up blazing fires until toward day when they had orders to retire.

"The night, although cloudless, was exceedingly dark, and, though calm, most severely cold, and the movement was so cautiously conducted as to elude the vigilence of the enemy." The line of campfires stretched along the Assunpink for about three miles. All along that distance men were busily and noisily using their entrenching tools.

The weather was again favoring Washington, coinciding with his flanking maneuver. Early in the evening his force appeared to be trapped in a desperate position opposite a far stronger enemy. Retreat across the clogged Delaware was out of the question and there were muddy roads on both flanks. Throughout the day, however, the weather-wise commander in chief had noticed the wind holding to the northwest, and although the temperature remained above the freezing point, a flow of cold air pouring into the area would surely mean a freeze at night, making the roads passable even with artillery pieces. And freeze it did.

"Night closed upon us," John Howland observed, "and the weather, which had been mild and pleasant through the day, became intensely cold."

Captain Stephen Olney also noted the sudden drop in temperature: "As the night advanced, it became extremely cold. . . . The roads, which the day before had been mud, snow, and water, were congealed now, and had become hard as pavement and solid."

As he set off with his company, Captain Rodney observed that the slushy terrain had been "frozen firm by a keen northwest wind," and that, following the whispered orders, "the whole army was at once put in motion. But no one knew what the General meant to do. Some thought we were going to attack the enemy in the rear; some thought we were going to Princeton." The time of departure, like many other details of the campaign, was variously reported. According to General Knox, it was "about one o'clock at night when we began to march and make this most extra manoeuvre. Our troops marched with great silence and order."

William Hutchinson, a seventeen-year-old militiaman from Chester County, Pennsylvania, was among the troops ordered to remain at the edge of the Assunpink. With a fellow militiaman he silently crossed the bridge to investigate the area where the enemy had made the three charges: "A certain Hugh Coppell and myself passed over the ground which they had occupied during the battle and their attacks upon us. Their dead bodies lay thicker and closer together for a space than I ever beheld sheaves of wheat lying in a field over which the reapers had just passed."

Another militiaman from Chester County, eighteen-year-old James Johnston, returned from guard duty and "found the army about to move." Many of the soldiers, he observed, "thinking they were about to be led against an enemy, threw away their knapsacks."

Later in the night, after the departure of Washington's force, Johnston was sent forward with a small party to reconnoiter the enemy's forward posts. Moving cautiously, they reached a point where they had "a full view of the Hessians sitting around their fires, smoking their pipes. A sentinel challenged." Johnston and the others "dropped to the ground and lay quiet until the sentinel was heard to resume his walk." They then "cautiously retrograded and made report."

At the house near the river that had been converted into a hospital, Dr. Cochran awoke before sunrise and, as Dr. Rush would later report, "went up to Trenton to inquire for our army." He returned in haste. The army "was not to be found"! It was time to flee; they were in danger of capture. As quickly as possible they hitched up horses to wagons and rode off with their wounded toward Bordentown, assuming that Washington had retreated in that direction. For having thus abandoned them, Rush would find fault with the commander in chief, observing that "a general should be great in minute things."

Some of Washington's troops had left Trenton by the Borden-town road, escorting the army's baggage to Burlington, farther down the river. Sergeant William Young and two of his sons were among those on that march. They had made a hurried departure from Trenton, and in the confusion one of the baggage wagons had been loaded with blankets that were soon to be sorely missed by some Philadelphia militiamen.

"As soon as night fell," Young noted in his journal, "our people lined the wood, made large fires. As soon as I could I came to them with the wagon, with the provisions and blankets, and staid with them till 12 o'clock. Then loaded our wagon, set out and joined my two sons whom I left in the wood with some of our men. . . . One o'clock ordered to move out with the baggage and proceed to Burlington, such a hurry skurry among all our waggoners. Some of our horses . . . got stalled which retarded our march." It would be noon by the time the baggage train would reach Burlington, and there Young, although "a good deal tired, blessed God am very well." That night he would record his usual thanks: "Blessed be the God and father of my Lord Jesus Christ for his protecting care over me and mine through this day."

Some of the inexperienced militiamen marching toward Princeton would, like Young, end up in Burlington. "During this nocturnal march," Captain Rodney noted, "I, with the Dover Company and the Red Feather Company of Philadelphia Light Infantry, led the van of the army, and Captain Henry with the other three companies of Philadelphia Light Infantry brought up the rear.

"The van moved on all night in the most cool and determined order but on the march great confusion happened in the rear. There was a cry that they were surrounded by the Hessians and several corps of militia broke and fled towards Bordentown. But the rest of the column remained firm and pursued their march without disor-der, but those who were frightened and fled did not recover from their panic until they reached Burlington."

And some of them—skittish recruits ready to fly at the first snapped twig—never stopped until they reached Philadelphia. So it was reported. Some of those who settled in at Burlington would come under the sympathetic but suspicious eye of Mrs. Margaret Morris on the riverbank. "I went into the next house," she would note, "to see if the fires were safe, and my heart was melted to see such a number of my fellow-creatures, lying like swine on the floor, fast asleep, and many of them without even a blanket to cover them. It seems very strange to me that such a number should be allowed to come from the camp at the very time of the engagements, and I shrewdly suspect they have run away—for they can give no account why they came, nor where they are to march next." Later her suspicions would be confirmed: "Upon my questioning them pretty close, I brought several to confess that they had run away, being scared. . . . There were several pretty innocent-looking lads among them, and I sympathized with their mothers when I saw them preparing to return to the army."

Like all of the troops on the march except the highest-ranking officers, Lieutenant Charles Willson Peale had no idea of where the army was headed. He and his company of young Philadelphians had been ordered to take their baggage out of the wagons "and at 12 were ordered to parade. By sending away the wagons and parading at midnight, I really expected a retreat."

After answering the hushed order to parade and then waiting in silence for about an hour, Peale and his company joined the long line marching off from the Assunpink: "We . . . directed our course through the woods, directly from the road, and, after some time northerly. By this, I expected we were going to surround the enemy." Farther on, Peale picked up some misinformation that was making the rounds: "After marching some miles I learned that we were going a by-road to Trenton, marching pretty fast."

But, according to young John Howland, it was slow going on that byroad, a mostly crude path hewn through a heavily forested area. Howland, on the march with the other Rhode Islanders who had agreed to stay beyond their enlistment period, would recall that "the march . . . was not by the direct road. A considerable part of it was by a new passage, which appeared to have been cut through the woods, as the stubs were left from two to five inches high. We moved slow on account of the artillery frequently coming to a halt or standstill, and when ordered forward again, one, two, or three men in each platoon would stand, with their arms supported, fast asleep. A platoon next in the rear, advancing on them, they in walking, or attempting to move, would strike a stub and fall." The tall stubs "stopped the movement of some of the guns and caused many a fall and severe bruise to some of the over-weary, sleepy soldiers."

This byroad, which led to the Quaker Bridge Road, was not acknowledged on any map (and in later years would disappear). Some stretches of it were mere shortcuts used by persons going from one neighborhood or farm to another. It was a narrow, rough route even in daylight and at some points it was all but impassable for horse-drawn wagons and cannon moving through the night. If the sudden plummeting of the temperature had not occurred, passage over this route would have been next to impossible.

One night earlier, four young men of the Philadelphia First Troop had explored the area while on mounted patrol. One of the troopers, John Lardner, said that they remained on the byroad "the whole night, occasionally going as high as Quaker Bridge. We found that the enemy had no patrols there, and that apparently they had no knowledge of it."

———— ◆◆◆ ————

CHAPTER 45

A Great Number of Rebels Fell

A British detachment of about a hundred men had been patrolling the Quaker Bridge Road for three consecutive nights. Because of an oversight, however, on the fourth night, that of January 2–3, the road was not patrolled. The men on duty there had been quartered near the Quaker Meeting House, about a mile and a half to the southwest of Princeton. On the morning of January 3, following orders, they marched off toward Trenton with the rest of Cornwallis's troops. They were not replaced and as a result the Quaker Bridge Road was left unguarded that morning all the way to the edge of Princeton.

Late in the afternoon of January 2, around the time when Lord Cornwallis's assault troops were attempting to storm the Assunpink bridge in Trenton, an astute and bold-spirited English officer named Charles Mawhood was leading his troops from Kingston to Princeton, a march of about three miles. They settled into quarters vacated by troops who had marched off toward Trenton with Cornwallis. It was during this changeover that the patrol post on the Quaker Bridge Road was overlooked.

Lieutenant Colonel Mawhood, a tough and reliable field officer, had served with distinction for twenty-four years. Like Cornwallis and like Commander in Chief William Howe, Mawhood had some years earlier expressed sympathy for the American cause and, like them, he had followed orders, despite his feelings, when he was sent across the sea to put an end to the colonial insurrection.

During the days preceding the rebels' attack on Trenton, Colonel Mawhood had taken quarters in a physician's home in Somerset Courthouse, about twelve miles north of Princeton. According to the physician, Mawhood "often expressed himself very freely, lamenting the American contest very much and pronouncing Lord North a villain for being the cause of it." On Christmas night, the physician said, Mawhood sized up the situation, "blaming the English generals for dispersing their army so much, and said that if he was in General Washington's place he would make an attack on several of the principal posts at the same time—that they were all so weak that he could certainly cut them off—and be in possession of all Jersey in a few days."

The next day an express rider arrived with news of the attack on Trenton. "Well, Colonel," a subordinate officer informed Mawhood, "Washington has executed your last night's plan already." So the doctor would later report to Captain Rodney.

In Princeton on January 2 Colonel Mawhood was in command of the three regiments of the Fourth Brigade—his own Seventeenth Leicestershires, the Fortieth Somersetshires, and the Fifty-fifth Westmorelands. That evening he received orders from Cornwallis to "escort the stores" to Trenton early the following morning with two of the regiments, the Seventeenth and the Fifty-fifth. That would leave the Fortieth and a smattering of other troops as a rear guard in Princeton.

Like the rebels, Mawhood's infantrymen had of late been living under circumstances that made them yearn for the comforts of home. In a journal he was keeping, George Inman, an ensign in the Seventeenth Regiment, expressed some widely held sentiments: "The season of the year being severe, snow on the ground and for nights having no other bed than hard frozen earth or ice and no other covering than a cloak oftentimes induced me to reflect on past times when I used to sleep on soft downy beds and with every comfortable necessary around me, amongst them friends whom I left, and which, perhaps, if I had remained, might still have enjoyed."

Such thoughts, however, did not interfere with Ensign Inman's duty. On the morning of January 3 he was up before sunrise and shortly thereafter he was riding out of Princeton as part of a long column of troops. Colonel Mawhood, in the vanguard, was astride a brown pony and as usual was accompanied by his two frisky spaniels. He was riding with some thirty dismounted dragoons, some mounted scouts, and cannoneers with two artillery pieces. The rest of the Seventeenth Regiment, about 250 infantrymen, trailed behind, followed by the leading elements of the Fifty-fifth Regiment, who were just leaving Princeton. Mawhood's force was advancing along the main stagecoach route, the King's Highway, also known as the Post Road (today's Route 206). The sun was about a half hour high as the vanguard passed over the wooden bridge over Stony Brook, about a mile west of Princeton, and proceeded up a steep hill about a quarter of a mile in length. Near the crest of the hill a mounted scout in the vanguard spotted a force of troops on the Saw Mill Road, about a thousand yards to the south, marching toward Princeton. Rebels?

"As this was in the grey of morning," British Captain Hall would report, "at their first appearance they were mistaken for Hessians; but their movements and other circumstances soon proved the mistake. Colonel Mawhood, who on the first intelligence rode forwards to reconnoitre, presently perceived that it was part of the rebel army making for Prince Town, and as readily suggested . . . that the enemy had slipt Lord Cornwallis in the night and by stealing a march meant to surprize that place."

Mawhood had two choices, according to Captain Hall: to take on the rebel force, strength unknown, or to demolish the bridge over Stony Brook, thus retarding the rebels long enough for his troops to push on and join Cornwallis as ordered. "But, reflecting that by such conduct the Fortieth Regiment, with the town and everything in it, must fall into the enemy's hands—and incapable of reconciling himself to the idea of flight before a people he had long since been accustomed to conquer and despise—these considerations determined him to make a stand. . . .

"As the enemy, who marched in columns, were but imperfectly seen in the woods and thick cover through which they passed, their numbers could not be guessed at with any degree of precision; and from this uncertainty and the probability of its being a strong detachment rather than the body of their army, he formed this resolution in hopes that a noble exertion of three British battalions might insure him some success, if not a victory."

Perhaps if he had known the size of the American force, Mawhood, with fewer than 300 troops, would have taken up a defensive position and called for reinforcements. However, with Washington's main body holed up in Trenton, how large could this force be? Moreover, they were only rebels, were they not? At them!

His decision quickly made, Colonel Mawhood dispatched a mounted scout toward the rear of his line of march with orders for the Fifty-fifth Regiment, its vanguard hardly out of Princeton, to turn back to the town and there, with the Fortieth Regiment, prepare to make a stand against the rebels. With about 250 infantrymen, some thirty dragoons and artillerymen with two cannon—in all, a force of 276—Mawhood turned back, recrossed the bridge over Stony Brook and at the first break in the wooded area along the Post Road turned right and and advanced in search of the rebel force.

From a house within view of the Post Road, Robert Lawrence had watched a short time earlier as Mawhood's Regulars marched past toward Trenton, "and in about half an hour's time we saw them coming back faster than they went. A party of them came into our field and laid down their packs there and formed at the corner of our garden about sixty yards from the door and then marched away immediately to the field of battle which was in William Clark's orchard. . . . It was plain within sight of our door at about 400 yards distance."

Presently, the troops leading Mawhood's charge found themselves within sight of a small rebel force. But more rebels—about 200 of them—were coming on, and behind them hundreds more—the whole damned rebel army! But even against such odds, Mawhood and his force continued to charge on, and his two cannon were quickly put into action.

"From this situation," according to Captain Hall, British artillerymen "began to cannonade the enemy as they were forming." The rebels, "soon after advancing in a large column, threw in their fire upon the right of the 17th Regiment, which did considerable execution. This fire was returned with great spirit and, after two or three volleys, the column of the enemy began to give way. . . . The 17th Regiment, rushing forwards with their bayonets, drove the enemy back in their charge. . . . Great numbers of the rebels fell in endeavoring to pass a fence . . . over which they had moved to the attack."

In the cannonading duel that ensued, a woman became one of the battle's first casualties. Her leg, Robert Lawrence would report, "was shot off at her ankle by a cannon ball. She was in one of the houses near the bridge on the main road in the hollow on this side

Stony Brook. It was thought to be done by one of General Washington's field pieces."

Lawrence and others who had come out of the house witnessed only the early moments of the confrontation: "The battle was plainly seen from our door. Before any gun was heard a man was seen to fall and immediately the report and smoke of a gun was seen and heard. And the guns went so quick and many together that they could not be numbered. We presently went down into the cellar to keep out of the way of the shot."

———◆◆◆———

CHAPTER 46

I Never Saw Men Looked So Furious

It had been a mutual sighting: around the same time that Mawhood's scouts caught sight of an American force advancing along a lower road toward Princeton, some Americans in that force spotted part of Mawhood's vanguard near the crest of the Post Road hill. Because the terrain in between was so thickly forested, neither side could determine the size of the opposing force.

A short time earlier, a few minutes after seven o'clock, the vanguard of the American force had crossed the lower bridge over Stony Brook and reached the area surrounding the Quaker Meeting House, about a mile and a half southwest of Princeton. The Americans had come this far without encountering any enemy patrols. There was evidence that enemy troops had recently occupied the area but none were in sight.

"The sun rose as we crossed the brook on a clear frosty morning," Captain Thomas Rodney noted. Here a halt was called so that the artillery pieces could be brought across the bridge. For some of the troops this was a time for a dose of liquid courage—a ladle of rum sprinkled with gunpowder. "The captain sent me a sergeant with a bucket full of rum," Sergeant Joseph White noted. "Every man must drink a half gill." White did not want any. The captain came by and asked if he had had his rum.

"No."

"Drink some. I have."

So White "took a little."

The morning, Major Wilkinson observed, "was bright, serene, and extremely cold, with an hoar frost which bespangled every object." With the coming of daylight Sergeant R noted that "the ground was literally marked with the blood of the soldiers' feet. Though my own feet did not bleed, they were so sore that their condition was little better."

Near the Quaker Meeting House, the Quaker Bridge Road branched in two. It was at this point, during the halt, that General Washington divided his army. As he had done in preparation for the attack on Trenton eight days earlier, he ordered General Sullivan's column to attack from one direction and General Greene's from another. First, Sullivan's troops wheeled to the right off the Quaker Bridge Road and entered Saw Mill Road, which led to the southern edge of Princeton. Then Greene's column continued northward on the Quaker Bridge Road toward the Post Road. General Mercer's force of about 120 was in the vanguard. "General Mercer with 100 Pennsylvanians and 20 Virginians," according to one of the Pennsylvanians, Lieutenant James McMichael, "were detached to the front to bring on an attack." Several hundred yards behind Mercer's troops came a large force of militiamen led by Colonel Cadwalader, then Colonel Hitchcock's New England Continentals. Greene's column, under Washington's plan, was to turn right upon reaching the Post Road and attack the town from the west. Along the way, as Captain Rodney noted, these troops were to "break down the bridge and post a party at the mill on the main road, to oppose the enemy's main army if they should pursue us from Trenton."

General Mercer was in full dress uniform—even wearing a cravat—and he rode with the advanced guard. At his side, advancing on foot, was Colonel John Haslet, acting as Mercer's second in command. Haslet no longer had his Delaware regiment; he and five others were all who remained of that once proud unit, the rest having gone home, with or without permission. Haslet had been ordered by the commander in chief to proceed home for a winter of rest and recruiting duty, but he had chosen to ignore the order so that he could be where he now was, advancing with about 200 seasoned Continentals and unaware that a British force was coming on toward them.

Captain Rodney said his company meanwhile "flanked the whole brigade on the right in an Indian file so that my men were very much extended and distant from each other. I marched in front and was followed by Sergeant McKnatt and next to him was Nehemiah Tilton. . . .

"General Mercer's brigade, owing to some delay in arranging Cadwalader's men, had advanced several hundred yards ahead and never discovered the enemy until he was turning the buildings they were posted behind, and then they were not more than fifty yards off."

Mercer "immediately formed his men, with great courage, and poured a heavy fire in upon the enemy, but they being greatly superior in number, returned the fire and charged bayonets."

Sergeant White and Captain Frothingham were positioned behind the left of the American line with their two artillery pieces, facing, in White's words, "the enemy's right, consisting of grenadiers, Highlanders, etc., their best troops." The oncoming British "were to the north of us. The sun shone upon them and their arms glistened very bright. It seemed to strike an awe upon us."

Were they not "nigh enough," Frothingham asked, to give the enemy a shot?

White: "Yes, I think so."

Frothingham: "You fire, and I will follow suit."

With the help of "a strong man," White got the cannon into position, then took aim and shouted "Fire!" The gun blasted its load into the enemy ranks. Frothingham followed with a blast from the other gun.

"Then," as White saw things, "the enemy began—both armies advancing towards each other, firing as fast as possible. We then loaded with cannister shot; they made a terrible squeaking noise. Both armies kept on marching towards one another until the infantry came to use the bayonets. . . . Our left line gave way.'"

Lieutenant James McMichael, a member of General Mercer's small force, would recall, somewhat inaccurately, that "the enemy, then consisting of 500, paraded in an open field in battle array. We boldly marched to within 25 yards of them, and then commenced the attack, which was very hot. We kept up an incessant fire until it came to pushing bayonets, when we were ordered to retreat."

At the outset, it appeared to Sergeant R that victory was going to be won quickly: "As we were descending a hill through an orchard, a party of the enemy who were entrenched behind a bank and fence, rose and fired upon us. Their first shot passed over our heads, cutting the limbs of the trees under which we were marching. At this moment we were ordered to wheel. As the platoon which I commanded was obeying the order, the corporal who stood at my left shoulder received a ball and fell dead on the spot. He seemed to bend forward to receive the ball, which otherwise might have ended my life. We formed, advanced, and fired upon the enemy. They retreated eight rods to their packs, which were laid in a line. I advanced to the fence on the opposite side of the ditch which the enemy had just left, fell on one knee and loaded my musket with ball and buckshot. Our fire was most destructive; their ranks grew thin and the victory seemed nearly complete, when the British were reinforced. Many of our brave men had fallen, and we were unable to stand such superior numbers of fresh troops. I soon heard General Mercer in a tone of distress, 'Retreat!' "

About thirty-six hours earlier in Trenton, within the hearing of Major Wilkinson, General Mercer had expressed his dedication to the cause, adding that "God can witness how cheerfully I would lay down my life to secure it." Now he was about to become one of the first victims of the charging British. After shouting "Retreat!" he was knocked from his horse and surrounded by British bayonets. "Call for quarter, you damned rebel!" one of the British shouted, but Mercer would not. Instead he drew his sword and attempted to fight back. He was stunned by the stroke of a gun butt, then bayoneted time and again. Finally, feigning death, Mercer heard one of his attackers say, "Damn him, he is dead. Let us leave him." (Mercer gave this account, according to Major Wilkinson, before dying of his wounds nine days later.)

The oncoming British appeared to be as inflamed with blood lust as some of the Hessians had been a day earlier in the action at the Assunpink bridge in Trenton. They were "screaming as if so many devils had got hold of them," according to an eyewitness.*

---

*A British officer had been fatally shot from ambush near Princeton the previous day. Cold-blooded murder, it was called, and some thought it accounted for the ferociousness of the British attack.

This is how William Howe, the British commander in chief, reported that incident to London: "Captain Phillips of the 35th Grenadiers, returning from hence to join his company, was . . . beset between Brunswick and Princetown by some lurking villains who murdered him in a most barbarous manner, which is a mode of war the enemy seem from several late instances to have adopted with a degree of barbarity that savages could not exceed." According to Major Apollos Morris, the British soldiers "were exasperated by hearing of the shooting of a captain . . . and his servant the previous day as he traveled unarmed."

After Mercer fell under the British charge, Colonel Haslet took over command and presently became a casualty himself. In Captain Rodney's words: "Colonel Haslet retired some small distance behind the buildings and endeavored to rally them but, receiving a bullet through his head, dropt dead on the spot and the whole brigade fled in confusion." In one of Haslet's pockets was the week-old order from Washington to go home on recruiting duty—the order Haslet had chosen to ignore.

Having routed the Continentals under Mercer's command, the British troops charged on with their bayonets toward the oncoming militia force commanded by Colonel Cadwalader, and they were now supported by heavy artillery fire. "At this instant," according to Rodney, "General Cadwalader's Philadelphia Brigade came up and . . . took post behind a fence . . . and so extended themselves that every man could load and fire incessantly. . . . On the hill behind the British line they [the British] had eight pieces of artillery which played incessantly with round and grape shot on our brigade, and the fire was extremely hot.

"Yet General Cadwalader led up the head of the column with the greatest bravery to within fifty yards of the enemy. But this was rashly done, for he was obliged to recoil, and, leaving one piece of his artillery, he fell back about forty yards and endeavored to form the brigade. . . . Some companies did form and gave a few vollies but the fire of the enemy was so hot the militia gave way and the whole brigade broke and most of them retired to a woods about 150 yards in the rear."

Perhaps it was rashly done, as Rodney said, but Colonel Cadwalader, as he would later report, "rode in front to the column and ordered the second divisions to double up to the right, the third to the left, and so on alternately. This was done in the face of the enemy and under a shower of grape shot. About half the first battalion was formed when they broke, fell back upon the column, threw the whole into confusion. I immediately rode around the left and formed a division, joined one man after the other to it, but the fire was so hot that they again broke."

This is how Lieutenant Charles Willson Peale, in the second wave of Cadwalader's troops with his young Philadelphians, noted the action: "The battalion just ahead of us began an exceedingly quick platoon firing, and some cannon [firing]. We marched on quickly and met some of the troops retreating in confusion. We continued our march towards the hill where the firing was, though now rather irregularly.

"I carried my platoon to the top of the hill and fired, though unwillingly, for I thought the enemy too far off, and then retreated, loading. We returned to the charge and fired a second time, and retreated as before."

In a screaming bayonet charge that would go down in regimental history, Mawhood's small band of infantrymen and dragoons had routed both the Mercer and Cadwalader brigades, numbering about 1,500. Along the way, the British refused to give quarter. Lieutenant Bartholomew Yeates, an eighteen-year-old member of the First Virginia Regiment, "received a wound in his side which brought him to the ground. Upon seeing the enemy advance towards him, he begged for quarter. A British soldier stopped, and after deliberately loading his musket by his side, shot him through the breast. Finding that he was still alive, he stabbed him in thirteen places with his bayonet, the poor youth all the while crying for mercy. Upon the enemy being forced to retreat, either the same or another soldier, finding he was not dead, struck him with the butt of a musket on the side of the head." Yeates would impart these details to Dr. Benjamin Rush before dying a week later.

"On our retreat," Sergeant R would report, "we had left a comrade of ours whose name was Loomis from Lebanon, Connecticut, whose leg was broken by a musket ball, under a cart in a yard. But on our return he was dead, having received several wounds from a British bayonet.

"My old associates were scattered about, groaning, dying and dead. One officer who was shot from his horse lay in a hollow place in the ground rolling and writhing in his blood, unconscious of anything around him."

Another American officer, wounded in the legs, became the victim of a British soldier who "came and knocked his brains out with the butt end of his gun," according to one of Sergeant William Young's informants. "A young lad that was wounded they stabbed three times in his side with his bayonet, which so exasperated our men that, seeing two Hessians behind a tree, ran at them, shot one and run the other through."

Captain Daniel Neil's company of East New Jersey artillery got off a few rounds but was overrun and surrounded by the enemy charge. Screaming imprecations, the British killed Neil, took one of his cannon, turned it around and opened fire on the fleeing Americans. Neil, too, suffered in the extreme in his final moments, according to General Greene: "The enemy refused him quarter after he was wounded. He has left a poor widow overwhelmed with grief. . . . Such instances paint all the horrors of war beyond description."

Captain John Fleming, only twenty-one but commanding the First Virginia Regiment, tried valiantly to get his men into formation as the enemy troops came on. "Gentlemen," he shouted over the din, "dress the line before you make ready!" But by this time the British were overrunning Fleming's position. "We will dress you!" one of the British shouted, and in short order Fleming fell to the ground mortally wounded.

William Shippin,* a twenty-six-year-old grocer from Philadelphia, and the father of three children, was also fatally wounded in the skirmish. He was the captain in command of a small company of marines who had joined the Pennsylvania militia in the action. He had had command of one of the vessels in Commodore Thomas Seymour's fleet in the Delaware, the fleet that had kept Colonel Donop from occupying Burlington. Margaret Morris had mentioned Shippin in her journal—"a captain, a smart little fellow"—as one of the Tory-hunters in her area.

Ensign Anthony Morris, Jr., a thirty-eight-year-old Quaker who was serving in defiance of the tenets of the Society of Friends, would die about three hours after the battle, having suffered three wounds, "one on the chin, one on the knee and the third and fatal one on the right temple by grape shot," as Dr. Jonathan Potts would report.

At one point in this action, Captain Rodney noted, "a field officer was sent to order me to take post on the left of the artillery until the brigade should form again . . . and to assist the artillery in preventing the enemy from advancing." The artillery Rodney was assisting was that of a militia captain named Joseph Moulder—two guns handled by some twenty boys recruited from Philadelphia's dock area. Would these inexperienced youngsters be able to stand firm in the face of the British onslaught? They would indeed, according to Rodney: "Two pieces of artillery stood their ground and were served with great skill and bravery."

Rodney himself barely escaped. He was at his post with about

---

*Apparently not related to the Shippen family.

fifteen of his men, "but I could not keep them all there for the enemy's fire was dreadful and three balls, for they were very thick, had grazed me. One passed within my elbow, nicking my great coat, and carried away the breech of Sergeant McKnatt's gun, he being close behind me. Another carried away the inside edge of one of my shoe soles; another had nicked my hat and indeed they seemed as thick as hail.

"From these stacks and buildings we, with two pieces of artillery, kept up a continuous fire on the enemy, and in all probability it was this circumstance that prevented the enemy from advancing, for they could not tell the number we had posted behind these covers and were afraid to attempt passing them. But if they had known how few they were, they might easily have advanced while the two brigades were in confusion and routed the whole body for it was a long time before they could be reorganized again, and indeed many that were panic struck ran quite off."

Like many another American officer, Captain Stephen Olney found it difficult to keep soldiers from running off as the British came charging with their bayonets. Olney was serving with a platoon in the Rhode Island regiment that had until now been led by Colonel Daniel Hitchcock. The colonel, who would die within a few days, had become so ill that he had turned over the command to Major Israel Angell. Just before the battle, according to Olney, Major Angell, "the only field officer present, made a short speech to the regiment, encouraging them to act the part that became brave soldiers worthy of the cause for which we were contending.

"We then marched a short distance with a wood upon our right, and partly in front, and the first notice that I had of the enemy being so near, they, to the number of thirty or forty, fired a full volley on the front of the column composed of Jersey or Pennsylvania militia, who broke and came running through our ranks. This had like to have disordered our march, but Captain Jeremiah Olney,* in a peremptory manner, ordered them to join our platoon. I was in this platoon and I seconded the motion, *in earnest,* so that with some persuasion and a few hard words, some ten or twelve of them complied, and the rest made off into the woods.

"When clear of the woods and other obstructions, our column

---

*Apparently an uncle of Stephen Olney's, but the relationship is not made clear in Stephen Olney's recollections.

displayed and marched in line. At this instant the enemy made a full discharge of musketry and field pieces loaded with grape shot, which made the most horrible music about our ears I had ever heard, but as they overshot, there were but few but what continued the march, looking well at the colors, which were carried steadily by Ensign Oliver Jencks, of Cumberland, (no fool of a job to carry colors steady at such a time).

"The enemy, perceiving we were not all dead and that we continued to advance in order with a reserved charge for them, turned their backs and fled in disorder. We pursued them."

It was Captain Olney's platoon and the rest of the New England troops being led by Major Angell who, according to Lieutenant Peale, saved the day: "I must here give the New England troops their due. They were the first who regularly formed and stood the fire without regarding the balls, which whistled their thousand notes around our heads." General Sullivan, though back on the Saw Mill Road at this time, would later claim authoritative information on the performance of the New Englanders: "When the [British] 17th Regiment had thrown 3,500 Southern [i.e., Pennsylvania] militia into the utmost confusion, a regiment of Yankees restored the day. This General Mifflin confessed to me, though the Philadelphia papers tell a different story."

Sergeant R was among the troops retreating as the New Englanders were coming forward. He said he discharged his musket "at part of the enemy, and ran for a piece of wood at a little distance where I thought I might shelter.

"At this moment Washington appeared in front of the American army, riding towards those of us who were retreating, and exclaimed, 'Parade with us, my brave fellows! There is but a handful of the enemy, and we will have them directly.' I immediately joined the main body, and marched over the ground again. . . . The British were unable to resist this attack."

General Washington had been riding with General Sullivan's column back on Saw Mill Road when he became aware that the Mercer-Cadwalader force was in serious trouble; this was not just a minor skirmish. Wheeling his horse about and calling to his aides and the First Troop Philadelphia Light Horse to follow, he raced to the battle scene, which was shrouded in a dense white cloud created by the concentrated fire. In "this moment of disorder," according to Major Apollos Morris, the volunteer from England, the commander in chief "was exposed to both firings for some time." This final charge, Ensign Beale noted, "was made by Washington in person, who carried the men to charge bayonet. This was done while we were marching down the hill and the party that we were opposed to, seeing that, ran without firing a gun." Colonel John Fitzgerald, one of the aides who had been riding with Washington, lost sight of the general in the action and covered his eyes with his tricorne, reluctant to witness His Excellency's fate. But Washington emerged from the smoky cloud unscathed and shouting an order to Fitzgerald: "Away, my dear Colonel, and bring up the troops!"

Hitchcock's New Englanders were soon thereafter joined by other battle-tested troops, including Colonel Edward Hand's Pennsylvania riflemen. Observing the advance of these men, Sergeant White was awestruck: "I never saw men looked so furious as they did, when running by us with their bayonets charged. The British lines were broken and our troops followed them so close that they could not form again."

Now the exhausted and greatly outnumbered enemy troops, with Americans charging at them from three sides, could only break and run. Some of them were captured and some slashed their way through American ranks with their bayonets. Most of them raced back toward the Post Road, the one from which they had come charging and screaming less than an hour earlier. Some fled back toward Princeton. It was all over, this part of the fighting.

"Having retreated a short distance," Lieutenant McMichael would recall, "we were reinforced, when we immediately rallied and with the utmost precipitation put our foes to retreat." General Greene also noted the turnabout: Cadwalader's Philadelphia militiamen "were broken at first [but] soon formed in the face of grapeshot and pushed on with a spirit that would do honor to veterans."

The battle lasted about forty-five minutes, according to most reports, and as John Armstrong, Jr., General Mercer's aide-de-camp, observed, "it was for fifteen minutes as hot as any amateur of the game would wish for."

After the firing ceased, Armstrong found Mercer in a state "bordering on insensibility." On Armstrong's greatcoat he was carried to a nearby farmhouse, where he briefly revived. "Beckoning to me," Armstrong later recalled, "he said in a voice and articulation much changed, 'Get ready a poultice of bread and milk.' This was soon prepared and about to be applied to the lower part of his face, which was at that time the only wounded part visible." Then, according to Armstrong, Mercer pointed to his abdomen, where three puncture holes were found and poulticed.

Later in the day, after the Americans had left the battle area, Mercer was abused by a party of British, according to Dr. Jonathan Potts, an army surgeon: "Would you believe that the inhuman monsters robbed the General as he lay unable to resist on the bed, even to the taking of his cravat from his neck, insulting him all the time."

———— ◆◆◆ ————

CHAPTER 47

We Suffered Much

In the final moments of the fighting outside Princeton, according to a British version, the men of Colonel Mawhood's Seventeenth Regiment of Foot wanted to continue to fight even when the odds became impossible. They "deliberately pulled off their knapsacks and gave three cheers, then broke through the Rebels, faced about, attacked and broke through them a second time. Colonel Mawhood then said it would be prudent, as they were so few, to retire; upon which the men one and all cried out, 'No, no; let us attack them again.' And it was with great difficulty their colonel could induce them to retreat; which at length they performed in the utmost order."

Because of the valor they displayed against the rebels, the members of the Seventeenth Regiment, also known as the Royal Leicestershires, came to be called "The Heroes of Prince Town," and for many years were glorified as such on recruiting posters in England.* The Seventeenth, it was reported, "consisting of less than 300 men, fell in with the rebel army of between 5,000 and 6,000, whom they attacked with all the ardor and intrepidity of Britons. They received the fire of the Rebels from behind a fence, over which they immedi-

*They were also nicknamed the Tigers, an appellation adopted years later by representatives of the college in Princeton.

ately leaped upon their enemies, who presently turned to the right about with such precipitation as to leave their very cannon behind them. The soldiers instantly turned their cannon and fired at least twenty rounds upon their rear, and had they been assisted with another regiment or two, the Rebels would have found it rather difficult to make good their retreat. This has been one of the most splendid actions of the whole campaign and has given convincing proof that British valour had not declined from its ancient glory. Of Colonel Mawhood, their gallant commander, and of his conduct too many encomiums cannot be said."

According to this version, Mercer, the seriously wounded rebel general, was astonished by the bravery of Mawhood's small force: "When he was taken up by our people [Mercer] asked how many the numbers were who had thus attacked him and, upon being told, he cried out with astonishment, 'My God, is it possible? I have often heard of British courage, but never could have imagined to find such an instance as this!'"

George Inman, the ensign who had been longing for home and a soft, downy bed, was among the few officers of the Seventeenth who escaped serious injury. "We attacked their center column," he would report, "and drove them to their main body but, they rallying, we were obliged to retire after making such an exertion as we were able to proceed to our army, then lying at Maidenhead.

"We suffered much. Out of 224 rank and file that marched off the parade at 5 o'clock that morning we sustained a loss of 101 rank and file, killed and wounded . . . , I being the only officer in the right wing of the battalion that was not very much injured, receiving only a buck shot through my cross belt which just entered the pit of my stomach and made me sick for the moment."

The outcome might have been different, Inman felt, if the Seventeenth had received help from the two other regiments of the Fourth Brigade: "The enemy proved too powerful for us, the 55th giving way and retired to Prince Town, where the 40th Regiment were posted, and both regiments quitted that town, retiring before the enemy to Brunswick."

Captain Thomas Dowdeswell singled out one of those regiments as being blameworthy: "The 40th Regiment did not do themselves any credit by the early retreat they made towards Brunswick on the first alarm."

CHAPTER 48

Not a Man Among Them But Showed Joy

As the outnumbered but stubborn British force finally began to give way, Washington's troops, sensing victory, followed in close pursuit. General Cadwalader had, at last and at great personal risk, "collected some of the brigade and some New-Englandmen," and advanced in the face of heavy fire. The British, he said, "gave us several heavy fires, in which two were killed and several wounded. I pressed my party forward, huzzaed, and cried out, 'They fly, the day is our own,' and it passed from right to left.

"I fancy the enemy found it impossible to escape, as our troops all began to rally and join in the pursuit. They all dropped their packs and flew with the utmost precipitation and we pursued with great eagerness."

In the final minutes, according to Thomas Rodney, "General Washington having rallied both General Mercer's and General Cadwalader's brigades, they moved forward and, when they came to where the artillery stood, began a very heavy platoon fire on the march. This the enemy bore but a few minutes and then threw down their arms and ran."

"It's a fine fox chase, my boys!" a jubilant General Washington shouted as he rode along with the pursuers, including his escort party, the mounted Philadelphia troop, and Colonel Hand's riflemen. Many of the British were captured during this chase. In one of the day's most unusual maneuvers John Donaldson, of the Philadelphia troop, and a lieutenant named Simpson accounted for the capture of about twenty of the enemy. "In the ardour of the pursuit," Major Wilkinson would report, Donaldson "separated himself from the troop and as the infantry could not keep up he found himself alone and liable to be shot by any straggler of the enemy who would not surrender. Yet, unwilling to slacken his pace, he mounted a Lieutenant Simpson behind him, who, whenever a fugitive threatened to be refractory, jumped off and shot him. In this manner three men, whilst taking aim at Mr. Donaldson, were knocked down and his life saved. But he made a score of prisoners, whom he sent to his rear after disarming them."

On the battlefield, now suddenly quiet, an officer approached Sergeant R. "Sergeant R——, you are wounded," he said. No, said the sergeant, for, like many a combat soldier before and since, he "never expected to be injured in battle." But the officer was right: "On examination I found the end of my forefinger gone, and bleeding profusely. When and how it happened I never knew. I found also bullet holes in the skirts of my coat, but, excepting the slight wound of my finger, was not injured."

The battlefield was a gory sight—the dead, the dying and other wounded lying in grotesque positions on the frigid turf. "The ground was frozen," Sergeant R noted, "and all the blood which was shed remained on the surface, which added to the horror of this scene of carnage."

The unidentified Princeton scholar serving as a militiaman reacted similarly when he came upon the scene a few hours later. He and the rest of his small militia company had waited in ambush near Pennington in the hope of capturing some of the fleeing enemy troops. The scholar and his men had set out early from Pennington that morning, according to his journal, "towards Trenton till sun half an hour high, when we heard the engagement begin towards Princeton. We then immediately marched back to Penny Town waiting some time for intelligence. Made two or three movements and lay in wait some time in the woods for the enemy. But they, having got intelligence of us by some Tory, returned another road and so escaped us." Around three in the afternoon "we came to the field where the battle was fought. Had a most dismal prospect of a number of pale, mangled corpses lying in the mud and blood. I felt gloomy at the awful scene."

Octogenarian Robert Lawrence and the others who had taken cover in their cellar about a mile west of Princeton emerged shortly before the firing ceased: "Towards the last of the battle seven [British] Regulars was seen from our door to fall at once. . . .

"Almost as soon as the firing was over, our house was filled and surrounded with General Washington's men, and himself on horseback at the door. They brought in with them on their shoulders two wounded [British] Regulars. One of them was shot in at his hip and the bullet lodged in his groin, and the other was shot through his body just below his short ribs. He was in very great pain and bled much out of both sides, and often desired to be removed from one place to another, which was done accordingly and he died about three o'clock in the afternoon. They was both used very tenderly by the Rebels (as they call them). The other also bled much and they put a cloth dipt in vinegar to the wound to stop it. . . .

"As soon as the battle was over, General Mercer . . . was carried into Thomas Clark's house with several other wounded men. And above twenty was carried into William Clark's house. Two of them dyed soon after they was brought in. Sixty was carried to Princetown but how many of them were Regulars, I know not. By an account that a neighbour gentleman sent to me there was thirty-one Regulars found dead in about the field of battle and nineteen Provincials, and one hundred and seventy-five taken prisoners of the Regulars and Hessians.*

"General Washington's men came into our house. Though they were both hungry and thirsty, some of them laughing outright, others smiling, and not a man among them but showed joy in his countenance. It really animated my old blood with love to those men that but a few minutes before had been courageously looking death in the face in relieving a part of their country from the barbarous insults and ravages of a bold and daring enemy."

After leaving the Olden house, General Washington came upon a wounded British soldier, lying on the frozen field. According to a contemporary account, Washington, "after enquiring into the nature of his wound, commended him for his gallant behaviour, and assured him that he should want for nothing that his camp could furnish him.

"After the General left him, an American soldier who thought he was dead came up in order to strip him. The General, seeing it, bid the soldier begone, and ordered a sentry to stand over the wounded prisoner till he was carried to a convenient house to be dressed."

The column commanded by General Sullivan, after a pause, was now advancing along Saw Mill Road toward the southern edge of

---

*Losses of just the British Seventeenth Regiment were listed as 13 killed, 53 wounded and 35 missing or captured—101 casualties out of 246 men. In all, according to General Howe's report, the losses included 1 captain, 1 sergeant, and 16 rank and file killed; 1 captain, 1 lieutenant, 2 ensigns, 5 sergeants and 48 rank and file wounded; 1 captain, 1 lieutenant, 2 ensigns, 5 sergeants, 4 drummers and 187 rank and file captured or missing. Howe's return omitted, perhaps among others, a lieutenant and 9 enlisted men of an artillery unit who were killed.

American casualty reports were also inconclusive. Washington estimated his loss "in slain" as "6 or 7 officers and about 25 or 30 privates; the number of wounded is not ascertained." Writing from Princeton two days following the battle, Dr. Jonathan Potts estimated that the American killed were 16 and the British 23.

Princeton. According to Major Apollos Morris, Sullivan had earlier sent forward "a battalion detached to post itself beyond the town and prevent the escape of any toward Brunswick." Now he called this force back to join the march on Princeton. Soon after Sullivan's column resumed its advance, Morris would report, some troops of the British Fortieth "appeared pouring out of the back gate of the college and taking possession of a dike which extended from thence down the hill."* The troops of the British Fortieth, joined by some members of the Fifty-fifth, were about equal in number to Sullivan's force. However, with the Americans coming on and effectively supported by the two artillery pieces, the British defenders broke and ran. Another fox chase was on.

This was not as routine an action as would be reported, according to General Sullivan. "It seems to have been forgot," he would complain, that while the British Seventeenth was engaging the Mercer-Cadwalader troops, "six hundred Yankees had the town to take against the 40th and 55th Regiments, which they did without loss owing to the manner of the attack. . . . Newspapers and even letters don't always speak the truth. . . . No men fight better or write worse than the Yankees."

In the town the end came quickly. Several of the British who had not succeeded in breaking away toward Brunswick had joined others already ensconced in Nassau Hall. As the Americans came on, the British fired from the windows but they were able to hold out for only a few minutes.

Captain Alexander Hamilton brought his artillery pieces forward and opened fire. One ball landed against a wall of the prayer hall and knocked the portrait of King George II to the floor; another bounced off an outside wall of the building and barely missed the horse ridden by Major Wilkinson.† This was followed by an attack on the front door led by Captain James Moore, a resident of Princeton whose home had been plundered by the enemy.‡ The

---

*This area, known as Frog's Hollow, included what are today the sites of the Princeton Inn Dormitory and the Princeton Theological Seminary.

†Ashbel Green, of the class of 1783 at the College of New Jersey, noted that during his undergraduate days the belief was definitely accredited that a cannonball from an American gun "took off the King's head." The nick in the outside wall is still visible.

‡Moore later claimed, in seeking damage payment, that the enemy had carried off calf skins, sheep skins, and other goods valued at more than £750, a huge sum.

door gave way and soon a white flag of surrender was flying from one of the windows. It was all over.

The captured British—"a haughty, crabbed set of men," according to Sergeant R—streamed out of Nassau Hall along with some liberated Americans. "General Washington's army," as Robert Lawrence got the story, "took all the Regulars in town prisoners, and discharged their Continental prisoners that they had confined in the College . . . among whom . . . was about 30 of our Countrypeople that were accused either of being Rebels or aiding . . . them."

Among the other British captured was a sergeant named Burk, who was taken as he attempted to hurdle a fence behind Nassau Hall. He and other members of his company had heard that morning that Cornwallis's troops had defeated the rebels and in fact were coming into Princeton with Washington himself among their prisoners. "When we were taken," Burk later informed an American guarding him, "it was a warm, very foggy morning. We had eaten our breakfast and were in the college yard, stripped, with our coats and hats off, playing ball, and as to having any fear about an enemy, we felt as safe as if we had been in the kingdom of heaven. But at once we heard the sound of men's feet tramping, and I stooped down and looked under the fog, and I could see their legs as high as their hips, not more than six rods from us. Not a moment was left to look for our coats and hats."

Burk ran off and tried to climb over a fence: "I sprung and threw my breast across the top rail. At that instant, a ball from a fieldpiece struck in the middle of the rail. I was at one end and another man at the other end of the rail. The ball took the rail in two in the middle, and I was cast to the ground swift, and gave me such a jar, I thought myself mortally wounded, and, to sum it up, you see we are all prisoners."

"This," Captain Rodney would report of his entering Princeton, "is a very pretty little town. . . . The houses are built of brick and are very elegant, especially the College which has 52 rooms in it. But the whole town has been ravaged and ruined by the enemy." What Rodney did not add, or perhaps did not know, was that successive units of American troops had done much of the ravaging before the enemy troops arrived.

For a time in Princeton there was concern about the whereabouts of General Washington. Had he, like Mercer and Haslet, been a casualty? "When the troops were assembled in Princeton," Major Wilkinson recalled, "the absence of the General . . . excited strong emotions of alarm for his safety." Then Washington rode on to the scene; he had been with the troops rounding up the fleeing British—on the "fox chase."

Many of the soldiers had drunk their ration of rum before the battle and were showing the effects of the ration and post-battle drafts. Sergeant R, however, apparently observed none of this: "In this battle and that of Trenton there were no ardent spirits in the army, and the excitement of rum had nothing to do in obtaining the victories. As I tried powder and rum on Long Island to promote courage, and engaged here without it, I can say that I was none the less courageous here than there."

Plunderers among the troops in town were busily engaged in their specialty. Princeton was full of damned Tories, some figured, and used this as an excuse for looting. Enemy stores and equipment were considered fair game, and Sergeant R was among those who carried off items abandoned by the enemy: "In this battle my pack, which was made fast by leather strings, was shot from my back, and with it went all the little clothing I had. It was, however, soon replaced by one which had belonged to a British officer, and was well furnished." (A few days later, the pack would be on the back of another plunderer: "It was not mine long, for it was stolen shortly afterwards.")

Three brass artillery pieces had been abandoned by the British, according to Colonel Cadwalader. There were not enough horses to carry off two of them but, he noted, Major Thomas Proctor, of the Pennsylvania State Regiment of Artillery, made a good exchange: "He left an iron three-pounder and brought a brass six-pounder."

The Americans also loaded in their wagons whatever ammunition could be carried off. Then they set fire to the ammunition they had to leave behind, creating huge clouds of smoke that lasted through the day.

Major James Wilkinson was among those who partook of legitimate plunder. The troops, according to him, found "some shoes and blankets, which were very opportune, and for my own part I made a most seasonable acquisition in a breakfast at the provost's house, which had been prepared for a mess of the 40th Regiment, who, the steward informed me, were sitting down as the fire commenced."

One of the less legitimate plunderers was said to be an artillery officer, Captain Joseph Crane. According to an official report, he took "a box . . . from the enemy containing hard money" and was "suspected of converting the box and contents to his personal use."

Sergeant Joseph White partook of a British breakfast, and then some: "I went into a room in the college and locked myself in. I saw a plate of toast, a tea pot and everything handy for breakfast. I sat down and helped myself well. I was very hungry, marching all night and fighting in the morning. I felt highly refreshed.

"After I was done, I looked round the room and saw an officer's coat. I went to it and found it a new one; the paper never taken off the buttons, was plated or solid silver, I could not determine which, lined with white satin." White also carried off a "small gilt bible" and, for some reason, some female apparel: "a silk skirt, an elegant one, and a pair of silk shoes."

In their hasty departure the British had left many other prized items. Blankets, dozens of them, had been left behind. "Orders came," according to Sergeant White, "for all the men to throw away their dirty old blankets and take new ones." There were so many barrels of flour that the Americans did not have room for all of them on their wagons: "The barrels of flour were great indeed. After filling all the wagons, they knocked the heads out of the remainder and strewed it about the ground. The women came and looked at it, but seemed afraid to meddle with it. I, being nigh, told them to scoop it up by aprons full before the enemy come.

"I had rolled a barrel to the ammunition wagon and told the captain that I was only going to that house, pointing to it. I should be back in a few minutes.

"I engaged a woman to bake me some cakes. I asked if she had any daughters. 'What do you want to know that for?' said she." White answered by saying he was "steady as a pious old deacon," and persisted with the question: How many daughters did she have?

Two, the woman finally said.

"I have got presents for both," White said. "When I come again I will bring them."

After a while White was back at the woman's door: "I went to see how the cakes come on, and carried my presents. 'Here, mother,' said I, 'are the presents. Call your daughters.' She went to the stairs and called 'Sally, come down.' But she come part of the way and stopt. I went to the bottom of the stairs and said, 'Sally, come down. Here is a present for you.' She came. 'Here, try this petticoat on,

and if it fits you, keep it. Tell your sister to come. I have got
something for her.'

"She came. I told her to take the shoes and try them on; if they
fitted her, to keep them."

She kept them, and her sister kept the petticoat.

A short time later, back with his company, White heard the order
to form the line and march off in a half hour: "I ran to see if the
cakes were done. The woman said the oven was heating. I could
have some in an hour's time."

But that, as things turned out, would be too late: "An express
arrived and informed us that the enemy were marching quick time
after us." White and his cannoneers joined the long line marching
out of Princeton on the road to Kingston.

Charles Willson Peale and his young Philadelphians, along with
other units in Greene's column, had halted outside Princeton following the battle, but now, with the British approaching from the
direction of Trenton, they were on the march again: "We were
resting on our arms, waiting for leave to enter the town to refresh
ourselves when we heard the sound of cannon in our rear. We
thought it was at Trenton, but finding it approached nearer, we
perceived the enemy close upon our heels. We now began to march
on through the town. I expected we should be collected in order
when we got to the back of the town, but we still continued on."

So did Captain Thomas Rodney and his small company: "As soon
as the enemy's main army heard our cannon at Princeton (and not
'til then) they discovered our manouvre and pushed after us with all
speed and we had not been above an hour in possession of the town
before the enemy's light horse and advanced parties attacked our
party at the bridge, but our people by a very heavy fire kept the pass
until our army left the town."

The party at and near the Post Road bridge over Stony Brook was
made up of militiamen from Northumberland County, Pennsylvania, commanded by Colonel James Potter. They were supported by
Captain Thomas Forrest's two artillery pieces and they had been
ordered there by Washington to "hinder the [British] Regulars
passing over and to pull up the bridge." Some troops detached from
Potter's regiment and headed by Major John Kelly, of Union County, Pennsylvania, were taking down the bridge, a crude span made
of logs. With crowbars and other instruments the militiamen took it
apart, plank by plank, prying the logs free and tipping them over

into the ice-crusted stream. But before they could complete the job, the vanguard of the British coming on from Maidenhead approached the crest of the hill leading to the bridge. Here the enemy got their field pieces in place and fired. With grapeshot and cannonballs falling around them, Kelly's men dropped their tools and raced off. Kelly remained to complete the job. He kept hacking away at the planks until a ball struck the beam on which he was standing and dumped him into the stream's jam of ice and logs. Somehow he extricated himself and raced through the continuing fire and on to Princeton without being hit.

Captain Forrest's two artillery pieces were now exchanging shots with the enemy's big guns on the other side of Stony Brook and Colonel Potter's militiamen were firing their muskets at the oncoming enemy vanguard. Unable to get across the bridge (only the stringers, long pieces of timber that had connected the planks, remained), the British troops had to wade, hip-deep in places, through the frigid water. Having crossed, they proceeded to rout Potter's troops and captured Potter himself, who had been wounded in the firefight. More British troops arrived and crossed the brook, reinforcing the vanguard and helping to force Captain Forrest's cannoneers to retreat toward Princeton. Instead of advancing farther, however, the British, with more and more troops arriving, halted here and assembled in battle formation, the officers apparently having decided not to risk facing a numerically superior force of rebels in the town. Cornwallis's troops were meanwhile coming on from Trenton.

———— ♦♦♦ ————

CHAPTER 49

They Arrived in a Most Infernal Sweat

Sergeant Thomas Sullivan, of the British Forty-ninth Regiment of Foot, had spent the night with the rest of General Alexander Leslie's brigade in and around Maidenhead, about halfway between Princeton and Trenton. "Upon hearing the firing at Princeton from

Maidenhead," he noted, "Brigadier General Leslie sent an immediate express to Lord Cornwallis, who was [in Trenton] with the advance troops; and our brigade and the guards got on the march."

Approaching Stony Brook, Leslie's troops paused on high ground overlooking the brook before descending the steep stretch of the Post Road leading to the bridge. "A party of rebels were formed on one side on the bridge and another party cutting it down," Sergeant Sullivan observed. "The Fifth Battalion, which marched in front of the brigade with two six-pounders, engaged them from the opposite side and in a few minutes drove them from the bridge, which they had cut down, and they retreated into the woods. We crossed the river [Stony Brook], wading up to our waist and formed upon the hill."

As Leslie's brigade waited in battle formation near Stony Brook, Cornwallis's troops were marching quick time from Trenton. A highly chagrined Cornwallis accompanied the leading troops. Around daybreak at his quarters outside Trenton, he had learned to his dismay that Washington's army had decamped during the night—to Bordentown, it was at first believed. Then, as Captain Ewald noted: "We heard a heavy cannonade in our rear, which surprised everyone. Instantly we marched back at quick step to Princeton."

Captain Hall, in Trenton, had also heard the firing: "A heavy cannonade, a little after daybreak, effectually roused us from our slumbers, and announced the rebels' attack on Prince Town. . . . As soon as day appeared and discovered to Lord Cornwallis that the gross of the rebel army had given him the slip by moving in the night—which the cannonade soon after heard near Prince Town now confirmed—there remained no room to doubt of the enemy's design, and excited apprehensions that we had not yet felt the full weight of the blow for though the sacrifice of the three regiments at that place appeared more than probable, and became an object of momentous concern, yet it sunk on the reflection of the loss of Brunswick, which was an event much to be dreaded, for its defenceless situation and the weakness of the garrison, now exposed to the ravages of the rebel army. . . .

"Our generals, about 8 o'clock in the morning, had so far got the better of their surprise that they set the army in motion, and though it was so late before they began their march, the advanced guard entered Prince Town as the rear of the enemy left it."

Cornwallis's main body of troops, as General Knox later learned, approached Princeton "in a most infernal sweat—running, puffing, and blowing, and swearing at being so outwitted."

"In the afternoon," according to Captain Ewald, "the entire army reached Princetown, marching in and around the town like an army that is thoroughly beaten. Everyone was so frightened that it was completely forgotten to even obtain information where the Americans had gone. But the enemy now had wings, and it was believed that he had flown toward Brunswick to destroy the main depot, which was protected by only one English regiment. Hurriedly, the army was issued three days' rations of biscuit and brandy, left behind the stores, all the sick, the wounded and the greater part of the baggage and moved with . . . haste toward Brunswick." This was a march of about five hours, Ewald observed, but there was such a great quantity of stores and baggage to be brought to Brunswick that the job required a thousand wagoners, who would not reach Brunswick until the following evening. "If the enemy had pursued them with only a hundred horsemen, one after another would have been captured."

Ensign Thomas Glyn, on the march from Trenton with Lord Cornwallis, noted that the army, after fording Stony Brook, "came to the ground where the action had commenced. None of the enemy were to be found. . . .

"The magazines at Prince Town were burning. The Hessian Grenadiers . . . and Lieutenant Colonel Mawhood from Maidenhead joined us." (Mawhood had retreated from the battlefield into Princeton and then by a circuitous route had made his way toward Maidenhead.)

"On the approach of his lordship [Cornwallis], General Washington retreated from Prince Town and proceeded [toward] Brunswick." So Captain Charles Stedman would report. "Notwithstanding the expedition that General Washington used in his march to Brunswick, yet his rear was hard pressed by the van of the English army. He therefore resolved to relinquish his designs on Brunswick and crossed the Millstone River, breaking down the bridge at King's Town to evade a pursuit.

"The army under Lord Cornwallis, harassed and fatigued, declined pursuing the enemy and proceeded to Brunswick."

Before leaving Princeton, Cornwallis designated the critically wounded General Mercer as a prisoner on parole. He also took time, as Ensign Inman observed, to visit his wounded and sick soldiers and to leave a flag of truce with them. Moreover, as Dr. Benjamin Rush would later charge, Cornwallis provided more care for his wounded men than the American officers did for theirs. The British commander, according to Rush, "left five privates and one surgeon to attend the wounded men he was forced to leave behind him." As for the American wounded, including General Mercer, Rush would add, "I am sorry to say nothing of this kind was done by our generals."

"Some of the British wounded did not seem to expect any quarter," Major Apollos Morris was informed by some American officers. "The greatest part" of the British wounded, according to Morris, "lay on the ground where the corps were first drawn up, and near their knapsacks and two pieces of cannon."

Between thirty and forty British dead and wounded were strewn over the battle area, according to Morris, and fifty-six wounded soldiers were left behind in Princeton when Cornwallis's main body set off for Brunswick. Some of the fifty-six had been wounded before the battle. All would be taken prisoners about a week later.

One of the most seriously wounded was Captain John McPherson, a Scottish officer serving with Mawhood's Seventeenth. He would languish in Princeton for more than a year before dying. Another British captain, and casualty, reportedly participated in a series of events related by Robert Lawrence. As Mawhood's troops set off that morning from Princeton, "one of their captains . . . compelled a man that lived near Princetown to go with him and his company to show them the way to Trenton. The man was very loath to go and went slowly. Upon that the captain bid him step along nimbly, for if he did not he swore he would run him threw with the drawn sword that he had in his hand. . . . They went on about a mile and General Washington's army being discovered put them into a consternation and he got from them. The captain was found in the field of battle dead and carried into the man's house that he had insulted in the morning."

Cornwallis's troops continued to arrive in Princeton throughout the afternoon. "We had a very severe march that day and all the following night," Ensign Inman said, "passing over the field of action about 4 o'clock that afternoon through Prince Town and with the whole army to Brunswick where we got on the 4th about nine in the morning."

As usual the looters busied themselves along the way and, according to Robert Lawrence, they fought among themselves over the booty. Among their targets were the loaded packs that men of the Seventeenth Regiment had abandoned on the field of battle. Late in the afternoon, Lawrence observed, "[British] Regulars and Hessians from Trenton begun to plunder their fellow soldiers' packs, taking out what they pleased and leaving the rest in the dirt. . . ."

A fifty-nine-year-old blacksmith was one of the plunderers' victims, according to Lawrence. "Four or five of the soldiers . . . perceiving that he had a good pair of new shoes on his feet . . . took him prisoner and conveyed him about a mile back to the rest of their company. . . . His shoes was pulled off and one of their own men put them on his feet and compelled the poor old captive to march with them without shoes in his stockings all the way from Princetown to Brunswick."

William Clark's house, to which some twenty wounded men, most of them British, had been carried, was the scene of an atrocity recorded by Lawrence. Some British soldiers insulted Clark's "sick and feeble wife and robbed her of the cloak that she wore over her shoulders in bed. She asked them if they robbed women of their clothes and one of them swore that if the Damned Rebel Bitch said a word more he would run his bayonet threw her heart and they plundered the house of most of the valuable goods and then drew their bayonets and run them threw the feather bed that the sick woman lay on and swore that there was Rebels that was hid under it, but damn them they would fetch them out. This they continued to do until they spoilt the bed. And all the while there lay above twenty men upon straw in the next room. . . . Most of them were [British] Regulars, all groaning with the pains of their wounds and some of them in the very agony of death for two of them died either at that time or soon after. Thus those hardened wretches went on without having the least compassion either on their wounded fellow soldiers or the helpless woman."

By the time such plunderers had their fill and set off for Brunswick, Princeton was a despoiled village. "You would think it had been desolated with the plague and an earthquake," Dr. Rush would observe the next day, "as well as with the calamities of war. The college and church are heaps of ruin; all the inhabitants have been plundered; the whole of Mr. [Richard] Stockton's furniture, apparel, and even valuable writings, have been burnt; all his cattle, horses, and hogs, sheep, grain and forage have been carried away."

Before the main body of Cornwallis's corps left Princeton, a large

British force from Brunswick arrived in the town. During the morning, according to Captain Thomas Dowdeswell, word had been received in Brunswick of the rebels' attack on Princeton. He and his company were immediately ordered to prepare for the sixteen-mile march to Princeton as part of a force that included, according to Dowdeswell, "the British Grenadiers, the 16th Light Dragoons and the 1st Battalion of Guards." These troops set off "with the utmost expedition but did not arrive soon enough to come up with the rebels. However, we retook all the guns we had lost in the action."

Dowdeswell and the rest "made a forced march" back to Brunswick along with Cornwallis's main body of troops, departing late in the afternoon. Having made arrangements for the care of his sick and wounded, Cornwallis "was determined to make a forced march to achieve Brunswick, had General Washington marched to possess it or to recover General [Charles] Lee," Ensign Inman observed. "We marched at five in the evening, a very hard frost and snow on the ground. The bridge at Kingston being demolished occasioned some delay. Our men were so fatigued, having had nothing to eat for two days and no rest, that with difficulty we accomplished this march of eighteen miles. We arrived at daybreak on the 4th at the heights above Brunswick and remained there several hours, should the enemy have showed any disposition to attack us, we were prepared for them, but, finding every thing quiet, the troops . . . marched into cantonments."

Members of the garrison at Brunswick had been relieved to learn that night that the oncoming troops were those of Cornwallis and not of Washington. "We had repeated accounts that Washington had not only taken Princeton but was in full march upon Brunswick," an officer there noted in his diary. "General Matthew now determined to return to the Raritan landing-place with everything valuable, to prevent the rebels from destroying the bridge there. We accordingly marched back to the bridge, one half on one side, the remainder on the other, for its defence, never taking off our accoutrements that night."

Captain Ewald had high praise for the rebel general Washington and anything but praise for Cornwallis's generalship: "This brilliant coup . . . which gave Washington the reputation of an excellent general, derived simply and solely from Lord Cornwallis's mistake of not marching in two columns to Trenton. Had one column marched to Crosswicks by way of Cranbury, the American general would have had to abandon Trenton and still would have remained in a too unfavorable and precarious situation, since he had no depot for his new army in our vicinity. Then Lord Cornwallis would have needed only to pursue him steadily, whereby his army, lacking everything, would have been destroyed in a few days."

It was Colonel Donop, according to Ewald, who wisely suggested that the army approach Trenton from two directions. However, against such a feeble enemy, Cornwallis apparently thought the single-column approach along the Post Road would be sufficient. "The enemy was despised," Ewald commented, "and as usual we had to pay for it."

CHAPTER 50

O, That We Had 500 Fresh Men

General Washington and most of his troops remained in Princeton for about an hour and a half after the battle ended. Some troops meanwhile marked time outside the town, and on the battlefield a detachment supervised by Captain John Polhemus took on a grisly job. "I was left behind," Polhemus later recalled, "to secure stores and bury the dead with assistance of a small guard, which they did by hauling them on sleds to great holes and heaping them in."

In the town, fatigued but happy soldiers bartered for food, scrounged for British souvenirs, and wandered in search of rum or whatever else might turn up. For some, as Major Apollos Morris noted, the order to march off came so suddenly that there was no time to imbibe. The troops, Morris observed, "arrayed their prisoners, taking paroles of two or three sick officers, had not time even to distribute the rum found in store, tho' much wanted, before a firing was heard on the Trenton or Maidenhead road. This was from the advanced parties of Lord Cornwallis's army. . . . General Washington, judging what it was, assembled all that were in or near the town, sent officers after those engaged in pursuing, and, leaving everything taken but the prisoners and a few necessaries which were distributed amongst those who happened to be near the place where they were found, marched . . . till he passed Kingston bridge, ordering it to be taken down."

Farther on, after advancing about two miles along a road that paralleled the eastern bank of the Millstone River, Washington's troops reached Rocky Hill. Here it appeared for a time that the British army was about to catch up with them. A party of British light horse suddenly appeared at the crest of a hill on the other side of the river. It was just a reconnoitering detachment, as things turned out, but at first it was feared that it was the van of Cornwallis's main body of troops.

The British horsemen, according to Captain Rodney, had taken the road "on the left of the Millstone and arrived on the hill, at the bridge on that road just as the van of the American Army arrived on the opposite side.

"I was again commanding the van of our army, and General Washington, seeing the enemy, rode forward and ordered me to halt and to take down a number of carpenters which he had ordered forward and break up the bridge, which was done and the enemy obliged to return."

A halt was called at Rocky Hill just before the road branched in two. Here, as there had been following the victory at Trenton eight days earlier, there was a discussion about whether or not to make a further strike against the enemy. Should they continue along the road paralleling the river, away from the likely path of the British? Or should they take the road to the right and march on to attack the depleted enemy garrison at Brunswick? The British were keeping their prize captive, General Charles Lee, there, as well as stores and ammunition.

Such a strike, however, was not to be. "It was proposed at Rocky Hill," Major Apollos Morris would report, "to make a large detachment for Brunswick, but the men were too much fatigued to hope to affect anything in time. They had been almost constantly on their legs from the time of their parading at Trenton, without sleep, baggage or provisions more than for the day."

In Major Wilkinson's words: "It was the desire of the commander in chief and the inclination of every officer to make a stroke at Brunswick, which had been left with a small garrison. . . . But our physical force could not bear us out; the men had been under arms eighteen hours, and had suffered much from cold and hunger. The commander and several general officers halted at the forks of the road in Kingston, whilst our troops were filing off to Rocky Hill, when the exclamation was general, 'O, that we had 500 fresh men to beat up their quarters at Brunswick.' But the measure was found to be impracticable and we proceeded down Millstone River." The troops' destination was Somerset Court House (Millstone), about twelve miles north of Rocky Hill.

Along the route of march, Lieutenant Peale and his company, with some other troops, almost lost their way: "We took a wrong road, going to the right when we should have taken the left. Here, halt was cried through the army. I heard some rumors that the [British] Light Horse were coming, and some soldiers fixed their bayonets. At last we were informed that we must return and go to the left, which distance we shortened by going through the woods. The roads had now become very sloppy, and the troops so fatigued that many stopped by the way. Some of my men declared they could go no further. I told them of the danger of falling into the hands of the enemy, yet this could not induce all to keep up."

One of those who failed to keep up was a member of the Third Battalion of Philadelphia Associators named Hood. As he would later report, he "went to a farmer's to get some refreshments, fell asleep and waked in the morning, the Army was gone."

Captain Stephen Olney found his men to be hungry, fatigued, but uncomplaining upon arriving at Somerset Court House: "The two last nights' march, the first through mud, snow and water, the last over frozen ground, with the hardships of the day, seemed to have nearly exhausted both men and officers—some of whom were almost as bad as barefoot. Though we were rather short of provisions, no one complained, and we had been too busily engaged to think of hunger; and we rejoiced to find ourselves so much better situated than we were the preceding night at Trenton."

Captain Rodney kept most of his company together ("a few lagged behind") and arrived at Somerset Court House "just at dusk." There he learned of a curious escape just made by a British force: "About an hour before we arrived here 150 of the enemy from Princeton and 50 which were stationed in this town went off with 20 wagons laden with clothing and linen, and 400 of the Jersey militia who surrounded them were afraid to fire on them and let them go off unmolested and there were no troops in our army fresh enough to pursue them, or the whole might have been taken in a few hours.

"Our army was now extremely fatigued, not having had any refreshment since yesterday morning, and our baggage had all been sent away the morning of the action at Trenton, yet they are in good health and in high spirits."

John Howland and his fellow Rhode Islanders in Colonel Daniel Hitchcock's regiment "marched quick, as the advance guard of the British army . . . were said to be close in our rear, following us, as they supposed, to Brunswick. . . . But in three or four miles we turned a square corner and proceeded north toward Somerset Court House. The British continued on to Brunswick. Ten or eleven o'clock at night we arrived at the Court House." Here, about fifteen miles north of Princeton, the prisoners taken at Princeton were locked up. The captives were among the few, according to Howland, lucky enough to have shelter: "It will be remembered that this was the third night's march, and under arms or marching all day. There were barely houses sufficient for the quarters of the Generals and their attendants. The troops took up their abode for the rest of the night on frozen ground. All the fences and everything that would burn was piled in different heaps and burnt, and he was the most fortunate who could get nigh enough to smell the fire or smoke."

Charles Willson Peale arrived at Somerset Court House with only a few of his young Philadelphia militiamen. Many had dropped out of the line of march and fallen to the ground exhausted. At Rocky Hill, Peale had "stopped to collect as many of them as I could, and got several. I there received orders from Colonel Cox to continue as far as I could as the enemy was only seven miles distant from us. Three miles further we should receive further orders."

Eventually, "having continued on our way pretty briskly, got to Somerset Court House, expecting to have quarters in the court house but found it was already occupied by the prisoners."

Here Peale "pushed on to a tavern a little further and got my men into a loft amongst a fine heap of straw, where some Hessians had lain. This was gladly accepted by them who, at other places, were dainty, refusing to go into a house where soldiers had been quartered for fear of their vermin. Now they were glad to lie down and were asleep in a few minutes."

But there was to be no rest for mother hen Peale, not at least until he could collect some food for the next day: "I could not get a single man to go with me in search of provisions. I had the promise from

Colonel Cox of a barrel of flour and the use of an oven but could get nobody to assist me in bringing it to be baked.

"I then went to a house farther in town and purchased some beef, which I got the good woman to boil against I should call for it in the morning. I got a small kettle of potatoes boiled where we lodged. . . . I then laid myself down to rest amongst the men on the Hessian straw and thought myself happy though the room was as full of smoke as if to cure bacon, some New England troops having made a fire in an old chimney that conducted all the smoke to us. However, by covering our head with our blankets, we rested for the night."

In the court house, where British prisoners were sheltered, Lieutenant Elisha Bostwick, of the Rhode Island regiment, observed the prisoners under his care: "They were spreading their blankets upon the floor for the night's lodging. I saw a woman or two with them. I enquired into it and was told that it was sometimes allowed a Sergeant to have his wife with him who drew rations the same as a soldier, were very serviceable and supported virtuous characters." About midnight when all was still one of the prisoners, a Scot, arose and sang a song called "The Gypsy Laddy."

This is how Bostwick, who seems to have confused "laddy" and "lady," recalled some of the lines:

Will you leave your houses, will you leave your lands,
And will you leave your little children a-a-h
Will you leave your true wedded Lord and lying with a Gypsy Lady a-a-h . . .

Yes, I will leave my houses, I will leave my lands
And I will leave my little children a-a-h
I will leave for you my true wedded Lord and lying with a Gypsie Lady a-a-h

The singing soldier, according to Bostwick, "then lay down again. The tune was of a plaintive cast and I always retained it and sung it to my children."

———— ◆◆◆ ————

Epilogue

"It was," James Wilkinson observed, "the desire of the Commander in Chief and the inclination of every officer to make a stroke at Brunswick, which had been left with a small garrison."

What if General Washington's troops had been able to follow up the Trenton and Princeton victories with a strike at Brunswick? Would it have ended the war? Washington was among those who thought so. "In my judgment," he wrote to Congress on January 5, 1777, "six or eight hundred fresh troops upon a forced march would have destroyed all their stores and magazines, taken (as we have since learnt) their military chest containing 70,000£ and put an end to the war."

For this period the speculative game of "What if . . . ?" has many ramifications. What, for example, if General Lee had *not* been captured and his troops had not joined Washington's? What if, in advance of the first battle at Trenton, Colonel Rall had taken the American threat seriously and taken such precautions as installing those two artillery emplacements? What if the Hessians had, as had been their practice, sent patrols out on the River Road early in the morning of December 26? What if General Ewing's militiamen had succeeded in crossing the Delaware to Trenton during the night of December 25–26? Would they have been vanquished after being discovered by Hessian guards near the river's edge? Would the three Hessian regiments, once alerted, have been ready for action when Washington's troops reached the Hessian outposts west and north of Trenton? What if Rall had retreated to the far side of the Assunpink and made a stand there? (Colonel Donop thought he had the answer to that one: "All who know that region agree unanimously that if Colonel Rall with his brigade had retired over the bridge and destroyed it after crossing it, he would have been safe.") What if, during the night following the second battle at Trenton, the British had sent out patrols to investigate reports that American troops along the Assunpink were on the move? What if there had not been the sudden drop in temperature that froze the mud and slush and thus facilitated the movement of Washington's troops and artillery from Trenton to Princeton? What if the hundred Hessians patrolling the Quaker Bridge Road outside Princeton had remained on duty for just a few more hours—long enough to discover the oncoming Americans? What if the British dragoons in that area had been on the job? ("Had our Light Dragoons patrolled the Allens Town Road during the night of the 2d," British Ensign Thomas Glyn wrote in his journal, "the enemy's movement round the left of Lord Cornwallis's corps could not have taken place without our notice.")

Furthermore, what if the British and Hessians had not victimized New Jersey inhabitants, "friends of government" as well as rebels, and what if the British had provided humane treatment for their prisoners in New York? Like the instances of misbehavior in New Jersey, the atrocities committed by the British in the crowded prisons were widely publicized. "The dispute," Colonel Joseph Reed observed early in 1777, "is now advanced to such a height and the inhumanity with which it has been conducted by the British generals has created such an inveteracy between the two countries as no reconcilement can ever efface." General Horatio Gates agreed: "Had General Howe seen to it that the prisoners and Jersey inhabitants, when subdued, were treated with as much humanity as Sir Guy Carleton exercised toward his prisoners, it would have been all up with the Americans."

Finally, what if the Sergeant R's, the Sergeant Whites, the Captain Rodneys, and the rest had, like the majority of able-bodied American males, managed to avoid army duty? Carrying out Washington's newly developed strategy, they avoided open battles with the superior enemy, retreated without loss, and took the enemy by surprise. They demonstrated that in the right circumstances they could hold their own against British and Hessian professionals. They kept a dying revolution alive. A long, hard road lay ahead but never again would America be seized by such panic as spread through the states in December 1776; never again would the American cause be in such jeopardy as it was in December 1776.

Lieutenant Colonel William Harcourt, commanding officer of the party that captured General Lee, indicated new respect for the rebels: "Though it was once the fashion of this army to treat them in the most contemptible light, they are now become a formidable enemy."

In a letter he wrote to Lord George Germain on January 20, 1777, General Howe conceded that the "untimely defeat at Trenton has thrown us further back than was at first apprehended, from the great encouragement given to the rebels," and indicated a major change in plans: "I do not now see a prospect of terminating the war but by a general action."

Writing to Thomas Paine, General Greene observed: "The two late actions at Trenton and Princeton have put a very different face upon affairs." In Philadelphia, Congressman Robert Morris declared that "these feats have turned the scale."

Marching homeward from Morristown, where he was "sick of the smallpox," Sergeant R also noted the change. The weather in the Morristown area "was extremely cold, and we suffered from its severity. We stayed three or four days and then marched through New Jersey towards New York. The inhabitants manifested very different feelings towards us from those exhibited a few weeks before, and were now ready to take arms against the British."

Those were to be the last of Sergeant R's words known to history. His name has never come to light.

Sergeant John Smith faded similarly into oblivion in the ensuing years, as did Sergeant Joseph White, Sergeant William Young, and most of the other members of "the little band that faced the storm."

At Crosswicks on December 31, the day after Sergeant Smith and the rest of his unit agreed to serve beyond the term of their enlistment, he made this note in his diary: "Before day, was ordered to turn out again with our packs as tho we were to march. We then received orders to draw 3 days provisions and to cook it all, which we obeyed again, hearing the enemy were returning towards us. It soon began to rain and was very—" Here this diary ends, its final pages having apparently been torn away.

Smith continued to serve in the Continental Army and to keep other diaries in 1777 and 1778. His notebooks turned up many years later in Marietta, Ohio. On a label attached to them someone had written: "Revolutionary Journal of Smith, father of old man Smith at Joseph Backus."

Sergeant Joseph White was anxious to return home to Massachusetts after the action at Princeton but he was persuaded to stay on: "I got entirely wore out. I wanted to know of the captain why we were not relieved. I told him I was willing to do my share of the duty, but not all. 'I suppose they think us the best fellows,' said he.

"The term of my enlistment being out, General Knox addressed the artillery in a pathetic manner to stay two months longer. Most of our regiment did. The captain said to me, 'Do persuade the men to stay two months, until the new recruits learn how to handle the cannon. Have you put down your name?' I said I had not made up my mind. However, I put my name down to stay until the first of March, 1777. If I had left it when my time was out, I should have escaped many dangers and sufferings I experienced that winter."

Finally, the last day of February arrived: "I told the captain . . . that I should set out for home the next morning. I wanted him to give me a discharge and a month's pay. 'Step here,' said he, 'and take your pay. You are crazy to leave us now. Colonel Knox is made Brigadier General and two regiments more are to be raised, and every sergeant will have a commission. Your name is third on the list for one. You will be at least a captain lieutenant and, I think, a full captain,' said he. I told him that I should go home; did not care about a commission.

"All our officers met that evening and gave me very flattering discharge.

"I left the army and in about two weeks time marched home safe and sound." On the trip home he disposed of the "elegant sword" he had found next to a dead Hessian officer at Trenton: "At Hartford I met with a young officer. I sold [it] to him for eight dollars."

The next and apparently the only other thing known to history of Joseph White is that he was destitute at the time, in 1818, when he applied for a veteran's pension. In the application he listed personal property worth a total of $61.55. Before forwarding the application to Washington, a local judge wrote this message on it: "A decrepit soldier 63 years old can not do much at any labor." Eventually judged to be in sufficiently impoverished circumstances, White was granted a pension of eight dollars a month for the remaining years of his life.

Sergeant William Young and William, Jr. (his two other sons had gone home) remained in Burlington until January 8, 1777, when they were ordered to set off for Morristown, some seventy miles to the north, with the rest of their company. In Bordentown and Trenton Young found "the houses . . . torn in a shocking manner and all the valuable goods taken." In Trenton, the first overnight stop, there were "a number of horses lying on the ground dead belonging to Howe's train." On arriving at Morristown, he noted the usual shenanigans ("Our men uneasy on account of their staying. A great deal of swearing and taking the Holy Name of God in vain") and gave his usual thanks ("Blessed be God for his kind providence over me and mine").

In the course of a dreary fortnight in the Morristown area Young slept, on a typical night, "but poorly on account of the ungodly behavior of our men." He washed his own and his son's shirts and jackets as well as a "very raggy" handkerchief. He noted "great uneasiness among the Cumberland militia to go home, General Mifflin persuading to stay till Monday next. Few consent." One day he saw "General Washington just riding by," and on another he saw an old man suspected of Toryism all but lynched by an angry mob.

Finally, it was time to set off with his son and the rest for Philadelphia and home. It turned out to be a march of four days. At the first stop, "the people where we quarter with this night" were "somewhat shy of us." A few nights earlier some American troops "behaved very rudely, insulted the people of the house, and other ways used them ill. This shows that only one bad man causes a great many honest men to suffer."

At Abington, a village about twelve miles north of Philadelphia, it was snowing heavily when, around six p.m., they stopped "at a certain gentleman's house in comfortable expectation of quarters, which begged to be in the kitchen, and cover for our baggage, which he resolutely refused, and used some unkind expressions." He even refused "the loan of tubs to feed our horses in." However, a bit of friendly persuasion brought results: "I told him I only wanted to lay at the kitchen fire a few hours till the moon rose. It still snowed fast. At first [he] refused our men warming themselves," but then "the gentleman came and kindly offered my request. . . . At length put our baggage under his shed, our horses in his stable. Lay down by the kitchen fire. Very comfortable after eating some warm bread and milk.

"Rose about 3. . . . Set out about 4. Reached home and found my family all well to my great satisfaction, about 10. And now what shall I say? Surely God has been good to me and mine. Blessed be God my health is preserved through all the fatigue of this winter's campaign."

On the February day when young John Howland left Chatham, near Morristown, for his home in Rhode Island, he was still making do with the old shoes he had bought from a Dutch woman while on the march from the north. Howland and the others in Colonel

Christopher Lippitt's regiment left for home "by detachments, or small guards, as it was said we could better find lodgings or shelter for a night on the road. Our paper wages, forty shillings the month, was never paid fully, and we received nothing to bear our expenses home.

> " 'Some had to beg their bread
> Through realms their valor saved.' "

On the way home, Howland and his fellow soldiers met Mr. J. J. Hazard, an agent sent by the state of Rhode Island "with a quantity of shoes for those he should meet who were barefooted. We met him at Peekskill, and there he presented me with a new pair, and there I left what remained of those I bought of the Dutch woman, and with the new ones, after being detained in that neighborhood three weeks by sickness, I traveled home to Providence."

In 1830, more than a half century later, "John Howland, Esq.," as he was addressed, was still living in Providence, and apparently not in poverty. On November 24, 1830, he appealed to government officials, not in his own behalf but for some members of his regiment who had applied for pensions. Howland described them as "poor, infirm old men who in the prime of their youth, by the side of Washington, defended the pass at Trenton Bridge, and made these what they now are, independent states. And why are they excluded? Because the Secretary of War, Mr. Calhoun, thought they had not been nine months in the service of the United States. Is it possible? Can it be possible?"

John Greenwood, the young fifer afflicted with the camp itch, went home to Boston after the first battle at Trenton. He remained at home about two years, then went to sea. Eventually he settled in Manhattan, married, and raised a son, who became a doctor. Greenwood died in his sixtieth year at the family residence, 13 Park Row. Of him a friend recalled: "He was a venerable man of great originality and shrewdness of mind on all subjects, a great reader and deep thinker, generous and chivalrous in disposition, of ready wit and full of anecdote and lore of the past. In his profession [not specified] his expert and adroit workmanship, bold ingenuity and resources under all difficulties, acquired him a reputation that left him without a competitor."

James Monroe, the eighteen-year-old Continental Army lieutenant from Virginia, Charles Willson Peale, the militia lieutenant from Philadelphia, and Thomas Rodney, the militia captain from Delaware, were among the combatants of whom history was to hear more—a great deal more in Monroe's case. After being wounded in attacking the Hessian cannoneers in Trenton, Monroe recuperated for several months at a private home in Bucks County, Pennsylvania. Later, he took part in such battles as those at Brandywine, Germantown, and Monmouth, and advanced to the rank of major. After resigning his commission late in 1778, he embarked upon a career in government that was to take him to the White House as the fifth president of the United States. On completing two terms, he retired in 1825 at the age of sixty-seven. He lived six more years, ailing much of the time and at one point in such dire financial straits that he had to sell his home and move in with his daughter. He died almost broke but with his reputation as soldier and statesman intact. In 1968, however, he was to be outrageously denigrated when, in a book called *Burr*, Gore Vidal disposed of the young Virginian in these words: ". . . the burly Lord Stirling . . . was always attended by his aide James Monroe, whose principal task during the Revolution was to keep His Lordship's cup filled until it was time to put him to bed.'"*

During the long, cold days following the battle at Princeton, Charles Willson Peale continued to devote himself to the needs of his young Philadelphians: "I hurried my men up and carried them to eat their breakfast of the beef and potatoes I had provided." "I went into town and got a barrel of flour and engaged a negro woman to bake it." "Many of the men . . . were entirely barefooted. I got a raw hide to make them moccasins. . . ." "Went to Mr. Livingston's to beg some sugar for Billy Haverstick, who is very unwell. . . . I got him an emetic of Dr. Crockrin [Cochran]."

One day Peale went into Morristown "and got a barrel of flour, and put stones in the fire to bake our bread on and, before night, got some beef and made sumptuous meals. The men were very industrious, in baking, all the forepart of the evening. The place which fell to our lot was rather steep and nothing but a heap of

---

*Through the voice of Burr, Vidal also denigrated the herculean efforts of artilleryman Henry Knox, describing him as "fat, slow-moving, crafty . . . never entirely certain which end of the cannon you lit," and as General Washington's "plump favorite." Dr. Benjamin Rush described Knox as "a brave, sensible, enterprising man. I saw his behaviour at the battle of Trenton; he was cool, cheerful and was present every where."

stones. I found it to be a very hard lodging place. When one part of my body was hurt by the points of these stones I would change my position to get relief, and was continually moving the entire night, now and then making the fire better."

Back home in Philadelphia late in January 1777, Peale continued to serve the common cause by way of various homefront duties and resumed his career as a painter. He also resumed the siring of children; in all there were to be seventeen, of whom nine would be named for painters, including Rembrandt, Rubens, and Angelica Kauffmann. Peale's younger brother and protégé, Jamie, went on, after completing his army service, to become one of America's most popular painters of miniatures.

Following the action at Princeton, Captain Thomas Rodney and his Delaware company marched to Pluckemin and, after two days there, on to Morristown, where "Lieutenant McCall, who was left or lagged behind us at Trenton, rejoined us. By his story he came with the rear of the army to the battle of Princeton but was not in the action and, meeting the body of Colonel Haslet, was about to bury him when a number of our officers who he took to be [British] Light Horse appeared on the hill, which frightened him so that he did not stop until he had crossed the Delaware. . . .

"But eight or ten of the Light Infantry of the 2nd Battalion of Philadelphia say he came on the ground with them and as soon as the bullets began to fly he ran as hard as he could for the woods." (It was Lieutenant McCall who had charged Private Martinas Sipple with running off in the face of the enemy near the Assunpink bridge in Trenton.)

On January 10 the company, to Rodney's disappointment, began to break up: "The time that my men enrolled for expired today and most of them seemed determined to go home, upon which I went to General Cadwalader and brought him to our quarters and he informed them of the necessity of their staying a few days longer." But, as Rodney reported on January 14 in a letter to his brother Caesar, most of them went home anyway: "My company has stained those glorious lorrels which they gained in a four weeks severe duty. Most of them were in the hottest of the Battle at Prince Town without receiving a wound. . . . But this morning all of them but Tilton McGermet (and Bullen and McKnatt who are sick) set off home. I could not prevail on them to stay longer." In passing, Rodney noted a typical complaint of the time: "The Pennsylvania militia now here have sent a spirited letter to their Council of Safety insisting that they shall make every man turn out that is able to bare arms (except those who pretend Conscience) under pain of confiscation and banishment, that they make such the fate of all Tories and the militia will support them in it."

Rodney himself left for home a few days later and on the way stopped at Philadelphia to see the Fishers, the Tory in-laws who had advised him to join the British. They were, he found, "all gloomy. I reminded them that they were mistaken and that all was accomplished that I had foretold them but they affected not to believe it and I left them and from Philadelphia came on home where I found all well on the 28th of January 1777."

Within a short time Rodney bought 1,200 acres of land, one of a series of speculative purchases that would eventually lead to his being jailed. In the years to come Rodney would hold some high judicial positions and serve five terms in the Continental Congress. In 1791, at the age of forty-seven, however, he experienced financial difficulties. His creditors, including one of his Tory in-laws, Samuel Fisher, brought suit and had him jailed for fourteen months. Years later, Rodney was named U.S. judge for the Missouri territory and there he again speculated heavily in land, this time without going to jail.

Congressman Robert Morris, whose overnight fund-raising helped to keep Washington's army alive at a crucial time, would also eventually land in debtors' prison. Reputed to be the richest man in America, he continued in his role as fund raiser throughout the war. Colonel Joseph Reed, among others, questioned whether Morris was using government funds for his own speculation or risking his own money in behalf of his country. In any case, Morris came to be known as the "Financier of the Revolution."

Following the war, he declined appointment as President Washington's secretary of the treasury but served in the Senate from 1789 to 1795. Meanwhile he speculated heavily in western lands, ultimately overextending himself to the point where his financial empire collapsed. Early in 1798 he was arrested on the complaint of a creditor and jailed. President Washington, who was living in what had been Morris's stately Philadelphia home, visited Morris in jail, but even his influence was apparently not enough to effect his old friend's release. Morris remained in jail for three and a half years. He died about five years later, an obscure and pitiful figure.

Lieutenant Joseph Hodgkins, of Ipswich, Massachusetts, also came to a pitiable end. By January of 1777 he had had enough, having served "this glories cause," as he called it, since the spring of 1775. While marching ever farther from home, he had a few months earlier learned from his distraught wife that his infant son had died. In an answering letter he had assured her that he had "no thoughts of ingaging again."

Now, however, after serving thirty-eight days beyond the term of his enlistment, he changed his mind. Before leaving Morristown in February 1777 and setting off for home, he signed on for three years as a captain in the Continental Army.

Often during the period of his reenlistment his lonely wife would plead for his return: "I am very full of trouble on account of your not coming home. . . . I am very low in spirits, almost despair of your coming home. . . . I have got a Sweet Babe almost six months old but have got no father for it."

Hodgkins would write a typical reply on January 5, 1778, from Valley Forge: "I believe I have as great a desire to come home as you can possibly have of having me for this winter's campaign beats all for fatigue and hardships that ever I went through." He might "try to get a furlough in about a month but I am not certain I shall be sucksesfull in my attempts, therefore I would not have you depend on it."

In closing, Hodgkins referred to their recently born daughter: "You say you have named your child Martha and you did not know whether I should like the name. But I have nothing to say. If it suits you I am content. I wish I could have the satisfaction of seeing it. So I must conclude at this time by subscribing myself your most affectionate companion till death. —Joseph Hodgkins."

Like many of his former comrades in arms, Hodgkins would end his days all but destitute. He was survived by only one of his eleven children. He held numerous town offices in Ipswich and he eventually rose to the rank of colonel in the local militia. He worked for years as both shoemaker and farmer, but by the time he reached his eighties he was sorely in need of a pension. Time and again he went to court to prove that he needed the pension, but it was not approved until a few months before he died, in 1829, at the age of eighty-six.

At her home in Northampton County, Pennsylvania, in January 1777, Jean Rosbrugh had five children, the youngest not a year old, and no father for them. Their father, the Reverend John Rosbrugh, lay buried in Trenton.

For a few years Mrs. Rosbrugh managed to raise her children

without having to apply for aid, but by 1784 she was poverty-stricken. In an appeal to the Executive Council of the Commonwealth of Pennsylvania, she reported that her husband, "to encourage the militia . . . to go out in defence of their bleeding country, in the latter end of the year 1776, offered himself to accompany them to Philadelphia," and that "he was inhumanly murdered by the enemy at Trenton on January 2d, 1777," and that she was "left a widow with five small children, in circumstances tho' at that time somewhat good, yet now, by the inconstancy and fluctuating state of the late circulating currency, rendered very distressing."

Mrs. Rosbrugh told of applying several times for relief and of being turned down each time. "To whom shall she complain of her wrongs? Or where shall your memorialist with her fatherless children look for redress of their grievances . . . ?"

Eventually, help was on the way: "half pay of a chaplain . . . which is ten dollars per month."

Mary Peale Field, the opportunistic widow and mistress of White-hill, on the Delaware below Bordentown, would never need governmental aid. She survived the war unscathed and with her property intact. She lived on at Whitehill and eventually saw a son and a daughter both marry into the aristocratic Richard Stockton family of Princeton. Annis Boudinot Stockton, Richard's widow, was residing at Whitehill with Mrs. Field at the time of her death in 1815.

On Christmas Day, 1776, as had become her daily custom, Mrs. Field presided at tea for her new friends. Joseph Galloway was there. So were the Reverend Jonathan Odell, who had escaped the Tory-hunters in Burlington, and "several English and Hessian officers." General Washington's surprise attack on Trenton one day later put an end to these visits: "In the night of the next day," Mrs. Field noted, "they, with the army and several followers of it, took a precipitous flight at about one o'clock. . . . Several Jersey Volunteers [Americans serving with the British] were taken prisoners. None of our acquaintance for they kept close to the main body of the army."

In mid-January 1777 a British officer who had been captured at Princeton "came upon his parole on purpose to see us and seems in good spirits." The officer said he was ashamed to talk of the performance of some of the British regiments but he spoke "highly of General Washington and his troops. In short," Mrs. Field noted, "he is one of them people that appears happy in giving merit its due."

Her guest Joseph Galloway sailed with his daughter to England in 1778 after the British evacuated Philadelphia. His wife remained in Philadelphia and never saw either of them again. In 1778, a year before she died, all of the property she hoped to save for her daughter was confiscated. Galloway asked for permission to return home but his petition was rejected. He died in his early seventies, still convinced that America would have been better off if the colonies had adopted his 1774 Plan of Union with Great Britain instead of going to war.

Margaret Morris, at her home on the Burlington riverbank, heard on January 5, 1777, two days after the battle at Princeton, that Captain William Shippin, "who threatened to shoot my son for spying on the gondolas, is killed. . . . What sad havoc will this dreadful war make in our land!"

January 9: "We hear today that our troops have driven the English to Brunswick. . . . The report of poor A. [Anthony] Morris being killed is confirmed by an officer who was in the battle."

January 11: "Weather very cold, and the river quite shut. I pity the poor soldiers now on their march, many of whom will probably lie out in the fields this cold night. What cause have I for gratitude that I and my household are sheltered from the storm!"

By January 15 there occurred—about three weeks late—something that the Hessians in Trenton, eager to reach Philadelphia, had hoped for: the Delaware River froze over. "I was a good deal affected this evening," Mrs. Morris noted that night, "at seeing the hearse in which General Mercer's body was carried over the river, on the ice, to be buried at Philadelphia."

As a good Quaker, Mrs. Morris continued to maintain her neutrality throughout the war. She lived on to the age of seventy-eight and in her final years was carried by admiring grandchildren in a sedan chair to services at the Burlington Friends Meeting House.

After having escaped the Tory-hunters in Burlington with the help of Mrs. Morris, Jonathan Odell departed, never to return to the town where he had served as a popular Anglican clergyman for a decade. As a regimental chaplain and in other positions, he remained with the British throughout the war. As a secret agent he helped in 1780 to expedite the treasonable correspondence between Benedict Arnold, by then a major general, and Major John André.

He produced much-quoted verses that lauded the British and lampooned America's leading figures. At the war's end in 1783 Odell, his wife, and three children went to England. A year later they settled in New Brunswick, Canada, where he died in 1818 at age eighty-one.

Of the almost 30,000 German mercenaries who took part in the Revolution—more than half of them Hessians—about 18,000 eventually returned to their homeland. Some 7,000 died in America of wounds or disease and, despite the occasional hanging of a soldier caught in attempting to desert and the threat of severe punishment, about 5,000 deserted, hundreds in order to take advantage of land grants offered by the Americans, and many to marry local girls.

Colonel Donop, the ladies' man, apparently never again met with the beautiful widow, nor did he return home to resume his career in Frederick II's court; on October 22, 1777, he was mortally wounded during an attack on Fort Mercer, on the Delaware below Philadelphia.

Johannes Reuber, the young grenadier who idolized Colonel Rall, and the rest of the enlisted men captured at Trenton were escorted to Lancaster, Pennsylvania. According to an inventory made on January 10, 1777, 315 of the 830 prisoners there had been tradesmen: 89 weavers, 49 tailors, 38 shoemakers, 15 carpenters, nine butchers, and, among other specialists, a barber and two bookbinders. The shoemakers, among others, were promptly put to work at their trade. Most of the prisoners, such as Grenadier Reuber, were sent off to work on farms. Reuber apparently detested the work, for after being exchanged in 1778 he wrote in his diary: "Finally we were with our Hessian brothers again. What happiness and pleasure there was now for we were freed once and for all from our slavery." Reuber served to the end of the war and, late in 1783, he was back home in Hesse-Cassel after a two-month trip across the Atlantic. On November 27, 1783, he and the rest of his regiment were inspected by the Landgrave, and the commanding officer of the regiment accepted five Hessian flags that had been lost at Trenton on December 26, 1776, but regained during the fighting near Charleston, South Carolina, in May 1780. Reuber served some twenty more years in the army and was pensioned in 1816.

The Hessian officers captured at Trenton were escorted under guard to Baltimore, then to Virginia. Lieutenant Jacob Piel of the Lossberg Regiment reported that a curious crowd gathered as he and the others waited on January 9, 1777, to cross the Susquehanna River: "They had come to see monsters, and they were vexed when they found that we resembled human beings." A few days later: "We arrived at Baltimore. We were fortunate to meet some French officers who became very friendly with us. . . . We would have liked to spend the period of our imprisonment here, but Congress decided to send us to Dumfries in Virginia."

In Dumfries, Fredericksburg, and other Virginia villages some Hessians became romantically involved. Lieutenant Andreas Wiederholdt of the Knyphausen Regiment was at first highly critical of the Americans he met in Virginia; the dregs of America, he called them. He was especially critical of the way some black slaves were treated: "The barbaric treatment they receive from some is a disgrace to mankind, and being a witness to it horrifies me. The Americans have no such feelings despite claiming to be sensitive and hospitable." While quartered with a family in Fredericksburg, however, Wiederholdt fell in love and when, in September 1779, he had to leave for the north to be exchanged he experienced a sad parting. On the eve of departure, "a fair one who was much inclined to me, and whom I shall always respect and honor, said: 'Would to God that you could stay here, and that I might never be so unhappy as to be torn from you, as will happen tomorrow and perhaps forever! But go where duty and honor call you, and be ever happy!' " Good soldier Wiederholdt went, but not happily.

In the weeks following the battles at Trenton and Princeton, Captain Johann Ewald met a young woman named Jeannette Van Horne in Brunswick and was apparently smitten. In letters written to her in French over an eighteen-month period he signed off with such terms as "your fervent adorer" and declared, among other things, "It is you, Mademoiselle, it is you upon whom depends my great happiness, and since you are the cause of my remaining in America after the peace, you are the foundation of my bright fortune." Perhaps, as the war lengthened, the ardor faded on one side or the other. In any case, Ewald did not remain in America after the peace. He and the jagers of his company fortunate enough to have survived the years of hazardous duty returned to Hesse-Cassel in the spring of 1784, eight years and nine days after leaving for America. Ewald found the man who had fattened on their services, Frederick II, to be less than appreciative. Eventually disillusioned with military service in Germany, Ewald went to Denmark, where, en route to the title of General von Ewald, he became a national hero, celebrated for his military exploits in song and verse. He died there full of honors in his seventieth year.

He would never forget the welcome he and the heroic jagers received when they arrived in Hesse-Cassel at midday of May 18, 1784: "After the regiments had been inspected by their sovereign, they marched to their permanent quarters. The Jager Corps was reduced at once, despite its faithful and well performed service. His Serene Highness the Landgrave and his entire suite did not bestow a single, special, gracious glance on any officer. The subsidies had expired. We had willingly suffered eight years in America for the selfsame money. All services performed were forgotten and we poor 'Americans,' who had flattered ourselves with the best reception, were deceived in our expectations in the most undeserved way. Then envy stretched out its claws to us. We became agitated, muttered in our beards, cursed our fate, and bent our proud backs under everything, because it could not be otherwise.

"Thus ended the American war,
and thus was the soldier
treated by his sovereign
in Hesse.
Amen!"

---•••---

Notes

This book has been researched and written mostly with the general reader in mind, and the notes and bibliography that follow are signposts for sources that the general reader may wish to pursue: the narrative of Joseph White, for example, and the diaries kept by such soldiers as Thomas Rodney and Johannes Reuber. The notes and bibliography are not all-inclusive, but they cover the main sources used and provide collateral information and suggestions for further reading that may be of interest.

The book has been written, too, in the hope that history buffs and even scholars of the American Revolution will find in it a new insight or two and perhaps some new sources relating to the New Jersey campaign.

The reader should note that in some cases the spelling and punctuation in the documents cited have been modernized for purposes of clarity.

PART ONE: A GAME PRETTY NEAR UP

Chapter 1
Ye Should Never Fight Against Your King

Joseph White's engaging but, alas, overly laconic narrative was published long after the events described, and so were the recollections of Alexander Graydon. White printed his brief pamphlet in 1833 on his own little press, valued at twenty dollars, and noted on the cover that it was "Published at the earnest request of many Young Men." An original copy is in the Library of Congress; the narrative is more readily available in the June 1956 *American Heritage* magazine.

Graydon's detailed memoir, published in 1818, is, I think, one of the most lucid and intelligent accounts we have of the American Revolution. One of his most interesting recollections is of how his mother succeeded not only in getting through to New York from Philadelphia but also in negotiating his release from a British prison.

John Adlum recorded the details of his capture at Fort Washington in a diary, one that he continued to keep as a prisoner of the British. Unlike most of the Americans captured, he was not subjected to confinement in a hellish prison. Instead, he served as a sort of orderly or waiter for Colonel Robert Magaw and other officers captured at Fort Washington.

White, Graydon, and Adlum will be heard from again in coming chapters.

Chapter 2
All Who Are My Grenadiers, Forward!

Lieutenant (later Captain) Wiederholdt's candid observations about the Fort Washington battle and the subsequent New Jersey campaign are included, in translation, in Stryker's *The Battles of Trenton and Princeton*, Part II. This is an extensive appendix that includes letters, orders, brief biographies, accounts of court-martial proceedings, rosters, diary selections, and other useful material, much of it by or about the Hessians. "In 1877," Stryker wrote in his preface, "I crossed the ocean to examine the official records at Cassel, Germany, and in 1892 I caused a most exhaustive search to be made in the State Archives at Marburg, Germany, by competent men, and secured copies of all documents filed there (some 1,100 pages of manuscript, certified under seal as correct) which bear directly on the conduct of the Hessian force in New Jersey."

Stryker's main text has been faulted by scholars for mixing legend ("Tradition says . . .") with fact. He must be credited, however, with making available a great deal of material that was new at the time his book was published, in 1898, only a few years before his death.

Speaking of the Hessians, Rodney Atwood's *The Hessians*, published in 1980, includes much fresh material and provides in its appendixes full statistics on the Hessians in America and a bibliography listing manuscript sources available in both German and British archives. The author presents a balanced view of the Hessian auxiliaries and does a scholarly job of updating a volume that for years was the standard work on the subject: Edward Lowell's *The Hessians and Other German Auxiliaries of Great Britain in the Revolutionary War*, published in 1884. Atwood also includes many brief "human" bits, such as Lieutenant Bardeleben's description of the departure scene.

Johannes Reuber, a private during the New Jersey campaign but often identified as a corporal, a rank he later earned, kept a no-nonsense diary throughout his more than six years in America. He wrote in a dialect difficult for a non-Hessian to comprehend and he rendered many English terms phonetically; Trenton, for example, was recorded as Drendaun. One copy of the diary is in the special collections of the Rutgers University Library and another is in the manuscripts collection of the New York Public Library. Herbert H. Freund of Lancaster, Pa., translated the New York copy into English, and "slightly edited" parts of his translation are available in *Journal of the Johannes Schwalm Historical Association* 1, Numbers 2 and 3.

Chapter 3
A Set of Rascals Skulked Out of the Way

During the early stages of researching this book I intended to present General Washington only through the eyes of others, such as Sergeant White. For the most part I have done so, but Washington was to such a degree the dominant figure throughout the New Jersey campaign, holding things together through the force of his personality, that the story cannot be told without hearing from him.

The diary of Andrew Hunter, one of several Presbyterian clergymen on duty with the Continentals, is in the manuscript collection of the Princeton University Library.

For a brief biographical sketch of Stephen Kemble (and many others mentioned in this book), see Mark Boatner's *Encyclopedia of the American Revolution*, an essential research tool for anyone writing about the Revolution. This 1,290-page volume covers the persons, issues, and events in American history from 1763 to 1783.

Adrian Leiby's well-researched volume on the Hackensack Valley provides background on the military situation there as well as the ongoing "civil war" between Whig and Tory partisans. The Annuals published by the Bergen County Historical Society in 1970, 1975, and 1976 also contain a great deal of relevant material.

Chapter 4
Spare the King's Subjects

For many years, translated bits and pieces of the journal of the remarkable Captain Ewald turned up in writings about the American Revolution, especially in footnotes. Ewald wrote four detailed volumes about his experiences in America. Joseph Tustin worked for a dozen years translating, editing, and annotating them, and in *Diary of the American War* produced what has been called—and rightly so, I think—the most important volume on the American Revolution published within the past century.

Donop reported on the taking of Fort Lee in a detailed letter to General

Heister, commander of all the Hessians in America, and told the "small curious story" in a postscript. His report is identified as "Letter A" in the large and important collection of Hessian material in translation to be found in the library of the Morristown (N.J.) National Historical Park.

Stirke made almost daily entries in a small notebook between June 1776 and April 1778. It is now part of the Lloyd W. Smith Collection at the Morristown Park library. An edited version of Stirke's journal was published in the June 1961 *Maryland Historical Magazine.*

Lieutenant (later Captain) Heinrichs recalled the orders given Cornwallis in a letter written about fourteen months later. It is to be found, in translation, in "Extracts from the Letter-Book of Captain Johann Heinrichs of the Hessian Jager Corps, 1778–1780," *Pennsylvania Magazine of History and Biography* 22 (1898), pp. 137–43.

The British, Leiby noted in his Hackensack Valley volume, "knew very well that the Americans had passed the same point shortly before; they nevertheless chose deliberately to take the abandoned fort and not to pursue the retreating garrison."

For details of the taking of Fort Lee, see John Spring's "The 1776 British Landing at Closter," in the Bergen County Historical Society's 1975 Annual, pp. 27–42. See also Major Donald M. Londahl-Smidt's "British and Hessian Accounts of the Invasion of Bergen County 1776" in the society's 1976 Annual, pp. 35–79.

Chapter 5
Whether They Will Obey Orders, God Only Knows

The eyewitness of the arrival of Washington's army in Hackensack and its departure is quoted in the Reverend Theodore Romeyn's book about the Hackensack church.

Governor Livingston's response to Washington, his appeal to the militia colonels, and his comment on the Philadelphia Associators are in Volume I of his Papers.

Chapter 6
Their Army Is Broken All to Pieces

Glyn's journal is in the special manuscript collections of the Princeton University Library.

Chapter 7
No Lads Show Greater Activity in Retreating

"As Mr. Monroe was in that retreat, it may not be improper to insert here a notice which he took of it in a message to Congress, May 2d, 1822." So

Monroe wrote (as he often did, in the third person) in his autobiography, recalling the arrival of Washington's troops in Newark.

Governor Livingston was in Burlington when he issued the order to Colonel Smith on November 21, 1776. He was still there on December 7, when he dispatched five of Colonel Stephen's prisoners to Philadelphia to be disposed of by Congress.

Extracts from the letters written in Newark by the two Continental officers (and newspaper notices quoted in later chapters) are in *New Jersey Archives*, Second Series, Volume 1, *Documents Relating to the Revolutionary History of the State of New Jersey*, edited by William S. Stryker. This volume contains extracts from American newspapers published in 1776 and 1777.

"All who were in that march alluded to the 'Mud Rounds' as a time of great suffering and hardship," according to an authoritative source quoted in Grace Croyle Hankin's *True Stories of New Jersey* (Philadelphia: John C. Winston, 1938).

Chapter 8
The Rebels Fly Before Us

For more on Cavalier Jouet and the Elizabethtown scene, see Theodore Thayer's *As We Were: The Story of Old Elizabethtown* (Elizabeth, N.J., 1964). Jouet later barely escaped being hanged and was forced to leave the country. He returned home to a cool reception by the townspeople in 1795.

Chapter 9
They Perpetrate the Grossest Robberies

Howe's narrative, first published in 1779, has been reprinted in Partridge's *Sir Billy Howe*. Little is known of the flashing Mrs. Loring beyond her affair with Howe. General Clinton's criticism of Howe's moves in New Jersey had the benefit of hindsight. It appears in *The American Rebellion: Sir Henry Clinton's Narrative of His Campaigns, 1775–1782*, edited by William B. Willcox (New Haven: Yale University Press, 1954). Kemble's journal is included in *The Kemble Papers*, in the Collections of the New-York Historical Society.

Chapter 10
A Push for Philadelphia?

Jerseymen willing to serve in the army had begun to go on duty in November 1775. During that month two battalions of Continental troops, known as the Jersey Line, reported for duty in and around New York, according to Stryker's *Officers and Men of New Jersey in the Revolutionary War*.

By December 1776 the first battalion of the so-called second establishment was organized and three other battalions were being recruited in answer to a call from Congress.

Michael Graham narrated his experiences years later in applying for a pension. His application is among the 80,000 on file in the National Archives in Washington, D.C. They are indexed and available on microfilm. Graham's narrative and scores of others taken from the pension applications are to be found in John Dann's remarkable collection, *The Revolution Remembered*.

Colonel Patterson reported on his largely wayward battalion in letters to George Read. They are excerpted in *Papers of the Historical Society of Delaware*, Volume 2, Number 14 (Wilmington, 1895). Washington's letters are in the Fitzpatrick and Sparks collections under the dates indicated in the Bibliography listings. Captain Carver's letter is in Moore's *Diary of the American Revolution*, p. 357.

PART TWO: NOT ALL FIRE AND FURY

Chapter 11
As the Fire Came Closer, Many Drew Away

Though on the "wrong" side, James Moody was a genuine hero whose exploits were described in his own narrative and authenticated by superior officers.

In his autobiography, quoted here and more extensively later on, Dr. Rush provides some insightful views of the 1770s. Dr. Thacher's journal is useful but less detailed than Rush's. Judge Jones survived the Revolution unscathed, although known as a stout Loyalist. Ethan Allen marched to Canada in search of further glory but instead was captured and taken to a prison in England. Congressman Morris, a perceptive "insider," corresponded frequently with General Washington.

Chapter 12
The Devil of Desertion

Colonel Thomas's discouraging report is in *The Papers of William Livingston*, Volume 1. General Sullivan's salty comments on this and later occasions in the New Jersey campaign are in Volume 1 of his *Letters and Papers*. Congressman Thornton's and other letters dealing with the problems of this period are in Burnett's *Letters of the Members of the Continental Congress*.

Trapnell's violent and profane resistance to authority is reported in detail in *Archives of Maryland, Journal and Correspondence of the Council of*

Safety, Volume 26 (Baltimore: Maryland Historical Society, 1897). The same volume includes testimony about defiance of authority by Guyton and others.

The slave Samuel served, off and on, as a substitute for various owners, into the 1780s. After the war ended, he "applied and demanded" his freedom from farmer Casper Berger, one of the masters for whom he had served. "He sold me to Peter Ten Eyck for £100, a slave for life. Ten Eyck sold me to Rev. John Duryea for £92.10. I lived with him two and a half years and he sold me to Peter Sutphen for the same money. Lived with him and his for two years as slave. Then lived with mistress for one year. I agreed to pay him from the proceeds of my labor £92.10. I paid it and bought my freedom after the additional servitude of 20 years under different masters." Samuel took on the last name, in turn, of each master, and spent his final years as Samuel Sutphen. His is one of many unusual accounts to be found in Gerlach's *New Jersey in the American Revolution*.

PART THREE: A HANDFUL DAILY DECREASING

Chapter 13
They Don't Want to Finish the War!

Joseph Galloway was to become one of the most vociferous critics of Howe in such writings as *Historical and Political Reflections on the American Rebellion* and *Letters to a Nobleman on the Conduct of the War in the Middle Colonies*, written a few years later. He also criticized Howe in testimony given to a committee in Parliament. On Galloway's *A Letter from Cicero*, Joseph Sabin commented (in *Bibliotheca Americana*, Volume 7, p. 187): "Mr. Galloway here accuses Lord Howe and his brother, Sir William, of having most flagrantly, shamefully and wickedly betrayed the trust reposed in them in command of the British naval and land forces in America."

Chapter 14
The Enemy's Approach Alarmed Our Fears

John Witherspoon, the only clergyman to sign the Declaration of Independence, had come from Scotland to Princeton in 1768 to head the college. In Scotland, Dr. Benjamin Rush had allayed Mrs. Witherspoon's fears about coming to America and had influenced Witherspoon's decision to accept the offer of the college presidency. Under his leadership, the College of New Jersey produced many ardent supporters of the colonial cause. Not to be outdone by the Boston Tea Party, the students at Princeton held a "tea party" on campus in which the "steward's winter store of tea" was burned. In April 1776 when the grim news of Lexington and Concord arrived, the students organized a militia company of fifty men. "Every man handles his musket," one student observed, "and hastens in his preparations for war." With the news of the Declaration of Independence, Nassau Hall was, according to the *Pennsylvania Packet* of July 15, 1776, "grandly illuminated and INDEPENDENCY proclaimed under a triple volley of musketry, and universal acclamation for the prosperity of the United States." For more on the Princeton scene around this time see Wertenbaker's *Princeton 1746–1896*.

Houston, the supposed author of the *Campaign Journal*, was professor of mathematics at the College of New Jersey, and later a member of Congress. In the summer of 1777 he, President Witherspoon, and one tutor composed the faculty, and only a few students were in attendance.

Chapter 15
The Rebels Were Always Barely Ahead of Us

Muenchhausen, who arrived in America on August 12, 1776, as commanding officer of a grenadier company, was appointed Howe's aide-de-camp on November 18, 1776. He kept his diary on a daily basis and aimed at objectivity. "Be assured," he wrote on July 7, 1777, "that, to the best of my knowledge, I do not write anything that is not the truth, and, since I am at English headquarters, I think one can certainly put as much faith in my diary as in anyone else's." The diary was addressed to Muenchhausen's brother, an official in the royal court of Hannover, Germany, and it was dispatched to him in eleven parts. The diary is in the Main Archives of the State of Lower Saxony in Hannover. A handwritten copy, in German, is in the New York Public Library's manuscript division.

While serving with Howe, Muenchhausen was invited to leave Hesse-Cassel service and join the British service. Despite assurances of steady promotion, he declined the offer, but he did wear a British uniform during the eighteen months he served under Howe.

Ernst Kipping's translation of Muenchhausen's diary is one of a dozen fine books on the American Revolution published by Sam Smith's Philip Freneau Press.

Chapter 16
They Pillaged Friend and Foe

Excerpts from Domine Romeyn's journal are in the Bergen County Historical Society's 1970 Annual, pp. 19–33. The eyewitness account of the plundering in Piscataway is from Dunlap's *History of the American Theatre*, and is quoted in Stryker, *The Battles of Trenton and Princeton*, p. 25.

The Reverend Alexander McWhorter, pastor of the Presbyterian Church in Newark, headed the committee appointed by Congress to report on enemy atrocities in New Jersey. McWhorter accompanied Washington's troops in the retreat across New Jersey and remained with them in the Bucks County encampment. The report was published in the *Pennsylvania Evening Post* on April 26, 1777.

Chapter 17
We Sustained an Orderly Retreat

Jackson's *The Pennsylvania Navy* offers detailed information about the boats patrolling the Delaware.

Anderson's *Personal Recollections* was written in 1819 as a series of letters to a nephew in answer to a request "to fight battles over again on paper."

A great deal of information about the long and active life of Charles Willson Peale is to be found in the two biographical works by Sellers. Another good source is Silverman's *Cultural History*. The diary kept by Peale during the campaign is in the library of the American Philosophical Society in Philadelphia. It was published in Volume 38 of the *Pennsylvania Magazine of History and Biography*.

Sergeant Young's diary was published in Volume 8 of that magazine and McMichael's is in Volume 16.

Chapter 18
Neither Boats Nor a Ferry

Stedman, one of Howe's severest critics, later plagiarized many lines of Galloway's criticism of Howe. For more on Howe and his brother Richard as "peace commissioners" as well as military officers, see Gruber's *The Howe Brothers and the American Revolution*.

Chapter 19
A Neighborhood of Very Disaffected People

Stryker's book on the Trenton and Princeton battles and Fitzpatrick's *The Writings of George Washington* are good sources for details about the various encampments in Bucks County.

In covering this period, however, Stryker accepted a questionable story about John Honeyman. According to "a well-established tradition," Stryker reported, Honeyman allowed himself to be captured by American soldiers and taken to headquarters in Bucks County. There, according to a report for which no documentation has been found, Honeyman briefed

Washington on the vulnerable condition of the Hessians occupying Trenton and environs.

Ward's *The Delaware Continentals* is an excellent source for information about Haslet's regiment.

Chapter 20
Sad Work This Day

The headquarters journal covering Donop's activities from the time of his arrival in Trenton to the final day of 1776 is generally known as "Donop's Diary." One translation of the diary is in the library of the Morristown National Historical Park and another is in the New York Public Library. On the back of the first page of the translation in the New York Public Library there appears, in longhand, this note: "Copy of Journal which was found in the Despatch Box of the late Col. Von Donop, it being written in the hand of Captain Wagner . . ." Donop was mortally wounded in the action at Fort Mercer, N.J., on October 22, 1777.

Mrs. Morris kept a record of the events of this period in a lengthy letter, later sent to her sister. The letters of her friend Odell describing his plight are in Hill's *History of the Church in Burlington, N.J.*, pp. 307–18.

Chapter 21
They Called Us Damned Rebels

Greenwood's memoir was "written from memory in New York February 14, 1809, by a person who was in the Revolutionary War . . . relating naught but facts, so strongly imprinted upon the mind as never to be forgotten."

Chaplain Avery's diary covering this period is part of the collections of the Connecticut Historical Society, in Hartford. I worked from a typescript of the diary prepared by John M. Mulder (now president of Louisville Presbyterian Theological Seminary) when he was a faculty member at Princeton Theological Seminary. *The Papers of David Avery, 1746–1818*, which includes the war diary, edited by Mulder with the assistance of Milton J. Coalter, was reproduced in thirteen reels of microfilm in 1979. The microfilm and a typescript of the diary are in the Speer Library of Princeton Theological Seminary.

Wilkinson's memoirs are in part unreliable and at times self-serving. This is particularly true of the last three of the four volumes, which cover his later years. Following the Revolution, he earned a reputation as scoundrel and double-dealer; some considered him a traitor. As of December 1776, however, he had performed creditably as an officer and somehow had the knack of being on the scene when history was being made. Before publishing his memoirs in 1816 he visited many of the battle areas where he had served.

Lee's letter to Gates is in the Lee Papers in the library of the New-York Historical Society.

Chapter 22
Tell Them General Lee Submitted

Tarleton's capture of Lee and later exploits in the South, where his name became anathema to his American victims, are covered in Bass's *The Green Dragoon*. "As a leader of cavalry," Christopher Ward wrote of Tarleton, "he was unmatched on either side for alertness and rapidity of movement, dash, daring and vigor of attack. As a man, he was cold-hearted, vindictive, and utterly ruthless. He wrote his name in letters of blood all across the history of the war in the South."

Bradford's account of the capture of Lee is in Ezra Stiles's diary.

Chapter 23
Our Army Forms a Chain

"Enclosed you have a translation of part of a Hessian journal found at Trenton, in December last; you may depend upon its being genuine, and may insert it in your Evening Post, if you think proper." So read the note accompanying the translated part of the anonymous Hessian's journal. It was published on July 26, 1777, in the *Pennsylvania Evening Post* and reprinted in *New Jersey Archives*, Second Series, Volume 1.

Chapter 24
Are Our People Fast Asleep?

Lacey's memoirs were published in the *Pennsylvania Magazine of History and Biography*, Volumes 25 and 26. Letters and reports from Bucks County by Cadwalader, Bayard, Morris, Williams, and other officers are in *Pennsylvania Archives*, First Series, Volume 5, and other material related to the New Jersey campaign is in Second Series, Volume 1.

Chapter 25
Some Winter Quarters Indeed!

A translation of the part of Wiederholdt's diary dealing with the New Jersey campaign was published in the *Pennsylvania Magazine of History and Biography* 22 (1898), pp. 462–67.

In 1876 William S. Stryker published a pamphlet that sketches the Trenton of 1776 street by street. Titled *Trenton One Hundred Years Ago*, it is in the reference department of the Trenton Free Public Library.

Chapter 26
The Worthy Inhabitants Were Seized Upon

Mary Peale Field, a relative of Charles Willson Peale, reported on her experiences in a long and somewhat disjointed letter covering domestic happenings from December 8, 1776, to January 2, 1777. It was published in the June 1943 *Princeton University Library Chronicle*. Introducing it, Carl Van Doren wrote: "She seems to have been on the side of the Americans in sentiment but to have taken it for granted that as a noncombatant she was not to be molested."

Chapter 27
Our Worst Fears Were Soon Fulfilled

The account of the Reed family's experiences in Trenton is based on an elderly woman's recollections as recorded by her granddaughter, Susan Pindar Embury. It is second-hand reporting and probably embroidered a bit, but it is one of the very few accounts we have of what it was like to have Hessian soldiers suddenly burst into one's home.

Martha Reed, later Mrs. John Shannon, "had many recollections of the early troublous days," Mrs. Embury wrote, "but the most interesting of all her reminiscences was associated with the famous 'Crossing of the Delaware,' and the evacuation of Trenton by the British—and this I shall endeavor to relate as nearly as possible in her own words." Mrs. Embury put the words on paper in 1875 under the title "A Grandmother's Recollections of the Old Revolutionary Days." Copies are to be found in the Trenton Free Public Library and the Princeton University Library.

The account—four typewritten, single-spaced pages—ends with this paragraph: " 'Study your history, child,' the dear old Grandmother would add, with moistened eyes. 'Learn all that you can about those troublous days, and about the brave men who risked, and gave, their lives for their country and made it what it is, a blessed land, and, above all, thank God for Washington.' "

The manuscript of Robert Lawrence's narrative "was purchased in 1901 by the Library of Princeton University at the sale of the late General William Scudder Stryker's collection," according to Varnum Lansing Collins, who edited the narrative for publication in 1906. "It had been given to General Stryker by Governor Charles S. Olden of New Jersey who believed it to have been handed down in his family from the day of its composition a hundred and thirty years ago. It consists of twenty-four folio numbered pages, the final paragraph of which was written on April 18, 1777. The manuscript is brown with age and has suffered from exposure and careless handling."

Chapter 28
Philadelphia Made a Horrid Appearance

Rodney's diary has the ring of truth, not found in various embellishments written in later years.

Early in 1776 McKean had advocated in Congress steps toward reconciliation with England. He gradually changed his mind, however, and worked effectively in behalf of the movement for independence. It was at his behest and initiative that Caesar Rodney rode through the night to cast the Delaware delegation's decisive vote for independence.

Pertinent excerpts from Sarah Fisher's diary are to be found in "A Diary of Trifling Occurrences," edited by Nicholas B. Wainwright, in *Pennsylvania Magazine of History and Biography* 82 (1958), pp. 411–65. On December 22, 1776, shortly after Thomas Rodney's departure from Philadelphia, Mrs. Fisher noted: "At meeting an Epistle read . . . entreating Friends not to join in the present measure. William Brown preached an excellent sermon and prayed for the King."

For displaying what Congress described as "a disposition highly inimical to the Cause of America," her husband, Thomas, was arrested, along with other Quakers, on August 31, 1777, and eventually exiled to Virginia. "Three men came for him," Mrs. Fisher wrote, "and offered him his parole to confine himself prisoner to his own house, which he refused signing. They then told him he must go with them, & be confined to the [Masonic] Lodge."

John Howland recalled his wartime experiences many years later (1830) in an extensive letter written in support of a friend's claim for a pension. The letter was reproduced in the appendix of Benjamin Cowell's *The Spirit of '76*, published in Boston in 1850.

Wade and Lively's *This Glorious Cause* contains letters written by Hodgkins to his "Loven Wife" from "May ye 7 1775" to "Jany 1st 1779." This is his final line: "I have no news to write so I shall take the freedom after wishing you a happy new year to subscribe myself Dear Wife your most affectionate companion Till Death.—J Hodgkins."

Chaplain Rosbrugh's letters and the account of his march to Philadelphia are in Clyde's *Rosbrugh*. Rosbrugh married at about nineteen, after the family arrived in America. His wife died in childbirth and so did the child, their first. There is a gap in his story until 1761 when, at forty-seven, he was studying for the ministry at the College of New Jersey in Princeton.

He married Jean (sometimes spelled Jane) Ralston circa 1766 and they had the first of their five children about a year later.

Chapter 29
A Country Filled with Tories and Informers

Reed's narrative, published in Volume 8 of the *Pennsylvania Magazine of History and Biography*, is only a few pages in length but it provides a great many interesting details about the situation as Christmas approached. Rush described his visit with Washington in a letter to Richard Henry Lee.

Chapter 30
What Was There to Fear from the Rebels?

Galloway's criticism of Donop for remaining in Mount Holly was plagiarized by Stedman.

The young widow in Mount Holly has not, to my knowledge, ever been identified. Joseph Tustin, the translator of Ewald's diaries, has made several attempts to identify her but has not come up with the answer. One of the theories he pursued was that the woman who charmed Donop was Betsy Ross, a twenty-four-year-old widow best known as a seamstress and flag maker. At this writing it is still only a theory. For more on "The Mysterious Widow of the Revolution," see Tustin's article under that heading in the *Bulletin of the Gloucester Country Historical Society* 17 (December 1979), published in Woodbury, N.J. "Whoever she was," Tustin writes, "the beautiful widow of Mount Holly deserves the nation's thanks, be it two hundred years late."

Grant's letter of December 21 to Rall, and other letters of this period to or from Donop and Rall, are to be found in the appendix of Stryker's *The Battles of Trenton and Princeton*.

PART FOUR: SOME LUCKY CHANCE MAY TURN UP

Chapter 31
Boats Were in Readiness

The weather proved to be a major factor in the attack on Trenton and in subsequent action. For detailed information about the weather during these crucial days I have relied on veteran meteorologist David Ludlum, who has specialized in the effects of weather upon events throughout the Revolution. In a letter written on January 6, 1777, Colonel Donop observed that Washington was "favored by the worst sort of weather" in attacking Trenton. "Because of the high wind, the rain and the sleet, no one heard the musketry fire at the outposts." The letter, in translation, is quoted in Hans Huth, "Letters from a Hessian Mercenary," *Pennsylvania Magazine of History and Biography* 62 (1938), pp. 495–96.

The diary thought to have been written by Fitzgerald is in the appendix of Stryker's *The Battles of Trenton and Princeton*. The Reverend Cooley's account and notes are in the manuscript division of the Princeton University Library.

Ensign Robert Beale claimed to have participated in a Christmas Night attack on a Hessian outpost, possibly the one led by Anderson, although he did not mention any Hessian casualties. In *Revolutionary Experiences* Beale wrote: "I was ordered on a detachment commanded by Captain Wales to cross the river and show ourselves to the Hessian picket at Trenton. As soon as we had crossed the river, Captain Wales gave me command of twelve men to lead on in advance. I did so, and showed ourselves to the Hessian picket, who fired upon us. We immediately retreated with all speed.

"When we reached the river, that part of the army immediately under the command of General Washington was coming over."

Beale was a member of the Fifth Virginia Regiment, in General Stephen's brigade.

John Polhemus continued to serve in the army until he was captured by a band of Tories in August 1778 and imprisoned. In a memorial written in 1829 by his grandson, Charles L. Pascal, it was noted that his extensive property in Rocky Hill, N.J., "was wrenched from him to pay the debts he incurred in raising and equipping troops." His remarkable story, as told in the memorial, is to be found in Cleon E. Hammond's biography of John Hart (Polhemus's father-in-law), published by the Pioneer Press, Newfane, Vt., 1977.

Chapter 32
Take Care Now and Fire Low

Paine's *The American Crisis* was a series of sixteen pamphlets written between 1776 and 1783. In *The Complete Writings of Thomas Paine*, Philip Foner declares of Crisis I that "Washington ordered it read to his men," and adds: "Even Paine's bitter enemy Cheetham admitted that it had a dynamic effect on the Revolutionary cause. 'The number,' he writes, 'was read in the camp to every corporal's guard.' " This may be true—Crisis I was published in the *Pennsylvania Journal* of December 19, 1776, and in pamphlet form four days later—but I have not been able to find any documentation for the assertion.

In his autobiography, Monroe described the incidents en route to Trenton and the attack on the Hessian artillerymen. Following the battle, he was taken to a private home in Bucks County, where he spent several recuperative weeks before rejoining the army.

Francis, the former slave, wrote a narrative of about 3,000 words in applying for a pension in 1836. He was then living in Flemington, N.J. He received a pension. His account is included in Dann's *The Revolution Remembered.*

Chapter 35
Der Feind! Heraus!

"What plans had Colonel Rall made in case his regiments were attacked?" "Why did not Colonel von Donop march to their assistance and was there no communication existing between Bordentown and Trenton?"

These were among the questions raised following the Trenton disaster by Friedrich II, Landgrave of Hesse-Cassel, the man who had hired out the defeated troops. He raised the questions in a series of letters to General Knyphausen in which he ordered the establishment of a court-martial to look into the debacle. The court-martial was not completed until 1782. The witnesses put most of the blame on Rall and Dechow, both dead. The ensigns and lieutenants testifying agreed "that the disaster at Trenton was due to the neglect of Colonel Rall." Three majors found that "the examination shows nothing more to us than that Colonel Rall neglected to take the necessary precautions." So it went in the testimony of most of the other officers. The three regiments were eventually exonerated.

The letters from Friedrich II, the findings of the court-martial, and the report the Hessian War Commission submitted on April 15, 1782, to His Serene Highness are all to be found in the appendix of Stryker's *The Battles of Trenton and Princeton.*

Chapter 36
Your Country Is at Stake

The casualness of service as a Continental officer at this crucial period and the severity of the storm are illustrated in *The Revolutionary War Memoir and Selected Correspondence of Philip Van Cortlandt,* edited by Jacob Judd (Tarry-town, N.Y.: Sleepy Hollow Restorations, 1976, pp. 39–40). Colonel Van Cortlandt arrived at the Bucks County encampment on Christmas Eve, accompanied by his servant. On Christmas morning, he wrote, "my horse was foundered in such a bad manner as not to proceed. In the course of the day Capt. Benj. Pelton . . . and I, suspecting that the capture of the Hessians at Trenton was contemplated by Genl. Washington, I took my servant's horse and with the Capt. proceeded towards Trenton as storms of hail, snow and rains came on and I lost my way but seeing after some time a light I made a House where a Quaker lived and he informed me that I was three miles from Trenton and perhaps might get lost again but was welcome to remain with him. I did so and at the break of day heard the firing which soon terminated in the capture of the Enemy."

In the eventful days that followed he rode off to make "a short visit in Philadelphia." It should be added that Van Cortlandt went on to serve with distinction into the year 1783.

In addition to making notes in his diary, Thomas Rodney described the march to Bordentown and subsequent events in letters to his elder brother. They are in *Letters to and from Caesar Rodney, 1756–1784.*

Chapter 39
Haussegger Said It Was Mutiny

Haussegger, accompanied by waiter Housman, arrived in New York shortly after being, as he put it, "captured," and one night visited the house where Colonel Robert Magaw, the former commandant of Fort Washington, and other captured American officers were living. At the door Haussegger identified himself to Corporal John Adlum, who had been captured at Fort Washington and was serving as an orderly to the officers.

Adlum, as he later noted in his diary, "ushered him into the midst of our gentlemen officers who were listening to some [stories] of the famous Col. Ethan Allen, who was always a very welcome guest at our lodgings.* But I was much astonished to see Housacker's appearance operate on our officers as suddenly as an electric shock would. . . . From a pleasant hilarity it was turned to a dead silence and all were waiting in anxious silence to know the cause of his being here. One of the gentlemen asked him if there was another battle fought. He replied, 'No. I went to reconnoiter at Princeton and I was with ten men taken by the Hessians.' "†

Under instructions from the skeptical officers "to make particular inquiry [of waiter Housman] how Col. Housacker was captured," Adlum led Housman to an upstairs room and fixed him a hot toddy. The young men had been acquainted back in their home town, York, Pa.; Housman's brother was the Adlum family's butcher. "After some time," Adlum noted, "Col. [Samuel] Miles came up, and Housman gave us the . . . particulars" (of Haussegger's defection).

---

*Allen, who had been captured by the British shortly after his success at Fort Ticonderoga, was still a prisoner and had recently been brought back from imprisonment in England.

†Haussegger's reply indicates that he was "taken" before the second battle at Trenton, which was fought on January 2, 1777.

Following the Revolution, Adlum (who eventually earned a commission as a major) was able to authenticate Housman's account: "I afterwards became acquainted with Colonel Weltner and Captain Hubley. They were both promoted and they both corroborated and confirmed Housman's account so far as Colonel Weltner, when Major, of usurping the command, and Captain Hubley informed me that it prevented him from being taken prisoner."

According to Douglas Southall Freeman (*George Washington*, Volume 4, p. 343), Haussegger "surrendered under somewhat suspicious circumstances." In his *Historical Register*, Francis B. Heitman reports that Haussegger was "superseded" on March 19, 1777, "having joined the enemy." Captain (later General) John Lacey, who had served with Haussegger in the north and who had visited him the night before the attack on Trenton, noted in his memoirs: "In a few days from that time, he went over to the enemy between Trenton and Princeton." Haussegger was eventually paroled to his home in Lebanon, Pa., where, at the behest of General Washington, he was carefully watched. ("I thought it exceedingly proper," Washington wrote to General Gates on February 12, 1777, "that his conduct, after his return home, should be marked with some degree of vigilance and cautious attention by our Friends in his Neighbourhood, but in such a way as not to afford him room for suspicion.") Haussegger died in 1786, somehow having escaped court-martial.

Chapter 44
A Profound Silence to Be Enjoined

Major Adam Hubley, Jr., described the skirmish at Monmouth Courthouse in a letter written in Bordentown on January 4, 1777. It is in The Papers of the Continental Congress, National Archives, Washington, D.C., and is reprinted in Ryan's *A Salute to Courage*, pp. 60–61.

Commenting on General Washington's flank movement, Douglas Southall Freeman wrote: "To assume that Washington put his Army behind the Assunpink on the 30th of December and that he did not know on the evening of the 2nd of January how he could leave that position is to charge him with complete stupidity at a time when all his other moves were brilliant" (*George Washington*, Volume 4, p. 375).

Chapter 45
A Great Number of Rebels Fell

In Somerset Courthouse, a few days following the battle at Princeton, Rodney got the story of Mawhood's prediction from the physician whose home had briefly served as Mawhood's quarters.

Chapter 48
Not a Man Among Them But Showed Joy

Ashbel Green's comment appears in the October 1854 *Presbyterian Magazine*, page 470.

Chapter 50
O, That We Had 500 Fresh Men

The account of Washington's intervention in behalf of the wounded British soldier was published in the *Pennsylvania Packet* of January 22, 1777, and is to be found on page 268 of *New Jersey Archives*, Second Series, Volume 1. Sullivan was neither the first nor last officer to think his own men did more than their share of fighting. In a letter written on February 13, 1777, he lauded the performance of his Yankee troops at Princeton and looked back to December 26: "Believe me Sir the yankees took Trent Town before the other troops knew any thing of the matter." In at least two other letters written in 1777, he claimed that his troops took Trenton before receiving "any kind of assistance" (Sullivan, *Letters and Papers*, Volume 1, pp. 320, 468, 575).

Acknowledgments

Author J. C. Furnas once told me that his idea of heaven was to have free access to the open stacks of the New York Public Library. I share in that feeling, and during the course of researching this book I have been fortunate enough to have what must be the next best thing: free access to the open stacks on all six floors of Princeton University's Firestone Library. Not entirely free of late; seventy-five dollars a year, but well worth it, especially with the expert help and advice provided by Frederick L. (Ted) Arnold and other members of the library staff, to whom I am deeply grateful.

I am grateful, too, for the help received from four astute historians, all of them, fortunately for me, living within an hour or two of my home: Joseph Tustin, Samuel Stelle Smith, John M. Mulder, and Dr. Kemble Widmer. Mr. Tustin not only gave me access to the manuscript and notes of his fine translation of the journals of the remarkable Hessian Captain Johann Ewald but also led me to other essential sources that helped my research. The late author and publisher William Sloane was, I think, not exaggerating when he described the translation of the Ewald diaries by Mr. Tustin as the most important contribution to our understanding of the American Revolution published in the past century. Sam Smith not only gave me permission to use selections from four of his first-rate books dealing with the New Jersey campaign but also provided sound words of guidance. Professor Mulder, of the Princeton Theological Seminary (now president of Louisville Presbyterian Theological Seminary), made readily available to me all of the material he had gathered on Avery, the Congregational minister who marched with the troops of General Gates to Bucks County, Trenton, and Princeton. Dr. Widmer, retired state geologist of New Jersey and a highly regarded military historian, gave me the benefit of his many insights into the New Jersey campaign.

In researching this book I also used the facilities of many institutions, among them the New Jersey Historical Society; the New-York Historical Society; the Library of Congress; the National Archives; the Morristown National Historical Park; The Lawrenceville School; the Princeton Theological Seminary; the David Library of the American Revolution, where I benefited from the scholarship of the director, Joseph J. Felcone II; the Trenton Free Public Library, where I was assisted by Miss Veronica Cary, Harold Thompson, Mrs. Nan Wright, Richard Reeves, and Miss Peggy Walsh; and the New Jersey State Library, where I received help from former state librarian Roger H. McDonough, state archivist Dr. William C. Wright; Mrs. Rebecca Colesar, Ms. Mary Alice Quigley, Ms. Bette Barker, Ms. Janice Caldwell, and David Munn. Bernard Bush, executive director of the New Jersey Historical Commission, gave me the benefit of his erudition, and so did Richard Waldron and Peggy Lewis, members of the commission staff.

I am also indebted to Mark Lender of the Rutgers University faculty for access to his papers on the sociology of Washington's army; to Dr. Aida Koch and Joseph Koch for translating parts of the diary of Grenadier Reuber; to Ray Walters for running an author's query in *The New York Times Book Review* that elicited some helpful sources; and to Mrs. Annette Carter, Miss Diane Hamilton, Robert C. Kuser, Jr.; Mrs. Lavinia Melton, Dr. Gordon Myers, Ronald Rinaldi, Carl Schielke, H. Kels Swan, Frederick W. Bogert, the late Thomas Jefferson Wertenbaker, Jr., Martin Winar, and Mrs. Gladys D. Wright.

For encouragement beyond the call of duty and for many hours at the typewriter I am indebted to my wife, Marjorie, and I acknowledge the invaluable assistance of three Viking Press editors, Alan D. Williams, Charles T. Verrill, and Virginia Avery.

Select Bibliography

Adlum, John. *Memoirs of the Life of John Adlum*. Edited by Howard H. Peckham. Chicago: University of Chicago Press, 1968.

Anderson, Enoch. *Personal Recollections of Captain Enoch Anderson, an Officer in the Delaware Regiments in the Revolutionary War*. Edited by Henry Hobard Bellas. Wilmington, 1896. Reprint. New York: Arno Press, 1971.

Atwood, Rodney. *The Hessians: Mercenaries from Hessen-Kassel in the American Revolution*. Cambridge: Cambridge University Press, 1980.

Bakeless, John E. *Turncoats, Traitors, and Heroes*. Philadelphia: J.B. Lippincott, 1959.

Barber, John W., and Howe, Henry. *Historical Collections of New Jersey: Past and Present*. Newark, N.J., 1844. New Haven, Conn., 1868. Spartanburg, S.C.: Reprint Co., 1966.

Barnsley, Edward R. *Historic Newtown: A Booklet Prepared for the Celebration of the 250th Anniversary of Newtown, Bucks County, Pa*. Newtown, 1934.

Bass, Robert D. *The Green Dragoon: The Lives of Banastre Tarleton and Mary Robinson*. New York: Henry Holt and Co., 1957.

Bauermeister, Carl Leopold. *Revolution in America: Confidential Letters and Journals 1776–1784 of Adjutant General Major Bauermeister of the Hessian Forces*. Edited by Bernhard A. Uhlendorf. New Brunswick, N.J.: Rutgers University Press, 1957.

Beale, Robert. "Revolutionary Experiences of Major Robert Beale." *Northern Neck of Virginia Historical Magazine* 6 (December 1956): 500–506. An excerpt describing the actions at Trenton and Princeton is in Ryan's *A Salute to Courage*, 55–58.

Beatty, William. "Journal of Capt. William Beatty, June 1776–January 1781." *Maryland Historical Magazine* 3 (1908): 104–19. Also in *Historical Magazine*, 2nd ser., vol. 1 (1867): 17–85.

Bergen County Historical Society. Annuals, 1970, 1975, 1976. Bergen County Historical Society, River Edge, N.J.

Bill, Alfred Hoyt. *The Campaign of Princeton, 1776–1777*. Princeton: Princeton University Press, 1948.

———. *New Jersey and the Revolutionary War*. New Brunswick, N.J.: Rutgers University Press, 1964.

Bliven, Bruce, Jr. *Under the Guns: New York: 1775–1776*. New York: Harper and Row, 1972.

Boatner, Mark M., III. *Encyclopedia of the American Revolution*. New York: David McKay, 1966.

Bostwick, Elisha. "A Continental Soldier Under Washington . . ." Edited by William S. Powell. *William and Mary Quarterly*, 3rd ser., vol. 6 (1949): 94–107. Original in Yale University Library.

Boudinot, Elias. *Journal; or, Historical Recollections of American Events during the Revolutionary War*. Philadelphia: F. Bourquin, 1894. Reprint. New York: Arno Press, 1968.

Boyd, Julian P. *Anglo-American Union: Joseph Galloway's Plans to Preserve the British Empire, 1774–1788*. Philadelphia: University of Pennsylvania Press, 1941.

Brown, Wallace. *The King's Friends*. Providence: Brown University Press, 1965.

Burnett, Edmund C., ed. *Letters of Members of the Continental Congress*. 8 vols. Washington, D.C.: The Carnegie Institution of Washington, 1921–1936.

Burrows, John. *Sketch of the Life of Gen. John Burrows, of Lycoming County*. 1837. Reprint. Williamsport, Pa., 1917.

Butcher, Herbert B. *The Battle of Trenton*. Princeton: Princeton University Press, 1934.

Chamberlain, William. "Letter of General William Chamberlain." *Proceedings of the Massachusetts Historical Society*, 2nd ser., vol. 10 (1895–1896): 490–504.

Clyde, John C. *Rosbrugh, a Tale of the Revolution, or, Life, Labors and Death of Rev. John Rosbrugh*. Easton, Pa., 1880.

Commager, Henry Steele, and Morris, Richard B., eds. *The Spirit of 'Seventy-Six*. New York: Bobbs-Merrill, 1958.

Crary, Catherine S., ed. *The Price of Loyalty: Tory Writings from the Revolutionary Era*. New York: McGraw-Hill, 1973.

Cresswell, Nicholas. *The Journal of Nicholas Cresswell, 1774–1777*. New York: Dial Press, 1924.

Dann, John C. *The Revolution Remembered: Eyewitness Accounts of the War of Independence*. Chicago: University of Chicago Press, 1980.

Davidson, Marshall B. *The Horizon History of the World in 1776*. New York: American Heritage Publishing Co., 1975.

Dowdeswell, Thomas. "The Operations in New Jersey: An English Officer Describes the Events of December 1776." *Proceedings of the New Jersey Historical Society* 70 (1952): 133–36.

English, Frederick. *General Hugh Mercer: Forgotten Hero of the American Revolution.* New York: Vantage Press, 1975.

Ewald, Johann. *Diary of the American War: A Hessian Journal.* Translated from the German, edited, and annotated by Joseph P. Tustin. New Haven: Yale University Press, 1979.

Field, Mary Peale. "A Recently Discovered Letter of the American Revolution." Introduction by Carl Van Doren. *Princeton University Library Chronicle* 4 (June 1943).

Fitzpatrick, John C., ed. *The Writings of George Washington.* Vol. 6, *September 1776–January 1777.* Washington, D.C.: United States Government Printing Office, 1931–1944.

Fleming, Thomas. *1776: Year of Illusions.* New York: W.W. Norton, 1975.

Flexner, James Thomas. *George Washington: In the American Revolution.* Boston: Little, Brown, 1967.

———. *Washington: The Indispensable Man.* Boston: Little, Brown, 1974.

Foner, Philip S., ed. *The Complete Writings of Thomas Paine.* 2 vols. New York: Citadel Press, 1945.

Force, Peter, ed. *American Archives: Fifth Series, Containing a Documentary History of the United States of America from the Declaration of Independence, July 4, 1776, to the Definitive Treaty of Peace with Great Britain, September 3, 1783.* 3 vols. Washington, D.C., 1848–1853.

Freeman, Douglas Southall. *George Washington: A Biography.* 7 vols. New York: Charles Scribner's Sons, 1948–1957.

Galloway, Joseph. *Historical and Political Reflections on the Rise and Progress of the American Rebellion.* London, 1780.

———. *Letters to a Nobleman, on the Conduct of the War in the Middle Colonies.* London: J. Wilkie, 1780.

———. *A Letter from Cicero to the Right Hon. Lord Viscount H—e.* London, 1781.

———. *An Extract from a Reply to the Observations of Lieut. Gen. Sir William Howe, on a pamphlet entitled Letters to a Nobleman.* London: J. Paramore, 1781.

Gerlach, Larry R. *New Jersey in the American Revolution, 1763–1783: A Documentary History.* Trenton, N.J.: New Jersey Historical Commission, 1975.

———. *The Road to Revolution.* Trenton, N.J.: New Jersey Historical Commission, 1975.

———. "Soldiers and Citizens: The British Army in New Jersey on the Eve of the Revolution." *New Jersey History* 93 (Spring-Summer 1975).

———. *William Franklin: New Jersey's Last Royal Governor.* Trenton, N.J.: New Jersey Historical Commission, 1975.

Glyn, Thomas. Ensign Glyn's Journal on the American Service with the Detachment of 1,000 Men of the Guards Commanded by Brigadier General Mathew in 1776. Bound original. Manuscript Division, Princeton University Library.

Graydon, Alexander. *Memoirs of His Own Time*. J.S. Litell, ed. Philadelphia: Lindsay and Blakiston, 1846. Reprint. New York: Arno Press, 1969.

Great Britain. Parliament. House of Commons Committee on the American papers. *The Examination of Joseph Galloway, esq. by a Committee of the House of Commons*. London, 1779. Reprint edited by Thomas Balch. Philadelphia: Seventy-six Society, 1855.

Greenwood, John. *The Revolutionary Services of John Greenwood of Boston and New York, 1775–1783*. From the original manuscript, with notes by his grandson, Isaac J. Greenwood. New York: The DeVinne Press, 1922.

Gruber, Ira D. *The Howe Brothers and the American Revolution*. New York: Atheneum, 1972.

Hall, John. *History of the Presbyterian Church in Trenton, N.J.* New York: A.D.F. Randolph, 1859. Reprint. Trenton, N.J.: MacCrellish and Quigley, 1912.

Haven, Charles C. *Thirty Days in New Jersey Ninety Years Ago*. Trenton, N.J.: State Gazette office, 1867.

———. *A New Historical Manual Concerning the Three Battles at Trenton and Princeton*. Trenton, N.J.: W.T. Nicholson, 1871.

Hawke, David Freeman. *Benjamin Rush: Revolutionary Gadfly*. Indianapolis and New York: Bobbs-Merrill, 1971.

Heath, William. *Memoirs of Major General Heath*. Boston: Thomas and E.T. Andrews, 1798. Reprinted as *Heath's Memoirs*. New York: A. Wessels Co., 1904. Reprint. New York: Arno Press, 1968. Freeport, N.Y.: Books for Libraries Press, 1970.

Heitman, Francis B. *Historical Register of Officers of the Continental Army*. Rev. ed. Washington, D.C.: The Rare Book Shop Publishing Co., 1914. Reprint. Baltimore: Genealogical Publishing Co., 1969.

Hills, George Morgan. *History of the Church in Burlington, N.J.* Trenton, N.J.: William A. Sharp, 1876.

[Houston, William Churchill?]. *A Campaign Journal, from November 29, 1776, to May 6, 1777*. In Thomas Allen Glenn, *William Churchill Houston (1746–1788)*. Privately printed in Norristown, Pa., 1903.

How, David. *The Diary of David How*. Cambridge, Mass.: Houghton, 1865.

Howe, William. *The Narrative of William Howe*. 2nd ed. London: H. Baldwin, 1780.

Hunter, Andrew. *Diary, 1776–1779*. Bound original. Manuscript Division, Princeton University Library.

Huth, Hans. "Letters from a Hessian Mercenary." *Pennsylvania Magazine of History and Biography* 62 (1938): 488–501.

Hutton, Ann Hawkes. *The Year and the Spirit of '76*. Philadelphia: Franklin Publishing Co., 1972.

Inman, George. "Ensign George Inman's Narrative of the American Revolution." *Pennsylvania Magazine of History and Biography* 7 (1883): 237–48.

Irving, Washington. *The Life of George Washington*. New York, 1855. Edited and abridged by Charles Neider. New York: Doubleday, 1976.

Jackson, John W. *The Pennsylvania Navy, 1775–1781: The Defense of the Delaware*. New Brunswick, N.J.: Rutgers University Press, 1974.

Johnston, Henry P. *The Campaign of 1776 around New York and Brooklyn*. Brooklyn: Long Island Historical Society, 1878.

Jones, E. Alfred. "The Loyalists of New Jersey: Their Memorials, Petitions, Claims, etc. from English Records." *Collections of the New Jersey Historical Society* 10 (1926). Republished from *Proceedings of the New Jersey Historical Society* (1926–1927).

Jones, Thomas. *History of New York during the Revolutionary War*. Vol. 1. New York: New-York Historical Society, 1879.

"Journal of a Pennsylvania Soldier, July–December, 1776." *Bulletin of the New York Public Library* 8 (1904): 547–49.

Kemble, Stephen. *The Kemble Papers*. 2 vols. New York: New-York Historical Society, 1884–1885.

Ketchum, Richard M. "England's Vietnam: The American Revolution." *American Heritage* 22 (June 1971).

———. *The Winter Soldiers*. Garden City, N.Y.: Doubleday, 1973.

Kipping, Ernst. *The Hessian View of America 1776–1783*. Monmouth Beach, N.J.: Philip Freneau Press, 1971.

Lacey, John. "Memoirs." *Pennsylvania Magazine of History and Biography* 25 (1901): 1–13, 191–207, 341–54, 498–515; 26 (1902): 101–11, 265–70.

Lawrence, Robert. *A Brief Narrative of the Ravages of the British and Hessians at Princeton in 1776–77*. Edited by Varnum Lansing Collins. Princeton: The University Library, 1906. Reprint. New York: Arno Press, 1968. (Author not here identified.)

Leiby, Adrian C. *The Revolutionary War in the Hackensack Valley*. New Brunswick, N.J.: Rutgers University Press, 1962.

Livingston, William. *The Papers of William Livingston*. Vol. 1, edited by Carl E. Prince. Trenton, N.J.: New Jersey Historical Commission, 1979.

Lowell, Edward J. *The Hessians and Other German Auxiliaries of Great Britain in the Revolutionary War*. New York: Harper and Brothers, 1884. Reprints. Ann Arbor, Mich.: University Microfilms, 1960. Williamstown, Mass.: Corner House Publications, 1970.

Ludlum, David M. "The Weather of American Independence: The Loss of New York City and New Jersey." *Weatherwise Magazine*, August 1975; "The Weather of Independence." *Weatherwise Magazine*, April 1976.

Lundin, Leonard. *Cockpit of the Revolution: The War for Independence in New Jersey*. Princeton: Princeton University Press, 1940. Reprint. New York: Octagon Books, 1972.

Mackenzie, Frederick. *The Diary of Frederick Mackenzie*. Vol. 1. Cambridge, Mass.: Harvard University Press, 1930.

McCarty, Thomas. "The Revolutionary War Journal of Sergeant Thomas McCarty." Edited by Jared C. Lobdell. *Proceedings of the New Jersey Historical Society* 82 (1964): 29–46.

McCormick, Richard P. *New Jersey from Colony to State*. Princeton: Van Nostrand, 1964.

McMichael, James. "Diary of Lieutenant James McMichael, of the Pennsylvania Line, 1776–1778." *Pennsylvania Magazine of History and Biography* 16 (1892): 129–59. Also in *Pennsylvania Archives*, 2nd ser., vol. 15, pp. 195–218.

Monroe, James. *Autobiography*. Edited by Stuart Gerry Brown, with the assistance of Donald G. Baker. Syracuse: Syracuse University Press, 1959.

Montross, Lynn. *The Reluctant Rebels: The Story of the Continental Congress 1774–89*. New York: Harper, 1950.

————. *Rag, Tag, and Bobtail: The Story of the Continental Army*. New York: Harper, 1952.

Moody, James. *Lieutenant James Moody's Narrative of His Exertions and Sufferings*. London, 1783. Reprint. New York: The New York Times, 1968.

Moody, Sid. *'76: The World Turned Upside Down*. New York: The Associated Press, 1975.

Moore, Frank. *Diary of the American Revolution, from Newspapers and Original Documents*. 2 vols. New York: Charles Scribner. London: Sampson, Low, 1860. Reprint. New York: The New York Times & Arno Press, 1969.

Morris, Apollos. *Major Apollos Morris's Manuscript Account of the Trenton-Princeton Campaigns*. Jared Sparks Manuscript Collections, no. 53, Revolutionary Miscellany, Harvard University Library.

Morris, Margaret. *Private Journal Kept during a Portion of the Revolutionary War*. Philadelphia, 1836. Reprint. New York: The New York Times & Arno Press, 1969. "The Revolutionary Journal of Margaret Morris." *Bulletin of the Friends Historical Society of Philadelphia* 9. Philadelphia, 1919. *Margaret Morris: Her Journal, with Biographical Sketch and Notes*, by John W. Jackson. Philadelphia, 1949.

Morris, Richard B. *The American Revolution Reconsidered*. New York: Harper and Row, 1967.

Muenchhausen, Friedrich von. *At General Howe's Side 1776–1778: The Diary of General William Howe's aide de camp, Captain Friedrich von*

Muenchhausen. Translated by Ernst Kipping and annotated by Samuel Smith. Monmouth Beach, N.J.: Philip Freneau Press, 1974.

New Jersey Archives, 2nd Ser., Vol. 1, *Documents Relating to the Revolutionary History of the State of New Jersey; Extracts from American Newspapers, 1776–1777.* Edited by William S. Stryker. Trenton, N.J.: John L. Murphy Publishing Co., 1901.

Owen, Lewis F. *The Revolutionary Struggle in New Jersey, 1776–1783.* Trenton, N.J.: New Jersey Historical Commission, 1975.

Partridge, Bellamy. *Sir Billy Howe.* New York: Longmans, Green and Co., 1932.

Peale, Charles Willson. "Journal by Charles Willson Peale, Dec. 4, 1776–Jan. 20, 1777." *Pennsylvania Magazine of History and Biography* 38 (1914): 271–86.

Prince, Carl E. *William Livingston: New Jersey's First Governor.* Trenton, N.J.: New Jersey Historical Commission, 1975.

Quarles, Benjamin. *The Negro in the American Revolution.* Chapel Hill, N.C.: University of North Carolina Press, 1961.

Reed, Joseph. "General Reed's Narrative of the Movements of the American Army in the Neighborhood of Trenton in the Winter of 1776–1777." *Pennsylvania Magazine of History and Biography* 8 (1884): 391–402.

Reed, William B. *The Life and Correspondence of Joseph Reed.* 2 vols. Philadelphia: Lindsay and Blakiston, 1847.

———. *The Life of Esther DeBerdt, afterwards Esther Reed.* Privately printed, Philadelphia, 1853.

Reuber, Johannes. *Tagebuch des Grenadiers Johannes Reuber aus Niedervellmar vom amerikanischen Feldzug.* Edited by F. W. Junghans. *Hessenland* 8 (1894). Copies in Manuscript Collections, New York Public Library and Rutgers University Library. Translated by Herbert H. Freund. *Journal of the Johannes Schwalm Historical Association* 1, Numbers 2 and 3 (Lyndhurst, Pa., 1979).

Robertson, Archibald. *Diaries and Sketches in America.* Edited by Harry M. Lydenberg. New York: The New York Public Library, 1930.

Rodney, Caesar. *Letters to and from Caesar Rodney, 1756–1784.* Philadelphia: University of Pennsylvania Press, 1933.

Rodney, Thomas. *The Diary of Captain Thomas Rodney, 1776–1777.* Papers of the Historical Society of Delaware, Vol. 1, Paper No. 8, 1888. Reprint. New York: DaCapo Press, 1974.

Romeyn, Theodore Bayard. *Historical Discourse on the Occasion of the Reopening of the 1st Reformed (Dutch) Church, at Hackensack, N.J., May 2, 1869.* New York: Board of Publication, R.C.A., 1870.

Rush, Benjamin. *Autobiography.* Edited by George W. Corner. Princeton: Published for the American Philosophical Society by the Princeton University Press, 1948.

————. *Letters.* Edited by Lyman H. Butterfield, Princeton: Published for the American Philosophical Society by the Princeton University Press, 1951.

Ryan, Dennis P. *New Jersey's Whigs.* Trenton, N.J.: New Jersey Historical Commission, 1975.

————. *A Salute to Courage: The American Revolution as Seen through Wartime Writings of Officers of the Continental Army and Navy.* New York: Columbia University Press, 1979.

Sabine, Lorenzo. *Biographical Sketches of Loyalists of the American Revolution.* 2 vols. Boston: Little, Brown, 1864.

Scheer, George F., and Rankin, Hugh F. *Rebels and Redcoats.* Cleveland: World Publishing Co., 1957.

Schuyler, Hamilton. *A History of St. Michael's Church—Trenton.* Princeton: Princeton University Press, 1926.

Sellers, Charles C. *The Artist of the Revolution: The Early Life of Charles Willson Peale.* Hebron, Conn.: Feather and Good, 1939.

————. *Charles Willson Peale.* Philadelphia: American Philosophical Society, 1947. Reprint. New York: Scribner's, 1969.

Serle, Ambrose. *The American Journal of Ambrose Serle, Secretary to Lord Howe, 1776–1778.* Edited by Edward H. Tatum, Jr. San Marino, Calif.: Huntington Library, 1940.

Silverman, Kenneth. *A Cultural History of the American Revolution.* New York: Thomas Y. Crowell, 1976.

Smith, John. "Sergeant John Smith's Diary of 1776." Edited by Louise Rau. *Mississippi Valley Historical Review* 20 (1933): 247–70.

Smith, Samuel Stelle. *The Battle of Trenton.* Monmouth Beach, N.J.: Philip Freneau Press, 1965.

————. *The Battle of Princeton.* Monmouth Beach, N.J.: Philip Freneau Press, 1967.

————. *The Hessian View of America.* Monmouth Beach, N.J.: Philip Freneau Press, 1975.

Sparks, Jared, ed. *The Correspondence of the American Revolution: Being Letters of Eminent Men to George Washington.* 4 vols. Boston: Little, Brown, 1853. Reprint. Freeport, N.Y.: Books for Libraries Press, 1970.

————, ed. *The Writings of George Washington.* Vol. 4, *July 1776–January 1777.* Boston: 1834–1839. Reprint. New York: G.P. Putnam's Sons, 1889; Boston: Little, Brown, 1958.

Stark, Caleb. *Memoir and Official Correspondence of General John Stark.* Concord, Mass.: G.P. Lyon, 1860.

Stedman, Charles. *The History of the Origin, Progress, and Termination of the American War.* 2 vols. London, 1794.

Stevens, Benjamin F., ed. *Facsimiles of Manuscripts in European Archives Relating to America 1773–1783.* 25 vols. London, 1889–1895.

Stiles, Ezra. *The Literary Diary of Ezra Stiles*. Edited by Franklin P. Dexter. New York: Scribner's, 1901.

Stirke, Henry. *A British Officer's Revolutionary War Journal, 1776–1778*. Edited by S. Sydney Bradford. *Maryland Historical Magazine* 56 (June 1961).

Stryker, William S. *Official Register of the Officers and Men of New Jersey in the Revolutionary War*. Trenton, N.J.: W.T. Nicholson, 1872. Reprint. Baltimore: Genealogical Publishing Co., 1967.

———. *Trenton One Hundred Years Ago*. Trenton, N.J.: MacCrellish and Quigley, 1878; Naar, Day and Naar, 1893.

———. *The Battles of Trenton and Princeton*. Boston and New York: Houghton, Mifflin, 1898. Reprint. Spartanburg, S.C.: Reprint Co., 1967.

Sullivan, John. *Letters and Papers of Major-General John Sullivan*. Edited by Otis G. Hammond. Vol. 1, *1771–1777*. Concord, N.H.: New Hampshire Historical Society, 1930.

Thacher, James. *A Military Journal during the American Revolutionary War*, Hartford, Conn.: S. Andrus and Son, 1854. Reprint. New York: Arno Press, 1969.

Tilghman, Tench. *Memoir of Lieut. Col. Tench Tilghman*. Albany, N.Y.: Albert J. Munsell, 1876. Reprint. New York: Arno Press, 1971.

Trevelyan, George Otto. *The American Revolution*. Edited and with an introduction by Richard B. Morris. New York: D. McKay and Co., 1964.

Van Doren, Carl. *The Secret History of the American Revolution*. New York: The Viking Press, 1941.

Wade, Herbert T., and Lively, Robert A. *This Glorious Cause: The Adventures of Two Company Officers in Washington's Army*. Princeton: Princeton University Press, 1958.

Ward, Christopher. *The Delaware Continentals, 1776–1783*. Wilmington, Del.: History Society of Delaware, 1941.

Webb, Samuel Blachley. *Correspondence and Journals, collected and edited by Worthington Chauncey Ford*. Vol 1. New York, 1893. Reprint (3 vols.). New York: Arno Press, 1969.

Wertenbaker, Thomas J., ed. "The Battle of Princeton." In *The Princeton Battle Monument*. Princeton: Princeton University Press, 1922.

———. *Princeton, 1746–1896*. Princeton: Princeton University Press, 1946.

Wheeler, Richard. *Voices of 1776*. New York: Thomas Y. Crowell Co., 1972.

White, Joseph. *An* [sic] *Narrative of Events, As They Occurred from Time to Time, in the Revolutionary War; with an Account of the Battles of Trenton, Trenton-Bridge, and Princeton*. Charlestown, Mass., 1833. In *American Heritage* 4 (June 1956). Original in Library of Congress.

Wickwire, Franklin, and Wickwire, Mary. *Cornwallis: The American Adventure*. Boston: Houghton Mifflin, 1970.

Wiederholdt, Andreas. *"Tagebuch des Capt. Wiederholdt von 7 October 1776 bis 7 Dezember 1780."* Edited by M. D. Learned and C. Grosse. *Americana Germanica*. Vol. 4, 1901. New York, London and Berlin, 1902. A translation of "The Capture of Fort Washington" by Wiederholdt is in *Pennsylvania Magazine of History and Biography* 23 (1899). A translation of Wiederholdt on the New Jersey campaign is in *Pennsylvania Magazine of History and Biography* 22 (1898).

Wilkinson, James. *Memories of My Own Times*. 4 vols. Philadelphia, 1816.

Young, William. "The Journal of Sergeant William Young." *Pennsylvania Magazine of History and Biography* 8 (1884): 255–78.

Index